TE DUE

THE MANAGEMENT OF BANK FUNDS

THE MANAGEMENT
OF BANK FUNDS

Roland I. Robinson

Professor of Financial Administration and Economics
Graduate School of Business Administration
Michigan State University

Second Edition

McGraw-Hill Book Company, Inc.   1962

New York   San Francisco   Toronto   London

THE MANAGEMENT OF BANK FUNDS

53279

III

Preface

Twelve years ago I offered the original version of this work for publication with a considerable diffidence. Most of the collegiate courses in commercial banking then offered emphasized operating techniques. This approach seemed sterile to me; I thought operational practices were best learned on the job. This text grew out of the effort to change the emphasis—to explore the unique control problem of commercial banking: the management of bank funds so as to maintain liquidity while maximizing profits. I was not at all sure, however, that this approach would be acceptable to other teachers. Experience, happily, has been favorable to the change. Collegiate courses in commercial banking have moved a gratifying distance in the new direction, at least if catalogue descriptions can be used as a guide.

The financial climate has changed greatly in the eleven years since the first edition of this text was published. Demands in money markets have shifted from congenital ease to a general state of tightness relieved only occasionally by cyclical downturns. New competitive factors have emerged in the financial community. Banking profits have become much more generous, but banking costs have marched every step of the way upward with them. Finally, the philosophy that governs the teaching of business and financial subjects has changed greatly in most schools. Trade school aspects are given less attention, and the leading schools of business now try to prepare their graduates

v

to apply their knowledge in a rapidly changing world. This new edition aligns itself fully with the new philosophy; it is offered as a work in applied economics.

The debts incurred in preparation of the first edition have not been outlawed by any intellectual statute of limitations. In addition, new ones have accumulated. Many users have sent me suggestions and given me encouragement. Two persons must be singled out for special mention: Hobart Carr and Lawrence Ritter, both of New York University, have been penetrating but creative users and critics.

It is usual to end a preface with an author's assumption of undivided responsibility for residual errors and shortcomings. At the risk of seeming fatuous I must do more than repeat this truism. Shortcomings do remain, but their remedy would have required a different and very much longer book. That book would be based on a thorough empirical investigation of the managerial practices that are, in fact, used in modern commercial banking. Anyone who shares the feeling that this would be worth doing and who commands the necessary resources should be encouraged to do that job. It needs doing.

Roland I. Robinson

Contents

PART VI. PROFIT MANAGEMENT

Part I

INTRODUCTION

1

The Business of Banking

Modern commercial banking is an exacting business. The rewards are modest; the penalties for bad banking are enormous. If banking has come to be regarded as a "conservative" business, it is for good reasons. Banks have to "conserve" their position and their assets; they can afford little or no waste.

All financial institutions must operate within rather narrow profit and loss margins. The amount of capital which can be profitably employed in finance is usually modest in relation to the aggregate sums dealt in, and modest capital means that losses must be minimized. The obligation for safety and prudence which bears on all financial institutions is particularly severe for commercial banks. Commercial banks are great monetary institutions, important to the general welfare of the economy. More than any other financial institution, they have a vastly sobering and exacting responsibility: they must be ready to "pay on demand," without warning or notice, a good share of their liabilities. While this obligation in its most extreme form is not often encountered, banks must, as a matter of course, expect rather large fluctuations in the demands on their liquidity—variations which they must honor without strain or delay. Most businesses can enjoy some slack in their affairs; commercial banks can afford almost none. Since commercial banks must make a living by putting the money at their disposal to work, they are faced with the problem of making a living without jeopardizing the safety of their institutions. The art of commercial banking is solving this basically conflicting requirement: that of being safe and yet profitable.

Because commercial banking is more of an art than a science, this book must immediately admit to a modest and limited purpose. This purpose is to suggest a philosophy of the central problem of commercial banking—the management of its funds—and to offer some comments on the art of this business. An art, since it requires experience, wisdom, and judgment, can be learned only by doing. Its practice requires experience. The most that this book can accomplish, therefore, is to indicate the problems and describe some of the ways in which they have been handled. It cannot be a substitute for the final teacher of all arts: experience and practice.

The business problems which commercial banks have in common with other businesses—such as promotion, personnel, and accounting—are not touched on here; they can be studied in other more specialized treatments of those subjects. There are, of course, special commercial banking aspects of each of those subjects; but it is believed that those special aspects may be studied more profitably as phases of the major subject of which they are a part—for example, bank personnel problems as special cases of personnel administration—than they can be surveyed here.

ORGANIZATION OF SUBJECT

We have already stated the basic purpose of our inquiry: to describe methods of achieving the most profitable employment of commercial-bank funds consistent with safety. Our method of attack will be relatively simple. We shall measure, as far as measurement is feasible, the needs of safety and then discuss the employment (or investment) of funds which will meet these standards of safety and at the same time yield the maximum return. Priorities in the use of funds will be discussed in a later section of this chapter. These priorities will give us the pattern for our entire study; the major sections of this book follow the order of their presentation.

This study of the business aspects of commercial banking has been pitched at the level of banking policy formation. In general terms, it concerns itself with what the executive officers think about and not with what the employees do. Many of the problems of banking operations have already been excluded by narrowing our focus to the central problems of commercial banking. Even within the areas that we touch, the emphasis will be on the "whys" and not on the "hows." We take the view that the ways of doing things are best learned by doing; there is no substitute for such experience. The function of a book or of any outside study is to make the functional explanations clear. It may often be observed that business practitioners follow rules of behavior, the reasons for which they do not understand. It is possible for a person to do certain tasks well without understanding just why his methods of operation succeed while others might not. The unthinking follower of rules, however, may be lost when conditions about him change even slightly.

The emphasis on the hows and the neglect of the whys might not be too damaging in a field which changed slowly. Where ways of operating are about the same for long periods of time, "rules of thumb" may work quite successfully. A house painter probably can do pretty well with paint mixing without being a color physicist or a paint chemist. But in business procedure the fields of operations are constantly changing. The form of financial institutions changes; the public view and the regulation of business change. The functional nature of finance evolves with time. The practitioners of commercial banking who know only the hows would be badly off when faced with new developments; they know only one way of operating and not what to do when this one way fails them. Those who know the whys are vastly better equipped to shift with the changing times, to know when the old rules are no longer infallible, and to see when modifications are needed.

It must be admitted at the very beginning that by limiting our purpose in this way, we are not being very helpful to those just beginning a career in commercial banking. They are likely to be in banking departments of fairly narrow purpose: they will be working on the books, posting or "spreading" statements in the credit department, working in some "outside" department, or will have a similar function. This book will not help them much in their present job. It will deal, as we have said, with what the leading executive officers do or rather why they do what they do, the policies they frame, the judgments they make.

This emphasis has its advantages. The early jobs in commercial banking, just like the early jobs in almost any complicated business, are bound to be narrow and to be best learned on the job. If the person engaged in learning these jobs understands how they are related to the total problem of commercial-bank management, he will be that much better prepared to learn these special jobs with dispatch and understanding.

FOCUSING ON THE INDIVIDUAL BANK

All the commercial banks in the country—the commercial banking system—are collectively the most important part of our monetary system. Commercial banking in this total sense is the central subject of study in "money and banking" courses. Many first-rate texts about this subject have been written and are available for the student. But this is not the area which we propose to study.

Each bank is managed separately. The normal focus of the managerial problem in banking is a bank, not the system of banks. That will be our point of view, the focus of our examination. This focus will be reflected in a number of ways. The volume of deposits in the commercial banking system as a whole depends on the volume of banking reserves and the amount of credit (loans and investments) extended on the basis of these reserves. With unimportant exceptions, which we shall not examine here, the line of causation in the banking system runs from the asset side of the balance sheet to the liability side. The amount of liabilities *depends*, we might say, on the volume of assets. This is all fully expounded in every text on money and banking. For the individual bank, the line of causation runs the other way. Each bank gets its deposits and then puts these funds to work. The causation is from liabilities to assets. As every operating banker knows, the first step is to attract deposits, the second step is to employ the funds brought in.

Both lines of analysis are true; the sole difference is in the point of view. Since we are dealing with the policies for management of funds in the individual bank, we shall follow the second line, not because it is truer than the first, but because it is the view appropriate to our purpose.

There are other differences between the banking system as a whole and the individual bank. If we were to consider the liquidity of the banking system as a whole, for example, we should have to talk about the operation of the Federal Reserve System and the Treasury and of the general monetary scene. What is liquidity for one bank is not liquidity for the banking system. Since our point of view is that of the individual bank, we shall talk about liquidity policies appropriate for the single bank.

Even though this text does not deal with the problems of monetary economics, bankers are strongly urged to study this subject at some time. Many of the business factors with which bankers must concern themselves are determined by the aggregate workings of our monetary and financial system. The amount of funds available to the individual bank is usually an indirect reflection of central banking policy: the extent to which the Federal Reserve is supplying banking reserves. The interest rates prevailing on securities and even on loans are another reflection of these factors. General economic developments are all influenced by the stabilization policies of the government. The strategies, if not the tactics, of bank management are closely geared to the expected nature of general financial and economic developments.

UNIT BANKING IN THE UNITED STATES

The business of banking in the United States is conducted to a considerable extent by unit banks, that is, by banks the physical location of which is limited to one site. Branch banking is practiced in a certain number of states and urban areas, but nevertheless unit banking is the most common form of bank organization in our system.

Many fail to recognize the enormous disparity in size among banks in the United States. Considerable differences are found in size of banks in such countries as Great Britain and Canada. Their largest banks are from ten to a hundred times the size of their smallest banks. In the United States the largest commercial bank is ten thousand times as large as not just one small bank but the 1,200 smallest banks in the United States!

With so much disparity in size and in location it becomes extremely difficult to generalize about the managerial policies appropriate for individual banks. The manager of one of the smaller clearing banks of London probably would be able to assume control of one of the larger banks, possibly one a hundred times as large as his own institution, and still be immediately prepared, on the basis of his experience, to make appropriate managerial decisions. This general applicability of experience is not as true of our system. Unit banks in rural areas, though prosperous and progressive in managerial policies, are so different from the large money-market banks that it would be difficult to exchange managerial personnel without a considerable intervening period of indoctrination.

This disparity in size will be dealt with in several ways in this text. At some points the comments will be broken into parts, some applying only to smaller banks and some applying to the larger ones. Other times the practice will be to limit generalizations to matters that are applicable to banks of all sizes. The necessary result is that some observations on managerial policies will be more guarded and less general than we altogether prefer.

HOW "COMMERCIAL" IS COMMERCIAL BANKING?

Still one more explanatory qualification must be made before we can get into the heart of our subject. Our opening comments have narrowed our attention to commercial banking. The tradition of commercial banking made the scope of credit operation much narrower than that now observed by commercial banks. Our intention is to deal with commercial banks as they are today. Extensive recognition will be given to the fact that savings banking has come to be a sizable part of so-called commercial banking. In our study of the forms of credit, we shall devote a great deal of attention to kinds which are far afield from the older traditions of commercial banking. In other words, our use of the word "commercial" is not so much logical as a matter of convenience; we mean by it just about what everyone else does when talking about commercial banks.

The word "commercial" came into wide usage when business was rather more "commercial" and less "industrial" than now. Times have changed; our banks are now rather more industrial than commercial. When the goldsmith and the Venetian banking systems were operating, there was much trading or commerce but little manufacturing or industry. The word "commercial," however, continues to be the recognized term in distinguishing our department-store banks with their industrial and consumer business from other types of financial institutions.

THE SOURCE OF BANK FUNDS

The balance sheet of a modern commercial bank is divided into parts about as shown in Figure 1-1. In the analysis of any business we may treat the liabilities as sources of funds, the assets as uses of funds. We have therefore shown in Figure 1-1 the three major sources of bank funds and their relative importance.

As is very evident, deposits are the main source of bank

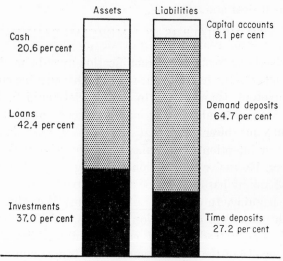

FIGURE 1-1. Division of the balance sheet of a modern commercial bank. (Adapted from estimates for all commercial banks as of June 30, 1960; see *Federal Reserve Bulletin*, October, 1960.)

funds. We must note one characteristic of deposits: the contract between a commercial bank and a demand depositor is an obligation which banks must observe scrupulously. The holders of deposit accounts assume it their privilege to draw down their accounts when they need funds and to let them grow when there is no immediate use for them. In other words, banks must expect deposit accounts to fluctuate, often to gyrate materially. While these fluctuations of individual accounts may be offsetting in part, a bank cannot depend on this always being true. In areas of economic concentration such as agricultural communities, banks must expect most of their deposit accounts to move in the same direction at about the same time, and therefore not be offsetting. Similarly, there are many other cases of deposit changes which are not offset in the individual bank. This, we shall find, is at the heart of the problem of protective investment in banks.

In the ordinary course of business, it is as important for an individual bank to get funds as it is to put them to work safely and profitably. We shall say very little about the first problem and a great deal about the second. Why? The art of attracting funds is important but, like so many other processes of salesmanship, it is an intangible beyond the purview of a pedestrian text on banking. Banks get funds by advertising for them, by direct solicitation, by contacts through their officers and influential directors; they get and hold them ultimately by furnishing the kind of banking services that depositors feel is what they want and should have.

This is very important. Our brief attention to it should not delude anyone into underrating its importance. The arts of advertising and solicitation are treated in other texts. The way to attract and keep influential officers and directors can hardly be taught by rule. The one contribution this text can make to the subject is to deal with two aspects of service which depositors prize. Depositors, even under the operation of deposit insurance, like to have their funds in a "safe" bank. We shall say quite a lot about this before we are through. Further, depositors, or some of them at least, prefer to keep their accounts where they can expect credit or borrowing accommodations when they have a legitimate need for such. We shall also have a great deal to say about this aspect of banking.

PRIORITIES IN THE USE OF BANK FUNDS

We started by averring that the essential banking problem is to resolve the conflict between safety and profitability in the employment of bank funds. Why is there a conflict? In its simplest form it can be seen by comparing the holding of cash with any form of investing funds. Since bank liabilities are payable in cash, it is obvious that cash is the premier banking asset. Any way in which the funds are otherwise used is not quite so good in the sense of immediate safety. Some investments of funds leave them in such shape that a recovery of cash can be both prompt and without chance of material loss. Such obviously superior assets involve a sacrifice: a lower interest income. Some forms of investment offer only a remote return of cash and the chance of loss both during the life of the investment instrument and at its maturity, but a particularly great chance of loss if an asset must be converted into cash (sold) before maturity. Here is the conflict: it is within this category of assets that the best interest returns are normally available. So the conflict between safety and profitability is the conflict between liquidity (the nearness to cash form) and the size of the interest return.

The division of banking assets between cash assets and earning assets and the division of earning assets between loans and investments, as shown in Figure 1-1, is the practice commonly followed in publication of banking statements. Unfortunately, it is not the most meaningful division possible. The degree of liquidity within earning assets, a vastly more important distinction, is left obscure. Occasionally individual banks show more than is required in published statements but not often or regularly.

The division between "loans" and "investments" is more conventional than logical. The usual concept of a loan is a credit transaction between a borrowing customer and the bank. Loans are frequently but not regularly short-term in maturity. An investment is an impersonal or open-market credit and, more often than not, of longer term than a loan. However, this distinction tends to break down under close examination. Some loans are syndicated among a number of lenders and are very nearly open-market obligations. Some investments turn out to have almost no market and are like long-term loans. Rather than involve ourselves with complex distinctions, we shall, throughout this treatment, speak of loans as being customer credits, negotiated directly by the bank holding them and not ordinarily subject to sale; we shall consider investments to be credit not always but primarily of longer maturities placed through the open markets and ordinarily subject to resale in these markets.

Our reason for making this distinction is that the institutional nature of commercial banks has been traditionally adapted to "lending" rather than to "investing" and, even though investments have come to occupy a large role in commercial banking, there is still much good sense in this traditional distinction. Because there are so many commercial banks, they tend to be close to the lending markets, closer than most other financial institutions. For the same reason, they are not so close to the central investment or capital markets.

The Schedule of Priorities

Having addressed ourselves to the question of safety versus profitability and also to the question of types of credit to which the commercial banking system is adapted, we are now in a position to suggest an order of priority for the employment of commercial-bank funds, an order which will dominate the discussion of the remainder of this study. Our sole guides in establishing this priority are two rules: (1) When there is conflict between safety and profitability, it is better to err on the side of safety, and (2) the commercial banking system should prefer the types of credit for which it is institutionally well adapted and should avoid those types for which it does not enjoy a natural advantage.

The highest priority: primary reserves. Before any other use of funds is considered, a commercial bank must provide itself with enough cash, that is, adequate primary reserves. Part of the reason is traditional. Commercial banks have the legal obligation to pay out their demand deposits without notice and "on demand," and "paying out" here means providing legal-tender currency—cash. Since the habit of the community is to depend on the commercial banks for its cash needs, a steady and expected inflow and outflow of cash is experienced by every bank. As we shall find, the amount of till cash kept by commercial banks is small, but it is nevertheless important. A further reason for keeping primary reserves is legal; for banks are required to hold some proportion of their deposits in cash form, depending on the legal jurisdiction in which a bank operates. In modern times the banks that are members of the Federal Reserve System keep their "required reserves" as deposits in a Federal Reserve bank, and, until very recently vault cash did not count as reserves. A further reason for keeping cash or primary reserves is the practical operating need of providing a means of paying or clearing checks and other credit obligations among banks. While a part of this clearing function is performed by the Federal Reserve System, much of it is still outside the System and is performed by the great city correspondent banks. Since there are other reasons for the existence of the correspondent banking system and the maintenance of balances with such banks, the full treatment of this part of our inquiry will be presented later; our purpose now is to note the position of such balances in the priority of employments.

Although our reason for putting cash or "primary reserve" needs at the top of the list is mainly that of safety, we must immediately note that there is much more than safety to this order. A great share of it is pure legal compulsion. While there have been cases in which bankers have depended on large cash holdings to make their banks safe, this is usually neither necessary nor even wise. To forgo income altogether may not be real safety in the long run. In other words, while cash enjoys the top position in priorities, we shall find that the usual rule of prudence is to keep as small a cash position as the law and ordinary standards of operation permit. In other words, the central provision for banking safety comes not in primary but in secondary reserves.

A moment's reflection on the nature of the central share of primary reserves—the required legal reserve—will make evident the reason why this seemingly contradictory fact is true. Since these reserves are required, they may not be depleted for any extended period to meet cash demands. In other words, only cash in excess of legal requirements or assets that can be converted into cash give a bank real flexibility in meeting its legal obligations.

The second priority: protective investment (secondary reserves). We have already disclosed a major reason for our second priority. To plan for all possible and remote contingencies of cash needs by adequate cash holdings requires a bank to forgo earnings needlessly; indeed for reasons of long-run safety, banks should have adequate earnings. It may be "safer," in all reasonable senses of the word, for a bank to provide for contingent cash needs by the investment of funds in a form which is fairly close to cash or which can be turned to cash without material impairment of the principal sum invested, than just to carry the actual cash. In such investment of funds, the primary purpose is that of safety. Amount of return takes second place. In some periods the amount of income conceded for this safety has been small, but in recent years when funds have been in active demand, the income on protective uses of funds has usually been considerably below that available on other uses of funds.

We have used two terms "protective investment" and "secondary reserves" without distinction. The phrase "secondary reserves" has enjoyed long and honorable usage in banking. These reserves are "secondary" to the "primary" or cash reserves. They have differed in one great respect: In the conventionally published balance sheets of banks, primary reserves are fully disclosed while secondary reserves are concealed. The so-called secondary reserve assets have usually been a part of the investment accounts, but some forms have been included in loan accounts. While study of the publicly available published forms tells us rather fully what the primary reserve policies of banks have been, there is surprisingly little known about secondary reserve policies.

An added title has been used here because the banking usage of the phrase "secondary reserves" has been obscured by an ambiguity which makes the idea of "protective reserves" perhaps more exact, even if uncommon. Banks really have two uses of their protective or secondary reserves: (1) for likely and indeed almost forecastable cash needs, (2) for remote, unlikely, but possible cash needs. The first use may be illustrated by ordinary seasonal shifts in deposits. Many banks know that their deposit total will go down at certain times during the year and can plan ahead for this decline. The second use may be illustrated by the possibilities of bank "runs." Banks know from hard experience that depositors can become frightened and that this fright becomes a social malady passing from person to person so that the depositors end up by mobbing the bank and asking for a conversion of their accounts to cash, not because they need the cash but because they fear for the safety of the banks. While deposit insurance has made bank runs almost a thing of the past, a bank might, in its computations of safety, allow for this possible but remote contingency.

The importance of making this distinction is that the protective employment of funds for the two uses may follow a quite different pattern. Accordingly we shall establish two subclasses within our second priority:

Protective reserves for expected cash needs—expected deposit shifts and loan demands; protection for deposit accounts that are very likely to fluctuate even though this move is not altogether "expected." These reserves might be labeled "working" secondary reserves.

Protective reserves for remote but possible cash needs— deposit moves due to fluctuations in the business cycle, runs, local depressions of sensitive industries such as agriculture and the like.

The third priority: customer credit demands. Once a bank has made itself safe, it should devote itself to the business for which it is best fitted. Traditionally, banks were primarily direct lenders to their customers. They invested in open-market securities only to the extent that safety required. If this were still possible, it would be a good practice.

A clear recognition of this priority will help in making one point of our later discussion abundantly clear. We shall argue that, in credit, the standards applied by commercial banks to loans do not need to be so high as those applied to investments. We shall argue that commercial banks often are required to take material risks in lending and should take them. We shall also argue that in open-market investments commercial banks seldom have any business taking more than minimum risks. Commercial banks are strategically located for lending. They know a great number of moderate-sized customers intimately; they can extend loan credit and collect it where other lenders could not. In the investment market they are not so strategically located. For example, face to face with insurance company competition a commercial bank is vastly better equipped to make customer loans; working through loan agents and with few offices the insurance companies just could not do so well. When it comes to open-market investment, insurance companies, greater in size and with more stable liabilities, have an advantage over most commercial banks.

Thus we introduce our fourth and last priority with a note of caution.

The fourth priority: open-market investment for income. When a commercial bank has provided the liquidity needed for safety and has satisfied in full the local customer demand for loans, it can enter the investment markets with any remaining funds; indeed, in some cases it must do so in order to earn a minimum living. The emphasis on income need will come up for much discussion later on; this much we can anticipate. Income need of and by itself cannot be a good excuse for taking many investment chances. Banks which cannot make a satisfactory income from customer loan credit and safe—very safe—open-market investment of funds should seriously consider liquidation. When there is a need for income, this need cannot but have weight in investment policy. A bank which has a pretty satisfactory income from loans but still has some funds left over for income investment might forgo trying to maximize investment income and decide that the value of flexibility is worth more than a slightly higher current income. In other words, an adequately high income may be the foundation for opportunities for even higher income. By the same token, the bank which is hard pressed for income may, under some circumstances, bargain away its prospects for improved income in exchange for slightly better current income.

We have already argued that commercial banks are none too strategically located for operation in the open investment markets. We might add that a modern circumstance compounds this difficulty. The investment markets now reflect the heritage of two great wars and a great depression; public-debt obligations are important in these markets. Commercial banks, because of their monetary significance, are subject to rather more direct and detailed influence by public monetary and fiscal authorities. The commercial bank that leans heavily on the open investment markets for income will probably tend over the long run to live on a much more variable income and one that will tend to be quite skimpy if this nation should ever again suffer a prolonged period of slack economic activity.

ALLOCATION SYSTEMS AS SUBSTITUTES FOR PRIORITIES

Some banks manage their funds by direct allocations to various departments. For example, the manager of the money position may be allocated a certain number of dollars to be maintained in first-line secondary reserves, another sum may be allocated to the consumer credit department, and similar arrangements may be made for term loans and real estate loans. In a few cases the allocation of funds may be a comprehensive system embracing the entire asset portfolio with funds allocated either in fixed-dollar terms or as percentages of the total.

The top-management decisions that go into determining these allocations may be guided by exactly the same considerations reflected in the sequence of priorities discussed above. Systems of allocations, however, usually leave some unanswered questions. If allocations are made in fixed-dollar sums, unexpected developments may require revision of them. For example, if a bank with its funds allocated in dollar terms should suffer an unexpected loss of deposits beyond allocated secondary reserves, how should this loss be met? Should the liquidation of earning assets be proportionate in all segments or should it be concentrated in some segments of the portfolio? On the other hand, if allocations are expressed as percentages, they automatically imply a proportionate liquidation of all segments in the case of funds loss or a proportionate increase in the case of unexpected gain of funds. But is proportionate liquidation (or addition) logical? Isn't it possible that liquidation (or addition) should be more in some segments than in others? The logic of priorities in asset management suggests that a rule of proportionate change is suspect.

Allocation systems have the great merit of providing a clear and explicit form for the delegation of responsibility to middle-management officers of a bank. On the other hand, they leave unsettled the questions of how the optimum balance between liquidity and profitability can be maintained in circumstances, the character of which cannot be fully anticipated at the time when allocation plans are being framed.

2

The Economic Environment
of the Banking System

The banking system of the United States operates in an economic environment of strength, growth, and dynamic change. Change gives strong underlying support to financial development. An active and even aggressive financial system is important because a high rate of saving is needed. Change means that obsolescence becomes more important than depreciation; new methods mean new machines which, in turn, require saving. When functioning properly our banking system also assures the employment of savings in some productive form.

The other side of growth and change is that income and economic activity tend to be unstable. Growth and change account in part for the fact that the country does not always enjoy a high enough level of prosperity to employ all resources fully. With limited space, the subject of economic instability cannot be studied adequately; it can only be touched on lightly. A large literature is available, however, and specialized treatises cover almost any aspect one might wish to pursue. The purpose of this chapter is to inquire into some of the effects economic instability has on commercial banking and on finance.

Because economic instability is wasteful of resources and demoralizing for people, the principle of government intervention to reduce its severity has been widely accepted by persons of all political persuasions. It is now accepted, by all but a handful of dissidents, that governmental fiscal and monetary powers should be exercised in the interest of producing economic stability, or at least of avoiding the excesses of instability. The workings of monetary and fiscal policy have unusually direct effects on commercial banks and both will be examined in considerable detail later in this chapter.

THE FINANCIAL ENVIRONMENT

Apart from the general economic characteristics of the economy of the United States, a number of its special financial characteristics should be noted.

An Evolutionary Financial System

The financial system of the United States is an evolutionary one, changing constantly in response to new needs and new demands. New financial institutions appear, but more often existing institutions change their character to be able to meet new needs. The relative importance of various financial institutions constantly changes. Occasionally, a type of financial institution disappears; the fixed investment trust is one of the rare examples. The important conclusion for commercial banking to be drawn from this historical generalization is that competition frequently arises from quite unexpected and new sources. To survive, commercial banks must be adaptable in the provision of services. If older credit forms preferred by banks do not meet the changed needs of customers, it will be the banks —not the customers—who must adapt themselves. A complex economy demands a wide variety of economic and financial services. Unless existing institutions adapt to change quickly and adequately they will inevitably tend to lose their share of the total market.

To some extent commercial banks have already faced this problem and not solved it fully. At the opening of the twentieth century commercial banks were, by a very wide margin, the leading financial institutions in the United States. Whether measured by size or the qualitative importance of the financial services they rendered, they were considerably more important than all other types of financial institutions combined. Since that time commercial banks have grown but they have not grown as rapidly as other financial institutions. Commercial banks have lost somewhat in the competitive race. A number of other types of financial institutions are now enjoying a considerably more rapid rate of growth.

Another characteristic of our financial system is the volatility of its financial markets. Each business is vitally interested in the market in which its product or service is sold. A wheat farmer keeps track of week-to-week, possibly day-to-day, fluctuations in the Board of Trade prices or those of other grain markets. A manufacturer of household appliances is interested in the price policies of his competitors, to the extent of using extensive comparison-shopping devices to find out how trade-ins are valued, etc. A schoolteacher is always curious about the contracts of other schoolteachers. A banker is vitally interested in the price of what he has to sell—the use of money.

Bankers are interested in the money market because they are interested in the level of interest rates. There are not just two or three interest rates, but many. The *Federal Reserve Bulletin* lists almost two dozen interest rate series with weekly, monthly, or quarterly figures. These are the *leading* figures; the number of separate interest rates is even greater.

The market for money is not simple; it is complex. Part is open and well advertised; part is concealed in a multitude of individual and private transactions. Economists have long defined a "market" as any recognized arrangement or area for bringing buyers and sellers together. The more striking illustrations are the highly organized and centralized markets: the stock market, the grain market, and the various commodity markets. But any arena in which buying and selling takes place is a market. In that sense, a money market exists wherever a borrower and a lender get together: in the securities markets, where bonds are bought and sold; on the platform of a small country bank, where an ill-at-ease farmer sits and chats with the cashier until he finally admits that "he'd like to get a little money." Thus part of this market is an open, centralized, explicit market with promptly available quotations. Anyone sitting by a telephone can, without too much trouble, find out just what U.S. Government securities are yielding in terms of effective interest income based on market transactions of the past few minutes. Another part of the market is dispersed, without published quotations, and cloaked in secrecy.

To some extent all open and free competitive markets are characterized by a fairly great degree of volatility. Only where prices are administered by a few price leaders can short-run price fluctuations be avoided. The financial markets, however, are unusually volatile for a wide variety of reasons.

It is customary to speak of markets as being dominated by supply and demand; this is a truism of elementary economics. This trite observation, however, does not supply an adequate reason for the considerable volatility of financial markets. In financial markets demand is for credit, and supply ultimately comes from saving. Both factors are characterized historically by large variations. Furthermore, these markets are extraordinarily sensitive to expectations of the future: expectations as to changes in general business developments as well as expectations as to developments in the areas of public policy. This means, in effect, that commercial banks frequently operate in a market subject to extraordinarily sharp and quick price fluctuations. The highest ability of a bank manager is that of being able to change policy quickly when the economic climate of markets changes. The commercial banker who is unable to adapt himself to varying market conditions usually fails to take advantage of all of the opportunities open to him.

Federal Reserve Policy

Of all the factors influencing the financial environment in which commercial banks operate, Federal Reserve policy is the most important. The influence of the Federal Reserve System is partly direct and well publicized. However, it is also felt through channels that are not always immediately evident in the markets.

The reason the Federal Reserve operates so directly on the commercial banks is that it is the branch of government that manages money. Since commercial-bank demand deposits have come to be the most important kind of money in our economic order, management of them is a clearly recognized governmental function. This function is exercised by the Federal Reserve as the central bank for the nation. The central banking responsibility has sometimes been complicated by exercise of other and related kinds of authority, such as banking supervision and the provision of a number of important banking services, among them the clearing and collection of checks. These matters, however, are never more than incidental to the System's basic obligations.

The Federal Reserve, as the manager of money in the United States, is expected to limit the creation of new money when the economy generates more demand than can be accommodated by existing resources. On the other hand, when economic activity slackens, the Federal Reserve attempts to stimulate it by liberal dosages of newly created money. In other words, the Federal Reserve tends to operate almost directly counter to the changes in demands for credit likely to be encountered by commercial banks. Specifically, it makes banking reserves expensive and scarce at times when the demand for bank credit tends to be very high. On the opposite side of the business cycle it lowers the cost and increases the availability of reserves at the very times when the demand for bank credit tends to slacken.

It might appear to commercial banks that Federal Reserve policy tends to run counter to their business interests. This, of course, is not true; in the long run the interests of commercial banks are identified with economic stability. No responsible government could permit the power to create money to be governed solely by the demand for credit. Such a policy would exaggerate economic instability. Thus banks, subject to the money market pressures set in motion by central bank policy, must manage their affairs in such a way as to be prepared at all times to accommodate themselves to changes in this policy.

The operation of the Federal Reserve System has been described in great detail in other sources, and will not be covered here.[1] The way in which Federal Reserve policy is expressed may not always be immediately evident to bankers. A change in the discount rates of the Federal Reserve banks is a well-publicized fact known to all commercial banks. A more subtle and silent way of adjustment used by the Federal Reserve System is through open-market operations which take directions that may not be immediately evident to commercial banks. Even the most sophisticated money-market banks are sometimes in doubt as to the nature of prevailing policy. The net effect of open-market operations, however, is to change the volume of reserves available to the banking system as a whole. While shifts of funds among individual banks may explain either favorable or unfavorable experiences at the clearinghouse, when the Federal Reserve holds the supply of reserves in check, banks will tend to find adverse balances at the clearinghouse and in mail collections. On the other hand, when Federal Reserve policy is one of ease, banks will tend to find both mail clearings and clearinghouse balances favorable.

The initial impact of Federal Reserve credit action is either on the bank that buys from or sells to the open-market account of the System or on the bank that is depositary for the person or nonbanking institution that buys from or sells to the open-market account. When the bank feeling the initial impact adjusts its reserve position, this action shifts the impact to other banks within the banking system. As they take corrective action, the full effect is spread throughout the monetary system. This is the familiar "multiple expansion" process elaborated in all textbooks on money and banking.

[1] *The Federal Reserve System: Purposes and Functions* (4th ed.), published by the Federal Reserve System, Board of Governors, Washington, 1961, is recommended.

Fiscal Policy and Debt Management

Fiscal policy, the other part of the public weapon for economic stabilization, has less immediate effects on banks. A great many commercial banks (all the leading ones) maintain tax and loan deposit accounts for the Treasury. The rate at which funds are called from these accounts is often a factor of considerable significance in short-term planning of a bank's cash position. Many banks subscribe to new Treasury issues when offered even though they do not expect to hold them for long; it is a kind of underwriting activity. Banks naturally favor issues which they can pay for by a credit to their tax and loan account; the giving of this privilege is used by the Treasury Department as a way of inviting underwriting support from banks. These activities appear to be the principal contacts of fiscal activities on banks. In fact, however, the actual points of influence and contact are somewhat broader.

The general fiscal policy of the Federal government is expressed in the balance between its receipts and expenditures. An excess of expenditures over receipts tends to stimulate business. Such an excess is financed by an expansion of the public debt. This expansion of the public debt sometimes has a contractive influence but not enough to offset the spending stimulation. An excess of receipts over expenditures, which produces a budget surplus, tends to restrict private expenditures. The resulting surplus, when used to reduce the public debt, tends to have a slightly stimulative effect. The banking system may become quite aware of the shifts of funds through tax and loan accounts which tighten their reserve positions. On the other hand, it is by no means so evident to the individual bank when Treasury expenditures tend to put deposits into banks.

The result of both of these policies on the public debt is more evident to banks because the responsibility of the Treasury for either financing a deficit or using a surplus to retire debt is usually fully reflected in capital and money market developments. Since commercial banks are the most important underwriters of Treasury financing operations, they are directly concerned not only with the amount of such Treasury offerings but with whether the securities offered are appropriate for bank investment.

Banks are also concerned about the tax liabilities of their customers; deposits generally show a sharp seasonal drop around each quarterly tax payment date.

HOW THE ECONOMIC AND FINANCIAL ENVIRONMENT AFFECTS THE BANKING SYSTEM

The determinants of money market conditions follow the traditional classification of market factors: those bearing on the demand for money and those bearing on the supply of money. Because this is a field in which the causal factors get intertwined, an exact separation of what is a supply and what is a demand factor is not always possible. For example, Treasury finance and Federal Reserve policy have elements of both. With allowance for this ambiguity, the supply-demand classification will help to classify money market determinants.

The Demand for Money (or Credit)

The major demand for money comes from business firms; therefore, one of the leading factors of money market study is current business finance. What are the current plans for capital outlays? How are inventories growing or declining? What are the changes in current cash position of business concerns? Are their retained earnings likely to be adequate for capital outlays? Will prices advance so as to increase working capital needs?

The study of business finance has many ramifications; sorting out cause and effect is always difficult, often impossible. For example, suppose there is an observed increase in business inventories. An increase in physical volume may have been the cause but not necessarily; the increase in dollar amount may only reflect higher prices. But which caused which? Did the higher prices cause the larger inventories, or did the buying in an effort to maintain or increase inventories drive up the prices of goods? We thus find that a study of the money markets is not so much a purely financial survey as one that goes back to basic economic analysis. The study of general business conditions is necessarily the root and foundation of money market study.

Governmental units, both Federal and state, are often important demand elements in the money markets, dominant ones n time of war. The demand for consumer credit, in both installment and noninstallment form, is an important though far from leading money market factor. Although in recent years private foreign borrowing in our money markets has been moderate, there are times when it is an important demand factor.

Variations in Credit Demand

Bank borrowing is basically a marginal source of credit to a great many business concerns; consequently, business demand for bank credit tends to vary widely. Short-term business borrowing is frequently used to carry either inventories or receivables, both of which tend to fluctuate parallel to changes in the level of economic activity. Such borrowing, however, may fluctuate because of special circumstances not directly related to the level of business activity. For example, business borrowing may be used either to delay long-term borrowing, if interest rates are currently felt to be high, or possibly to anticipate later long-term borrowing. Such demands for bank credit, while not directly related to the level of economic activity, are certainly strongly influenced by it.

In recent years many large corporations have found that their smaller customers depend on the trade credit they extend to them (frequently with rather generous terms) as a vital part of their financing. This may require the larger companies to draw down their cash balances or to undertake larger bank borrowing. Since the amounts of accounts receivable outstanding tend to fluctuate with business conditions, such variations likewise tend to increase the already variable or fluctuating pattern of demand for bank credit.

Variations in the demand for credit may also be observed in the area of consumer credit. This is evident in the direct bank loans to consumers but it is even more sharply expressed in the indirect loans to consumers made through credits to sales finance concerns. The rather sharp movements in demand for credit of sales finance concerns is also expressed in their policies of maintaining lines of credit to cover the sales finance paper that they market directly in the commercial paper market.

Variations in the demand for bank credit pose particularly awkward problems of bank management because in periods of tight or inaccessible funds customers are likely to fall back on banks after failing to cover their requirements by other means. This is particularly true of the small and moderate-sized businesses that frequently are such an important part of the clientele of banks. To some extent small businesses appear to be more sensitive to fluctuations in economic conditions than large businesses. Wider swings in their activity seem to occur, and these create wider variations in their demand for bank credit.

Variations in Funds Available

The most important long-term supply element on the money markets is private saving: saving by individuals and the retention of earnings by business concerns. (The second seldom comes to the open capital markets.) It is rather artificial to speak of savings as a supply of money or credit, since it means that income has been diverted from consumption and made available for capital outlays. But, in the usual individual savings transaction, the saver builds up his savings in money and then turns the money over to someone who uses it.

For technical reasons which would go outside and beyond the scope of analysis employed here, the volume of saving in any given period always equals the capital outlay of the period. (The definition of "capital" implied here includes changes in unsold inventories of consumer goods.) This has no more meaning than saying that the number of shoes sold in any month equals exactly the number of shoes purchased. The two transactions are simply reciprocals of the same operation. Even though there is this sales and purchases equality, it is possible that the general demand for shoes may be tending to outrun or to fall short of the supply of shoes, and it is this balance of tendencies which determines shoe prices. So with saving and investment. The tendency of saving to exceed investment lowers interest rates; the tendency of investment to outrun saving raises interest rates.

The shrewd analyst of the money market does not content himself with the realized statistics of saving and capital demand; he looks to find out the general factors of current disposition to save or to make capital outlays. These fundamental factors are hard to judge. About the only facts available are taken from the surveys of consumer intentions to save and to consume, such as the Federal Reserve has sponsored.

Variations in the supply of bank reserves often come at awkward moments. Central banking policy tends to vary the supply of funds available in a direction opposite to the variation in credit demand. Deposit growth tends to be curbed by the Federal Reserve during periods of boom so that the balances available to individual banks no longer are growing. On the other hand, credit ease which is the policy of the Federal Reserve during times of slower business has the net effect of increasing deposits when the demand for credit is relatively slack. This conflict of tendencies is particularly important in the analysis of specific loan and investment policies.

Variations in Interest Rates

Bankers have one economic characteristic in common with farmers: the principal sales product of banks, which is short-term credit, has one of the most volatile prices in the entire economic spectrum. Figures 11-1 and 19-1 show the range of variations of short-term interest rates in the open markets and for bank loans over the past few years. The effect of variations in open-market interest rates is not fully reflected in the rate that affects banks most since the prime loan rate does not move as widely nor as promptly as open-market rates. Nevertheless, the connection between the two is relatively strong. A banker must recognize not only the direct connection between investment earnings and these open-market rates but the indirect influence of the rates on the bargains that he can appropriately make with customers.

The variations in interest rates not only affect the current earnings of banks but also have considerable effect on the value of securities held in bank portfolios. One of the principal objects of investment management, indeed, is to follow protective policies that will avoid the extreme risks implicit in fluctuations in interest rates and, if possible, to turn these fluctuations to their advantage.

Variations in Quality of Credit

Relatively short-term and quickly reversed fluctuations in business conditions do not have profound effects on the quality of credit. It could be said, for example, that since World War II variations in business conditions have had only slight effects on the over-all quality of credit. A longer historical view, however, shows that the quality of credit has been influenced by variations in business conditions and that these variations at times can have considerable curbing or dampening effect on banking activity. Unrealized losses or threats of losses in either loans or investments cannot help but limit a banker's room for maneuver.

MANAGERIAL PROBLEMS CAUSED BY EXTERNAL ECONOMIC ENVIRONMENT

All these aspects of the external economic environment in which the banking system operates find their expression in a variety of ways that will be considered in later chapters. The sections below, therefore, are little more than preliminary introductions to these later discussions.

Liquidity Management

Sizable changes in business conditions mean that a bank must maintain liquidity adequate to meet a wide range of contingencies. Liquidity requirements may become particularly compelling under two different types of circumstances which are at opposite ends of the scale of economic developments. A low level of economic activity normally means that liquidity tends to accumulate. In periods of great adversity it is possible, even if not likely, that some individual banks may be subject to sizable deposit drains. For example, an extreme drop in economic activity might cause banks in some areas to lose funds to the rest of the country and so lose liquidity. If times are so bad as to raise questions about the solvency of a bank, the pressure for liquidity can become even greater.

The opposite circumstance is the need to provide liquidity so that a bank can meet the loan demands of favored customers. This circumstance arises when a high level of economic activity prevails. This is the more real and more pressing type of liquidity requirement normally met in managerial operations.

Loan Policy

In one way or another many of the points that might be made with respect to the effects of external economic influences on loan policy have already been anticipated: the fluctuations in loan demands and the liquidity provision that must be made to meet them. It is worth noting, however, that loan policy may be influenced in other ways by the anticipation of likely fluctuations in external economic development. For example, if a bank tends to have customers of a given type or customers concentrated in particular industries, it may be wise to make extraordinary efforts to promote business in lines that either offset or minimize the risks implicit in areas of concentration that naturally appear in their institutions.

Loan policy may require the prudent banker to establish in good times quality standards which can be maintained in other periods. It is doubtful whether loans should be granted in periods of prosperity to customers who would be unwelcome in times of adversity. Even more specifically, it may be dubious wisdom to seek the business customers in lines that are likely to be unduly subject to unfavorable external economic developments.

Influence on Investment Policy

The influence of external economic events on investment policy is felt mainly in the nature of interest rate developments. A specific example will show the way in which interest rate relationships influence investment policy. As is well known (and developed in somewhat greater detail in Chapter 19), short-term interest rates fluctuate through a wider range than long-term interest rates. On the other hand, the prices of short-term securities fluctuate far less than those of long-term securities.

Not so well observed, but of considerable significance, however, is the fact that intermediate-term interest rates have recently fluctuated a great deal. They have fluctuated through so wide a range as to make variations in their prices almost as great as those of long-term securities. This fact could and probably should have a great influence on bank investment policy. In recent periods intermediate-term securities have sometimes been almost as risky to buy as long-term securities. By the same token, however, they sometimes offer considerably more promise of capital gains profits for a given degree of risk than is true of long-term securities. In other words, the policies that will be discussed in Chapters 18 and 19 suggest that the even spacing of maturities, a policy long widely recommended for banks, may not, in fact, prove to be as profitable as a more flexible investment policy. The potential improvement of return from the investment portfolio without extending maturity by taking advantage of variations in intermediate-term interest rates may be considerable.

The reasons that have accounted for these sizable fluctuations in intermediate-term interest rates lie outside the discussion at this stage. It is worth observing, however, that they have been an important expression of the variations in the supply of funds in the capital markets as well as variations in demand for such funds.

The discussion of variations in loan demand also has a bearing on investment policy. Since, as has already been made clear, investment policy is definitely subsidiary to loan policy, this means that, in effect, one objective of investment policy is to provide the liquidity needed to support appropriate loan policy. External events, in the form of changes in quality of credit as well as in interest rates, thus have a bearing on the formation of investment policy.

Earnings Management

Because of variations in the cycle of prosperity and recession, banks naturally must expect some variations in earnings. These variations in real earnings may also be complicated by variations in the time at which earnings are realized and reported. Some of these variations grow out of tax factors. For purposes of good stockholder relations, banks may be hesitant to encourage any sizable variations in earnings that might be produced by this combination of external economic developments and tax factors. Unfortunately, a bank that wishes to stabilize its earnings may fail to maximize them. A compromise that serves both objectives is not always possible to achieve in a fully satisfactory way.

Assurance of Solvency

A basic managerial problem created by the external economic environment is that banks must take precautions to assure their solvency, not only in periods of prosperity but also in periods of adversity. This is primarily a matter of the policy with respect to capital funds, but it also involves the policies with respect to liquidity and the control of quality in investment accounts.

3

The Individual Bank in the Banking System

The preceding chapter directed attention to the fact that the banking system is a significant part of our financial and economic system. The banking system is important in general economic analysis because it is the leading manufacturer of money. The state of business conditions is the central determinant of the rate at which the central bank (the Federal Reserve) permits the banking system to manufacture money. General economic conditions, therefore, influence the commercial banking system in a special way.

In this chapter attention will be directed to the role of the individual bank in the banking system. In this role it is subject to a number of external influences to which it must be responsive. This is particularly true of the unit banking system of the United States, in which the character of individual banks varies so widely. Experienced bankers take account of these variations though frequently in an instinctive or intuitive way and often without formal recognition of the problem. The major purpose of this chapter, therefore, will be to state as precisely and explicitly as possible the intuitive understanding of these points held by most individual bank managers.

DIVERSITY IN KINDS OF BANKS

Generalization about commercial banks in the United States can be misleading. More than 13,400 commercial banks operate throughout the country. They range all the way from several of the largest giants of commercial banking in the world (including the largest one of all) to banks so small that their survival would be in jeopardy in almost any other banking system.

Some of the differences are matters of location. Big banks naturally tend to be located in big cities. But big cities are not alike; big banks even in the same big city may be quite different in character. Some big banks have grown big by virtue of extending their business geographically by branch operations as well as by aggressive pursuit of business throughout the nation. In the areas where branch banking is prohibited, some banks have grown big by successful solicitation of national accounts in which physical location of the banking office is not important. Even where branch banking is permitted, a few banks have forgone the wider profit margins of retail banking to concentrate on being wholesalers of money.

Each bank should try to capitalize on the natural advantages of its location, on the nature of its existing customers, on the range of potential customers that it may solicit, and on the business connections it can make through its directors or through its correspondent relationships. Hard and fast rules cannot be made for individual banks in many of the matters dealt with here because opportunities vary so widely among banks.

CORRESPONDENT BANKING SYSTEM

The banking system of the United States differs from that of almost all foreign countries in that it depends on a complex web of correspondent relationships. City correspondents aid and complement their country correspondents;[1] they permit them to offer a full range of services to customers. In the absence of branch banking the individual country bank depends on its city correspondent in many ways. City correspondents perform the operational services of collecting checks, other cash items, and noncash items such as bond coupons and drafts. They also advise and assist their country correspondents on operational problems. In addition, city correspondents sometimes absorb "overline" loans which are too large for country banks to handle. At the other extreme country banks not having adequate local loan demand are sometimes granted participation in brokers' loans by their city correspondents in order to give them earning assets. Some city banks make markets in Federal funds more as a service to their country correspondents than as a profit-making device.[2] City correspondents also supply liquidity protection in other ways to their country correspondents. The many real advantages of a city correspondent relationship are usually paid for by a deposit balance, one that is frequently in excess of what is needed purely for liquidity purposes.

ECONOMIC CHARACTER OF AREA OF LOCATION

In the unit banking system that prevails in the United States the success of an individual bank is closely tied to that of the area in which it is located. Even where branch banking is permitted the maximum boundaries for branch operations are frequently so limited (such as to the city or country in which the head office is located) that the area of operations has dis-

---

[1] In the jargon of banking a "country correspondent" is not necessarily a small bank located in a rural village. Furthermore, it is not necessarily located in a "country" town as the term is (loosely) used in descriptions of legal reserve requirements. The so-called country correspondents of New York City and Chicago money-market banks include many large banks located in large towns.

[2] Most city banks, however, use their dealing in Federal funds to assist in managing their own liquidity position.

tinctive characteristics. Some areas experience large seasonal inflows and outflows of funds. Some depend on highly specialized types of economic activity; others are more diversified. Some industries and the areas in which they are predominantly concentrated tend to be far more sensitive to business cycle fluctuations than others. Great differences in the rate of economic growth exist among areas.

Seasonal Fluctuations

A seasonal variation is a repetitive movement of some magnitude that depends on or is caused by the season of the year. Weather and holidays cause seasonal movements. One is the product of nature; the other of man-made conventions. Business is influenced by seasonal factors, including the concentration of harvests, vacation habits, and traditional sales peaks. Some seasonal patterns are nationwide; others are local. Almost every area of the country has unique seasonal characteristics. Some are far more evident than others, but in almost all areas seasonal movements are great enough to merit special attention. The problems may be doubly acute for bankers because in certain areas the seasonal peak or peaks for loan demands almost coincide with the seasonal low point in deposits. In such circumstances a bank may have great difficulty in meeting loan demands at its peak season but have sizable amounts of idle funds in other periods. The banker who has a reasonably accurate knowledge of expected ranges of seasonal movements of these factors can plan offsetting arrangements. It is for this reason that reasonably precise knowledge about seasonal movements can be of value to bankers.

Several technical resources may be used by a banker to improve his knowledge of seasonal movements within his institution. A banker wanting outside assistance can take his problem to the service bureau of one of the large business machines companies. Most of these service bureaus are now equipped to compute statistical measures of seasonal variation. The charges for the service are moderate. The business research bureaus of some universities also have facilities for this work. A banker ambitious enough to undertake the job for himself may find help in any one of several standard textbooks on statistics.[3] Very simple methods are usually adequate for most purposes. By plotting the principal series, such as deposits or loans, on a chart with a horizontal cycle of one year and with the years superimposed, one on another, as in Figure 6-4, a fairly simple measurement of seasonals can be made visually without mathematical manipulation.

Since the seasonal loan is the traditional backbone of the commercial banking business, special interest attaches to the seasonal movements of loan demand in the area in which a bank is located. A banker might find it informative to maintain figures for the volume of loan applications, loans granted, and loan repayments as well as the balance sheet figure of loans outstanding in order to have a more complete understanding of seasonal movements in lending operations. A banker might also find that loan demands break down into subsidiary parts that have somewhat different seasonals. If one subsidiary type of loan has a natural seasonal peak that falls in the low point of the more major types of loans, a bank might concentrate its promotional efforts on this off-season type of loan so as to reduce the over-all seasonality of loan demand. Similarly, the seasonality of deposits as a whole may obscure the fact that important classes of deposits such as public funds have a quite different seasonal from other kinds of deposits. By careful observation of these differences in seasonality, and by a careful selectivity in his promotional activities, a banker can improve considerably his bank's competitive posture.

Business Cycle Influences

As the previous chapter developed at greater length, banking is much influenced by the swings in prosperity or slackness that have come to be known as the "business cycle." The busi-

---

[3] Such as W. A. Wallis and H. V. Roberts, *Statistics: A New Approach*, The Free Press, Glencoe, Ill., pp. 580–587, 1956.

ness cycle, however, is not a uniform national phenomenon; fluctuations vary both in character and in intensity from area to area. Banks located in areas dominated by heavy industries frequently experience far sharper swings both in loan demand and in availability of funds than banks serving the more stable consumer industries. Greater diversification of industry also tends to reduce the severity of local business fluctuations.

Unfortunately, appraising the character of local cyclical patterns is a rather complex problem for an individual banker to tackle. Outside resources may be needed to provide the necessary factual background. To an increasing extent the Federal Reserve banks and correspondent banks have become conscious of local differences in business vulnerability to cyclical developments and have studied the likelihood of local shifts in business conditions. Where studies have been made of regional characteristics such materials should be used.

There is relatively little defensive action that a banker can take against the basic risks of local business fluctuations. One prudent step, of course, is to provide the amount of liquidity needed to meet these local risks. The likelihood of such swings may influence many other decisions, such as judgments of risks in lending. For example, even the normal service industries which would be stable customers of banks in most areas may prove to have more-than-normal risks if their area is dominated by an industry having unusually sharp cyclical swings. Local grocery chains in a community dominated by a large but increasingly obsolete steel-producing company may be poorer credit risks than local grocery chains in growing communities.

Growth Potentials

The over-all growth of the United States is an amalgam of vastly different rates of growth in individual areas. Civic pride blinds some bankers to the relatively slow growth of the areas in which they are located. At the other extreme bankers in rapidly growing areas may come to depend on growth to cure the mistakes of overoptimism. Growth unquestionably has very great advantages for a bank. It means a lively loan demand and the comforting prospect of increased size in the long run.

Growth, however, can create thorny problems even if it tends to justify a tendency toward aggressiveness. An area of unusually rapid growth is frequently one in which there is a net import of capital from the rest of the country. A growing area attracts competition for the cream of the business but does not take care of the less glamorous local business. Growing areas also tend to be more unstable than those not growing rapidly. Banks in such areas may find themselves subject to unusual losses of funds by adverse clearing balances in times of difficulties. On the other hand, banks in areas of sluggish growth or possibly even dwindling areas may have difficulties in finding suitable employment for all of their available funds. Both circumstances have their special problems, but a clear recognition of the type of problem faced as well as the advantages of each circumstance is a necessary starting point for a bank in framing its over-all policies.

THE COMPETITIVE ENVIRONMENT

Most banks face competition in one form or another. The competitors may be other commercial banks, or they may be other types of financial institutions. Commercial banks not only compete one with another but may compete with other savings institutions, such as mutual savings banks, savings and loan associations, and even credit unions. The competition for funds may also be paralleled by competition for good loans, such as with government lending agencies or life insurance companies.

The existence of competition is the price most American businesses pay for relative freedom from regulation and restraint. The important issue is the way in which competition is dealt with in terms of general managerial policy. Some competitors of banks unquestionably have important natural advantages. Commercial banks, as department stores of finance, however, also have a strong basic position and should not let their courage sag simply on the superficial evidence that a given type of competitor has done fairly well with a given type of business.

Competition for Funds

Competition for the demand deposit business of a bank is necessarily with other commercial banks. Much of the competitive efforts of banks centers around this simple and self-evident aspect of banking. The promotional activities of a bank are frequently judged more by their relative success or failure in attracting funds than by any other criterion. It must be recognized, however, that subtle differences exist in the positions of individual banks. These differences would not be immediately evident to an outside observer. For example, the business connections of members of the board of directors sometimes account for the superior attraction of good and stable funds by certain banks. All bankers are sensitive to the extent to which directorships can open up competitive advantages for their institutions. It is possible, of course, to exaggerate the importance of this factor. The ability of directors to influence or control deposits may sometimes have led to the selection of directors who were otherwise of little help.

The competition for time or savings deposits is of a somewhat different character. This competition tends to be rather stronger between banks and other types of savings agencies than among commercial banks themselves. Savings is a type of retail business and is promoted by methods quite different from those used to build up demand deposits. Passbook savings may even require somewhat different tactics than certificate of time deposit. The bank that believes quite a bit of money in large unit blocks to be available may wish to emphasize the promotion of certificates of time deposit and to offer more attractive rates or terms for such deposits (at least in so far as Federal Reserve Regulation Q permits).

Competition for Loans

The competition for loans was quite intense in the thirties and in the early postwar years when banks were worried about adequate outlets for their funds. As the balance between the supply of funds and the demand for them shifted, however, this type of promotion tended to dwindle. But competition for loans is still very real; loans are still the most profitable of all types of bank earning assets. In most circumstances the heart of loan competition is not the rate of interest offered borrowing customers but more subtle factors such as prestige and service. Commercial banks have a special interest in meeting the loan needs of customers who normally can provide them with large deposit balances. In the long run customers with good average balances carry their own weight and provide the kind of two-way relationship on which commercial banks depend.

Rate differentials for customers can be a thorny problem. A clear-eyed view of customers usually indicates that some deserve far better rates than others. But can a bank differentiate between customers without bruising some feelings dangerously?

Character of Banking Competition

The business of banking, like many other parts of the American business scene, has become one in which competitive efforts emphasize quality of service rather than cheapness of price. Most banks try to offer superior service and, in fact, the service of banks has been greatly improved in recent years. On the other hand, the use of price as a competitive inducement is unpopular within the banking fraternity. This is particularly true with respect to the interest rates charged on loans. The same observation might be made with respect to the interest rates paid for time and savings deposits.

The uniformity of banking price is best exemplified in the application of the prime loan rate which covers a great proportion of the lending business done by large money-market banks. This rate is changed from time to time largely as the result of general money market ease or tension. A leading money-market bank generally initiates changes in its prime loan rate, and it is typical that almost all other leading money-market banks fall into line within a matter of hours or even minutes after such an announcement. Whatever rate is chosen is likely to prevail for some period (only twelve changes were made in the eight years between 1952 and 1959) and applies to a large part of the business done in bigger banks. Figure 11-1 shows prime loan rate changes during recent years.

There is less uniformity among banks with respect to the rates paid on time and savings deposits. To a considerable extent, however, Regulation Q of the Federal Reserve has had the effect of providing a ceiling on such rates. In periods of higher interest rates this ceiling has tended to minimize competitive pressures for making rate changes. Even in the absence of Regulation Q, however, rates paid on time and savings deposits tend to be uniform within a given competitive area even though large regional differences still exist.

The rates of interest charged on loans by banks outside money-market centers usually exceed the prime loan rate by some margin. Within a given area, however, interest rates on loans tend to be rather uniform among banks. Surprisingly enough, rates also tend to be uniform among customers even though they differ in their credit worthiness.

Competition with Savings Institutions

Commercial banks not only compete for funds with one another, they also compete with savings institutions. The rapid development of savings and loan associations in the postwar period is well known. Mutual savings banks have likewise been more vigorous competitors.

Commercial banks also compete with savings institutions for high-quality loans. Commercial banks have traditionally tried to maintain somewhat higher standards for credit granting than other financial institutions. These new and aggressive savings outlets, however, not only have frequently been able to secure a larger part of the flow of new funds but also have competed successfully for top-quality loans. Commercial banks have been viewed by some customers as "off-again-on-again" lenders. In contrast, savings intermediaries have often seemed to be more consistent sources of funds.

Commercial banks also compete with other financial intermediaries in supplying general financial services. Some savings intermediaries have devised payment systems by supplying cashiers' checks; some have offered safe deposit services. Judged by the needs of most individuals, they have become nearly full-line financial agents. The department store character of commercial banks has long been one of their important competitive characteristics. The increased range of services offered by other financial intermediaries may be a clear and effective threat to the unique quality of commercial banks.

Value of "Keeping in Step"

Banking usually encourages conformity and discourages heterodoxy; banks usually try to "keep in step" with one another. Banks scrutinize one another's financial statements in great detail and tend to justify their policies on the basis of similarity to policies followed by other banks. The influence of the supervisory agencies also tends to produce some measure of conformity. The result of this tendency toward conformity is to keep the individual bank from departing greatly from the standards set by the banking community. Innovation is not discouraged, but a banker must be surer of the justification of innovation than is true in most other businesses. Disapproval of his fellow bankers is a luxury few bankers can afford.

Loans-to-assets ratios furnish an illustration of this tendency toward conformity. In the early years after World War II any bank that had loans in excess of 50 per cent of its assets was conspicuous. It would have been referred to as a heavily loaned bank. Banks in areas having strong loan demands hesitated to allow their loans-to-assets ratios to exceed this level even though such would have been profitable. Most banks thought that doing so would arouse the suspicions of the examiners and would seem to depart from banking prudence. On the other hand, in the late 1950s many banks had not only reached but exceeded this loans-to-assets ratio considerably. New York City banks averaged nearly 65 per cent. With such ratios becoming common, the individual bank at this level no longer felt conspicuous. Now banks with low loans-to-assets ratios feel out of step. Banks with such ratios try vigorously to increase their loans to "keep up with competition."

The efforts of banks to keep in step not only is reflected in their policies with respect to loan ratios but may be observed in their policies with respect to capital and capital ratios and in their policies with respect to borrowing. In the early postwar years when relatively few banks borrowed, the disclosure of borrowings on a published statement almost never occurred. Any bank doing so would have felt quite conspicuous. In later periods when borrowing became more frequent, the reluctance to publish borrowings was far less compelling, though it did not vanish. Some banks that had formerly avoided borrowing changed their policies and borrowed frequently.

While part of the incentive for keeping in step grows out of each banker's observation of others, part of this discipline is enforced by the scrutiny of an important group of customers: the corporate depositors. Large corporations whose deposits exceed the $10,000 amount covered by deposit insurance undertake rather detailed scrutinies of the banks in which they carry balances. This scrutiny frequently includes preparing detailed statistical analyses of the financial statements of their depositaries. These analyses tend to use national averages as medians with which the situations of individual banks are compared. A bank that had a loan ratio of 50 per cent when other banks averaged 30 per cent might have been conspicuous in such an analysis. It might also have felt a bit out of line and have avoided increasing its loans further. On the other hand, when national averages passed the 50 per cent margin, a bank having a loan ratio of less than 50 per cent might have worried that in the eyes of its corporate customers it was not showing itself to be as active a source of credit as it should. It is worth noting, of course, that a shrewd corporate treasurer might have reasoned somewhat differently. He could argue that a bank with a low loan ratio had more unused lending capacity and so might be a better credit source.

DEVELOPING BUSINESS WITH EXISTING CUSTOMERS

Banks, like all other businesses, survive and prosper to the extent they keep a hard core of profitable customers. Although a great deal of promotional effort is focused on acquiring new customers, it is often possible that a bank may find it just as profitable to encourage or develop added business within its existing body of customers. In order to do this, however, it is important for a bank to have some knowledge of the economic characteristics of its customers. Very few businesses have access to as revealing knowledge of their customers as bankers. A prudent banker, therefore, seeks to improve this knowledge by formal methods as well as the informal ones of face-to-face contact.

Two banks, located across the street from each other, may have vastly different types of customers. Sometimes this is the result of past policies. Those money-market banks that only "wholesale" money are aware of the limited range of their customers; the number tends to be small. Other banks, however, may not have as clear reasons for the singular character of their customers. Factors such as religious affiliations or social connections or nationality of present or former officers may account for special concentrations of customers—concentrations that may persist long after the basic cause no longer operates. Customers may differ by income level; an effective trust department may attract high-income customers for a general banking relationship. A loan officer who is familiar with a given type of business and who has a following in it may attract members of that industry or specialty to his bank.

Although most bankers are aware of the special characteristics that exist within their banks, formal statistical surveys of customers sometimes reveal new facts, and sometimes (a more sobering matter) disclose that a supposed point of strength or concentration has been lost though the myth of its presence still circulates.

The decision whether to embark on direct lending to consumers on an installment basis should depend on the kind of customers a bank already has on its books. To cover overhead costs and to be profitable, this type of business requires large-volume operations. Whether or not such business will be profitable may depend more on the nature of the body of existing customers than on the number of new customers that might be attracted. If installment lending business of a size and character that was profitable could be developed within the body of existing customers, this could make the entry less hazardous. With this basic backlog of existing customers a bank would then have an opportunity to attract other business from outside this group.

Much the same thing probably has been true of agricultural lending in many banks. Farmers have been customers of rural banks for many years. Nevertheless, the rise of governmental agricultural lending agencies seems to have indicated that these banking connections failed to supply the full range of lending services expected by farmers. If the public agencies lending to farmers had had difficulties or encountered losses, this might have indicated that the business was of a sort that was neither appropriate for nor profitable to banks. However, since a great share of the business done by governmental lending agencies has proved to be surprisingly sound and profitable, the question may be raised whether in the past some bankers were not failing to develop the full business potential within the ranks of their existing customers.

The same opportunity also exists for real estate lending. A bank that has developed a time and savings deposit business has had ample opportunity to study the financial habits of a sizable group of customers that may become home owners. These customers may furnish an unusually valuable outlet for mortgage loans. The establishment of a prior customer relationship is the foundation of credit judgments of a quality not accessible to other lenders.

The primary point to be made by these illustrations is that the economic characteristics of a bank's existing customers, their business connections, their income levels, and their economic habits may be the best beginning point for developing new business.

INTEGRATED TOP-MANAGEMENT POLICY

One of the principal reasons why a bank may wish to pay particular attention to the way it fits into the financial and economic environment in which it operates is that it is useful for each bank to adopt a "top-management" point of view with respect to the totality of its efforts. It is quite obvious that most banks are limited primarily to the business that is accessible to them from their existing locations. A bank in a remote location can hardly aspire to undertake the wholesale banking that would be done by a large money-market institution. A bank should integrate its investment policies with its loan policies. If it has a clientele that offers the potentials of active and continuing loan demands, then a bank may treat its investments largely as liquidity reserves. On the other hand, a bank so located as to lack a continuing demand for loans may have to depend on investments for income to a much greater extent. Such a bank is forced to follow investment policies that emphasize income rather than liquidity.

Most bankers ultimately arrive at a balanced view of business potentials by an intuitive process of trial and error. The rationale of the point of view expressed here, however, is that top-management policy for a bank should be based on the totality of considerations such as those enumerated in this chapter. Such policy is then based on systematic logic and empirical evidence as well as on practical experience.

Part II

LIQUIDITY MANAGEMENT

Banks need liquidity because they can forecast the future only imperfectly. Uncertainty is the theme that pervades this section. After an initial chapter on general liquidity policies, the remaining chapters deal with the three basic levels of liquidity management. The first level is management of the money position, a day-to-day concern of every commercial bank. While focused on meeting the requirements of law, the practical problems of dealing with currency demands and day-to-day deposit variations are considered. The second level is the provision of reserves for seasonal and other intermediate-range needs that are reasonably certain to occur. The third level is consideration of liquidity management for remote contingencies that might or might not happen.

4

General Liquidity Policies

A primary responsibility of a commercial bank is to maintain an adequate degree of liquidity. This form of statement, although true, is not very useful until a more precise expression of what is meant by the word "adequate" is supplied. If a bank fails to maintain adequate liquidity, it faces obvious difficulties. On the other hand, if it maintains excess liquidity, it may retard earnings to the point where it cannot build up the capital needed to hold its relative position in the banking structure.

Although there is a tendency to speak of the basic need for liquidity as being the extreme contingency that a commercial bank might be forced to liquidate all of its deposits, this is not the practical possibility against which operating officers must plan. Variations in deposits and loan demands, neither under the control of management, measure the size of the liquidity problem. How great are the variations that have been experienced or may be expected? Variations in deposits are sometimes a product of the nature of business conditions, they may be due to seasonal factors, and some variations in deposits are of a largely random nature. Variations in loan demand also are affected by cyclical developments as well as seasonal ones and, in addition, have certain random qualities which cannot be anticipated. Although a banker may exercise fairly complete control of investments, he usually feels obligated to meet legitimate loan demands and certainly is under pressure to do so for good customers. By the same token, it is obvious that a bank must meet all variations in deposits that it encounters for whatever reason whether good or bad. Thus to measure the adequacy of liquidity it is necessary to estimate likely variations in deposits and loan demands.

The importance to earnings of adequate but not excessive liquidity is not merely in keeping funds invested; it also is to give bankers some latitude in investment policy. This latitude is necessary to take advantage of interest rate shifts. Interest rates fluctuate. Since low interest rates tend to be associated with low loan demands, there is a natural tendency for banks to acquire investments in periods of low yields which would tend to make an adverse average yield or investment if a passive investment policy were followed. Shrewd bankers attempt to vary the average maturity of their portfolios according to swings in yields so as to improve investment yield. Adequate liquidity is, therefore, more than mere protection; it gives the bank manager a chance to show his skill at money market management.

There are two ways in which a bank can prepare to meet liquidity needs: by holding cash and by having investments which can be converted into cash quickly, in sizable amounts and with negligible loss. Thus the first element in protective liquidity is the cash (primary reserve) policy of a bank. As we shall find, the cash reserves are determined mainly by legal and operating considerations and are rather less important in providing protective liquidity than are secondary reserve investments.

This chapter will disclose some of the reasons why protective investment of reserves is rather more important than cash holdings in framing liquidity plans. One reason we can assert immediately. Since most cash needs are uncertain both in timing and in amount, a bank would forgo income unnecessarily if it should try to provide all its needed liquidity by holding cash. The very uncertainty as to how much and when liquidity

will be needed argues for recapture of income from liquid
reserves to the extent which is safe and practicable.

DEPOSIT FLUCTUATIONS

The primary reason why banks need protective liquidity is
that they always face the possibility of material and unexpected losses of deposits. It must be emphasized again and
again that the larger part of commercial-bank liabilities are
demand liabilities; they can be withdrawn at any time without notice. In reality this demand characteristic may not be
so important as it appears. Many other financial institutions
have short-term if not demand liabilities; for example, the
notice period for savings banks is generally from 30 to 90 days.
While moderately different from a pure demand liability, the
difference is not great. About all it amounts to is a breathing
period for change of policy and negotiation of asset sales. The
significance of the savings classification of a deposit is the
implied intention of the depositor to keep his account fairly
stable. Historically, he has usually done so, though savings
depositors occasionally do withdraw their funds quickly. Runs
on banks have as often been caused by savings depositors as
by others. The practical fact is that demand-deposit holders
have the right to change the level of their balances without
notice, and they exercise this right frequently. Demand accounts do change both up and down for individual depositors,
for all the depositors of a given bank (and, therefore, the totals
for that bank), and even for the entire commercial banking
system. Thus the need for a protective investment policy. The
purpose of protective investment is to provide a cushion so
that these deposit changes neither embarrass a bank nor put
it under unusual pressure.

Causes of Deposit Fluctuation

If the chief reason for protective investment is to meet deposit fluctuations, the next question is: What causes deposit

fluctuations? Later on, we shall list the kinds of circumstances that account for and explain deposit fluctuation historically. At this point we must recall that bank lending creates deposits and the contraction of bank loans reduces deposits. While this describes the process within the banking system, it is not altogether true of the individual bank.

The careful student will recall that there is a great deal of difference between the explanation of deposit increase and decrease for a system of banks and that for a single bank. In a system of commercial banks, the level of deposits depends primarily on the amount of credit these banks extend in the form of loans made or of investments purchased. If banks extended no credit, they would have deposits only to the extent that people left currency with them instead of carrying it around in their pockets: in such a case, commercial banks would have 100 per cent reserves for all deposits. Banks have less than 100 per cent reserves only when they start extending credit. But since banks determine the amount of credit they extend, they would seem to *determine the volume of their deposits themselves*. If this is so, why should they fret and worry about protective investment?

Here we return to the difference between a single bank and the banking system as a whole. The banking system as a whole influences the level of banking deposits by the amount of credit it extends. Any one bank has little control over the level of its deposits (at least, not a direct control); its promotion and reputation influence deposits only indirectly. To illustrate the case in a simple fashion, suppose that all the banks in the United States except one, or all the banks in a small economically isolated community except one, should decide that they could extend some additional credit. There would be a general deposit expansion equal to the credit extended, and the one holdout bank would very likely share in this deposit expansion as well as other banks. Its decision not to join in the credit expansion would not limit its deposit expansion. It would be a beneficiary of deposits "created" by other banks and would pile up excess cash from these new deposits even if it did not join in the process of credit granting.

In reverse, suppose that all the banks in the country, or in an isolated community, except one should decide to contract loans or credit. Deposits would then contract with the credit contraction, and this situation would be felt by the one hold-out bank as severely as by the other banks. In practice, this single bank would probably have to join the general liquidation movement in self-defense.

Now we are equipped to discuss the subject with which we started: What are the circumstances that cause deposit variations of the sort requiring protective investment? There are two principal factors: changes in the aggregate of bank loans and investments and changes among individual banks in the distribution of deposits. These variations are of several kinds:

1. Business fluctuations, which cause the demand for bank loans to go up or down. This, in turn, affects the level of deposits.

2. Seasonal variations in the demand for bank credit and for currency to put into circulation, which cause bank deposits to fluctuate.

3. Relative population changes among areas—some parts of the country grow rapidly, others hardly at all.

4. Competitive shifts in which some banks grow at the expense of others.

5. Changes due to shifts in the relative prosperity of various depositors; for example, when there is farm prosperity, agricultural banks gain deposits more rapidly than do other types of banks.

Before we leave this section, one general warning should be given. Since we have implied that the commercial banking system is itself responsible, in a general way, by its policies of credit expansion or contraction for the level of deposits, it must have sounded as if the public as a whole had little or no influence on the level of bank deposits. This is not so. In the first place, banks cannot extend credit unless there is a demand for loans or unless there are borrowing corporations (or governmental units) offering their securities on the market or existing holders offering their holdings on the market. Second, the public must be willing to hold bank deposits and to treat them as money or as a money substitute. Credit expansion is a two-sided matter; the banks and the public both must concur in the process.

A second qualification, perhaps harder to understand, is in reality just as important. We have said—and it was admittedly an oversimplified statement—that the cash reserves are secured by banks to the extent that the public is willing to forgo carrying around currency in its pocket and to substitute the checkbook for the wallet. This was almost literally true before the Federal Reserve; now it is partly but not wholly true. Legal bank reserves for all member banks are now not only currency on hand but also their deposit balance at the "Fed." In this way, the volume of legal banking reserves is dependent not just on currency habits of the public but on a great variety of factors. If, by demanding cash from the banks, the public should reduce bank reserves and if this were not offset by some other factor such as an increase in Federal Reserve credit, then banks would have no alternative but to contract loans and therefore decrease deposit totals. In practice, however, the Federal Reserve does allow for currency movements in its supply of bank reserves, so this contingency has little relevance.

Time and Savings Deposits

As would be expected, time and savings deposits have a great deal less day-to-day volatility than is true of demand deposits. The degree of protective liquidity required, therefore, is less than that for demand deposits. On the other hand, experience has shown that under pressure of extreme cyclical events, as in the early 1930s, time and savings deposits may be subject to almost as great a decline as was experienced by demand deposits. The question may be asked, however, whether contemporary circumstances require a commercial banker to observe standards which would protect against a depression as severe as that of the early 1930s.

Discussion of this probability requires a separate treatment of passbook savings deposits and time deposits. Even if the extreme pressures of a great depression recurred, it is hard to believe that public policy would ever permit panic liquidation of true passbook savings deposit accounts. In general, therefore, a portfolio of assets with relatively low turnover is probably consistent with the protection of passbook savings deposits. Special short-term liquidity, of course, is not required for these deposits. One possible exception would be banks located in areas subject to special local circumstances that might create pressure on these accounts. For example, a bank with large savings deposits located in a steel-producing area which is subject to cyclical variability and occasionally to strikes might expect to experience pressure on these accounts from time to time.

Time deposits such as those in the form of certificates of deposits are considerably more volatile. These deposits are typically held by large depositors, such as foreign governments, corporations, or by state and local government. All these balances are in the hands of financially sophisticated persons who are disposed to compare the yields available on time deposits with those available on open-market instruments. These accounts, therefore, should be expected to vary through a fairly wide latitude and a banker should provide a reasonably thick protective cover of liquidity for them. Experience is the best guide and the record clearly shows that these accounts do vary. This variation is further aggravated by the Federal Reserve regulation of payment of interest on these deposits (Regulation Q) which tends to limit the rates paid in high interest rate periods and thus to curb bank competition for this type of money.

Influence of Business Cycles

Chapter 2 dealt at length with the problem of business cycles and their influence on banking policy. A certain number of

points, however, may be recalled at this stage. Prior to World
War II bank deposits moved with the business cycle: they went
up in periods of prosperity and declined in periods of recession.
Since then there has been a very great shift in the nature of
Federal Reserve policy. This shift has affected the pattern of
deposit changes materially. The exercise of a positive monetary
policy by the Federal Reserve through the control of deposits
has meant a tendency to release reserves whenever recessionary
signs appear but to hold reserves rather tautly during boom
periods. As a result, a large part of the growth in demand deposits has taken place during recessionary periods and relatively little in periods of boom. In other words, the cyclical
movements of deposits experienced in the past have almost been
reversed.

This phenomenon is something on which bankers can depend
in some measure in their general managerial policies. In planning ahead they can expect to experience relatively little deposit growth in boom periods. Individual banks may differ from
aggregate experience but most banks will tend to feel, as individual institutions, the pressures put on the banking system or
the ease allowed it. In recessions, when interest rates are low,
they may expect to find reserves increasing and a tendency for
deposits to grow. This expectation unquestionably raises problems for individual banks. New funds appear mostly in low-
interest-rate periods, which exposes them to dangers. These
dangers will be discussed in later chapters.

Future Business Cycles and Bank Deposits

The business cycle has been important in deposit variations
in the past, but will it continue to be as important in the future?
It is arguable that this is not the case. There are several reasons.
In the first place, the Federal Reserve is both better equipped
and more determined to offset the liquidity drains which cyclical downturns may put on banks. Banks could have reasonably
expected more help in the depression of the 1930s than they
received, but Federal Reserve policy was hampered by legal
factors and personal indecision in a way that is no longer true.

Another factor is the Federal government's fiscal policy. Although the wisdom of governmental action in the face of depressions and economic difficulties is often challenged, some form of action will be taken whenever economic difficulties appear. The replacement of dwindling loans and private investment securities by government securities in depression periods is likely to stay the reduction of bank deposits. Cyclical fluctuations in deposits, once very large, have been reversed in direction!

Seasonal Variation in Deposits

Chapter 5 will present an explicit treatment of the way in which seasonal variations may be analyzed in framing protective investment policy. Here our purpose is only to describe the nature and extent of seasonal variations in deposits and the degree to which seasonality is a factor in causing need for protective action.

For the banking system as a whole, there is little seasonal fluctuation in deposits. Since deposits in the entire banking system are dependent primarily on bank credit extension and on the currency habits of the public, these factors, as expected, explain what little seasonal variation can be found. A seasonal pattern in currency demands also prevails. Loan demands at banks show rather less seasonality, but they tend to expand in the summer and fall months and to contract in the early months of the year. To the extent they vary, so do deposits.

At individual banks there are much larger and more evident seasonal patterns. What is even more important, the seasonal pattern of loans and deposits, which is of necessity parallel for the banking system, sometimes tends to be the opposite at individual banks! The reason is obvious. Customers both draw down their deposit accounts and borrow when they need funds; they let deposit accounts build up and repay loans in slack seasons. Figure 6-2 illustrates such a case.

An adequate study of seasonality at individual banks has never been made. As a result, most of what is known about the subject is hearsay and random observation. It appears that the biggest seasonal variations in bank loans and deposits are in banks dependent on and located in one-crop agricultural areas. Sizable seasonal variation appears in summer and winter resort areas. There seem to be some other cases of seasonal variation for which good reasons are not immediately evident.

Because a true seasonal movement can be measured and predicted with reasonable accuracy—something that is impossible for business cycle variations—the matter is not one that need cause so much concern in bank management. The proper and careful handling of the seasonal factor, however, can make a fairly substantial contribution to profitability.

Long-term Deposit Changes

The amount of bank deposits in any given area is, naturally, related to the population and richness of that area. As some sections of the country grow, others recede or at least do not grow rapidly. The more-than-average rapidity of growth in both population and wealth of the West and the Southwest in the United States is a striking example of such change in relative standing.

Deposits change likewise. They follow, to a considerable extent, the fortunes of the community of their origin. There is often a tendency, however, for the bank deposits of a rapidly growing area to increase less rapidly than the wealth and income of these boom areas. Nor do deposits hurry away from a rich but atrophying area. In spite of the prodigious growth of the West Coast states during the war and in spite of spectacular gains by some banks, the area as a whole gained only from 9 to 13 per cent of the deposit totals of the nation. A rapidly growing area, while showing deposit increases, is likely to be one of an active demand for capital. Loans are in demand, and banks in such areas may turn away credit demands that would be gladly met in other areas. Often the growing industries of new and rich communities go to the older financial centers to meet their credit needs.

Shifts of this sort are slow. They do not pose a serious problem of protective investment for the banker in a receding com-

munity. He cannot, of course, afford bad credit risks or losses
any more than any other banker, but the liquidity demands of
this sort are so slow and slight that they amount to very little.
If a banker is aware of the sort of shift away from his community that is bound sooner or later to lead to this sort of decline, he would do well to adopt the general business policies of
a slowly liquidating enterprise such as a mining company ex-
ploiting a rich but shrinking vein of ore.

Competition for Deposits

One important reason for shifts of deposits among banks
is competition. While competition has sometimes been mild in
such matters as service charges and rather less often for loan
rates, there is active competition in most areas for volume of
business. Competition for deposits is keen and takes many
forms. Open advertising and solicitation are well known. Various kinds of business connections are exploited; city correspondents try to direct business to their country clients, and the
favor is sometimes returned. Bank directors are often chosen
with some regard for the business they can bring with them.

Competition is not the sort of thing that leads to sudden or
unexpected losses of deposits. Like the secular changes discussed above, it poses no serious liquidity problems. The difficulty may be that a bank which is losing out competitively
often may use unwarranted loan policies in a fruitless effort
to restore its position; but with a weakened loan position, it
may not be able to face further competitive losses.

LOAN DEMANDS

A second reason for protective liquidity is the shape and
character of a bank's loan demands. As we have already argued, loans should have a priority in the employment of funds.
Once a bank has ample protective assets to meet deposit variations, it should be prepared to lend the remainder of its funds,
investing only those parts that cannot be lent. The ability to

lend requires assets in a form that can be converted into available funds as promptly as the funds needed to meet deposit demands.

The greatest short-term reason why a bank experiences fluctuations in loan demands is the same one we have already encountered in the discussion of deposits—seasonal variations. In the next chapter when we undertake to estimate the liquidity reserves needed for seasonal reasons, we shall combine the deposit and the loan factors.

There is, of course, a reason why both should be affected. As we have already explained, the volume of deposits in the banking system as a whole depends to a considerable extent on the volume of bank loans. If one is subject to seasonal influences, the other is likewise affected. The problem is that, while these influences affect the entire banking system, they are not parallel in a single bank. The deposits of an individual bank do not depend on its loans to any great extent. If anything, the opposite situation prevails. A period of seasonally low deposits is very likely to coincide with a period of seasonally high loan demands, both factors which drain funds from a bank and use up or depend on liquidity reserves. Since a bank's borrowers are also likely to be among its leading depositors, this coincidence is most natural. Customers need to borrow when their deposit accounts have been depleted.

Being prepared for short-term loan demands, such as those arising out of seasonal influences, is rather more important than being prepared for longer term demands, such as those growing out of general boom conditions. A seasonal loan demand does not in and of itself indicate the operation of any forces which would tend to restore or increase the liquidity reserves of the bank meeting this demand, but an increase in loan demand due to great prosperity or boom conditions probably means that all banks are increasing their loans. This very fact tends to bring added reserves to all banks.

Thus, as we have said, if a bank "lends in step" with other banks, it is likely to have no particular liquidity problems. ("Lend in step" can be defined as increasing loans at the same rate as all banks in the commercial banking system.) There are, of course, important differences among banks. Some areas, and therefore the banks in those areas, are rather more unstable than the country as a whole. Banks in these areas are likely to find loan demands unsatisfied if they only "lend in step" with all banks in the banking system. Such banks would do well to provide themselves with more reserves for long-term uses than banks generally.

Loan Liquidation and Deposit Fluctuation

In analyzing the causes of deposit fluctuation, it was emphasized that the deposits *of any one bank* are *not* the result of the loan and investment policy of *that* bank but rather of the banking system. While this is true, certain reservations to this generalization should be recognized. Those reservations have been discussed earlier, but the point is so important that we repeat it in greater detail.

If a bank puts unusual pressure on its customers for loan repayment, it probably will discover that deposits drop more than would have otherwise occurred. Since the borrowing customers are almost always also depositors in the same bank, they are likely, under pressure, to draw down their deposit balances to unusually low levels to meet the collection pressure. Even where collection pressure is not excessive, there is a good chance that a more than proportionate part of loan repayments will come right out of the funds of the bank receiving the repayment.

Investments are bought and sold on the open market. No such direct relationship connects deposits and investments as exists between loans and deposits. Because of this internal relationship, liquidity plans of a prudent bank can depend on possible loan decline for a part (though only a part) of the deposit loss. In other words, loan and deposit variations even within a single institution are, to an appreciable extent, directly related.

These reservations in no way conflict with what has been said elsewhere. Banks should, so far as possible, always follow liquidity plans which will not require them to put pressure on good and solvent borrowing customers merely to restore the banks' liquidity. It is probably true that, without excessive collection pressure, a bank will find that loans settle some of its deposit disappearances. But this is not a dependable relationship.

HOW MUCH SHOULD BANKS DEPEND ON GOVERNMENTAL ASSISTANCE?

At a number of points in this chapter reference has been made to the influence of public policy on the liquidity needs of banks. It has been implied that the prevailing policy both of the Federal Reserve as a central bank and of the Federal government as a whole as expressed in its insurance of deposits, has put bankers in a quite different position with respect to liquidity management.

This is partly true. A drastic change has occurred in the environment surrounding banking, and much of this change is permanent. The era of panic runs on banks will probably never again be experienced. On the other hand, on governmental assistance dependence has certain dangers.

Federal Deposit Insurance Corporation (FDIC)

The weakness of the banking structure produced by "runs" which were sudden and irrational demands for cash brought many demands for correction. Although deposit insurance (a guarantee to depositors that their funds are safe and reasonably liquid) had been tried in many state plans and had in each case failed, one of the early New Deal measures was deposit insurance on a national basis. The insurance plan, as modified in course of time, is simple: an assessment is charged against all deposits and prompt availability of all deposit balances up to $10,000 is guaranteed. Although insurance to this limit is the only *legal* obligation of the system, there is doubtless some added moral responsibility, and the $10,000 limit is more formal than real. In practice, most banks have been fully protected;

few have been allowed to fail. Thus depositors with all sizes of accounts benefit by deposit insurance.

The FDIC has now passed through its formative stages. The insurance fund it has now accumulated is over $2.2 billion. The assessment rate has been drastically reduced. While banking difficulties such as we have experienced in the past could exhaust this fund, it is hard to believe that cumulative banking difficulties would be allowed to get under way. There is every reason to expect that the real function of deposit insurance is not indemnification for loss but for minimizing the losses. So far it has worked that way.

Federal Reserve Support of Liquidity

Since the Federal Reserve has promptly supplied liquidity in each of the modest recessions already experienced in the postwar period, it is widely expected that in any greater recessionary period the Federal Reserve would supply liquidity in even more generous amounts. The degree to which this would be done, however, is not one for which precise rules can be framed. The Federal Reserve would probably be unwilling to release liquidity in amounts that might be so great as to threaten inflationary developments in a following boom. The release of liquidity would usually tend to be relatively modest. For this reason the extent to which Federal Reserve release of liquidity can be depended on by individual banks is clearly limited.

A Suggested Rule

Over-all liquidity support can fairly be expected of government. The individual bank, however, must recognize that its position can be weaker than the national average and it should not lean on the hope of individual rescue by a governmental agency. The Federal Reserve would not supply liquidity in a degree that would support the individual bank that suffered far greater losses than the average of the banking system as a whole. The FDIC, if it takes over a bank, usually dislodges the existing owners and managers. Each bank, in planning its own liquidity requirements, may expect that the over-all liquidity policy will probably help it to some degree. However, to the extent that it might suffer sharper losses than other banks for special institutional or locational reasons, it should plan on being able to meet those needs by itself unaided and without evident strain.

5

Day-to-Day Management of the Money Position

The maintenance of minimum reserves in the form of deposits or vault cash by the management of liquid assets, in order to avoid excesses or deficiencies of required reserves, is generally thought of as management of the money position. To perform this function, a bank must make certain arrangements. First, it needs to keep a supply of assets so liquid that they can be converted into money the same day or the following day without material loss. Second, the factors that determine reserve requirements should be ascertainable by the accounting department promptly. The ammunition must be at hand and the target clear. Some aggressively managed banks also prepare projections of future reserve requirements. This is forecasting the financial weather with an economic radar. The period covered by projections may be anywhere from the next few days to several weeks ahead. The development of electronic computers and other devices has aided this form of planning. Reserve projections, however, can be made with the simplest of computing or statistical methods.

Money positions are managed in many different ways. The principal reason for variation among banks is differences in size and character of business done. In the discussion that follows the management of money positions for very big banks will be discussed separately and given more attention since the methods followed are complex. Money management at medium-sized and smaller banks is given less detailed treatment because the methods followed are less complex.

RESERVE AND OTHER CASH REQUIREMENTS

The several factors determining the amount of cash a bank must hold, and the form in which this cash is held, are partly legal and partly practical. The first step in reviewing the process of money position management, therefore, is to examine the element that is to be managed.

Growth of Legal Reserve Requirements

The need for adequate cash reserves has been universally proved wherever commercial banking has developed. Prudent bankers have usually developed standards for the maintenance of cash based on experience and practice. In the banking history of the United States, the profits of rapid expansion have often lured bankers beyond the bounds of prudence; our financial history is blemished with a number of episodes of wild and unrestrained bank expansion followed by dreary interludes of bank failures and banking reconstruction. Unlike most other countries (and partly because of this record), the legal requirement of cash reserves has come to be almost universal in the United States. In pre-Civil War days, bank notes were the most important bank liability; reserve requirement was usually related to bank-note liabilities. The famed Suffolk banking system was really the imposition of a reserve requirement, not by law, but by the leadership of a big Boston bank. Between 1837 and 1860, 11 states adopted legal reserve requirements for bank-note liabilities. The earliest reserve requirement against deposits seems to have been that of Louisiana in 1842, following a voluntary agreement among the banks to do the same made in 1839. The relatively favorable experience of Louisiana banks encouraged other states to adopt reserve requirements.[1]

The legally required reserve was incorporated in the National Banking Act when it was passed in 1863. The system was modified substantially when the Federal Reserve System was inaugurated, but the basic idea of a legal requirement was continued. Thus a part of the management of bank funds is to observe the legal requirements, and sometimes so to arrange affairs that the legal requirements are least burdensome.

A legal reserve requirement allows very little latitude for deviation from it. The penalties for deficient reserves are considerable, possibly involving the closing of a bank that shows persistent shortages. Thus we find the paradox: in practice, a bank cannot depend on its legal cash-reserve requirement to meet deposit shrinkage; this must come mainly from other assets. Where cash reserves are customary but not legally required, deficiencies can be tolerated for short periods, and so cash accounts are in reality more of a bulwark of protection. An important conclusion may be drawn from this circumstance: the real protective assets are the secondary reserves!

Prevailing Legal Reserve Requirements

The prevailing reserve requirements depend on the legal status of the bank involved. All national banks located in the continental United States and all state banks which voluntarily elect to become members of the Federal Reserve System observe reserve requirements of the Federal Reserve. Other (nonmember) banks usually observe state reserve requirements.

Each bank must be thoroughly familiar with and prepared to observe the primary cash-reserve requirements of the legal jurisdiction under which it operates.

State reserve requirements. State reserve requirements vary widely so that there is little use in trying to do more than summarize them here. Their chief characteristics are:

[1] R. G. Rodkey, *Legal Reserves in American Banking,* Michigan Business Studies, vol. 6, no. 5, 1934.

1. They usually count balances with other banks (correspondent accounts) as eligible reserves.

2. Vault cash and till cash may be counted.

3. In some states, Federal government and occasionally state securities may be used to meet reserve requirements.

4. A few of the states have incorporated in their administrative law the power to change primary reserve requirements and have vested this power in the hands of the bank commissioner or a state banking board, a feature usually patterned after the administratively variable reserve requirements of the Federal Reserve which are later discussed.

Federal Reserve requirements. The requirements imposed by the Federal Reserve Act and administered by the System are distinctive in a number of ways:

1. The two assets which meet reserve requirements are: a collected balance in a Reserve bank, and cash in vault. Negatively, this means that cash items in process of collection (whether with Federal Reserve or others) and balances with other domestic or foreign banks cannot be counted.

2. The basis against which the demand deposit reserve requirement is assessed is a complex called "net demand deposits." This magnitude is arrived at by totaling all demand deposit items and deducting from them all cash items in process of collection and balances in domestic banks subject to demand withdrawal. The purpose of this fairly complex formula is to arrive at an unduplicated total of the demand liabilities of the commercial banking system to the public.

3. The period for which reserves are required and the holdings of reserves are themselves averaged over a fixed period: a biweekly period for "country" banks and a weekly period for Reserve city and central Reserve city banks.[2] The daily aver-

[2] The National Bank Act of 1863 and all subsequent legislation on reserve requirements have used the terms "central reserve city," "reserve city," and "other" banks. This third category has come to be known as "country" banks. This use of country is not necessarily parallel to the usage of "country correspondent" mentioned in Chap. 3. Under legislation adopted in mid-1959, the "central Reserve" classification will go out of existence by July 28, 1962, unless abolished earlier by Federal Reserve action.

age includes Sundays and holidays. The deposits against which reserves must be maintained are averaged as of the *opening* of business, and the reserve balances are averaged for the *close* of business; thus a bank has a lag of one business day in which to correct or adjust its reserve standing on the last day of the reserve computation period.

4. The percentage requirements for maintenance of reserves are established by law, but fairly wide latitudes are allowed the Board of Governors of the Federal Reserve for changing these requirements as a matter of broad credit control.[3] The statutory requirements together with the authority for changing are shown in Table 1.

TABLE 1

Deposits	Statutory base, per cent	Change which can be made by Board of Governors under basic F. R. Act per cent
Net demand deposits		
Central Reserve city banks (New York and Chicago)*...............	13	10–22
Reserve city banks (about 60 cities)...	10	10–22
Country banks...................	7	7–14
Time deposits (all classes)............	3	3– 6

* This classification will cease to exist on July 28, 1962, unless abolished earlier by Federal Reserve action.

Change in Philosophy of Legal Reserve Requirements

Although this is fundamentally a treatment of the problems of bank management, primary reserve philosophy has enough bearing on managerial problems to make a brief excursion into that subject useful.

Legal reserve requirements originally were used to enforce higher standards of prudence on banks than they were disposed

[3] Those interested in pursuing the rationale for exercise of this power are directly referred to any first-class money and banking text

to impose on themselves. In the course of time this has been displaced by a new view. Since the Federal Reserve has been in operation, banks have often, indeed usually, carried rather larger cash reserves than were required by law. The chief form has been the maintenance of correspondent-bank balances, but banks have also sometimes carried larger reserve balances at the Federal Reserve than were legally necessary. Moreover, there have developed standards of prudence in the management of secondary reserve accounts so that banks maintain, in practice, a degree of liquidity that considerably exceeds the standard imposed by law.

Furthermore, the spirit of promotion and adventure that characterized bankers in the days of wildcat banking has largely passed; bankers are now, by reputation and by deed, rather cautiously disposed. There is no reason to fear that, if the legal reserve requirements were relaxed, there would be deterioration in standards which would endanger the solvency of banks or the soundness of the banking structure. A few banks might take advantage of the relaxation, but self-control would undoubtedly characterize the system as a whole. Under these circumstances, what good use is now served by the legal imposition of primary reserve requirements?

The purpose is not to enforce managerial prudence but rather to furnish a specific wedge for the imposition of legal controls on the total volume of bank credit, and therefore on the monetary expansion of the banking system. In the pre-Federal Reserve days when the reserve asset of last recourse was actual cash in vault (and often gold coin itself), an automatic limit was placed on bank credit expansion. Banks could not expand beyond the reserve multiple (the reciprocal of the reserve ratio) of the reserve cash that they could persuade the public to leave with them. This system had both advantages and dangers, but the signal of overexpansion was the very fact of loss of cash reserves. The Federal Reserve System was devised, among other things, to provide a degree of flexibility in the reserve structure that had not prevailed before.

Flexibility can be a good thing, but it can be overdone. Because the total of reserve balances with Reserve banks under the new system could expand rather more flexibly than by cash in vault under the old system, banks were less likely to be embarrassed in times of panic. Thus credit control by a central authority is more or less a corollary of the idea of a flexible reserve system. Credit control means control of credit granting by banks. But banks grant credit when they have an excess over their required reserves. They can, therefore, be influenced in credit granting by the *amount* of their primary required reserves, or by the *proportions* (*percentages*) they are required to maintain.

Thus, the modern view of reserve requirements is not that of enforcing standards of managerial prudence but rather that of providing a means to the broader end of credit control. This reinforces and explains what has been said before. The paradox of cash reserves is that they are among the least liquid of assets; they are primarily the device by which the granting of bank credit is held in reasonable bounds.

How Much Do Required Reserves Protect?

What has been said in the preceding paragraph and also at an earlier place in this chapter might lead to the conclusion that there is no real protection in cash reserves. This is an extreme view, even if correct in part. The purpose of this section is to spell out more exactly just how much protection is afforded by required and primary cash reserves.

For sake of illustration, assume that the primary reserves required by law (already discussed) and those required for reasons of managerial needs (to be discussed later in the chapter) should altogether amount to 20 per cent of demand deposits. If a bank suffers a loss of demand deposits—say, a million dollars for sake of illustration—does it mean that *none* of this loss can be met from primary reserves? Not necessarily. When there is a loss of a million dollars of deposits, the need for primary reserves has diminished by 20 per cent of the deposits, which is 80 per cent of the deposits lost—$800,000 in this case—which must be met from secondary reserves.

Cash in Vault

The amount of cash needed varies widely among banks, and at a given bank it varies widely from season to season. Experience teaches each bank when the heavy drains come, such as in harvest periods, the shopping days of the week, when the circus comes to town; also the times when a heavy cash inflow may be expected, for example, when a cash buyer of livestock comes through town. Rather sizable cash drains sometimes come most unexpectedly. The auction of a real estate property which, for legal reasons, requires that the binder payment be in legal-tender cash may lead to a sizable withdrawal (and just as sizable a return immediately after the auction when the unsuccessful bidders and the seller come back and redeposit the cash).

Since banks are the public cash depots, they must look at it as a service function not only to keep the cash on hand that regular and exceptional circumstances will call for, but also to keep it in the denominations and form that are demanded. Most banks replenish their cash supplies from the nearest Federal Reserve bank or branch, though some still get direct cash shipments from their city correspondents. The size of cash in vault, then, is frequently related to the distance between a bank and its cash source, distance here being measured in the time sense. Banks in the same block as a Federal Reserve bank can minimize their vault cash; those with slow transportation connections need to have larger reserves. The differences are indicated roughly (but only roughly) by the class of banks. As shown in Table 2, country banks have usually carried more cash in vault proportionately than all member banks.

True money-market banks frequently carry less than 1 per cent cash in vault, seldom more than 2 per cent. Reserve city banks vary rather more widely, sometimes being down to 1 per cent but more often averaging between 2 and 4 per cent.

Although member banks now can count vault cash in meeting reserve requirements, they frequently try to minimize these holdings. Not only is it a nonearning asset; it is also a problem of surety. It is the cash in vault that is seized by armed ban-

TABLE 2

CASH IN VAULT AS A PROPORTION
OF DEMAND DEPOSITS ADJUSTED

Year	All member banks, per cent	Country banks, per cent
1924	4.0	5.8
1929	3.4	5.6
1934	3.9	6.4
1939	3.3	5.3
1944	2.2	3.4
1949	2.1	3.1
1954	2.3	3.4
1959	2.6	3.7
1960	2.7	3.7

SOURCE: *Member Bank Call Reports.*

dits and absconded with by defaulting tellers. The least cash possible is the best principle, and most banks can be depended upon to observe this principle. Nonmember commercial banks are often particularly exposed to these hazards.

Correspondent Balances

Correspondent balances are those amounts deposited by a bank with its city correspondent. The balance may be kept with a city bank which handles check and other collection items for the country bank, or it may be a relatively inactive balance maintained for other reasons.

The practice of maintaining correspondent balances is uniquely American; it does not prevail in other banking systems to any great extent.

During the operation of the First Bank of the United States (1791 to 1811), this bank pursued the very sound but unpopular practice of presenting all the notes of private commercial banks it received to the issuing bank for redemption in legal-tender currency. It was sound because it limited the note issues of banks (deposit liabilities were small and uncommon at this time); but it was unpopular because it required banks to keep sizable specie reserves. After the lapse of this bank and during the regime of the Second Bank of the United States, less therapeutic note redemption was practiced and private banks indulged in an orgy of note overissue. The notes of banks, even wholly solvent banks, when remote from the money centers tended to go to a discount. The holders of such notes would naturally pay out the depreciated notes in trade transactions, where by custom they were accepted at par, and employ the better known notes of nearby banks (which were not at a discount) to provide their specie needs. Thus city banks felt themselves at a disadvantage; their notes were redeemed frequently while depreciated notes of country banks tended to stay in circulation. They felt that any practice which would bring the country bank notes up to par would work to their advantage. The plan devised to accomplish this was called the "Suffolk banking system" since the Suffolk Bank of Boston took the lead in putting it into effect. According to this plan the outlying Massachusetts banks were given the choice: arrange to have Boston funds available for the prompt redemption of notes as they were presented, or be prepared to meet sizable and unannounced counter presentation of these notes for redemption. This none-too-well-concealed threat led to the maintenance of what we would view as Boston correspondent balances.

The existence of correspondent balances was recognized by the National Banking Act and, according to the reserve requirements enforced by this act up until 1917, a portion of such balances could be counted as legal reserves by most banks.

When the Federal Reserve System was initiated, it was expected that correspondent balances would shrink. But the shrinkage was small. The services such as collection, which was expected to pass largely to the Federal Reserve, were still performed to a considerable extent by city correspondents. Table 3 shows the relative importance of these balances for several years during the past four decades.

The striking fact is that when banks find it difficult to employ their funds (1934 and 1939), these balances tend to

TABLE 3
BANKERS' BALANCES AS A PROPORTION
OF DEMAND DEPOSITS ADJUSTED

Year	All member banks, per cent	Country banks, per cent
1924	15.5	21.0
1929	13.0	15.9
1934	20.4	30.2
1939	21.4	36.5
1944	11.1	20.3
1949	11.2	18.4
1954	11.4	16.7
1959	10.5	16.2
1960	9.1	13.8

SOURCE: *Member Bank Call Reports.*

grow relatively large; but when there is a keen demand for funds (such as 1929, 1944, 1949, and 1959), the balances shrink. Thus the balances are to some extent a reservoir for idle funds.

There are no explicit rules for the size of correspondent balances. The suggestions range from 6 to 12 per cent of demand deposits and from 3 to 5 per cent of time deposits. In practice many banks are considerably below and above these margins. City banks welcome these accounts and make them a leading part of their business. The nearest rule they provide for the size of balance is arrived at by account analysis. By "metering" the charges for various types of activity and by giving an implicit credit for free and loanable balance, city correspondents divide between those accounts that are profitable and those that are not. It is uncommon for city correspondents to collect service charges from the accounts of country correspondents, but the "meter" of account analysis determines which accounts are encouraged and which are, if continuously unprofitable, finally discouraged.

In practice, a country bank, or even a middle-sized city bank which itself acts as city correspondent for some very small country banks, is frequently solicited for its account; if it listened to every city correspondent representative, it might open more accounts than it needed and keep more funds in them than necessary. But how many accounts are needed and how much should be kept in them? One prime difference is whether a bank "clears" (collects checks and other items) through the Federal Reserve or through a city correspondent. Those banks clearing through a city correspondent need to keep enough in their correspondent accounts to compensate for the activity thus created. If a bank will follow the city correspondent account analysis, the question will be answered in part. Should a bank try to clear through several accounts? If it gets sizable amounts due it from several important centers, it can get "available funds" a little more promptly by such action. For many banks this is a refinement of dubious profitability. A very few accounts are usually enough for clearing purposes.

Furthermore, a bank that is a member of the Federal Reserve System might find it more profitable to use the System's collection services. The small extra trouble in preparing cash letters for the Federal Reserve can easily pay off if this frees a sizable amount of funds for secondary reserve investment. When short-term interest rates are fairly high, this action yields profits.

A number of other factors enter into correspondent relationships. The city correspondent is expected to be a source of investment counseling. City banks are also sometimes traders in securities appropriate for bank investment, or even underwriters (where the law permits) for certain classes of securities such as municipal obligations. As traders and underwriters, they may be prepared to render special services for country correspondents. Furthermore, city banks may take over loans too big for small country correspondents to handle and at the same time give country correspondents participation in syndicated loans that otherwise would not be available to the country banks. The city banks also often furnish the service of "setting up" special-type loans (term loans, accounts receivable, or field warehousing credits) which the country banks are willing to make or participate in but which they do not have the technical facility to work out. Less important than formerly but not wholly unimportant, the city correspondent may be a credit refuge if times turn bad.

The use of correspondent balances for protective liquidity is primarily for middle-sized and smaller banks. The city correspondents in the great money markets hold rather small amounts due from other banks. They protect themselves more by secondary reserve operations. The very essence of money market tradition is for the bigger banks to hold relatively larger reserves and to use directly the mechanisms of the money market and the facilities of the Federal Reserve to channel liquidity (cash) out to their country correspondents. Thus liquidity management of the great banks follows rules somewhat different from those outlined here.

Collection Items

Any bank is bound to have a part of its assets tied up in cash items (checks drawn on other banks) deposited for collection by its customers. Theoretically, but not always in practice, these amounts are supposed to be dormant in customers' accounts until the collection process is completed. Since no bank takes any longer to collect these items than it can help, the amount of them held by the banking system and by the individual bank may be safely presumed to be the practicable minimum.

MONEY MANAGEMENT TECHNIQUES

The ways in which the cash or money position of a bank may be managed can be classified under either of two headings: (1) the purchase or sale of assets, or (2) borrowing. The assets purchased or sold include Treasury bills, a few other short-term Government securities, bankers' acceptances, and Federal funds. Borrowing may take the form of buying Federal funds in the Federal funds market or direct borrowing from the Federal Reserve.

As promised above, our discussion of techniques will treat large banks separately. Quantitative distinction between big banks and intermediate-sized banks is arbitrary at best; however, for this one purpose a convenient dividing line is provided by those banks that do and those that do not participate in the Federal funds market. In 1956 a Federal Reserve study indicated that about 150 large banks participated in this market, but since then the number of participants probably has grown. It is now believed that from 250 to 400 of the largest banks in the country have practical access to this market, possibly more.

The Federal funds market is the one in which Federal Reserve reserve balances are bought and sold. As mentioned below, this market is the principal reserve-adjustment vehicle of large banks. A bank may "sell" (lend) some portion of its reserves either by the direct process of an overnight loan which uses the mechanics of the wire transfer system, or by the less direct form of exchanging officers' checks, the seller's check being immediately payable in Federal funds with the buyer's check payable only through the clearinghouse (clearinghouse funds become available the following day).

Only fairly large banks participate in this market. The usual minimum unit for trading of Federal funds is one-half million dollars and some dealer banks prefer to trade in minimum amounts of one million dollars. Once the minimum level is reached, however, trades may be offered in multiples of $100,000. In other words, a bid or offer for $1.3 million of Federal funds would be allowable. Unless they are fairly large, selling (lending) banks cannot make unsecured loans of this amount because of loan limits. An unsecured sale of funds (a loan) to any one interest cannot exceed 10 per cent of a bank's capital and surplus in the case of national banks. (Other but similar rules apply to most state banks.) This size limitation means that a bank cannot sell a half million dollars of Federal funds effectively unless it has capital and surplus of about $5 million. Only about four hundred banks in the United States have capital of this amount or more. Buying and selling Federal funds on an unsecured basis is the normal method and is less complicated, though some purchases are made from smaller banks as collateral loans, by city correspondents, largely as a favor.

Banks that make use of this market in the management of reserve positions follow rather different policies than banks that are too small to make practical use of the Federal funds market. In this discussion, "large" banks means banks that have continuous access to the Federal funds markets both as buyers and as sellers.

Management of the Money Positions for Large Banks

The two most important instruments of liquidity used by large banks in the management of their money positions are Treasury bills and Federal funds. The relative importance of these two vehicles is indicated by the following facts: The 1956 Federal Reserve inquiry reported that daily Federal funds sales were between $600 million and $1.1 billion. The market has probably grown materially since 1956. A study of the Government securities market, also made by the Federal Reserve, showed that daily average bill trading was from $600 million to $1.4 billion in 1958. These volume figures, however, should be halved for comparative purposes since they include both purchases and sales. It is also known that nonfinancial corporations probably account for more of the bill volume than commercial banks. Federal funds transactions are seldom for more than one day, whereas bill purchases and sales have more lasting effects on reserve positions. This evidence, although inconclusive, suggests that large banks make extensive use of both vehicles for reserve position adjustments.

Government securities other than bills are also used, though less frequently. A few central money-market banks offer or recall loans to U.S. Government security dealers to adjust their reserve positions. These loans are made on a day-to-day basis and presumably have an impersonal or open-market character. Nevertheless, this vehicle is of limited application since only a few banks can make practical use of it. Loans to other types of security dealers should no longer be considered as having true open-market characteristics and are, therefore, a dubious vehicle for reserve adjustment. While some large banks have correspondent balances, they usually maintain these balances at levels which just compensate the other city correspondents for services performed. Unpredictable use of these balances would be considered passing reserve position headaches on to other bankers. It is generally not feasible, therefore, for large banks to make frequent and erratic drain on correspondent balances for the sake of management of money position.

In addition to Treasury bills and Federal funds, the method of last resort in money management is Federal Reserve Bank borrowing. "Fed" borrowing is not regularly used by most banks, and is not intended to be used regularly as one of the instruments for management of the money position. It is always available in case of unexpected developments, but it should be used sparingly for any less reason. This view is encouraged by Federal Reserve administration of discount operations. The prevailing character of Federal Reserve Regulation A, which governs the use of this facility, discourages banks from borrowing in very many consecutive reserve-adjustment periods except as special circumstances may force them to do so.

The administrators of the discount windows at the Federal Reserve banks have generally attempted to be relatively diplomatic in their relationship with member banks. Criticism for excessive use of discount facilities has usually been quite mild, at least in its early phases. Nevertheless, banks cannot help but be sensitive to any form of Federal Reserve criticism, particularly criticism on a point that might expose them to the unfavorable notice of other bankers such as the class A directors of Reserve banks. For this reason some banks have adopted the general policy of never borrowing.

This stiff-backed attitude, while understandable, undoubtedly puts an excessive strain on the other means used to manage reserve positions. Borrowing to meet truly unexpected circumstances is legitimate. While banks should plan to meet all cash needs that can be reasonably anticipated and expected in their liquidity management, there is no reason for them to meet wholly unexpected demands on their cash positions without borrowing. To do so would be to forgo earnings by holding excessive liquidity for remote periods of general uncertainty, such as those of international tension, or for times when the nature of business developments is unclear. These are conditions that may legitimately give rise to borrowings at the Reserve bank. Use of those facilities at such periods should not be avoided.

Some banks hesitate to show borrowings on published statements, such as those at the end of the year. This window-dressing convention is understandable, but whether under present conditions of financial sophistication it is wholly worthwhile is doubtful. Some progressive banks have knowingly allowed borrowings to show in their statements. So far as can be determined, they suffered no adverse effects as a result of this candid admission of engaging in a practice which, of course, was already known to exist by all financial sophisticates.

Relative interest rates determine which of the two principal reserve-adjustment instruments is used or how their use is combined. The Treasury bill rate fluctuates more continuously than the Federal funds rate and may be either above or below the Federal Reserve bank discount rate, as experience has shown. The rate on Federal funds frequently tends to hug and almost never exceeds the Federal Reserve discount rate though it may, from time to time, drop below it.

When the Treasury bill rate is above the Federal Reserve discount rate, banks prefer to keep their bills and to adjust reserve positions by purchasing Federal funds (borrowing) or by Federal Reserve bank borrowing. On the other hand, when the Treasury bill rate falls below the discount rate, banks usually find it more profitable to sell bills if they face a demand for funds unless it is a known demand for only one or two days. It is particularly true that if idle funds can be disposed of by the sale of Federal funds (lending), there is a special incentive for banks to adjust their reserve position by this device.

In the short-run or day-to-day sense, management of the money position simply means getting money as cheaply as possible when a reserve deficiency needs to be corrected, and employing money at as good a rate as possible when a bank is generating excess reserves. This form of statement puts the matter in too simple a light. Good money management means prudent preparation for future periods. A shrewd manager of the money position tries to look ahead to future loan demands, possible Treasury financing dates, and expected deposit movements so as to make actions in the present consonant with future developments. Money managers, more than other department heads in banks, are frequently engaged in trying to anticipate changes in Federal Reserve policy. Every money manager operates in an environment of short-term uncertainty. Most managers attempt to maintain a flexible position, and to be ready to move in the direction of greater or lesser liquidity, depending on what economic circumstances indicate.

If a need for funds at a later period is expected, a steady selling not only of bills but of other Government securities may be prudent when the Government securities market can absorb offerings at favorable prices, even though the proceeds are not needed in the reserve adjustments on the day of sale. A bank might find it advantageous to dispose of U.S. Government securities and to reinvest the funds in the Federal funds market immediately.

Most of the larger banks that are being discussed here are classified as "reserve city" banks and so must average their reserve requirements over the weekly period beginning Thursday and ending the following Wednesday night. As already indicated, requirements are based on deposits at the opening of business and these requirements are met by the holdings of reserves at the close of business. In other words, there is a one-day lag of the reserves over against requirements. This gives a little, but only a little, latitude in the settling of requirements. The final Wednesday of the reserve computation period frequently turns out to be a quite volatile day in the money markets. Federal funds rates may become very "sloppy," although occasionally the opposite situation prevails.

Although most banks normally borrow from their Federal Reserve bank for a 15-day period, they are, in fact, at liberty to repay this indebtedness at any time without interest loss. A very large portion of "Fed" borrowing is, in fact, prepaid. Accordingly, most banks generally wait until near the end of the reserve computation period before borrowing from their Federal Reserve bank. Early in the reserve computation period a bank may find it possible to sell Federal funds at the discount rate. On the final day, however, it may switch position and seek to buy funds. If unable to locate funds in the market, it may ultimately have to discount at the Federal Reserve bank. This, however, is considered poor management by some bankers who try to avoid having Federal funds dealings ever force them into Federal Reserve borrowing.

Although permitted to average reserves over a weekly period, many banks follow the policy of attempting to meet the requirements of each day of the reserve computation period as closely as possible. Some conservative banks plan to get somewhat "ahead" in the early days of the reserve computation period, intending to sell Federal funds on the final day. A few more daring banks apparently aim at a slight deficiency during the early days of the reserve computation period, hoping for "sloppy" money on the final day of the reserve computation period and the possibility of meeting requirements at a relatively cheap price.

Until recently dealing in Federal funds was viewed as a residual device for management of the money position. However, some banks now definitely plan to maintain a net sales position for Federal funds as a part of their investment portfolio. This investment vehicle has sometimes proved to be more profitable than Treasury bills as well as more liquid. A few large banks appear to have fallen into the position of being net borrowers in this market, presumably by default. This is not thought to be conservative money management.

Money Management
for Intermediate-sized and Smaller Banks

Management of the money position of smaller banks is necessarily somewhat less precise than that of large banks. Smaller banks use Treasury bills and other Government securities in the management of money positions but most of them are unable to participate in the Federal funds market. On the other hand, smaller banks can and do make more active use of correspondent balances in settlement of reserve needs. Smaller banks generally feel at liberty to draw on their city correspondent balances for adjustment of reserve position. In the solicitation of correspondent balances, city banks have encouraged country banks to take this view but have been known to complain of the results when such actions have unexpectedly forced them to scramble for funds. Borrowing from the Federal Reserve bank, however, is as much a last resort for small banks as for large. It is not only considered a last-resort action; quite a few country banks never borrow as a matter of managerial policy. This is too extreme a response to official Federal Reserve policy. Borrowing has a legitimate even if clearly limited place in liquidity management. It should be used to meet truly unexpected and unusual drains on individual bank liquidity.

Smaller banks that are members of the Federal Reserve System are permitted to average their reserves over a two-week period. Nonmember banks are governed by the requirements of state law and usually have more latitude about the observance of these requirements, since the matter is policed by the bank examiners in most cases rather than by periodic reports, as is true of member banks. Since country banks generally enjoy a somewhat greater degree of stability in deposits and suffer less erratic loan demands, they are a bit more able to anticipate their needs. Even though they do not, as a rule, engage in formal projection of reserve position, as is more commonly done by city banks, they usually have good informal knowledge of expected needs. Country banks also tend to end reserve computation periods with some excess reserves; this is considered a wasteful practice by city banks.

Although country banks enjoy a greater degree of day-to-day stability than intermediate-sized and larger banks, they probably experience wider seasonal swings and some of them suffer greater cyclical instability. The forward planning of reserve positions is quite important to such banks; the absence of it may lead to embarrassing results.

Reserve Projections

As already observed, those banks that manage their reserve position most astutely generally buttress their plans by projections of expected needs for some period ahead. Projections are never precise, but they help the money manager to determine whether it is more likely that he will want to increase or to lighten his forward commitments. A reserve projection is a forecast of the joint results of the factors that affect reserve position. These projections suffer from all the defects usually attributed to prophecy, but they are nevertheless useful. Circumstances in individual banks vary so widely that it probably would not be helpful to suggest specific work-sheet forms or procedures for the preparation of reserve projections. Only general suggestions are offered in the following paragraphs.

One of the most important issues is the length of the period ahead for which it may be useful to forecast. In many banks the useful planning period may be no longer than a few weeks. However, banks that are subject to large seasonal movements or are attempting to divide carefully the taking of capital gains and losses between tax years (a point covered in Chapter 20) may find it useful to extend their projections through the current calendar or fiscal year at all times, and as the end of the year is approached to add another quarter or half year to the current projections.

In preparing projections the principal factors to be allowed for are as follows:

1. The deposit balances of large corporations and their loan needs are an important consideration. Such elements as dividend dates, tax payment dates, and other seasonal characteristics of large corporate depositing and borrowing customers are frequently determinable facts.

2. The Treasury tax and loan account of the United States government should be planned for in advance. Its variations can be anticipated with some success. The dates at which amounts are added to these balances as well as the likely dates of withdrawal are predictable. This planning is particularly important for the bank that participates actively in new Treasury financing. Government security dealers usually can be helpful in anticipating likely Treasury financing dates and other Treasury factors such as calls on tax and loan accounts.

3. Timing of additions to and withdrawals from state and local funds can be anticipated with reasonable precision. Tax collection dates are known and expenditures are usually budgeted.

4. Residual deposit accounts may also have clearly expected seasonal movements. Chapter 6 will deal with the measurement and management of seasonal adjustments. At this point it is only necessary to call attention to the fact that estimation of expected seasonal movements of this residual can improve liquidity planning materially.

Methods of Adjusting to Seasonal Pressures

The Federal Reserve Bank of Philadelphia has published an interesting account of the methods used by the member banks in their district to adjust to seasonal reserve pressures.[4] The four principal methods used were: drawing on correspondent balances, the liquidation of investments, borrowing from Federal Reserve bank, and borrowing from the Federal funds market. Unfortunately, it is not possible to derive the relative dollar significance of these various vehicles from this pam-

---

[4] *The Seasonal Squeeze,* The Federal Reserve Bank of Philadelphia, 1960.

phlet. The evidence presented, however, generally confirmed the judgment made above: The principal method of adjustment is through Federal funds transactions; the liquidation of short-term investment securities is the second most important. This inquiry did not classify banks by size, but the primacy of

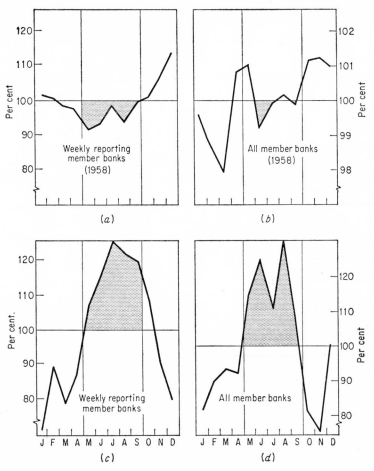

FIGURE 5-1. Banks adjust to seasonal pressures in a number of ways: (a) they draw down vault cash and correspondent balances; (b) they liquidate investments; (c) they borrow from others than the Federal Reserve; and (d) they borrow from the district Federal Reserve bank. (Source: *The Seasonal Squeeze*, Federal Reserve Bank of Philadelphia, 1960.)

Federal funds for large banks, and the sale of securities or correspondent balances for smaller banks, seem consistent with the evidence shown. A chart based on these relative figures is shown in Figure 5-1.

This account suggested that liquidation of securities was used more for liquidity needs that were somewhat further away, whereas Federal funds transactions were used for needs in the relatively near-term future.

6

Working Secondary Reserves

As the preceding chapter has brought out, bank needs for liquidity are caused by a wide variety of factors. Some of the needs arise because of well-defined movements in deposits through the seasons of the year. Other needs arise because of seasonal changes in loan demands. Banking operations also frequently exhibit a random quality; banks often face unexpected or unusual drains through the clearinghouse, or encounter unusual demands from borrowing customers.

Liquidity needs may also arise because of the swings in business conditions that occur from time to time. Although the United States government and other governments have adopted the policy of attempting to reduce the instability of the economy, this effort cannot be fully successful. Banks must expect some variations in business conditions, and the prudent banker is probably well advised to prepare for slightly more severe variations than those that many members of the public might feel to be the tolerable margin. Needs for liquidity are also caused by a variety of other incidental factors, such as possibilities of changes in reserve requirements or simply unexpected local and community developments.

These various liquidity needs may be separated on one score: some are quite likely to occur; others are of a more remote and uncertain nature. In the discussion that follows, therefore, the more likely needs are treated separately from those that are remote but possible. This chapter will deal with the likely needs for which banks should provide true working secondary reserves.

CAUSES OF EXPECTED SECONDARY RESERVE NEEDS

The principal cause of expected secondary reserve needs is seasonal movements of either deposits or loans. That subject will receive a large part of the attention in the remainder of this chapter. A number of somewhat less important points will be treated, however, including the nature of random deposit movements and certain unstable deposit accounts that have special characteristics and present special problems.

Seasonal Fluctuations as the Basis for Liquidity Needs

The phenomenon of seasonal variation may be observed in many ways. Agriculture is obviously seasonal. We all know about the Christmas bulge in retail trade. These two examples illustrate two major factors underlying seasonal variation. Some seasonal changes are due to nature's own annual cycle of weather. Agriculture is a seasonal business because weather and therefore growing conditions are "seasonal." Other kinds of seasonals are due to social or human conventions. Christmas is a traditional celebration. This second type of seasonal is subject to change because human and social conventions and habits can change, though slowly. For example, before the war it was customary for new automobile models to be introduced in the fall of the year. Few people bought cars during the summer months, and there was little automotive production. The plants were being tooled up for the new models. As a result, there was a summer slump in automobile production—a seasonal low. Later, the period for new models was changed to the turn of the year. The character of the seasonal pattern in the automotive industry was considerably modified by this change. When an industry operates at capacity, however, the degree of seasonal fluctuation is less.

To estimate the magnitude of seasonal variation is a problem familiar to students of statistics. It is also well known that the indexes of seasonal variation sometimes must be changed because of changing seasonal factors. When the date of the auto show was changed, the seasonal indexes were also changed. It is also well known that the estimates of seasonal fluctuation often go far wide of the mark; they cannot be refined beyond a certain point.

Seasonal fluctuation is necessarily an important aspect of banking operations. The tradition has been that the best loans were based on short-term transactions primarily for seasonal needs. The deposit accounts—at least the demand accounts held by business concerns and farmers—were likewise presumed to vary with the seasonal pressure for funds.

Banks located in large cities experience less seasonal swing because they deal with customers of many types. The seasonal peaks of some customers are offset by the seasonal valleys of others. Nevertheless, big banks may be subject to marked seasonal swings. For example, in 1950 the Chase National Bank (now the Chase Manhattan Bank) made a study of seasonality in its loans. Although more than a decade has passed since this study was prepared, the best evidence available suggests that it is still quite representative of existing circumstances. The Federal Reserve publishes weekly figures of commercial loans to selected industries by leading member banks. These figures indicate patterns quite similar to those in the Chase study. The Chase study showed that current commercial, industrial, and agricultural loans reached a seasonal peak of 12 per cent above the annual average in December and that they fell to a seasonal low of 11 per cent below the annual average in June. Some special types of loans were found to account for most of the seasonal swing. The big movers were:

Foodstuff loans

Tobacco loans

Finance, acceptance, and small-loan company loans
Department-store loans

The picture of these separate categories, as well as the seasonal movement of the current commercial, industrial, and agricultural loan account, is shown in Figure 6-1.

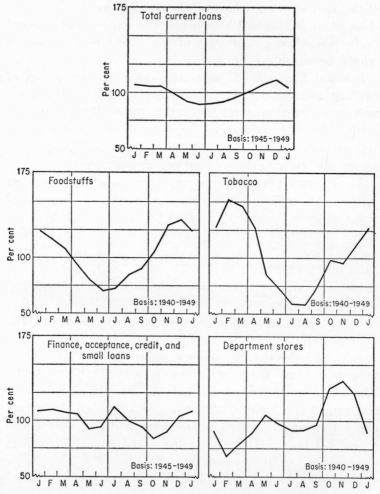

FIGURE 6-1. Factors expressing seasonal fluctuations computed from five years of raw data. (Source: Chase Manhattan Bank; then Chase National Bank, 1950.)

Coincidence of Loan Highs and Deposit Lows

Strong reasons exist for expecting that in an individual bank there will be an adverse coincidence of deposit declines and increases in loan demands. The reason may be found in the typical cash management habits of customers. Except as they may be restrained by compensatory balance rules, customers will tend to draw down deposit accounts before seeking loan accommodations. On the other hand, once loans are repaid deposit balances may accumulate. To the extent that a bank has a concentration of customers with similar economic char- acteristics, as would be true of single-industry communities, this concentration will tend to cause the peaks of loan demands to coincide with the valleys of deposits. Such a coincidence is quite evident in Figure 6-2. The kind of circumstance that would produce such a seasonal pattern could be found in a one-cash-crop agricultural community. When crops are being planted and grown, deposits will be drawn down and loan de- mand will increase. When crops are marketed, however, loans will be retired and deposits will tend to increase.

Several interesting conclusions may be drawn from Figure 6-2. While it demonstrates the general proposition that loan and deposit seasonals tend to move in opposite directions, it also shows that the coincidence is not precise. For example, the peak in the demand for loans comes in July, fully two months in advance of the low point for deposits. The low point of loan demand comes in February, one month before the de- posit peak in March. In other words, the offset is not exact.

Another interesting observation is the rather large amount of variation among years. The year 1958, which was marked by general increase of deposits in most banks, did not reflect such an increase at this particular bank.

Figure 6-2 is based on a hypothetical case, but it contains many demonstrated elements of reality. Seasonal indexes com- puted for a small Middle Western bank a number of years ago had a similar pattern. These indexes are shown in Figure 6-3. The seasonal movement of deposits at this bank were far

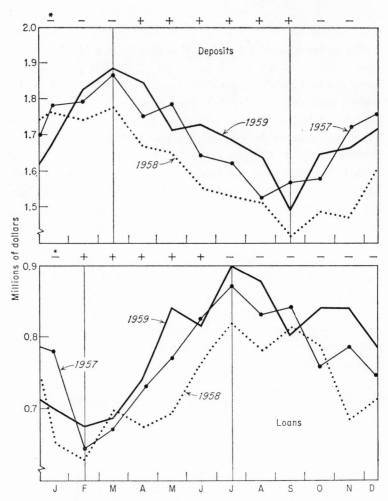

FIGURE 6-2. Demand deposits and short-term loans of a hypothetical bank. A "+" sign refers to need at that month for seasonal reserves; a "—" sign signifies that cash inflows are offsetting reserve need. (Source: *The Seasonal Squeeze,* Federal Reserve Bank of Philadelphia, 1960.)

more pronounced than those for loans. A reverse situation might prevail in other banks; in fact, the usual thing to expect would be more seasonal movement in loans than in deposits. This case also underscores the warning given above that the high point for loans may not coincide with the low

point for deposits, as is also true of the opposite pair of high
and low points.

One cause of seasonal liquidity needs experienced by banks
grows out of seasonal aspects of our tax systems. Some of
these needs are reflected primarily in the way in which customers draw checks on certain fixed dates to pay taxes, a point
which presumably has already been dealt with in the general
measurement of seasonal influences affecting deposits. These
seasonal movements are not necessarily regular, and an ob-
servant banker can sometimes improve on simple or mechanical measures of seasonal variation. For example, the quarterly

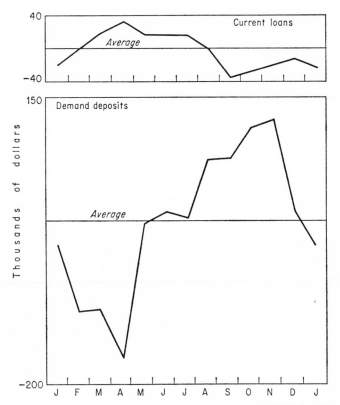

FIGURE 6-3. Seasonal variation experienced by a small Middle Western
bank. (Seasonals expressed in dollar terms were computed from month-
end statements.)

payment of corporate income taxes, while clearly seasonal in nature, often varies from average seasonal performance because profits themselves vary. If profits have been unusually high, a banker carrying corporate balances may expect unusually heavy tax drains. Therefore, a prudent banker in liquidity planning may sometimes vary his judgment of seasonal expectations based on known factors of this sort.

Taxes on personal property which extended to deposits may lead to tax-date deposit shifts, such as in the city of Chicago. Deposits there are subject to heavy but erratic personal property assessment. Under such circumstances bank customers may attempt to convert these deposits into some tax-exempt form or to remove them to a jurisdiction in which they are not subject to taxes. These seasonal movements may be quite sharp and require highly specialized liquidity planning by the institutions involved.

Random Deposit Movements

Seasonal movements of both loans and deposits can be fairly well anticipated as to when they will take place and roughly *how* large they will be; but there are also some types of deposit movements which, for lack of a better name, might be labeled "random." If the deposit figures by days or weeks for a given bank are plotted on a graph, some of the ups and downs will be unaccountable; they are random movements. Random movement of loan demand is rather less likely than for deposits. A bank is well advised to make some liquidity provision for deposit variability. Perhaps the best defense against randomness is being just a little more safe than logic demands.

The causes of random deposit movements are usually unidentified. If deposits fall off a bit in some given week, even though seasonal patterns do not suggest such a drop, it might mean only that a new seasonal force is at work. Recognition of random movements is, perhaps, a sort of clumsy effort at preparing for the unknown future.

Unstable Deposit Accounts

Apart from the seasonal and random factors in cash needs, there is much to be said for providing some protection against the movement of certain types of deposit accounts which are notoriously unstable. The leading illustrations of such accounts are:

1. Amounts "due to banks" are often irregular in movement. Since these accounts are primary reserves for the bank owning them, they are subject to unexpected and sizable use as need occurs.

2. "Public funds" are usually regarded as highly variable. This reputation may not be fully merited but it contains enough truth to make extra protection prudent. The tax and loan accounts due the Treasury of the United States often show considerable fluctuation, but the amounts due state and local governments sometimes are and sometimes are not variable. Where a given bank has state or local funds because of political connections, the instability of such accounts is particularly great. The shift of a large public account can come most unexpectedly, perhaps for no reason greater than the death and succession of a public official.

3. The accounts of "uninvested trust funds," "investment trusts," and "rich investors" are sometimes subject to extensive variation. A business corporation may have disposed of property and have deposit balances larger than needed for ordinary business purposes. These accounts are subject to large and irregular demands.

4. The "big" account in the "little" bank is another illustration. Many small towns have only one leading industry, possibly only one company. When this is true, the prosperity of the town is tied up with and dependent on it. Sometimes a town is built around the plant or branch of a large company headquartered elsewhere. While some companies are so clearly immobile that the bank carrying their account need not worry, this is not always true. Companies and the plants of outside

companies can and do move, sometimes quickly and with little notice.

A bank should always be prepared to lose its biggest single account without distress. If the account forms a sizable part of deposits, this plan may enforce a rather severe liquidity requirement, but in practice it pays. Any community which loses a large single company or plant will be sorely depressed. The bank will have other problems, and the loss of the one big account should not exhaust its defenses. That loss will probably mean that the bank needs even more protection.

It could be argued that this sort of hazard is one that might be treated as a more remote reserve need, and the argument would have merit. The reason for suggesting, however, that it is more nearly a situation for protection by working reserves is that the attending risks need as much protection as is feasible.

This circumstance also illustrates a case of general banking policy. While every bank has reason to welcome deposit accounts and particularly the big ones, the small banker should never make himself slavishly beholden to one big account. Not only are the risks considerable, but the earnings on it are not so lush as might be expected. A number of fairly big accounts are generally much better than a single giant; not that the giant should be accepted reluctantly, but the responsibility for it should be respectfully treated.

ESTIMATION OF EXPECTED RESERVE NEEDS

Practical bankers are well aware of seasonal fluctuations and estimate their banking impacts in a variety of ways. Methods of estimation commonly used, however, have been of a quite informal and sometimes rather crude sort. While such methods are probably adequate under most circumstances, at times more precise measurement is useful.

Rough Approximation of Seasonal Influences

The methods of rough approximation in practical use are usually a combination of head scratching and figuring on the back of an envelope that would be the despair of a theoretical statistician. These crude methods work; for those who do not wish to bother with the refinements of statistics they can be made to work again.

The practical banker is likely to say something like this: "Normally my September loans will run about $600,000 above my present (say, June) loans; my deposits will run off about $900,000 between now and October, ordinarily the low month. Guess I'd better have about $1,500,000 free for this purpose." A precisionist could point out to the banker that since the loan high and the deposit low do not coincide, he may not need the full $1,500,000. But this is meticulously academic. This way of figuring works, and any method that works is not to be scoffed at.

Chart Method of Estimating Seasonals

A banker need not use refined statistical methods to estimate likely seasonal influences with adequate accuracy. Very simple graphic tools can supply surprisingly accurate measurements of probable seasonal influences. Graph or cross-section paper (available in almost any stationery store) is the only special working tool required.

The horizontal scale on the graph or cross-section paper should be divided into twelve spaces if the banker proposes to make his measurement in monthly terms; into 52 spaces if he plans to use weekly figures. Total deposits, one year at a time, are plotted in the horizontal scale with the various years superimposed one upon another. In order to keep the years visible, separate multicolor pencils or other identifying devices may be used. It is seldom practical to put more than a half dozen years on a single chart, which is usually enough to bring out the seasonal pattern clearly; fewer may be adequate and certainly would be more understandable. The graphic demonstration of seasonal patterns in Figure 6-4 was limited to three years for purposes of clarity.

Such charts can be made directly in dollar terms. It is possible, however, to prepare the chart in "relative" form. This method involves a small amount of arithmetic manipulation. The dollar figures of loans and deposits are first arrayed on a work sheet and an average is computed for each of the years. This average is computed in the following way: The figure for each month or each week is divided by the annual average; the resulting figure is a "relative." The plotting of relatives is illustrated by Figure 6-4. The use of relatives gives a direct percentage measure of movement and is thus useful for comparison with other figures that may have a different dollar level.

Figure 6-4 was drawn up from three nonconsecutive years: 1952, 1955, and 1959. It is quite evident that approximately the same seasonal pattern prevailed through these years but the variations are still of considerable significance. In giving weight to the character of seasonal variations, it would always

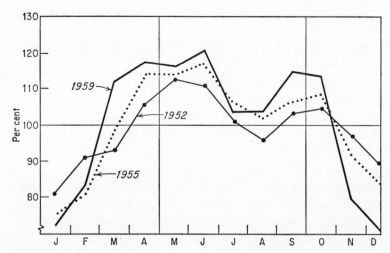

FIGURE 6-4. Seasonal factors of total loans expressed in relative terms. (Source: *The Seasonal Squeeze*, Federal Reserve Bank of Philadelphia, 1960.)

be more natural, of course, to give somewhat greater weight to the more recent year. The year 1959 shows the widest seasonal swings, suggesting that this bank might have to increase further its protection for seasonal variation in later years.

Statistically Prepared Measures of Seasonal Variation

Relatively few banks employ trained statisticians, but those that do so might well use their services for the preparation of formally derived indexes of seasonal variation. Moreover, banks not having access to such statistical skills within their own staff can have such indexes prepared for them by a number of outside sources. The business bureaus of neighboring universities will frequently perform this service for relatively moderate fees. The service bureaus of some electronic computer companies will prepare such indexes for a fee.

The measures of seasonal fluctuations prepared by professional statisticians or by the electronic computer programs are usually expressed as indexes or relatives. The operating banker may find it useful to have these indexes or relatives converted into dollar amounts. In turn, the dollar amounts may be expressed as absolute amounts or as amounts of variation around an average level. They may be secured by a relatively simple computation process. The basic dollar figure used may be an annual average of monthly figures. The relatives or indexes for each month are then multiplied by this base dollar figure. Variations about the average are computed by deducting the average figure from the monthly series computed above. Table 4 on page 110 illustrates the use of formally derived indexes of seasonal variation.

Estimation of Cash Needs
for Random Deposit Movements

When introducing the subject of random deposit movements, we observed that the nature of these movements could be best observed by inspecting a chart of deposits plotted from daily or weekly figures. For that same reason, the best and easiest determination of the rough importance of this factor is made by graphic methods. The method, very similar to the one used above, is about as follows:

1. Plot the weekly deposit figures for three or four years (excluding the special accounts, such as "due to banks" or public funds) on a chart of one year's span with the years superimposed one on the other.

2. By inspection, determine which of the broad movements is to be considered seasonal and therefore not included in this step.

3. By parallel marks, measure roughly the variation which might be considered random.

This is illustrated in Figure 6-5, which is based on the weekly figures of a moderate-sized city bank. The final results may be kept in absolute dollar amounts or may be treated as a percentage. Random deposit movements are roughly $150,000, or about 4 per cent of the deposit base.

Figure 6-5 shows one interesting characteristic: variations from year to year are not seasonal in character. Virtually no

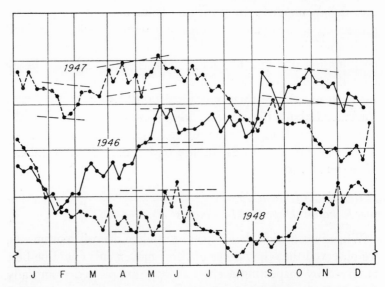

FIGURE 6-5. Random variation of deposits of a moderate-sized city bank in 1946, 1947, and 1948. Each vertical space equals $200,000.

detectable seasonal variations can be isolated for this particular bank, though up-and-down movements reflect the character of the random fluctuations against which a bank must protect itself in the conduct of its liquidity policy.

Estimation of Cash Needs
for Unstable Deposit Accounts

The nature of the accounts that should be classified within this group varies from bank to bank; the amount of protection no doubt has about the same characteristic.

Since the basis of calculation is crude at best, the way of determining needs is almost wholly a matter of judgment. An inspection of records of the past always helps. Accounts which have been unstable are likely to keep on in about the same way. About the best that can be suggested is that a liquidity policy should be determined in advance, including some rule such as "maintenance in working secondary reserves of one-fourth, or one-third, or one-half of accounts classed as unstable." It is hard to conceive of a case where more than half the dollar volume of such accounts should be protected; the needs may more often be one-third or even less.

FORMATION OF A LIQUIDITY PLAN

Once an estimate of the expected needs for working secondary reserves has been developed, it is necessary to convert these estimates into some kind of workable or effective liquidity plan. The function of this section is to suggest first a rather simple plan and then to outline a somewhat more formal plan.

A Rough Plan to Meet Liquidity Needs

The simplest and possibly the most straightforward way of preparing a liquidity plan is to add together the various requirements. For example, a banker might simply sum the peak of loan demands above average, the amount by which deposits are below average at their lowest, an allowance for random deposit fluctuations, and finally an allowance for possible losses

in unstable deposit accounts. For example, a very simple estimate would be as follows:

Peak of loan demands above average...............	XXX
Decline of deposits below average (80% of amount)*..	XXX
Random variations in deposits (80% of amount)*.....	XXX
Unstable deposit accounts (33⅓% of amount)........	XXX
Total.......................................	XXXX

* This assumes 20 per cent required reserves.

As this simple plan shows, the need for working reserves is
not equal to the total drains but rather to the amount that is
not already covered by primary reserves. In other words, if
the primary reserve ratio in a bank is 20 per cent, the working reserve required for the above would equal 80 per cent
of this total.

Precise Estimation of Seasonal Liquidity Needs

As indicated in the text, most bankers make rather crude
allowance for seasonal needs. Because there is no great regu-
larity to seasonal movements, this is usually adequate, but the
techniques of the statistician can be used to give somewhat
more refined results. Some banks, however, have the staff and
the facilities for such computations, and for them the detailed
work should be worthwhile.

The most effective way of explaining this slightly more
formal method of estimating the influence of seasonal fluctuations on banking liquidity is by use of a simplified illustration.
First it is necessary to introduce, as is done below, a highly
simplified assumed year-end balance sheet and a set of assumed
factors expressing seasonal fluctuations. These assumed data
are used in the calculations made in Table 4; the calculations
are explained in the following numbered paragraphs.

ASSUMED YEAR-END BALANCE SHEET

Cash....................	$2,000	Capital assets............	$1,000
Loans...................	2,730	Demand deposits..........	6,360
Investments.............	5,270	Time deposits............	2,640
	$10,000		$10,000

ASSUMED INDEXES OF SEASONAL VARIATION

Month	Loans	Demand deposits
January...............	90	102
February.............	96	99
March...............	87	96
April................	91	95
May.................	105	94
June................	109	93
July................	107	95
August..............	107	100
September...........	107	107
October.............	103	108
November...........	103	108
December...........	95	103

1. The first two columns of Table 4 reproduce the assumed factors of seasonal variation. The amounts for the month of December appearing in columns 3 and 4 are taken from the assumed balance sheet. Figures for the other months are computed from the seasonal factors. For example, the balance sheet showed loans of $2,730,000 and demand deposits of $6,360,000 at the year end. Taking the December seasonal factors, 95 and 103, the values for the other months are computed; that is, if a seasonal value of 95 is $2,730,000, then the seasonal value of 90 for January is $2,590,000, and 96 for February is $2,760,000, etc.

2. Since this computation is being made in terms of "funds seasonally released," we figure the amounts by which loans are less than the maximum month (column 5) and the amounts by which demand deposits are in excess of the minimum month (column 6).

3. Column 7 reduces the deposits in column 6 to the amount by which secondary reserves are expected to vary. This reduction is by the constant ratio of 80 per cent. This is because primary reserves in this bank were 20 per cent, leaving the remainder (80 per cent) to be covered by secondary reserve changes.

TABLE 4
ESTIMATION OF SEASONAL CASH NEEDS
(All dollar figures in thousands)

Month	Factors of seasonal variation for		Estimated seasonal variation in		Deficit in loans under maximum	Excess of demand deposits over minimum	80 per cent of Col. 6	Col. 5 + Col. 7	Col. 8 with lowest month equal to zero	Net change in Col. 9 starting at zero month
	Loans	Demand dep.	Loans	Demand dep.						
	(1)	(2)	(3)	(4)	(5)	(6)	(7)	(8)	(9)	(10)
January	90	102	$2,590	$6,300	$540	$550	$440	$980	$980	$+ 90
February	96	99	2,760	6,120	370	370	300	670	670	−310
March	87	96	2,500	5,930	630	180	145	775	775	+105
April	91	95	2,620	5,870	510	120	100	610	610	−165
May	105	94	3,020	5,810	110	60	50	160	160	−450
June	109	93	3,130	5,750	...	...	...	*	...	−160
July	107	95	3,070	5,870	60	120	100	160	160	+160‡
August	107	100	3,070	6,180	60	430	340	400	400	+240
September	107	107	3,070	6,610	60	860	690	750	750	+350
October	103	108	2,960	6,670	170	920	735	905	905	+155
November	103	108	2,960	6,670	170	920	735	905	905	0
December	95	103	2,730†	6,360†	400	610	490	890	890	− 15
Total	1,200	1,200								

* In this illustration the loan maximum and deposit minimum coincide. This is likely to happen, but it is not inevitable. When there is not a coincidence, column 9 is different from column 8 and lower by the amount of the minimum month. See text comments about this table.

† Taken from balance sheet; see p. 108.

‡ Since June is the "zero" month, net changes are figured from that date.

110

4. Column 8 is obtained by combining the loan "deficit" (which simply means the amount less than the maximum) and the deposit excess (the amount over the minimum), reduced by the amount of primary reserves carried. Seasonal peaks and valleys do not always coincide, as in this illustration. When they do, there is a zero month in column 8. When they do not, the low month is converted to a zero basis in column 9 in order to achieve this effect.

5. Column 10, which is computed by figuring the changes in column 9 following the zero month, serves to show a picture of the month-to-month amounts which either become "seasonally idle" (indicated by a plus, see comment 2 above) or constitute a "seasonal demand for cash" (indicated by a minus sign).

It should be borne in mind that, in this illustration, the amount being estimated is the volume of funds seasonally idle and therefore to be kept in secondary reserves. This is the opposite of the "seasonal cash demand" which was referred to several times in Chapter 5. A "seasonal demand for cash" is just the opposite of "funds made seasonally idle." For example, if loans go up and deposits go down in a given month, there is a "seasonal demand for cash"; if loans go down and deposits go up, then there is a "seasonal release of funds." The computation could be made in either form; the one used here is chosen because it corresponds to a computation of funds to be retained in secondary reserve form.

Putting Seasonally Idle Funds to Work

With a precise method of figuring the volume of funds that would be seasonally idle, a fairly precise schedule for putting these funds to work can be devised. Obviously they cannot be invested in long-term form if we follow good secondary reserve practice. With short-term obligations a precise investment schedule is not absolutely necessary. A quite adequate nonprecise rule is the following: Buy any asset with a maturity to qualify as a secondary reserve. When money is needed, sell some of these secondary reserve assets. If a bank wishes to be

very precise, it may wish to have a maturity schedule for its
secondary reserve assets held for seasonal purposes which will
correspond to the likely schedule by which these funds will be
needed. If such is wanted, it can be supplied quite readily.

For the month of December, Table 4 shows us that $890,000
should be held for seasonal requirements. This will be needed
when the minus figures in following months (meaning a need
for money) appear. These minuses are:

	In thousands
Month	*of dollars*
February............	$-310
April..............	-165
May..............	-450
June..............	-160

These requirements total $1,085,000, which consists of the
$890,000 on hand at the year end and the $90,000 which becomes available in January and the $105,000 which becomes
available in March. If we assume that these amounts are either
kept in cash form or invested in one-month obligations, then
the December maturity schedule could be:

In thousands of dollars
$220 in 2-month form
60 in 4-month form
450 in 5-month form
160 in 6-month form

The investment maturity for seasonally idle funds in subsequent months (months which are plus) can be stretched out
to cover the subsequent minuses.

7

Secondary Reserves for Remoter Contingencies

After a bank has provided the working reserves needed for likely and forecastable events, should liquidity reserves be arranged for other, more remote purposes? A number of circumstances would indeed seem to require more protective liquidity than that used for working purposes. The geographic areas in which banks are located vary greatly. Banks located in areas of rapid growth and intense development may reasonably expect to grow considerably faster than the nation as a whole. In declining communities, however, the situation faced by banks may be rather different. Does this require a special kind of liquidity policy? Another fear we may fervently hope is remote but which has never been eradicated is that of war. In an era in which nuclear disaster is always possible, must banks take special measures to prepare themselves for survival? The Federal Reserve may require member banks to meet higher reserve requirements. In recent years the Federal Reserve has had a considerable amount of unexercised authority to increase reserve requirements. On the other hand, increases have been made rarely.[1] Should a bank be prepared against other undefined contingencies that it cannot now completely anticipate?

[1] Between 1948 and 1951 reserve requirements were increased as well as decreased several times. After early 1951 several decreases in percentage required were allowed but no further increases were ordered until late 1960 when country-bank requirements were increased 1 percentage point at the time vault

113

All these possibilities must be considered, but one further circumstance towers above the others: liquidity problems associated with the business cycle.

The fluctuations of economic affairs which are none too accurately called the "business cycle" have caused more banking difficulties than all other circumstances combined. A chart of bank failures of the past would show ups and downs corresponding surprisingly well with the ups and downs of price levels and the levels of employment and income.

Formerly, when good times receded and were followed by bad times, the turning point was usually marked by so-called "crises" or financial "panics." Collapse of the banking structure was associated with these episodes and was popularly believed to be the cause of them. Banks were often unable to meet their liabilities in legal-tender cash (the "suspension of specie payment" was the phrase used to describe these episodes), and it was commonly believed that banking difficulties were one of the leading causes of these turns in economic conditions. When the Federal Reserve System was created, it was hoped that the causes of crises and financial panics had been removed and that we might thereafter enjoy economic stability.

The bitter disappointment of these high hopes demonstrated that the problem of economic instability is deeper seated and more profoundly caused than by banking and monetary affairs. Creation of the Federal Reserve System did not erase or change the fact that banks are greatly affected by alternations in economic fortunes. The pattern of the past, however, seldom recurs without variation.

BANK LIQUIDITY POLICY FOR THE BUSINESS CYCLE

The nature of business cycle influences on banking is one of the central features of the history of business fluctuations.

---

cash averaging about 1½ percentage points was made eligible to meet legal requirements. Thus even this action resulted in a net decrease in average requirements. However, critics of Federal Reserve monetary policy have urged a freer use of increases as well as decreases in such requirements.

This important subject has been fully treated in many specialized works; only a brief survey is practical at this point.

The Record of the Past

One of the initial purposes of the Federal Reserve System was to eliminate the monetary and banking factors that were thought to have caused business fluctuations. In part the System was successful in this endeavor, but not wholly so, as was demonstrated by the experience of 1933. The weaknesses in the financial system that brought on that collapse have certainly been reduced and possibly cured by such devices as deposit insurance and a new philosophy of Federal fiscal policy. Although financial panics may now have been eradicated, pronounced fluctuations in business conditions still occur. There was a sharp business downturn in 1920–1921, a cataclysmic downturn in 1929 which produced a recession of a number of years, a rather sharp downturn in 1937. All these downturns had sizable influences on banks. Bank loans were liquidated in each case, and a liquidation of loans produced and accompanied the decline in the volume of deposits.

The pattern of business fluctuations since World War II has been somewhat different. The Federal government adopted the policy of using its powers to offset the more extreme forms of business fluctuations, and so far the policy has been reasonably successful. Support of the Employment Act of 1946 has been affirmed in the planks of both major parties in every election since that time. Business fluctuations since World War II have been relatively mild. A mild downturn in business came in 1948, but it was largely cured before the end of 1949. Another somewhat more pronounced downturn in activity took place in 1953–1954, but recovery was reasonably complete before the year 1954 was ended. Still another decline started in 1957 but was cured by 1958. A mild decline appeared in 1960 and extended into 1961.

Figure 7-1, which compares industrial production for the durable and nondurable segments, shows clearly the effect of these postwar cyclical movements. The downturns, however,

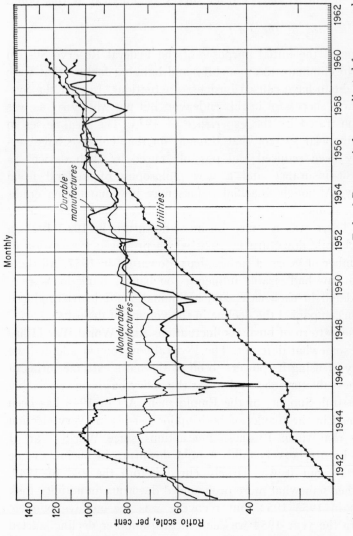

FIGURE 7-1. Industrial production, by major divisions, Federal Reserve indexes, adjusted for seasonal variation, 1957 = 100. (Source: Board of Governors of the Federal Reserve System.)

tend to be rather more clearly marked in industrial production than they are in total income or other factors.

General Economic Characteristics of Business Cycles

The phrase "business cycle" is possibly misleading since the record of the past shows that these events do not tend to have a repetitive character but change quite sharply from period to period. This record implies a warning against efforts at outguessing or forecasting the nature of business developments. One general characteristic of business fluctuations is that variations in sales of durable goods and other types of postponable purchases are greater than variations in the sales of the necessities of life. This is as would be expected. This means that as income increases (and therefore more is spent for luxury purposes and durable goods) business fluctuations might increase in magnitude.

This tendency may be offset. The determination and authority of government to offset business fluctuations has likewise been increased. It is not exactly clear how this balance of forces will resolve itself. Important changes in the character of cyclical fluctuations will probably take place as public anticyclical authority is exercised more confidently.

Several characteristics of business cycles are of special significance in the formation of banking policy. Interest rates tend to fluctuate through very wide levels during various phases of business fluctuations. Interest rates have always fluctuated through rather wide ranges but not with as great frequency as has been true in the postwar period. The somewhat milder nature of business fluctuations may have also meant that they recur with greater frequency. The more vigorous application of monetary policy to cure fluctuations may have led to a widening of the variations in interest rates, particularly short-term rates. The greater frequency of interest rate fluctuations may cause special problems for banks.

Banking Stake in Business Fluctuations

The comments made to this point on business fluctuations show that banking concern with them remains high even though public policy now attempts to moderate their character. Several reasons for banking concern may be cited.

In the previous chapter it was shown that there is a tendency for loan demand and deposits to behave cyclically as well as seasonally in a reciprocal way. The peaks of loan demand are likely to come when the level of business activity is high. The restraining policy of the monetary authorities is likely to curb deposit growth at just such times. On the other side of the cycle, the easing policies of the monetary authorities probably will tend to come when loan demand is somewhat slacker. It should also be observed that the relaxation of reserves which allows deposit growth is likely to come when interest rates are low. This gives rise to an investment problem. Banks will be tempted to commit their funds in low-interest-rate periods when security prices are high. Declines in these prices later when yields increase may tend to produce losses.

The new character of business cycle developments may mean that there is more strain on banking liquidity at the top of booms than at the bottom of depressions, as was true in earlier periods. The timing of this strain may be complicated by still another structural factor: Noncommercial-banking financial intermediaries have been of growing significance for many years. Some of these financial intermediaries are effective competitors for funds. Their competition is likely to be particularly effective near the tops of booms. In other words, unless banks can retain their competitive vigor they may lose more funds at the top of each boom than they recover in subsequent recessions.

Although a large or prolonged recession has not appeared in the postwar period, such is still possible. It seems quite likely that the Federal government could and would stop such a recession before it turned into a financial panic, and probably would avoid allowing any recession to become extremely deep. On the other hand, the economy may become less responsive to the stimulants of public policy than it was in the early postwar years.

As outlined in an earlier chapter, a severe depression would not affect deposits in the same way and to the same extent as in the past. For banks as a whole, the level of deposits depends mainly on loan behavior, variations in investment holdings, and the currency habits of the public.

It should certainly be expected that a severe depression would lead to loan contraction, which could be sizable. But in a depression it should be expected that bank investments would rise. While there might well be a slight shrinkage of corporate or other nongovernmental securities, holdings of Federal government obligations would probably increase, even if the total Federal debt were not growing. Experience shows that during depressions, fixed-income securities tend to drift from individuals to institutional investors. If the Federal government were running deficits, not at all unlikely during a severe depression, then bank holdings of Federal obligations would show an even greater tendency to grow.

The likely degree of currency hoarding should not concern banks as it did in the past. To an increasing extent, Federal Reserve operations have fully and exactly offset currency changes. It was the policy of the System from the beginning to do so with seasonal currency changes; during World War II currency was the main reason for growth of Federal Reserve credit. A continuation of this policy seems quite certain. If so, currency movements will affect banks as a whole very little.

In future depressions bank deposits probably will shrink very little, perhaps not at all. If depressions should be the occasion for deficits of size, this is particularly likely to be the case. The decline in the relative importance of bank loans affects banks in more ways than one.

All that has been said so far pertains to banks as a whole. Individual banks vary from the average experience of the banking system. That is likely to be true again in the future. During the Great Depression, some banks were subject to relatively small deposit drains. Since these same banks often found their loan accounts shrinking against their wishes, they accumulated unemployed funds. Other banks lost deposits rapidly and, even with pressure, could not realize very much from loan accounts.

Variations will certainly continue to occur; some banks will find idle funds an embarrassment; others will be equally troubled by a shortage of funds. If, for example, agricultural prices and income should decline more than other prices and incomes, then agricultural banks are likely to be under extra pressure.

It must be recollected, of course, that time deposits in the Great Depression fell off as much as demand deposits and relatively more rapidly. Whether this would happen again is difficult to predict. Startling as it might appear, it is not at all impossible that in a prolonged depression, banks with large proportions of time deposits might suffer more shrinkage than banks with mainly demand deposits. If the deposit totals are sustained by Federal government fiscal action tending to offset loan contraction, this offset would in the main take the form of demand deposit expansion. If the depression were not completely offset by governmental policy, there would probably tend to be some erosion of time deposits by those who had to use these funds to live on or to supplement reduced wage and salary incomes. (Fluctuations in gross dissaving are more significant in determining the volume of time deposits than changes in the rate of gross new saving.) If this happened, savings banks might suffer deposit losses while other banks were holding their own or even gaining. Curbing the growth of demand deposits during booms may lead to ever increasing emphasis on the competition for time deposits during the peak period of booms.

The conclusion that banks as a whole are likely to suffer less deposit pressure still yields some comfort for the individual banker. If the average deposit decline is not severe, even the hardest hit banks are less likely to be under so great pressure as before, and the investment markets for securities held by banks are less likely to be so demoralized as they became in the early 1930s.

BANK LIQUIDITY POLICY FOR OTHER PURPOSES

The Declining Community

While cyclical fluctuations are the leading factors in large and irregular total deposit movements, local factors play a role in some circumstances. Everyone is familiar with the dying community. The record can be read in many ways; the decline of deposits in such an area is usually a signal of general economic difficulties. Should a bank which finds itself in such an area arm itself with extra liquidity? Unless the decline is very rapid, such as that caused by the collapse of a boom town, the closing of a wartime shipbuilding boom, the exhaustion of lumber resources following a lumbering boom, the exhaustion of ore after a mining boom, the provision of special liquidity probably is not necessary. The history of declining communities is that, if they have existed for some time, people leave rather more slowly than industry; the decline of deposits will be less rapid than the decline of loans.

The problem of banks in such areas is not so much liquidity as income, a fact that is the clue to their real difficulty. If the pressure for income is excessive, they are likely to become less liquid than normal in an excessive reach for income by the extension of investment maturities. A bank in a declining community may not have any serious liquidity problem if it does not depart from fairly normal investment policies. A bank under pressure for income should seriously consider voluntary liquidation rather than take chances in its investment operations.

War and the Threat of War

Is the remote contingency of war one for which banks should prepare by extra liquidity? Asked differently, should a bank change its liquidity plans if there is increasing possibility of war? It is true that in the past war has usually caused special pressures on banks. Those located in countries that were the scene of hostilities were particularly subject to such pressures.

If and when war comes, what is the significance of this prospect for bank liquidity policy? Does the possibility of massive destruction by nuclear weapons present a circumstance against which any form of financial preparation is either feasible or wise?

As the military techniques of war have been changing, so have the fiscal techniques. Under modern circumstances, commercial banks in times of war have to follow closely the general pattern of governmental economic policy. While banks may not be allowed much choice, they are not going to be allowed to be victims of special liquidity problems. Individual banks need only be sure that they are not sharply out of line with the banking system.

Just before World War II, some banks sold off all long-term securities and became very liquid, not because of fear but because they expected interest rates to rise. They were mistaken; the interruption of their investment plans lost them income. The fiscal authorities did not and probably never will again permit interest rates to rise in time of war. There is little excuse for banks to change their plans materially toward more liquidity for recurrent war threats. If anything, a moderate move in the opposite direction would be more reasonable.

The Unstable Community

Apart from the other rather tenuous circumstances requiring protective secondary reserves, there is one circumstance of special significance for some banks. Some areas suffer wider ranges of up-and-down economic movement than the country as a whole. In the past, agricultural areas were of this kind. Farming banks were always going from rags to riches and back again. Policies for the support of agricultural income apparently have not changed this character greatly. The big single-industry community is also of this type.

A bank can best judge for itself whether its location falls in such a class by looking at its own record and the record of the community. Some care must be used in reading the record, but conclusions can be determined from relatively simple facts. The deposits of a bank, converted to relative form as described in the preceding chapter, may be compared with the deposits of all banks, also in relative form, to disclose the relative stability or instability of that bank's chief source of funds.

Possible Changes in Legal Reserve Requirements

All commercial banks that are members of the Federal Reserve System (and some nonmember commercial banks in states such as New York and Connecticut) are subject to primary cash reserve requirements which may be changed from time to time by the administrative authorities. The character of each bank's requirements depends on its classification. Some bankers take the view that whenever the existing reserve requirements are less than the administrative maximum, they should maintain liquidity reserves adequate to bring primary cash reserves up to the statutory maximum without resorting to borrowing or fundamental changes in investment plans. This is a defensible but extreme position.

The probability that increases in member bank reserve requirements will be used more frequently as an instrument of general credit policy will be determined more by political than by economic considerations. The policy heads of the Federal Reserve System have indicated fairly clearly their reluctance to use this instrument as a credit-tightening device. Nevertheless, a considerable number of respected monetary economists and congressional critics have urged its greater use.

Any change in policy that would involve a more frequent use of changes in reserve requirements would almost certainly be signaled well in advance of such actions. Rather than prepare now for possible increases in reserve requirements, banks might await more definite indications of a revived use. They should, however, be alert to the signals since slow reactors might find late adjustment painful and costly.

LIQUIDITY PREPARATION FOR REMOTER NEEDS

The somewhat less precise nature of the discussion in this chapter is a reflection of the greater difficulty of framing precise rules for "remoter needs" liquidity policy. The problems are of a less clear nature and not subject to quantitative determination. Nevertheless, a few general observations may be useful in this connection. The provision of liquidity for remoter needs is much more a problem of the protection of bank earnings than it is of the protection of a bank's ability to meet customers' cash demands. For example, it is possible to argue that if a bank can meet its expenses and dividend requirements in a satisfactory way it would do well to preserve all funds above those needed for primary reserves, for working secondary reserves, and for loan demands in a kind of intermediate secondary reserve. In other words, the residual priority mentioned in Chapter 1 might be vacated unless there should be serious earnings pressure of a short-term nature.

Reserves of this type do not need to be held in securities of the shortest maturities though they should clearly be of the highest degree of marketability. High-grade intermediate-maturity securities would qualify. Interest yields from these intermediate maturities of U.S. Government securities have fluctuated widely in the postwar period. At times intermediate maturities have produced higher yields than were available on long maturities. They offered very attractive investment opportunities for the banks that could take advantage of them. As might be expected, however, these excellent yields appeared mainly in periods of high loan demands and relatively few banks could, in fact, increase investment holdings under these circumstances. The secondary reserves for more remote needs, therefore, might be invested to maximize liquidity at the peaks of booms rather than at the bottoms of depressions, as was formerly the case. Banks are not invited to tamper with the quality of the liquidity portfolio, but they might consider varying maturity in an effort to maximize earnings. In effect, this is taking advantage of this liquidity segment as an instrument of positive policy formation instead of viewing it merely as a negative or defensive part of a banker's armor against an uncertain future.

When Is Liquidity Needed?

Earlier sections have emphasized the fact that several cyclical recessions occurred in the postwar period even though public policy tried to reduce or even eliminate such instability. This fact, however, does not mean that the banking defense to protect against their effects is the same as the defense formerly needed. Indeed, the principal lesson to be learned from postwar experience is that although the recessions were somewhat milder than in earlier periods, monetary policy has attempted to offset them in every case. The Federal Reserve has made added reserves available in times of depression and has limited the supply of reserves in times of boom.

As a result, banks no longer need to hoard liquidity during periods of high activity to protect against downturns in business activity. Rather, banks must expect to meet customer loan demands during booms without additions of liquidity to their reserves. They may also reasonably expect rather sizable additions to these reserves during recessions. The problem of banking policy, therefore, is to absorb new liquidity when it is released during recessions and to use it in such a way that it will be readily available for banking purposes when the succeeding boom emerges. In other words, the policies that had been appropriate before measures of public policy were so vigorously directed to the cure of business fluctuations are no longer appropriate and a new kind of liquidity timing must be followed.

One of the results of the policy of preserving the liquidity acquired during a recession in preparation for the succeeding boom is that it will lead to considerable instability of bank earnings. Total bank earnings probably will be increased in the long run by this policy but their timing will be somewhat more erratic. This result runs counter to the natural preferences of bankers and businessmen, who generally desire stable profits. If liquidity policy makes earnings more variable, then other policies that stabilize earnings are that much more important. For example, somewhat greater willingness to make term loans in boom periods combined with the will to curb such lending when rates on it are low would improve long-range earnings. These loans can continue during slumps to yield the high returns that had been negotiated during booms. They tend to support earnings during ensuing recessions. Even with the provisions for prepayment that are usually included in these loan contracts (which will be discussed in Chapter 14), sizable earnings support for the period when a bank moves into a period of recession nevertheless remains if adequate liquidity reserves were available during the preceding boom.

In the 1920s the fear was sometimes expressed that banks became too illiquid during booms to weather the following recessions. The fear might now be expressed that banks become too illiquid during recessions in an effort to sustain earnings to take advantage of the better earnings opportunities available during booms.

Part III

LOAN MANAGEMENT

Lending is the core function of commercial banking. The successful banker is a successful lender. The tools used to manage lending are credit analysis, budgeting, and supervision. Lending also has to be enlightened by a competitive but reasonable policy for interest charges on loans. These subjects are dealt with in the successive chapters of Part III.

8

General Loan Policies

The central business of commercial banks is the making of loans to customers. While banks engage in a large number of other financial activities and render a wide range of services to customers, direct lending is the primary function performed by them, the one in which they have a natural advantage over almost all other financial institutions.

Not only is customer lending the central service performed by banks, it is their most profitable type of business; it gives them the best available rate of return. More than that, compensatory balances produced by customer lending are one of the most important sources of funds for bank lending. The customer relationship in bank lending also accounts for many other kinds of profitable business. The impersonal granting of credit by purchase in the open market of a security or a piece of commercial paper is a unilateral transaction that generates little supplementary business. The balances held by customers when out of debt supply funds which banks can lend to other customers. The relationship between a bank and a customer may show net debit balance in one period, net credit balance in another. It is a two-sided relationship with positive advantages to both participants.

Commercial-bank lending, however, involves certain problems and even some dangers. Although banks might like to think of their borrowing customers as among the very best of business concerns, bank lending typically involves some credit risk. In addition, bank lending involves a number of timing problems. The loan demands of customers may tend to bunch in some periods so that a bank is unable to accommodate all of its customers. In other periods this bank might find it difficult to employ all of its funds. This alternation in strength of loan demand is of both a short-term and a long-term nature. Loan demand has sometimes been persistently high for considerable periods of time. Recent years have been of that character, as were also the 1920s. On the other hand, more than a decade intervened in the 1930s and during the war years when customer demand for loans fell considerably short of the capacity of banks to grant credit. Although customer loan demand has been generally high in recent periods, short-term alternations in the demand for loans have persisted. The individual bank, therefore, faces the problem of being able to satisfy the legitimate needs of its customers for credit during periods of peak loan demands. The solution of this problem is one of a bank's most difficult tasks.

PROFITABILITY OF LENDING

While the public service character of bank lending should not be neglected, banks should be anxious to make loans for reasons of profit. Almost every other function performed by commercial banks could be as well done by some other agency. Banks have no profit advantage in other lines; in some aspects, such as investment management, commercial banks probably are at a distinct disadvantage when their position is compared with that of other institutional investors.

However, banks can lend. That is the business they are best fitted for by tradition, organization, and position. No other existing agency could take their place. Without bank credit, many small and moderate-sized businesses would wither and die. Lending is not only a good social service, it is profitable. It is, indeed, the most profitable aspect of commercial banking. The rates realized on loans have always been well above those realized on investments. In the moderate-sized bank, the contrast is even greater.

Even allowing for the somewhat greater cost of servicing loans, the rate of return on them has usually been at least a half more than the rate of return on investments; sometimes it has been nearly twice as great. Since some portion of most investment accounts is devoted to liquidity protection, this comparison of rates of return is not altogether equitable. However, other factors must also be considered. Borrowing customers are also depositors and a well-managed loan account can augment the funds available to a bank, something that is seldom attainable from investments. Because large money-market banks are generally somewhat more successful in securing compensatory balances than are country banks, their net rate of return on loans realistically figured is probably closer to that obtained by smaller banks than an uninformed view of the statistics might indicate.

CHARACTERISTICS OF BORROWING BUSINESSES

Although the many favorable features of bank lending deserve mention, it has a number of sobering aspects. The businesses to which banks may expect to extend credit have some startling characteristics.

1. Borrowers tend to be of less than average profitability. This fact was clearly established by studies of the National Bureau of Economic Research made more than a decade ago.[1] It can be verified in the income statements of the corporations filing tax returns with the Bureau of Internal Revenue. A moment's reflection establishes the reasonableness of this fact, as startling as it may be at first thought. A profitable business has ample earnings with which to finance expansion or current needs. Less profitable businesses cannot finance their expansion

[1] N. H. Jacoby and R. J. Saulnier, *Business Finance and Banking* (a National Bureau of Economic Research study), Princeton University Press, 1947. See particularly the Summary, pp. 1–19, chap. 1, pp. 23–37, and chap. 6, pp. 152–167.

and companies sustaining losses may need outside help to keep their current position from deteriorating. Many specific circumstances lead to a tight current position (the usual signal that sends a business off to the bank for funds), but meager earnings or losses are frequent reasons.

For this reason, bank credit must be extended with great care. Commercial banks, contrary to popular impression, do not get their business from the premier business concerns but rather from a distinctly second-rate group. The financial (not moral) character of applicants for bank credit is often such that they could not secure funds from the investment markets. This means that unusual protective measures must be taken by banks to assure themselves that they are not assuming excessive risks. This is also a good pragmatic ground for the reluctance with which banks consider some long-term credit applications. Short-term credit can sometimes be safely extended where long-term credit would be too risky.

2. Another characteristic of businesses using bank credit is that they are repeat customers. The National Bureau of Economic Research found that about two-thirds of the business concerns indebted at any given time were likely to be indebted to banks the following year.

3. Still another characteristic is that businesses which seek bank credit are relatively small. While the traditional division of the financial markets between commercial banks and the securities markets has been between short- and long-term credit, there is much evidence that size is a more important point of difference. Those big enough to have a "name" in the central capital markets finance themselves in these markets whether their needs are long term or short term. Those who cannot command credit in the central capital markets content themselves with bank credit and adjust their affairs so that short-term borrowings fill their needs, even though they might, with more choices at their command, prefer long-term credit.

4. Business concerns using bank credit are often the moderately young businesses. The very young concerns have not yet

established sufficient stature to command bank funds. The older concerns have lived through their critical periods and have had time to accumulate earnings to do their own financing. It is the ones in between—those that have established their position and have not yet grown old—that are the best bank customers.

5. Growing concerns are more likely to use bank credit than those well stabilized. Growth is one of the very best of reasons to justify the extension of bank credit. It is a healthy sign and likely to be accompanied by other favorable characteristics. Growth combined with a strained current position may be a safe basis for the granting of bank credit. A dwindling business suffering losses, even though it has the remnants of a reasonably satisfactory current position, may be a poor customer in the long run.

LOAN POLICY AND THE ORGANIZATION OF LENDING

In the ordinary course of business, a bank awaits loan applications and then grants or rejects them. While a bank may be active in promoting applications and in soliciting business, it nevertheless plays a somewhat passive role in the lending operation. In the first place, customers that are most eagerly solicited probably have been given a thorough credit investigation prior to an application, and so there has already been a favorable if tentative credit judgment made of them.

Even though a bank acts on each case as it arises, it needs to have a variety of general lending policies and a considered internal organization for carrying them out. The ultimate legal responsibility for lending in every bank rests with the board of directors. Sometimes a few leading directors take an active role in credit granting, but in most big banks the primary responsibility for lending rests with full-time officers who are specialists in its various phases. To discharge their minimum responsibility faithfully, bank directors should establish a loan policy and delegate responsibility for its discharge to those who will carry it out.

A Written Loan Policy

A written policy, spread on the minutes of the bank, has its advantages; it can also have disadvantages. Policies may have to be changed or modified, and it is less awkward to change an oral than a written statement of policy. Whether formalized or not, it should be well known to all employees and officers who have responsibilities to discharge in this kind of work. We shall, in the following sections, consider some of the major points that must be a part of any well-integrated loan policy.

The few banks that have adopted a formal written loan policy usually have had it approved by the directors. This practice, however, is not at all common and some banks, after experimenting with such a policy, have abandoned the idea. The commonest reason for not having or for abandoning a written loan policy apparently has been that the process of writing out a policy was thought to lead to an excessive degree of rigidity and impaired flexibility. On the other hand, a few banks believe that it is advantageous to discipline both themselves and the loan officers by going through the exercise of committing the paper to general outlines of a loan policy. Arguments may be advanced for both positions. Neither one is necessarily right; the weight of experience certainly seems to suggest, however, that the written loan policy, though it may serve a useful purpose in some banks, is not necessary since it has not been adopted in many highly successful lending commercial banks.

Maximum Size of Loan Account

Two general standards are frequently applied in trying to determine the appropriate maximum size of the loan account at an individual bank. The ordering of priorities discussed in the opening chapter suggested that after a bank had set aside funds for primary reserves, and had established an adequate secondary reserve account, any remaining funds might be placed in loans. When converted into concrete terms this standard suggests that the loan account of a bank might be as much as two-thirds of its deposits, sometimes even more.

One limitation to this standard must be recognized. The capital account of a bank represents its ability to absorb losses. Since loans represent the most likely source of involuntary bank losses, the relationship of loans to the capital account is extremely important. Because the quality of loans varies greatly, no fixed ratio can represent what is considered to be a satisfactory loan-to-capital relationship. This margin, however, is scrupulously watched by those who stand in judgment of banking solvency, such as corporate treasurers, in choosing the banks to which they commit their working balances. A specific standard should not be set without regard to the quality of the loan account, but some feel that even a high-quality loan account should not exceed seven or eight times the capital account.

Maturity Policy

Banks have had, by tradition, a strong preference for the short-term business loan. To what extent is this preference still valid in view of modern circumstances? Other things being equal, a short-maturity credit instrument is more liquid than one with a long-term maturity. But to what extent are "other things equal"? A truly short maturity is one thing; a speciously short maturity has no relevance to our problem. The many banks that still write all loans on a 90-day basis regardless of the nature of the transaction are fooling no one but themselves. If the underlying transaction is long-term, the loan will tend to be long-term no matter what is written on the face of the credit instrument.

One of the most constructive characteristics of good loan policy is to grant maturities of a nature that borrowers can reasonably meet, and then expect them to be met. The use of repeated but uncertain renewals to discipline a borrower should be reserved for unusual circumstances. When there is a change in circumstances beyond the reasonable control and expectation of the borrower, a renewal presumably is justified. If a loan is drawn in terms of a specific plan of repayment (more will be said of this in connection with budgeting for bank credit), the borrower is much more likely to perform in a satisfactory manner than if he is subject to nothing more compelling than the vague threat of a loan maturity that "probably will be renewed if everything goes all right, that will certainly be renewed if the borrower's affairs deteriorate to the point that repayment is impossible, and that will be collected only in a difficult but not impossible situation!"

The preference among commercial banks for business credits is traditional, but the tradition is weakening. There was much common sense in the preference for business credit. Its great virtue was and is that, if well considered, it is truly "self-liquidating"; it produces the revenues with which to retire the credit. If banks must make some maturity concessions, the rule of tailoring each loan to the repayment prospects of the borrower is a good one.

What about the over-all maturity of the loan account? Should it be permitted to find its own natural level? This issue confronts bankers in two forms. In Chapters 14 and 16, where we discuss the two major forms of long-term bank credit—the term loan and the real estate mortgage—we shall consider the matter of appropriate maximum maturities for each of these two classes of credits. Should the average maturity of the loan account be determined by the proportion of these two inherently long-term credits in the total portfolio? Asked differently, what proportion of the loan account can be safely long-term?

The answer to these two questions is about as follows. A bank should make its liquidity plans on an over-all basis, not just by the character of the loan account. If a bank is so fortunate as to need no investments for income purposes but solely for secondary reserve purposes, then it might follow some rule of self-restraint and limit the proportion of long-term credits. But, as has been argued, assets other than loans are better for providing liquidity. If a bank has made good secondary reserve plans, it can probably afford to let the maturity of its loan account reflect the basic credit needs of its borrowers.

Self-delusion in Maturity Policy

A bank may appropriately plan to put some portion of its funds in long-term loans to business. It is quite another matter, however, for a bank to do a great deal of long-term lending in short-term form by allowing repeated renewals. Long-term credit, if planned in advance, may be made safe by a variety of protective provisions. When credit is extended in short-term form but with the implied expectation that renewal will be permitted, these protective provisions are absent. Even more important, the moderate degree of liquidity of term loans on which a bank can depend is absent from short-term loans for which the time of repayment is uncertain.

Unfortunately, the practice of allowing credit that is nominally short-term to become prolonged by repeated renewals is deeply entrenched in American banking practice. While the truth of this assertion is reasonably well known to practical bankers, research demonstration of it is based on relatively slender evidence. In 1955 the Cleveland Federal Reserve District included material relevant to this point in the loan survey they conducted in the fall of that year.[2] This inquiry showed that while only one-third of the notes held by the commercial banks in the Cleveland District had a stated maturity of one year or more, nearly two-thirds of the dollar volume of business loans outstanding was owed by borrowers who had been continuously in debt to the same banks for one year or more. In other words, about one-third of the credit at member banks in this district was for long-term purposes but had been made in short-term form. An even more extreme example of this disparity of form and reality was disclosed in the fact that whereas only 6 per cent of the loans had been written for a term of five years or more, about 25 per cent of the dollar volume of loans

[2] *Monthly Business Review,* Federal Reserve Bank of Cleveland, September, 1956.

outstanding was owed by borrowers who had been continuously in debt to the same bank for five years or longer.

If such a practice is faulty it can be said that the mistake was made when the loans were originally extended, not when they were renewed. The Cleveland survey showed clearly that the predominance of such credit was to industries in which credit needs were obviously of a long-term nature. If a banker extends credit to a customer without a clear-cut plan for repayment of the credit at the contraction of maturity, he can hardly blame the customer if he is unable to repay and seeks renewal at the maturity of the loan. No real liquidity exists in such credit and the loans not only are without the protection that may be formally provided in a term contract, but they give rise to an ambiguity with respect to the nature of performance expected of customers.

Stagnant loans are often well secured and quite safe; their only fault is that they may stay in a bank for an indefinite period. The best way to avoid this problem is to have a clear understanding of the true maturity of each loan and to encourage its refunding in some other form if long-term credit is really needed. This is particularly the case when stagnant loans are not accompanied by adequate compensatory balances.

Should Maturity Policy Shift?

Postwar bank policies with respect to loan maturities have shifted, depending on the nature of loan demand. During periods of lower loan demand banks have been willing to extend term loans, but in periods of high loan demand there has been a tendency to reduce term loans and to engage only in very short-term lending. This shift in policy is understandable; short-term lending presumably puts a bank in a somewhat more flexible position and possibly allows it to accommodate a greater number of customers. In addition, banks feel more comfortable by habit and tradition when engaging in short-term lending.

There are reasons, nevertheless, to question whether this is necessarily the most profitable policy over the long run. Term loans made at the height of loan demand unquestionably command higher rates of interest than those made when loan demand is slack. Such loans tend to stabilize earnings. Those banks that resist making term loans at low rates in periods of slack loan demand may be in a position to make rather large term loans at high rates when demand is high, thus providing themselves with portfolios to stretch out over succeeding periods of lesser loan demand. In any event, the prevailing character of liquidity needs brought about by existing Federal Reserve monetary policy suggests that the impairment of liquidity by making term loans in times of peak loan demands is not necessarily dangerous since there is little likelihood of liquidity demands being concentrated in periods of slacker business.

Risk Policy in Bank Lending

All credit extensions involve some possibility of loss. Since much bank credit is granted to marginal business borrowers, there is a sizable risk element. It is only the strategic position of banks and their ability to supervise credits rather closely that make bank loans tolerably collectible. Banks must constantly try to minimize losses. In spite of this, some banks doubtless go too far and, in the process of minimizing losses, do not extend credit which they properly should and appropriately could. The exact middle ground cannot be defined; the banking system nevertheless has a compelling responsibility to lend whenever there is a reasonable expectation of making the transaction pay out.

Since banks cannot, for the reasons given above, avoid incurring considerable risk in lending, they must employ every safeguard at their command. It can be said that

1. The majority of bank loans made should be collectible without extra supervision.

2. Of the loans that become "distressed," a large majority must be collectible without loss. Many loans which finally "pay out" have done so only because of skilled banking collection.

3. When losses must be taken, they should be minimized. Every bank that runs a normal loan business is going to have distressed loans, some of which will lead to losses. A large loss

on any one loan, however, is likely to be a sign of some fault in the lending procedure.

Specialization by Type of Loan

Some banks get to be known as "textile" banks, "meat-packing" banks, or the like. This often grows out of the fact that one of the leading loan or executive officers gains a reputation, a competence, and the contacts needed for getting business in these lines. Location sometimes plays a part. The reputation of specializing in certain types of loans has both advantages and disadvantages. The advantage of being able to operate confidently in a given field is considerable; not only is it a safeguard for the bank itself but it helps to attract business. Such specialization has the disadvantage of leading to less diversification than is wholly desirable. Since unit banking limits loan diversification geographically, the further limitation produced by specialization may put a bank's loan account in a particularly concentrated and vulnerable position.

The matter is not one about which general rules can be framed. The kind of business a bank can attract is limited by its background, the interests and connections of lending officers, and other related factors. Even if some degree of loan concentration is unavoidable, it can be offset partly by promoting business in contrasting industries. A bank that specializes in heavy-industry loans might improve its balance by seeking credit outlets in some field such as textiles, or in some consumer-goods line not subject to the same cyclical influences.

Loan limits for special types of loans. Although the rule for the size of the total loan account should be a liberal one, as argued above, does the same argument apply to special types such as real estate loans, consumer credit loans, or term loans? This is not an easy question. It is sometimes settled by law. In the case of national banks, the total volume of real estate loans is limited to 60 per cent of time deposits or 100 per cent of capital and unimpaired surplus, whichever amount is the greater. The problem is the same one met in diversification of the investment account, a matter to be considered at length later.

The problem met by a bank in concentrating on loans is much more difficult than in the case of investments. A bank cannot pick and choose among loan alternatives. Except for very large banks loans to remote borrowers are not practicable, and local loans tend to violate the rules of diversification. Since business or industry of a given type often tends to be concentrated in a given area, a bank may have to accept a large undiversified block of risk in the major business risk of the area. Loans of the same type tend to be concentrated in point of time. The demand for real estate loans tends to be high when there is a great deal of construction activity. This also tends to concentrate the maturity of real estate loans; "spaced" maturity plans for these loans are not practicable.

The problem is essentially insoluble. Perhaps the best solution is a good protective income investment policy. The risks of concentration in lending cannot be avoided or even much minimized, but they can be held within tolerable margins if the general liquidity of a bank is ample and if its income investment risks are not likely to cause trouble when the loan account is having its bad days.

Fitting Loans to Borrowers' Applications

One of the problems of general loan policy is to lend the right amount to each customer. While customers unquestionably have some notion of the amount of credit they want, discerning bankers often find that the amount appropriate and useful to them may be quite different from the amount for which they apply. It is obvious that some customers seek far more credit than is appropriate, but some customers are timid and fail to ask for an adequate amount.

One of the functions of the discerning banker is to analyze the real credit needs for the borrower and to extend the amount of credit that is appropriate to the circumstances. In the long run this action is very much in the interest of borrowers. If too much credit is extended, it may lead to difficulties in repayment. If too little credit is extended, the customer may be pinched and have to come back for another extension or curb business activities in an unnatural and probably unprofitable way.

Banks may not always be aware of the number of borrowers who come to them fearfully. While some of this timidity has disappeared, cases of it still occur. There are times when the banker might, after a full review of circumstances, encourage a customer to apply for a larger loan than he has asked for, perhaps on a rather different basis of borrowing. When good constructive business can be done, the banker should find and promote it. Selling credit, if it is really to the borrower's interest, is a proper banking function.

It was said above that the banking system has a particular responsibility in the financing of a new and growing enterprise. This is constructive lending in that it encourages and assists in the building of new businesses. A modest part of a loan account can be used for this purpose.

The argument for constructive loans is stronger than merely economic or community responsibility; it is a matter of considerable profit. Good and satisfied customers stay with a bank for a long time. The best business is that which keeps on coming back year after year. But the time to secure the allegiance and good will of customers is before they have grown so large and so obviously desirable that everyone seeks their patronage. A sympathetic policy on credit in the early phases of a business may make a vast difference in its success or its failure. The recollection of such a sympathetic policy is bound to have all sorts of favorable results.

The Compensatory Balance

Banks sometimes require and usually expect customers borrowing on an unsecured basis to maintain a deposit balance bearing some relationship to the aggregate amount borrowed or the maximum line of credit. Sometimes this requirement is used as a way of differentiating among customers: some customers are expected to observe the minimum rules without fail; others are given more latitude. In considering a new loan application, the banker may be influenced by the size of the applicant's prior deposit balances. The requirement for unsecured borrowing varies moderately, running from 10 to 20 per cent of the maximum borrowing or credit line.

The way in which the requirement is applied seems to vary from bank to bank. The ordinary rule is that "on the average" or "over the course of the year" the deposit balance must equal the specified minimum. Some banks seem to apply the rule in an even more rigid fashion and expect the balance to be maintained at the minimum or not to fall below it while the borrower-depositor is indebted to the bank. This second form is, of course, much more burdensome to the borrower because the part of the year when he has to borrow is naturally the time when he would be most disposed to draw his balance down to a minimum.

The compensatory balance is more often enforced in times of credit stringency and in city banks than otherwise. There seems to be a far from uniform view as to the desirability of the practice. Some banks view it as a necessary practice. In order to be able to lend, they must have deposit funds, and borrowers must be so disciplined as not to shirk their part in giving the bank lending power. A few take the view that a compensatory balance is an interest-raising device. If a borrower has access to only 80 per cent of the funds he borrows, the 4 per cent he pays on his loan (let us assume) becomes an effective rate of 5 per cent for the money he can actually use. (This is figured $0.04/0.80 = 0.05$.) But this calculation is partly spurious. Since most customers would keep some cash in any event, their cost is not increased in the way this computation suggests.

The compensatory balance also has some advantages for a bank in dealing with a borrower whose credit is not above reproach. As will be mentioned later, the legal right of offset means that a bank can use all the deposit balance a bank customer has with it to offset a portion of any loan to this customer; the bank then becomes a general creditor for the remainder of the loan. By virtue of this device, the bank tends to get slightly better settlement than if it were just a general creditor of the bankrupt customer. This will be illustrated in a later section of this chapter.

When Should Compensatory Balances Be Required?

Many banks enforce compensatory balance requirements only while a loan is outstanding. Application of the rule in this way, particularly if it leads to higher balances than the borrower ordinarily would keep, has the effect of increasing the income from loans. On the other hand, if a banker is anxious to provide himself with funds for lending to others, he might put more emphasis on the maintenance of compensatory balances during periods when a business is out of debt. In other words, the enforcement of compensatory balance rules to lines of credit rather than to credit outstanding has a great deal of merit. If business concerns maintain balances during the periods that they are out of debt, these funds are clearly available for other users. Maintenance of a compensatory balance rule while they are in debt may only lead the borrowers to request more credit than otherwise would be needed. If this request is granted, the bank does not have possession of any added funds.

THE INTERNAL ORGANIZATION
OF A BANK FOR LENDING

The lending function, being an important one, is usually exercised only by the top bank officers. (In a legal sense, bank loans can be made only by bank directorates.) The differences among banks in internal organization depend to a great extent on their size. Big banks typically have a large number of specialized loan officers. In some banks, the organization of lending functions is quite detailed.

Geographic vs. Functional Organization
of Lending Activities

A very small bank typically has no diversification of function in its organization for lending nor does it need any. The two or three top officers are generally familiar with the entire lending activities of the bank and are prepared to take care of all aspects of customer credit requests. The organization of lending in larger banks, however, frequently requires a considerable amount of complexity. The process of credit analysis is delegated to a credit department, whereas negotiations with borrowing customers is conducted by specialized loan officers.

One of the aspects of this division of labor is the relationship of the credit department to the lending officers that face the public. Credit departments typically analyze the financial statements and prepare the other analytical tests. They may but do not always make recommendations about new credits and keep track of outstanding loans. Loan officers, who deal face to face with the borrowing customers, generally assume a large share of the responsibility for the judgments made with respect to the extension of credit, sometimes the full responsibility. In very large banks it is typical that loan officers may be given authority to extend credit up to certain limits or in certain circumstances without seeking approval of any higher authority. On the other hand, many banks require some form of review of all credit extended.

The division of loan officers among various lines of credit may be on either a geographic or functional basis. The organization of a credit department along geographic lines has some operating advantages in that it may make it possible for loan officers to visit many borrowing customers conveniently without traveling great distances. In addition, it allows the selection of loan officers who have special contacts in the area of the country assigned to them.

The functional organization of lending operations, on the other hand, has the advantage of allowing loan officers to acquire a far greater degree of technical knowledge of the specialized areas in which they are extending credit. This may result in some geographic overlap of customers served by various loan officers and may require somewhat more travel, but many banks feel the other advantages outweigh this one disadvantage. Some banks manage to have a combination in which they use each loan officer in the way that maximizes his contribution, whether it be by virtue of a unique geographic tie or standing or because of special knowledge of some industry.

Once upon a time an applicant for bank credit was expected to be humble in his relationship with his banker. Bargaining about interest rates or other borrowing terms was almost unknown. The popular picture of the banker was that of a hard-hearted fellow who liked to say "no." Though this is a great exaggeration, there is enough truth in it to provide a moral for modern public relations experts.

Now the scene has changed. The picture of the successful bank lending officer has changed greatly. He is a salesman at heart, albeit a salesman with a sense of financial prudence but more disposed to view the applicant's case favorably than not. Still another way to look at a successful bank lending officer is to think of him as a financial expert who can take the loan applications as they come in and, by reworking them, find some way to grant credit that is both safe for the bank and sound for the borrower. The credit officer is the one who can make safe loans out of dubious applications. The penalties for mistakes, including mistakes of overconservatism, are greater than they used to be.

Credit Department Organization

Almost every good-sized bank has a credit department. In small banks, the routine functions of the credit department are usually performed by part-time clerks. There is seldom an independent credit review, as is given by credit departments in big banks. In a small bank, the chief executive officer is likely also to be the loan officer.

The credit analysis function will be described at greater length in the following chapter (Chapter 9); only a few brief points will be made here. Credit analysis has become a complex science. It involves a detailed review of financial statements and of ratios derived from them and of cash-flow estimates. Credit information is checked against actual performance. How well are various individuals keeping up their credit

standing? Credit departments have two large routine functions: (1) the maintenance of files of financial statements
embellished with the derived figures and ratios used for analysis and (2) credit correspondence. Aside from these routine
functions, credit departments of the larger institutions are
likely to take an active part in the granting of credit. Officers
and employees in credit departments are independent of the
officers who meet the public and deal with loan applications.
This independence is expected to make their credit judgments
disinterested.

The matter can be summarized somewhat this way: If the
loan officer is supposed to be a salesman at heart, the credit
department is expected to be more of a critic. Also, the credit
department is expected to keep a continuing check on the borrowers after they are on the bank's books and to call attention
to any deterioration in their affairs.

One of the great tools of modern banking is the credit file:
an organization of all pertinent credit data in such shape that
a reviewing officer can quickly get a broad picture of the
analyzed firm. The form of the credit file varies from bank to
bank.

*Credit Department Experience as Training
for Loan Officers*

In many banks the credit department is used as a training
ground for the young men who are expected to graduate into
loan officers. There is unquestionably merit in this practice
since credit analysis is a useful prelude to the administration
of lending. On the other hand, the practice may result in
somewhat lower prestige for credit departments. It may also
mean that a larger portion of the ultimate credit judgments
will be delegated to loan officers rather than to credit departments. This form of organization also fails to take advantage
of the fact that some bank officers are highly skilled analysts
by talent and temperament but without the personality and
poise needed to meet borrowing customers face to face. The
typical solution is to organize the credit department so as to

keep officers of this type in charge of credit analysis permanently but to rotate under them for training a steady stream of young men with the latent special talents of loan officers.

LEGAL FACTORS IN BANK LENDING

It is not entirely accidental that so many lawyers have been recruited into banking. The handling of trust and deposit accounts and the making of loans involve many questions of law. Some of the elements are quite uniform; others vary from state to state. The legal factors set down here present no more than a brief sketch. Any person going into banking would do well to acquaint himself with the banking laws prevailing in the jurisdiction in which he works. This section can serve only to indicate a few of the leading features of law as they relate to bank lending.

In the first place, most banks are subject to rules of *loan limits*. These limits do not appear in all state laws, and the form varies. For national banks the rule is, roughly, that the loan to an unsecured borrower shall not exceed 10 per cent of capital and unimpaired surplus. There are several exceptions: loans secured by longer term U.S. Government securities, by goods in storage, by livestock are limited to 25 per cent of paid-in and unimpaired capital and surplus. Loans on U.S. Government securities with maturities of 18 months or less are not subject to this limitation. Open-market obligations such as drafts, commercial paper, bankers' acceptances are also subject to no limit whatsoever.

Since loan limits are stated in terms of capital and surplus, banks sometimes transfer amounts from undivided profits and other capital accounts into surplus or declare stock dividends so as to increase their loan limits.

Loans on a bank's own shares. National banks and most state banks are prohibited from lending on their own shares. Whether prohibited or not, it is bad practice. If permitted to the extent that a bank had capital outstanding, such a bank could exist with no capital whatsoever.

Loans to examiners are prohibited for obvious reasons.

Loans to a bank's own executive officers above an amount of $2,500 are prohibited at member banks. If an executive officer secures a loan from any other bank, he must report it to his board of directors promptly. This provision has obvious merits, but from time to time it seems to create a problem in securing directors who might also be considered executive officers although having some outside interests.

The responsibilities of directors in making loans are complete. Even though in practice the work of lending and the actual process of deciding "yes" or "no" are delegated to other hands, directors cannot evade the ultimate legal responsibility for making loans. Many times this is discharged by the desultory reading of all loans made since the preceding directors' meeting followed by a blanket motion for approval. Sometimes the responsibility is discharged by the use of set lines of credit, which are determined before any credit is extended, by formal action of the directors.

Loans to corporations can be made only if the bank has satisfactory evidence that the corporate powers permit borrowing, that the loan would not be in violation of some other contract entered into by the corporation, that the specific loan is authorized by the directors of the corporation, and that the officers negotiating the loan are authorized by the corporation to execute the necessary guarantees and obligate the corporation for the credit.

Sometimes a loan can be made only if other creditors will agree to *subordination* of their claims. This is particularly true of loans that involve a concern which is in some difficulties. It means that the other creditors agree to subordinate their claims to those of the bank in the event of liquidation. The bank or other creditor to whom other claims are subordinated is said to be a preferred creditor.

As mentioned before, a bank can claim the right of *offset* which means that it can apply any deposits it holds for a debtor against the claims the bank has on this debtor in the event of bankruptcy. This gives the bank a slightly preferred position. For example, if a bank held a $1,000 deposit due a bankrupt debtor who owed the bank $5,000, the bank could apply the $1,000 against the loan and then claim the remaining $4,000 as an unsecured creditor. This explains in part why banks are fond of the compensatory balance requirement. Thus, if the other assets of this debtor (assuming no other preferred creditors) were liquidated to realize only $10,000 against a total of $20,000 of claims—50 per cent return to unsecured creditors—the bank would realize 60 per cent on its total claim, whereas it would have realized less than $52\frac{1}{2}$ per cent if it had been forced to turn over the deposited funds of the bankrupt debtor for distribution to all unsecured creditors.

When secured loans are made, the banker must be sure that he really has a valid and enforceable claim on the security, that he has a real *bailment* on warehoused goods, that his *mortgage* or *deed of trust* on real estate can be made effective in the event of default, that the *endorsements, guaranties,* and *pledges* he exacts can be made to stand up under juridical review.

Loans for the purpose of *purchasing or carrying securities* are regulated by the Federal Reserve. This is for the purpose of avoiding large-scale excesses in speculation. The legal limits within which the Federal Reserve can set "margins" is from 40 to 100 per cent; that is, the buyer must put up these amounts; the lender can supply the remainder, which would be from 60 to 0 per cent. These are loans for purchasing and carrying the securities, it should be emphasized. The banker can ask for collateral in the form of these securities without regard to margin rules prescribed by the Federal Reserve if the loan is for some other purpose, such as business needs, buying a car, or the like. In order to be safe, the bank, in making such a loan, would do well to secure some form of certification or warranty from the borrower that the purpose of the loan was not for purchasing and carrying securities.

9

Credit Analysis

Most banks have some recognized system by which loan applications are analyzed. In a small bank, this process may represent little more than the reflections of the cashier as he listens to a verbal request for a loan. In the big metropolitan money-market banks, credit analysis usually involves a detailed and complicated system: all credit applications are probably in written form, and the record of the applicant is subjected to scrutiny, often with considerable accounting and statistical detail.

A generation or more ago credit standing was a matter of word-of-mouth reputation: "So-and-so was thought to be worth about so much, he was reputed to pay his bills promptly, and he was highly regarded by his associates." During this period very few businesses published financial statements; even stockholders were given less information than is now considered appropriate.

Times have changed. One of the great advances is in business accounting, which has grown enormously both in detail and in dependability. Financial statements have become more revealing and usable, and the practice of releasing and even publicizing financial statements is more common. Much can be learned about a business from its statements. This can be done even by those who know only elementary accounting. The analysis of financial statements for determining credit worthiness has opened up new markets for commercial-bank credit.

Since this chapter is concerned with credit analysis, the subject matter will be mainly the objective tests that can be applied to a business concern. This is not to imply that the basic foundations of credit have changed drastically from those of former times. The good credit of an individual or of a business is still *both the willingness and the ability* to meet obligations as they fall due. In this chapter we shall deal with ability mainly; but the willingness, the character of honesty and intention to pay debts, is of undiminished importance. This is quite obvious in a man, less so in a corporation. But the corporation is, after all, nothing but an artificial shape for the operations of flesh-and-blood individuals. The character of those who dominate the affairs of a corporation is as important as the objective analysis of financial strength.

THE C'S OF CREDIT

The student of banking is almost sure to have been exposed at some stage to the C's of credit, the number of which varies —three, four, five, or six, depending on the ingenuity of the author in alliteration. The three most often mentioned are character, capacity, and capital. Others sometimes added are collateral, coverage, and condition. Clever fellows no doubt have thought of others and could devise more.

In modern credit analysis, this sort of classification has about the same standing as a farmer's almanac in the scientific study of meteorology, but as crude reminders, these points are not without merit. The problem of credit analysis is primarily that of forecasting both the willingness and the ability of the creditor to pay his debts. Judgment of the second factor (ability to pay) is the general area of scientific credit analysis. The moral foundation of credit, willingness to pay is nevertheless very important. Because it cannot be treated so objectively as the other credit factors is no reason for neglecting it. Many old-fashioned bankers got along pretty well without scientific credit analysis, and their success was due, to a considerable extent at least, to their skill in judging character.

JUDGING THE BORROWER

The art of credit judgment, too narrowly construed, focuses a great deal of attention on the credit, less on the debtor. The judgment of financial factors is only a part of a larger complex of credit factors. Whenever a bank grants a loan to a new customer, the bank, by this act, assumes some responsibility toward the new customer. Banking is like other businesses: a large share of its volume and a very great share of its profits come from repeat business. Therefore a bank can afford to spend both time and money in the process of getting started with the right customers.

What, then, is it that a bank wants in its customers? The answers are relatively simple:

1. The only good customers are the basically honest ones. The first of the C's is always character. A bank needs to deal with reliable customers; it can seldom have money dealings with any others.

2. The best customers are those who are prosperous. This may be a matter of industry as well as the personal character of the applicant.

3. The competent practitioner of a craft, trade, business, or the like is obviously the preferable choice. Customers in stable lines of business tend to do better than others.

4. The financial affairs of the applicant should be in good order.

In the consideration of bank credit applications, the analysis is analogous, in a general way at least, to that of investment analysis. As in long-term investment analysis, there are two steps: (1) a consideration of the industry which the applicant represents and (2) a consideration of the applicant in comparison with others in the field. The industry analysis is probably more important for long-term investment than for banking; the differences among industries show up slowly. For example, the best local traction company of earlier decades might have turned out to be a poor risk in contrast with a relatively less well-situated chemical or oil company. But it is possible that bank credit can be extended to an industry long after the prudent long-term investor should have fled it. This is, however, admittedly dangerous and not by any means always true.

Even if the extender of bank credit does not have to take so long a view of industries as does the long-term investor, a loan officer must know the industries to which he lends money for a wide variety of reasons. Accordingly, in this chapter there is a discussion of analysis at the industry level before a consideration of credit analysis in purely financial terms.

CREDIT ANALYSIS: INDUSTRY LEVEL

The particular industries in which bank credit officers must interest themselves are those located nearby and in need of bank funds. A few metropolitan banks lend on a country-wide basis, but this is the exception rather than the rule. Many industries use little bank credit and are not important applicants.

Some industries, such as the petroleum industry, have come to be so important as borrowers that banks have hired specialists acquainted with their technology, finance, and leaders. Some bank officers have made an outstanding reputation for themselves, built up a good business for their employing bank, and secured a strong personal following by becoming "experts" in a new field. The study of industries is therefore recommended to the aspiring bank credit officer: those industries which are local and offer an opportunity for the bank in which he is employed.

Industry analysis is something that cannot wait until the loan application appears. A good credit department keeps abreast of the industries that are local to it and even of the leading companies whether or not they are customers of its bank. That is the reason why the "economics" intelligence office is so often an adjunct to or connected with the credit department of banks, and possibly why college-educated bank trainees are so often started in credit departments.

The methods and problems of industry analysis are so diverse that a short treatment can be no more than suggestive of the attack that should be made. Here we shall emphasize those factors with which banks, unique among investment or credit agencies, should be familiar.

Price History

Short-term credit is intimately related to the problems of commodity prices. Every business has inventories of some size; in certain lines, such as liquor aging, the size of inventory is determined by deep-seated and invariable technological requirements. The prices of raw materials have an influence on the probable success of moving existing inventories through the usual processing and sale channels. Prices of the final products have a bearing on the profits and recovery of costs.

Some prices are much more stable than others, often because of the sensitiveness of the industry to the influences of the business cycle. In other cases, the kind and character of competition in a field may be strongly determinative of price history.

Prices in certain industries seem to have a steady trend. For years it was assumed that there was a steady upward drift of land prices; that if one waited long enough, even a bad real estate loan would be bailed out. This sometimes proved to be a false expectation; at least the upward drift has at times been halted for such a long period that harassed lenders on both high-priced urban and farm lands were not rescued.

More refined price problems are often of particular significance in certain fields. Some industries buy their materials in markets of great stability but sell their products in a market of considerable price volatility. Thus a decline in prices produces a severe pinch for them. The opposite circumstance is that of an industry in which raw material prices are volatile but the prices of final products are relatively stable; the chewing-gum and soft-drink industries are excellent illustrations. Still another circumstance which may have particular price relevance grows out of the variations among industries. In some industries labor costs are a large proportion of total costs; in others they are relatively small. (NOTE: This does not refer to high or low wage *rates*.) Since there is a great deal of inflexibility to wage rates (at least downward), an industry with a high proportion of labor costs can be treated as one in which raw material prices are inflexible.

The Business Cycle and Specific Industries

The variations in prices referred to in the preceding section are usually, though not invariably, a product of fluctuations in business conditions. Aside from price influences, there are many ways in which the cyclical fluctuations in business are of consequence for the banker.

Although prices go up in good times and down in bad times, within a specific industry price history and susceptibility to cyclical influence are not necessarily related. Stable prices are often found in unstable industries, also unstable prices in stable industries. The industries that produce raw materials (metals, fuels, etc.) and the industries that produce durable goods (machine tools, automobiles, farm equipment, etc.) are cyclically unstable, but some of their prices are fairly stable. On the other hand, those industries that produce "necessitous" perishable goods for direct consumption are fairly stable cyclewise, for example, food products, tobacco products, and similar goods. But prices for many of these products are highly volatile.

The extension of bank credit to an industry which is cyclically unstable presents two quite unrelated problems: (1) Companies in an unstable industry are, for reasons beyond their managerial competence, often seriously embarrassed. In other words, bank loans in such an industry, even those well made, may turn out to be "slow." (2) The more soundly financed companies in an industry which is notoriously variable over the phases of the business cycle are likely to have no bank credit needs in bad times. They liquidate a good part of their current assets, pay off debtors, and prepare to ride out the economic storm.

Thus a bank dealing with industries which are particularly susceptible to cyclical influences is likely to have trouble at two extremes: frozen credits and excessive fluctuation of loan volume.

Growing or Stagnant Industries

One of the great enthusiasms of long-term investment analysts over recent years has been for "growth" industries. The relevance of this factor for long-term investment is obviously much greater than for short-term credit. Bankers should avoid the losses that result from staying with stagnant industries too long. The advance of technology in recent years has meant that many companies could not maintain their relative standing without substantial research facilities. Growth industries also present problems of credit analysis. Growth often corrects for errors of judgment, but the rates of obsolescence in growing industries are high. The profits of new methods may be great, but so are the costs.

Competitive Relationships

In an earlier section it was explained that competition or its absence may have an important place in industry credit analysis. The credit analyst who understands the competitive structure of a given business is often equipped to form a judgment as to the prospects of the individual concern that appears as a credit applicant. In still another way, a banker may often be able to take a longer and broader view of competitive problems than the customer in the heat of the business battle; he may be able to counsel the customer to his advantage.

Industry credit analysis also requires some attention to marketing problems. While the credit analyst might find that marketing problems are not directly related to those of bank credit, the character of a borrower's marketing operations is an important influence on his success and his capacity for repaying bank loans. In the field of retail and wholesale credit where banks have long been so important, marketing methods are particularly important.

CREDIT ANALYSIS OF A BUSINESS

Just what does a bank ask from an applicant for credit? It wants assurance that the credit granted *can* and *will* be repaid. On the basis of the facts, is it likely that the business *can repay the debt according to the contractual terms in the regular course of business at maturity?*

This point seems abundantly simple, but it bears emphasis because of a mistake sometimes made. It is thought by some that the purpose of financial credit analysis is only to judge if the credit *can* be repaid. The important qualifying phrase "in the regular course of business" is not considered. Bankers will ultimately profit and serve a social function only if they help their borrowers. To extend credit to a business under conditions that make the collection possible only with strain on the business serves no one—neither the business, nor the bank, nor the public at large.

Business borrowers often have a natural bias of optimism. This is a good fault and is not to be discouraged. Business leadership needs a certain amount of confidence. It takes courage and faith to undertake business risks. But this very temperament may mean that the applicant-borrowers do not adopt a wholly detached view of their capacity to repay. The banker cannot afford the luxury of a sanguine view.

Thus the basic function of credit analysis is more than just to look at the record of the past (though that is important); it should also determine, so far as existing facts permit, the probability that the loan can be repaid in the ordinary course of business. This requires imagination. It requires the use of tools of financial analysis that look toward the future: budgeting, cash-flow estimates, and *pro forma* statements.

Credit grantors have sometimes avoided losses by requiring wide margins of safety. There have doubtless been many rejections of good loans because the margins of safety were not wide enough. When there were plenty of loan demands, this was a tolerable practice. With present competition such a lender is likely to end up with few loans and low profits.

The Paradox of Credit Analysis

The applicants for bank loans are those who need, or think they need, funds. Thus the businesses with ample working capital are not applicants. Those who do apply are not in so good a relative position. This is not to say that the use of bank credit is to be considered a sign of weakness, but it is significant that many very strong concerns seldom need or apply for bank credit. Users of bank credit may be strong, but the fact that they need credit demonstrates that they are not so strong as those in similar situations who need no credit. Since the need for funds is relative, the applicants who "need" the funds most are almost certain to be the most doubtful ones. Those who need the funds least are likely to be the safest applicants.

There is, therefore, this paradox of credit analysis: the analyst deals, not with the average of business concerns, but with those somewhat below average!

Credit Analysis for Various Situations

Borrowers sometimes apply for funds to carry them over a seasonal peak. The task of the banker is then fairly simple: he looks at the past record of the borrower, discusses plans for seasonal activity in the current period, and makes an estimate of how far amiss the plans of the applicant could go without impairing his ability to repay the loan. How much unexpected price decline could be afforded? How much deflation of his optimistic sales plans could take place without jeopardizing the credit? Are the other affairs of the applicant in such condition (does he have adequate fixed-capital equipment, for example) that he can do the volume of business he hopes to do?

Questions of this sort are quite different from those that would be asked if the credit were for working capital purposes to be retired out of earnings, or for an equipment loan, or for a term loan. These questions, taken in their literal and direct sense, furnish the banker with the starting point for his analysis. Credit analysis has to be adapted to the type of credit involved. Sometimes it is used to determine the type of credit needed.

The Tools of Financial Credit Analysis

The advance of accountancy has given credit grantors much more precise and dependable tools of analysis. A generation or more ago, many bankers carried their credit files in their head; when they died or left their banks, they took these "files" with them. Now it is a more orderly business.

The financial statements. The foundations of scientific credit analysis are three basic accounting statements: the balance sheet, the income statement, and the cash-flow analysis. For proper use in credit analysis, these statements should be prepared according to standard and accepted accounting practices. To assure this, many commercial banks require that the financial statements filed with them (at least, the annual ones) shall be prepared and certified by a recognized public accountant. Sometimes banks even issue instructions as to the form in which statements should be submitted.

Even with the advances of modern accounting, every person familiar with financial statements will recognize the need for care in interpreting these statements. The banker should inquire about all unclear and ambiguous items.

The analysis of financial statements is more and more in comparative form. The direction in which a business is going is almost as important as its present level. A concern with strained working capital may be a dubious credit risk, but if it has been improving its position from an even more strained one, there is a very good chance that it can work out its problems. A concern in about the same condition, but having arrived at it by deterioration, is really in much weaker shape. As a result, the use of comparative statements in credit analysis is widely practiced by banks.

The number of years for which comparison is useful is more often dictated by expediency than by logic. Credit files (discussed below) usually provide space for as many years of statements as a concern remains a customer of a bank. When a credit file is started, the bank may attempt to secure statements for the preceding three to five years; sometimes it also seeks a statement for some date a number of years back—a depression year or one reflecting great strain.

The "current" sections of financial statements filed with banks should be prepared with unusual care. In recent years the dependability of financial statements in this regard has improved so that a certificate by a reputable accountant can usually be accepted by a bank without much further attention. However, a rather close check of all dubious parts of the current assets and a determination that all current liabilities are in fact included in that section are worthwhile for noncertified statements.

Because monthly, quarterly, and other interim statements are not always prepared by outside accountants, banks should scrutinize these statements with special care. In recent years several notorious cases of businesses which deteriorated rapidly between the dates of audited statements have come to light.

Ratio analysis. Ratios have become an important part of credit analysis. At least two dozen of them have been proposed at one time or another for this purpose. The matter of ratios may have been badly overdone, particularly by those who have not pondered their meaning and their interpretation. A few ratios, well understood, are far more valuable than a great clutter of little-used figures.

Ratios are the statistician's device for facilitating the comparison of magnitudes that change in absolute value. A business grows, and its dollar figures are several times those of a number of years ago. Growth is fine, but what about the *relative* position of, let us say, current assets and current liabilities? When the word "relative" crops up, then ratios are used to supply the answer. Since a ratio is a fraction, the same proportionate or relative growth of both numerator and denominator leaves the numerical value of the ratio unchanged.

If the student is anxious to pursue the study of the numerous ratios that may be used in financial statement analysis, there are many excellent and authoritative sources for doing so. Here we shall consider only a few.

The commonest by all odds is the *current ratio*, indicated above. It is the ratio of current assets (numerator) to current liabilities (denominator). The long-standing tradition has been that this ratio should have a numerical value of 2 or more; we shall see that this is an unnecessarily rigid standard. These same two figures are used for the computation of a closely related financial figure, net working capital; that is, current assets minus current liabilities equals net working capital, sometimes called "net current assets."

Since inadequacy of working capital is a very common weakness of business and because the provision of commercial bank credit is uniquely related to this problem, there needs to be a complete understanding of just what the current ratio and the amount of net working capital mean. It has already been pointed out that the current ratio often varies seasonally. Additions to current assets, matched by equal additions to current liabilities, reduce the current ratio but leave the net working capital unchanged. In other words, the current ratio may not be comparable from season to season; the net working capital is more likely to be.

Qualitative differences among current assets exist but they are of less importance among liabilities. Some current assets are fluid and capable of adjustment to business needs; some are less so. Cash is the very essence of liquidity, but other types of current assets, such as inventories, are sometimes far from liquid. Inventories of style or highly fabricated goods often cause losses. Balance sheet valuation of inventories has been one of the major subjects of lively accounting debate. The valuation system used for inventories may have a considerable bearing on the significance of a ratio.

The variability of the current ratio while net working capital remains constant can be seen from a very simple arithmetic example. Suppose that a business concern starts with the following current items in its balance sheet:

Current assets		Current liabilities	
Cash	$320,000	Notes and accounts payable	$300,000
Accounts receivable	80,000		
Inventory	200,000		
Total	$600,000	Total	$300,000

The current ratio is 2 (or 2 to 1 as some prefer to say), and the net working capital is $300,000 (that is, $600,000 minus $300,000). If the business should elect to use $200,000 of its cash to pay off an equal amount of notes and accounts payable, the current ratio would jump to 4 to 1; but net working capital would remain unchanged. Is the business stronger or the same? On the other hand, suppose that as a result of a seasonal increase in sales, both accounts receivable and inventory increased, the total increase of the two being $300,000 with the current liabilities increasing an equal amount. Now the current ratio is $1\frac{1}{2}$ to 1, but net working capital is still unchanged. Is the business stronger or weaker? or the same?

Because the current ratio can be "adjusted," a business financial manager is frequently tempted to "window dress" his statement—to pay off liabilities at about the time a statement is to be drawn off for credit analysis. For this reason, a bank often has more reason to watch net working capital than the current ratio.

Another test of considerable importance is the "quick asset" ratio, or "acid test" as it is sometimes called. This is the ratio of current assets, not including inventories (often called "dollar" assets), to current liabilities. This is a test of the ability of a business to meet the demands on it without liquidation of inventory.

Still another test used extensively in credit analysis is the ratio of receivables to net credit sales. This tests the promptness with which receivables are collected. In order to reduce this to a more relevant form for analysis, it is sometimes expressed in terms of *days required for collection of receivables*. The formula used to derive this form is:

$$\frac{\text{Accounts receivable} \times 360}{\text{Net annual credit sales}} = \text{days accounts were outstanding}$$

As a specific example, assume receivables at the year end of $20,000 and net credit sales during the preceding year of $150,000; then it may be presumed that, on the average, it takes 48 days to collect the accounts:

$$\frac{\$20,000 \times 360}{\$150,000} = 48 \text{ days}$$

There are a number of flaws in this rough computation. One of the most important is that the amount of receivables outstanding at the end of the fiscal year when statements are drawn off is very likely to be at a seasonal low. Where fiscal years do not correspond to the calendar year the fiscal year end chosen is usually a low point to facilitate inventory taking. Net credit sales, however, are for the full year; there is no seasonal factor in such a figure. As a result, the computed average number of days in which receivables are collected is quite a bit less than the true average. A precise method would require the use of a daily average figure of receivables. This is quite beyond the possibility of accounting records for most concerns. Unless unusual shifts occur near the time when the accounting statements are drawn off, the relative level of this figure may give a good year-to-year comparison even if its absolute level is rather too low (or high, as it may be if there is a seasonal bulge near the end of the accounting statement period).

One of the problems in dealing with this ratio is that separate figures for credit sales are often not supplied. When such is the case, a ratio figured on the basis of total sales has little meaning for absolute level unless one has a rough idea of the proportion of credit to total sales. If a credit applicant avers that credit sales are "about 40 per cent of total sales," and the "number of days" computed on the basis of total sales is 20 days, then it may be estimated that the true level is about 50 days. Thus,

$$20 \times \tfrac{100}{40} = 50$$

or

$$20 \div 0.40 = 50$$

Even without an estimate of the proportion of credit to total sales, a comparison of the average collection period computed on the basis of total sales may indicate roughly whether collections are staying the same, improving, or deteriorating.

Another ratio of importance in credit analysis is that of *inventory turnover*. The rough form for computation of this turnover—sales divided by inventory—is defective. The valuation bases for sales and inventories are inconsistent because sales are at retail prices and inventories are valued by a variety of rules, but mostly below retail price. Some exceptions may be found; department stores often value inventories at retail prices.

There are two ways to compute this ratio in usable form:

1. Divide the cost of goods sold by the inventory at cost, or

2. Divide sales by the inventory converted to the selling price.

If neither one can be prepared, then the ratio can be corrected by still another device. The average markup is known for many lines, particularly retail lines. The uncorrected ratio of sales to receivables can be divided by the markup plus one. Assume an uncorrected ratio for inventory turnover of 6 based on sales of $1,500,000 and inventory at cost of $250,000. Also assume that the average markup in this field is about 50 per cent. The corrected turnover is 4. Thus,

$$6 \div (0.50 + 1) = 4$$

The chief trouble with this method of correction is that a change in the composition of sales is likely to change the average markup.

Rapid inventory turnover is generally advantageous; holding more inventory than is needed is a form of speculation. But some fine profits have been made out of such "speculation."

During World War II, some of the most successful stores were those which had merchandise when others did not. They got it, more often than not, by flying in the face of conventional rules of expediency before the war and buying everything in sight. It is hard to condemn a policy which has worked as well as this has—sometimes. Perhaps bankers should not be concerned with this exception; perhaps the only concerns which can afford to take the sort of chances reflected in this are those with adequate funds for self-financing without recourse to the banks.

It should be recollected that the character of inventory turnover should be used to moderate the interpretation of the current ratio. A high inventory turnover may be grounds for accepting a lower current ratio than might otherwise be safe; a slow inventory turnover means that the minimum for the current ratio should be higher.

Other ratios or derived figures are also used in credit analysis. Their significance is often overlapping with those already given. Some of these are:

1. Inventory to total current assets. This ratio is a test of the quality of current assets; a low ratio of this may excuse a low current ratio. It reflects much the same thing as the acid test.

2. Current assets divided by sales. This turnover of current assets is a curious mixture; its meaning is often ambiguous.

Certain other ratios reflect operating results rather than financial position and so are used more in longer term credit analysis:

3. Operating ratio: expenses of business and cost of goods sold to net sales. The arithmetic reciprocal of this ratio is the gross profit ratio.

4. Net profits to sales.

5. Net profits to net worth.

6. Net worth and funded debt to fixed assets. This indicates the extent to which long-term needs for capital have been financed with long-term funds.

7. Excess of net worth and funded debt over fixed and "other" assets. This is a test of the amount of working capital provided by permanent capital. The figure is often identical, or almost so, with net working capital.

8. Sales to net worth: the turnover of net worth.

Cash-flow Analysis

Most bank loans are repaid from the flow of cash generated in the ordinary course of business. Occasionally bank loans may be repaid by refunding, as when a public utility uses long-term borrowing proceeds to repay bank debt incurred in plant construction. Except in such cases one of the revealing tests that may be applied to a business loan application is to determine the adequacy of cash flow to meet the proposed loan repayment plan.

The measurement of expected cash flow is also useful in determining the appropriate maturity for a projected loan. If a borrower requests too short a maturity he is almost certain to encounter repayment difficulties. It is far better for both banker and borrower to anticipate correctly the period a loan is outstanding. The measurement of cash flow also can reveal unsuspected characteristics of a projected plan of bank borrowing. If a business is growing very rapidly a bank loan requested for ordinary working capital purposes may prove to be, in fact, awkward to repay though the business is profitable. If the rate of growth is rapid, both inventories and receivables may grow so fast as to absorb all the cash accruing from the profits and noncash charges. On the other hand, a business frequently can repay indebtedness while operating without a profit. A cash-flow statement that measures the ability of a business to repay debt may substantiate the possibility of a safe short-term credit extension to an unprofitable business.

The methods of measuring cash flow vary. Since excellent but detailed methods are described in a number of texts on business finance, a similar exposition will not be presented here.[1] The direct method of measuring cash flow is about as follows: to forecast sales for the future period over which the loan will be outstanding and then to estimate the passage of these sales through accounts receivable into cash receipts. From this sum cash expenses, including tax payments, scheduled repayments on other indebtedness, and any planned increases in inventories, are deducted. The residual may be considered the amount of cash probably available for payment of the added indebtedness now being considered. An indirect method of measuring cash flow is to add depreciation and other noncash charges to net profits and then to adjust for any changes in receivables and inventories. (An increase in receivables or inventories reduces expected cash flow and vice versa.)

These methods of measuring cash flow may be used to judge potential cash coverage of either short-term or long-term indebtedness. In the case of long-term indebtedness profits and depreciation charges are relatively much more important, and variations in accounts receivable and inventory less significant, in determining the contour and size of cash flow. In the case of very short-term indebtedness, however, profits and depreciation charges are less important and short-term variations in accounts receivable and inventories are of substantially greater importance in determining the contour and size of cash flow.

A conservative lending standard would be one in which cash flow rather amply covers the expected schedule of debt repayments. A two-to-one ratio in which scheduled repayment of indebtedness did not exceed one-half of projected cash flow should protect against most financial hazards. In certain cases this standard may be excessive, particularly in the case of loans to businesses with highly predictable cash flow such as stable merchandising enterprises or sales finance operations.

[1] B. B. Howard and M. Upton, *Introduction to Business Finance*, McGraw-Hill Book Company, Inc., New York, 1951; Robert W. Johnson, *Financial Management*, Allyn and Bacon, Inc., New York, 1959, chap. 4.

Use of the Pro Forma Statement

When a credit application is analyzed, the position of the business *before* the credit is granted is only a part of the story; the rest is what the financial statements will be like after the credit has been received and used.

The accountant's device of the *pro forma* statement can be used here. The application of the device is relatively simple; it amounts to adding in the expected changes made by the proposed credit after it has been applied. For example, suppose an applicant presents the following statement in support of a request for a loan of $20,000:

Assets			Liabilities	
Cash.............	$ 4,000		Accounts payable.........	$15,000
Accounts receivable	16,000		Mortgage...............	8,000
Inventories.......	15,000		Net worth...............	37,000
Total current assets.....		$35,000		
Fixed assets.............		25,000		
Total assets...........		$60,000	Total liabilities.........	$60,000

The purpose of the loan is "to retire the mortgage and improve the working capital position." On inquiry, it develops that the improvement in working capital means that about half of the remainder of the loan proceeds after paying the mortgage will be used to build up cash balance while the other half will be used to reduce the accounts payable. There is no thought of increasing inventories.

The statement is rearranged as in the accompanying form to reflect the expected changes; the result is a *pro forma* statement the purpose of which is to reflect the new situation.

After giving effect to the loan, the current ratio, which before had been 2.3:1, is now 1.4:1. The acid test changes from 1.3:1 to 0.9:1. Net working capital, notwithstanding the idea that the loan is partly to increase working capital, is reduced from $20,000 to $12,000.

Simple as this illustrative statement is, these changed circumstances are far from evident except to the most practiced observer. The use of the *pro forma* statement is often as eye-opening for the applicant as for the credit analyst.

Assets and Liabilities	Present statement	Changes made by proposed loan	*Pro forma* statement reflecting condition after loan
Cash................................	$ 4,000	$+ 6,000	$10,000
Accounts receivable.............	16,000	....	16,000
Inventories......................	15,000	....	15,000
Total current assets...........	$35,000	+ 6,000	$41,000
Fixed assets....................	25,000	....	25,000
Total.......................	$60,000	+ 6,000	$66,000
Accounts payable...............	$15,000	$− 6,000	$ 9,000
Notes payable..................	......	+20,000	20,000
Total current liabilities........	$15,000	$+14,000	$29,000
Mortgage.......................	8,000	− 8,000	
Net worth......................	37,000	....	37,000
Total.......................	$60,000	$+ 6,000	$66,000

Reports of Credit Agencies

The judgment of credit has long been of so much consequence in the mercantile field that specialized agencies make a business of furnishing credit reports. Dun & Bradstreet is a consolidation of some of the older agencies. Other credit reporters of a more specialized or regional nature may also be used. A credit agency has the advantage of extensive files and long experience. It keeps in constant touch with business concerns. If a person goes through bankruptcy and then moves to a new place and starts in business, concealing his past, this may be brought out by an agency report. Agency reports can only help, however; they cannot relieve a banker of his responsibility for final credit appraisal.

An agency report may be used as a supplement, a way of being assured that the banker has not overlooked some important aspect. The standard rating manuals also have the advantage of giving an independent judgment. Agency reports, of course, have much more meaning in urban areas than in small towns and villages. In villages, the banker often acts as a part-time reporter for the mercantile credit agencies; he can get nothing more or better from them than what he himself reports. In cities, the agencies employ their own credit-reporting staff. These specialists go into the firms and often, by virtue of their training, are able, in addition to securing formal financial reports, to observe a direction of business affairs not evident to less experienced observers.

Trade Checking

When an applicant approaches a bank in seeking credit, one of the things usually asked of him is a list of the names of his chief suppliers—those from whom he buys. The bank may then take the liberty of corresponding with these suppliers to ask about the payment habits of the applicant. Is he prompt? Does he take all cash discounts? Is he a satisfactory customer in general? To put it in blunter terms, does he "chisel" on merchandise returns and claims of defects? Does he engage in other sharp practices?

Trade checking is one of the expected business courtesies. Replies are given in confidence, and reputable concerns do not request them unless the promise of strict confidence is expressed or implied. Since preparing replies takes time, responsible banks do not check the trade without having good reason to do so. By the same token, banks undertake to give prompt and accurate reports to those who have legitimate reason for checking with them about their customers.

In addition to pure trade checking, a certain amount of cross checking occurs among banks. Multiple borrowing lines are usually cross-checked to avoid an unusual and possible fraudulent expansion of debt at a number of banks by a single borrower.

Miscellaneous Sources of Credit Information

Certain other sources of credit information are used by credit departments of banks. Most cities have local credit bureaus mainly for the use of merchants. A credit bureau is usually primarily concerned with persons rather than with business concerns and so is used by banks mainly in granting consumer credit. These bureaus usually are nonprofit associations and so, to participate, a bank might have to become a member and make a member's flat contribution. In addition there is usually, but not always, a charge for each report requested. On the other hand, the bank as a member is expected to furnish to the credit bureau reports covering its experience with customers.

Credit bureaus sometimes also cover or "report" on business firms. When this is so, the service is of particular use to banks, especially those which make small-business loans. In fair-sized urban areas, a single bank might find it hard to keep in touch with all its small-business customers; a credit bureau can be helpful in such circumstances.

Other sources of credit information include legal notices in newspapers, court records of judgments, recordings of liens, and sometimes even reports from private investigators.

The Credit File

The formal bank credit file is a way of making use of some of the other tools we have discussed. There are almost as many forms of credit files as there are ambitious banks. A credit file may be almost anything from a card file to a large, complex record. They almost always include standard forms for the financial statements and the ratios derived from them. Officers' reports of interviews and recommendations are usually included. The credit file will probably also contain an analysis of past borrowing and of deposit balances. It may include related correspondence or copies of it.

While credit departments have larger responsibilities than merely maintaining up-to-date credit files, that is one of their major responsibilities. Credit files are a matter of time and accumulation; after a period they become an invaluable record. A retiring loan officer should leave the bank with records so good that another loan officer can step in and familiarize himself with the clients handled by his predecessor rather quickly.

But some credit files have grown so large and complex that their use is thereby restricted.

The Exchange of Credit Information among Banks

Although banks are business competitors in the granting of credit, they recognize their interdependence in making credit judgments. It is obvious that, particularly against unscrupulous borrowers under multiple lines, banks would have inadequate defenses without some exchange of information. So, very much through the valuable offices of the Robert Morris Associates,[2] banks now have established practices and a recognized code of ethics for the exchange of credit information. The form of credit correspondence and its ethical restrictions are widely recognized. A bank wishing to be a part of the recognized community of bank credit grantors would do well to canvass the advantages of taking a formal place in this system of exchange.

Putting the Tools of Credit Analysis to Work

The means by which the complex tools of credit analysis can be made effective in practice depend, not so much on the nature of the tools, as on their user. Bank lending, even with these aids, is still an art. Rules cannot replace judgment; no mechanism can reduce the lending process to a routine. Ever bigger telescopes and more refined cameras have increased the penetration of astronomy, but astronomers cannot afford to become more automatic, less imaginative. Bank lending is just as hard a business as ever; the gain is primarily that of precision.

Banks must be more precise in lending. In the first place, they have thinner capital equities than in days gone by. The shock of losses is magnified many more times. Also, the social tolerance of a banking system that excludes deserving but marginal borrowers is less than it used to be. If banks do not want

[2] The Robert Morris Associates is an association of commercial-bank credit officers formed in 1915 as an offshoot of the National Association of Credit Men. It has furnished valuable statistical material to credit departments; in turn it depends on these departments for this material. A publication of the Associates, *The Credit Department: A Training Ground for the Bank Loan Officer,* is of particular interest to those engaged in bank credit work.

to be displaced by other agencies, possibly governmental ones, they need to make loans to those who can use the credit profitably—profitably in both a social and a business sense.

As has been said before, lending is the prime excuse and reason for commercial banking. Because banks cannot afford to lend with any less precision than their very best, better tools of credit analysis put more, not less, strain on the elements of discretion that rest in the hands of the tool users—the bank lenders.

Diagnostic Credit Analysis

The effective bank lender is skilled in business finance. He is a kind of financial doctor. Interpretation of financial statements is a kind of diagnosis; the credit recommendation is a kind of prescription. Since banks are still primarily short-term lenders, though less so than they theoretically used to be, their part in business finance has to do mainly with working capital needs.

When a bank loan officer has a full set of comparative financial statements and the relevant ratios, what does he look for? The very fact of a credit application carries with it the implication of working capital need. What is the basis of the need? Is it a temporary and justifiable use of bank credit? Or are there forces working to deplete the working capital of the concern? Working capital need can grow out of many different kinds of circumstances:

1. *Fast growth.* A very fine concern growing rapidly may find that growth itself is a cause of shortage in working capital. If earnings are good, this shortage may be restored before long, although further growth may upset all planning. This is a very good reason for bank lending. Still the banker should be sure that the need is not more for long-term and funded credit. Working capital may have been diverted for the purchase of fixed capital equipment; the restoration of this may take longer than is within the reach of an ordinary commercial-bank loan. (This is not an argument against long-term loans.)

2. *Losses.* The concern that is not covering its money costs

will tend to drain working capital. This furnishes a very poor foundation for credit; still, as we shall discuss below, the kind of losses due to general swings in business conditions may be temporary and can be weathered by the business. A bank finds it hard to desert an otherwise good customer because he has run into bad times and incurred some losses.

3. *Dividends and proprietary withdrawals.* If a concern distributes more than current earnings, with an adjustment for depreciation and similar charges, working capital is depleted. This is inexcusable as a basis for bank credit extension.

4. *Fixed capital expansion not funded.* As mentioned under growth above, this is a common situation in business. When a business is in good shape and earnings are high, the management may be anxious to undertake expansion of equipment and facilities without waiting for the long-term financing of it. This depletes working capital. If it is the cause of a credit application, there may be a legitimate foundation for lending, but the lending may have to be in long-term form.

5. *Seasonal peaks.* This is the traditional prime excuse for bank credit. In any highly seasonal business, the managers may need far more gross working capital at the peak season than they would have profitable employment for in the dull or bottom periods. This is an excellent occasion for the extension of bank credit. The only thing wrong, from the banker's point of view, is that there is not enough business of this sort.

Each of these circumstances can be read from the financial statements. It is for this sort of picture, and others not mentioned here, that the credit analyst must look. As in all analysis, a combination of these circumstances may be true of the same credit applicant. There is no rule for sorting out multiple effects.

It is for this reason that an imaginative examination of financial statements is so necessary. It is only by going behind the figures into matters of implicit business policy that the credit analyst can get at the heart of his problem. The combination of statement analysis with interview or visit to the credit applicant's quarters may be very revealing. Sometimes the problem of getting at the financial truth about a business is not so much due to secretiveness as it is that the leaders are not articulate; they do not express themselves clearly. Many business concerns have fixed policies which have never been formulated in so many words; they have grown up, perhaps in the mind of the dominant owner or manager.

To penetrate to such policies, and to find the truth about the financial affairs and policies of a given concern, credit analysis must be a combination of psychoanalysis and detection.

One of the great rewards for good credit analysis is not just in the reduction of loss to the bank which practices it. The customers of banks, the businessmen who come for credit, are often fine engineers, effective business leaders, or persuasive salesmen; but they are often not financiers. Caution, the temperamental hallmark of finance, is often the very quality which makes a poor businessman. The banker fits in here as an informal financial adviser to his customers. The purpose of credit analysis at the time of a loan application may not be to choose between acceptance or rejection, but rather to determine what kind of advice should be given. Should the customer be granted his request unaltered? Should it be modified materially? If so, how should it be altered? Should he be advised not to press the application?

Flexibility in Credit Judgment

Credit analysis has to move with the economic climate. Each business must be judged against the prevailing conditions of business and general income or prosperity of the community. This is not true of just any one credit judgment but of lending policy as a whole. When times are good, almost all businesses are likely to show profits—to look good. But this may be the very time to start the more careful scrutiny of financial statements, for a general hardening of credit policy. When times are very bad, even good businesses produce losses and show signs of distress. There is often an agonizing judgment for a commercial banker to make. Shall he support customers who have been good customers and loyal to his bank in the past when they get in the twilight zone of survival–nonsurvival? There are no easy answers. The good credit analyst is a good economic analyst, but that is not enough. In the end there has to be a certain amount of blind guessing.

Reshaping Credit Applications

The analysis of financial statements, as already indicated, often shows that the applicant–borrower is asking for short-term credit when his real need is for long-term credit. A constructive lending officer may reshape a loan application to reflect what is good for the borrower and safe for the bank. This is, in effect, an illustration of furnishing financial advisory service.

A bank that has a fixed maximum fund for term loans might be tempted to lend on a short-term basis even though the need were long-term. Should it do so? In general the answer is "no." If the need is for long-term credit, the granting of it in temporarily short-term form may mean only that the formalities of a limit have been evaded. The realities have a way of breaking through the fictions of form. If the credit is for essentially long-term purposes, it is likely to turn into just that, no matter what action the bank takes.

10

Supervision, Budgeting, and Handling Distressed Loans

It has been said that a bank never makes a bad loan, that loans get bad only after they are made. This is, of course, partly true; but the moral implied by it is important: banks cannot make loans and then forget them. A necessary part of their lending function is to keep abreast of the loans outstanding.

The supervision of loans, like the making of them, is usually the responsibility of more than one department of the bank. The credit department continues to secure and analyze the statements of customers indebted to the bank. The lending officer keeps track of his clients. When special problems in connection with outstanding credits arise, they may have to be referred to the higher echelons of bank management, just as in the case of new credits.

The process of statement analysis, which is so important at the time a credit is granted, is equally important after the loan is made and the funds are disbursed. If, as has been suggested, a definite budget plan has been worked out between the bank and the borrower, a review of statements to find out the extent to which this plan is being followed is of the greatest importance.

Budgets are necessarily flexible instruments of estimation.

178

Banks cannot expect their customers to follow them precisely. In the review of actual events a line must always be drawn between the elements of activity that are within the control of the borrowing customer and those that are not. If the estimate of sales in a budget does not pan out, the sales forces of the borrower may be exhorted to more activity; but sales cannot be forced. On the other hand, an estimate of expenses or of capital outlay is fully or largely within the control of the borrower. Large variations from budget plans should not only be explained but corrected, if possible.

The intervals at which statements are secured from borrowing customers naturally depend on the prior arrangements made with them and the state of their accounting records. One of the common practices in the case of distressed credits is that of requiring financial statements (perhaps with some parts on an estimated basis) to be filed with the bank at frequent intervals, often monthly. If this is good practice for distressed credits, it is almost as good for credits that are still in good standing. No hard and fast rule can be stated, but a bank is doing its customers no disfavor if it requires the preparation and analysis of statements at an interval no greater than the bank itself feels necessary for proper review of the credit.

The handling of these periodic statements is carried out in the credit department and is not unlike the routine followed for customers from whom loan applications are anticipated.

When a loan starts to show signs of distress, a difficult choice arises: to collect it, or such part as is recoverable by strong-arm tactics, or to arrange a "workout" of the credit. This is one of the hard-bitten choices that all bankers face sooner or later. It is a choice for which there is no satisfactory answer, only a range of more or less unsatisfactory compromises.

If, as we have averred above, the primary art of commercial banking is that of finding ways to make loans, then an art of hardly less importance is that of working out distressed credits without loss to the creditor bank and in the best interests of competent and conscientious customers.

SOME CHARACTERISTICS OF LOAN LOSSES

In order to be active and aggressive in lending, commercial banks must face the probability of some loan losses. The very best and most profitable banks expect such losses. The route to profitability, however, requires that losses be held within relatively small margins. Only by this means is it possible to have an active lending program without exposure to excessive risk.

Research on bank losses has been relatively infrequent in recent years because of excellent business conditions and low aggregate losses. One study of such losses, however, supports the idea that the proper policy is to expect some loan difficulties but to curb the losses that result from them.[1] This study showed that the two types of credit most likely to give rise to losses or charge-offs were consumer loans and business loans. Loans on farm lands and mortgage loans had quite good records. Losses on consumer credit were concentrated primarily in banks that engage actively in such business and did a large volume of it. The successful institutions, however, kept the frequency of loss within small margins by alert collection procedures and other protective devices. In the case of business loans the range of loss was somewhat greater. Some banks' losses on business loans were negligible, but at a few banks they were quite large. Business loans may expose a bank to larger losses than almost any other type of credit if not carefully safeguarded. Successful banks did not avoid losses altogether but rather contained them within relatively small margins. A further interesting fact revealed by this inquiry was that banks with a high degree of specialization in lending tended to have moderate-sized but carefully controlled losses in their lines of specialization. One further point of some interest revealed by this study was that the loss rates of very small banks averaged somewhat less than those of large banks; however, greater variation among loan

---

[1] "Loan Loss Experience at Member Banks of the Seventh Federal Reserve District, 1957 and 1958," by Mary T. Petty and Theodore H. Schneider, Research Department of the Federal Reserve Bank of Chicago, 1959.

loss rates was found at small banks. Some had negligible losses but a few had fairly sizable ones. Large banks tended to cluster more around the average.

Loan losses are clearly related to the character of external economic developments. In the absence of a severe depression, bank lending policies have not been rigorously tested for almost a generation. However, public policy would probably never again permit banking liquidity to drop to the point at which banks were forced to put pressure on borrowers beyond those consonant with the requirements of good banking and collection policies. Without such unreasonable pressure, the chances of ultimate losses probably can be kept within tolerable margins by the standards of credit quality now enforced.

SUPERVISION OF OUTSTANDING LOANS

Near the end of this chapter when we are dealing with the collection of "hard" or "slow" loans, the difficulties of this process, the agonizing frustrations of it, will be evident. Many of the agonies and frustrations of slow and distressed credits can be avoided by the proverbial "ounce of prevention"—good loan supervision. A good loan is not only made good; it is kept good.

Visiting the Borrower

In discussing the lending procedure, it was suggested that a visit to the premises of the applicant is a good idea; it is fully as useful to visit the premises of those customers already on the books. While it takes an experienced observer to appreciate— sometimes almost to sense intuitively—just how things are going, this is an art that bankers need to cultivate. A good borrower whose affairs are in fine shape is almost always glad to see his banker, proud to show him how things are going. He appreciates the interest in his affairs and often makes use of the occasion to seek advice. The visit is a good-will builder.

A visit to a customer whose affairs are not going so well may be a bit chillier, but this is just the situation a banker needs to inspect. If he can find out early just how his customers' affairs are developing, he can often avoid the more strenuous problems of workouts and liquidations. All the old saws about "a stitch in time" and the like apply to this case.

What are the things that a banker might expect to look for on a visit? The conditions that may not be reflected in the financial statements? Several follow:

1. The general state of repairs and maintenance of plant and equipment. Inadequate maintenance is often an early sign of distress.

2. The state of employee and junior officer morale. Those inside a business know, partly by intimacy, partly by instinct, just how a business is going. Morale is often a product of this situation. It is an intangible characteristic but one to which the competent observer trains himself to be sensitive.

3. The physical evidences of materials and finished goods inventories. Interim statements of concerns are usually not audited or certified and, sometimes it must be admitted, fraud is resorted to under the pressure of difficulties. The overstated inventory is one frequent way of inflating financial statements. Highly trained observers soon get to have a "feel" for discrepancies between the claims of statements and the actual affairs.

General Business Policy and Advice

More and more, banks are becoming aware of the fact that general business conditions have a profound influence on their own affairs and those of their customers. The number of banks that maintain economic advisory services has increased greatly. A number of them issue "letters" or monthly bulletins of general business and economic analysis.

In supervising credits already outstanding, a banker may find that this process is one of the very best sources of "feel" for the state of business. These findings may be useful in dealing with other customers. If a bank is in constant and intimate touch with its customers, it may soon develop a sensitivity to the state of business. How fast are current orders coming in?

How are credit collections? What are price prospects? What is the current state of market demand?

If a bank is sensitive to business developments, it can: (1) revise its own loan and credit policies and (2) advise its customers similarly. While a bank cannot assume the management of its borrowers' affairs, it can help. Borrowers are not always (though sometimes) ungrateful for being restrained in their periods of high optimism. A flexible bank policy is likely not only to save the bank trouble and headaches, but also to save its customers similarly.

Keeping Track of Deposit Balances

Once a bank has granted a credit, it can learn a great deal by inspecting the deposit balance maintained by the borrowing customer. Since an agreement on the minimum balance that should be maintained by the customer is good lending practice, the way in which this agreement is observed gives some clues to his affairs. A bare minimum balance may be a bad sign; some surplus over it is to be considered a good sign.

The bank can also often tell by activity in the account the rather general progress of the borrower. While it is not the business of a bank to snoop into the affairs of its borrowers, it has a legitimate right to keep posted on them through these channels.

Checking with Other Creditors

In granting a credit, checking with other creditors is, as we have outlined before, one of the major tests of a borrower. This continues to be an important test after the credit has been granted. Is the customer continuing to take all discounts? Is he prompt in his payments or does he try to chisel a few days?

The checking of other creditors is useful and important, but it should not be overdone. A formal credit check puts a burden on other concerns and should be made sparingly. Informal checking is usually adequate. Formal checking often is to be avoided because it may start to cast doubts on a quite satisfactory debtor. When other creditors receive repeated requests for credit information, they may be disposed to start wondering just what it is that prompts this frequency of inquiry.

Special Supervision for Term Loans

The supervision of ordinary short-term bank loans has many problems; that for term loans even more. Because of the longer time involved, the need for careful scrutiny of the business reports as they are received is all the greater. Since the analysis of term credits emphasizes earnings more and current position less, the analysis of earnings factors is to be emphasized.

When a term loan is accompanied by a loan agreement, one of the specific supervisory tasks is that of checking to be sure that the agreement is being observed. The maintenance of current position, the payment of taxes, the maintenance of property in good condition, the agreed limitation of dividends or other distribution of profits, all should be verified.

Minor deviations from the exact terms of the loan agreement are sometimes found. Even though minor, it is usually desirable to secure a remedy of such deviations. There are exceptions. For this reason a loan agreement should contain a provision spelling out the fact that forgiveness of some lapses from the contracted conditions of the loan does not condone other defections or continued defection of a given sort.

BUDGETING

The basis of commercial-bank credit to business is some sort of plan which promises to produce both income and cash. The second of the two—cash—must be emphasized, because it is the stuff with which debts are repaid. The ability to earn a profit is not necessarily proof of ability to repay debts; indeed profitable but expanding businesses are often the most "hard up" while dormant old ones may be profitless but quite liquid.

Modern accounting techniques have been developed, not only for keeping a record of the past, but also for planning or looking into the future—financial budgeting. Budgeting can be a very useful device in commercial-bank lending. The budget looks not only at profits but also (sometimes, primarily) at expected cash flow. The cash-flow budget is the future tense of the cash-flow analysis described in the preceding chapter.

Budgeting for Ordinary Loans

The most ordinary short-term business loans involve rudimentary budgeting. The business wants money for some deal which will produce cash with which to repay the loan. Implicit in this simple statement are all the parts of a business budget. It need not be written to be real. Often the business affairs of even a fairly modest borrower are such that the cash-flow plan cannot be compressed into such simple terms. It is then that the more formal techniques of budgeting come to be of assistance.

A business in which finances are none too closely controlled may apply for a bank loan only when it needs cash. The business operators, confident of their enterprise, may feel quite secure in promising to repay the bank after some customary period. The business may appear to have such ample earning power that it seems to be a fine and deserving risk. Yet a credit advanced under circumstances of no greater assurance than this may result in many difficulties. If the business is expanding its capital assets, there may be no near-term prospect for enough excess in the cash flow to repay the loan for which an application has been made. The current application may, in fact, prove to be simply the first of a series of further requests for more cash and long-continued requests for renewals.

Budgeting is the technique for putting all the circumstances that might affect future balance sheets, income statements, and cash-flow analyses in an orderly form. In concrete terms, it may be said that a budget answers these questions in reasonably satisfactory form:

1. How much credit is needed?
2. When will it be needed?
3. Once granted, how long will the need continue?
4. When and how fast can the loan be repaid?

In other words, the budget has the advantage of being a fairly precise agreement between borrower and bank as to the purpose of the loan. It is a much more satisfactory expression than that which can be crowded into a line on the application form: "Purpose of the loan is . . . ."

Budgeting also has the merit of distinguishing clearly between the case of a credit that is truly seasonal and one that represents a chronic deficiency of working capital. The importance of this in credit analysis cannot be overstated. For example, a present or projected weakness in current position may be wholly forgivable if it is the result of seasonal factors. A loan could be hazarded under such circumstances that would be unthinkable if the weakness of the current position were chronic.

Budgeting in Term Lending

The discussion so far has related to the application of the budget to ordinary short-term business lending by commercial banks. In long-term lending, budgeting is even more important. Budgets for term loans will be discussed in greater detail in Chapter 14, but certain points may be profitably added here.

In the ordinary term loan, cash flow is perhaps just as important as in a short-term loan. The test of a good loan, after all, is that it is repaid according to contract terms. But the determinants of cash flow over long periods are not quite the same as those for short periods. Earnings and depreciation charges loom rather larger in such circumstances; seasonal factors are less important.

The application of budgeting to term lending is chiefly of interest because it gives the lender one of the most powerful of analytical weapons known to credit management. It furnishes the natural link between banker and borrower, the platform for the delivery of such financial help, advice, and assistance as the bank can give.

The "Workout" Budget

When a credit has deteriorated but the bank does not wish to displace the existing management, the budget often becomes the tool for liaison between the banker and the embarrassed borrower.

Where basic business strength is good but where financial mismanagement has been the cause of embarrassment, a period of penance almost always has to follow, during which the husbandry of liquidity becomes the leading feature of operations. Under these circumstances the creditor bank can often gain by using the business talent of, and good will attaching to, the borrower if his integrity is adequate. The bank can supply the financial supervision. The budget is the specific tool of instruction and discipline by which the bank can enforce its will on the borrower.

The Banker's Application of Budgeting

Many borrowers do not have the sort of skilled accounting help needed for budgeting. The banker may be forced to supply it. This is true of small-business lending and of agricultural credits.

In order to suggest how bankers may proceed, the following illustrations are simple but fairly concrete in detail. It is not the purpose of this section to discuss the actual technique of budgets; that is adequately covered elsewhere. For the purposes of this section, it is adequate to identify them and to discuss their application to the credit problems of commercial banks.

A simple budget is a projection of past accounting records; it forecasts future gross income (usually sales) based on the records of the past; it forecasts outlays required for the expected or projected level of sales; and finally it makes the adjustments of these and related asset conversion factors, including plans for capital outlays, into a general scheme descriptive of the cash flow.

Suppose that a banker should receive a visit and a verbal credit application from X, the sole proprietor of a small building supply and lumber yard. X, acquainted with bank practice, comes armed with the balance sheet shown at the top of the next page.

X COMPANY, MARCH 31, 19—

Assets		Liabilities	
Cash....................	$ 1,500	Accounts payable.........	$ 7,500
Accounts receivable.......	4,000	Proprietor X..............	16,500
Inventory................	12,000		
Current assets..........	$17,500		
Fixed assets..............	6,500		
Total..................	$24,000	Total..................	$24,000

The cash, except for a small imprest till cash fund of $100, is all deposited in this bank. This statement presents a current ratio of 2.3:1 and an acid test ratio of 0.7:1 both fairly satisfactory. X explains that he wants $5,000 for about six months to take the discounts on accounts payable. He expects that the loan can be repaid early in the summer after the spring sales, which normally run fairly high. On inquiry it develops that sales are expected to average around $4,500 a month, but on closer questioning X agrees to about the following schedule of expected sales and purchases:

Month	Sales	Purchases	Month	Sales	Purchases
April........	$3,000	$2,000	July........	$7,000	$2,000
May........	4,000	2,000	August......	4,000	2,000
June........	6,000	2,000	September...	2,000	2,000

The present high inventory is due to the expected large spring sales. X's plans for purchases, developed after inquiry, are fairly modest as shown by the second column in the above statement. It also develops that about one-half of his sales are for cash and the remainder for credit. The credit portion is again divided into halves: one-half paid in the month following sale and the remaining one-half in the next month. Amounts running longer than this or presenting a collection problem are, according to X, trivial.

Conversation with X develops the fact that, on the average, his markup for goods is about one-third (the "cost of goods sold" is 75 per cent of sales price), and the regular selling and other current expenses of his yard are about $800 a month, including X's own withdrawals.

The banker is now equipped with almost all the financial data needed for a budget. But other facts must be included if the picture is to be reasonably complete. The banker, noting that this is a single proprietorship, asks X if he has any personal or other debts not shown in the statement. X replies that there is a small amortized mortgage on his house which is paid out of his regular withdrawals from the business. This fact, though a relevant credit consideration, does not need to be brought into the budget. The banker also asks X if he has any plans for unusual capital expenses for the business or the expectation of making any extra withdrawals for himself from the business. X responds by disclosing the plan that, after the high and profitable spring sales, he had hoped to spend $1,500 for yard improvements in August and September. He is also being pressed by his wife for a new car; he would prefer not to buy "on time" but hopes to have enough profit, about $1,600, in the business to pay for a car in June, possibly.

The banker now reduces the sales estimates to expected cash inflow as follows:

Cash receipts	April	May	June	July	August	September
Total sales...........	$3,000	$4,000	$6,000	$7,000	$4,000	$2,000
Cash sales, one-half...	1,500	2,000	3,000	3,500	2,000	1,000
Accounts receivable collections:						
One-half paid first month..........	2,667*	750	1,000	1,500	1,750	1,000
One-half paid second month......	.....	1,333*	750	1,000	1,500	1,750
Total cash receipts....	$4,167	$4,083	$4,750	$6,000	$5,250	$3,750

* It is assumed that two-thirds of the $4,000 of receivables held at the end of March will be collected in April and one-third in May.

The next step is to put together a very simple budget. Using the schedule of cash receipts already worked out and assuming that all purchases take the form of accounts payable which are paid promptly so as to take cash discounts (2 per cent for payment in 10 days, net 60 days), the following is a general financial plan or budget:

Budget items	April	May	June	July	August	September
Cash on hand at start...	$ 1,500	$2,517	$3,840	$ 4,230	$ 7,470	$ 9,210
Proposed loan..........	5,000					
Cash receipts (schedule above)...........	4,167	4,083	4,750	6,000	5,250	3,750
Total cash receipts....	10,667	6,600	8,590	10,230	12,720	12,960
Cash payments:						
Accounts payable (purchases less 2%).	7,350	1,960	1,960	1,960	1,960	1,960
Expenses and owner's drawing..........	800	800	800	800	800	800
Yard improvement...	....	....	....	....	750	750
Owner's special withdrawal (car).......	....	....	1,600			
Repayment of proposed loan............	....	....	....	....	....	5,150*
Total cash payments..	8,150	2,760	4,360	2,760	3,510	8,660
Cash on hand at end of period............	2,517	3,840	4,230	7,470	9,210	4,300

* Loan plus interest at 6 per cent for 6 months.

Several points about this plan are of interest to the observing financial analyst. The proposed purchases look small in comparison with the sales. Is this an underestimation of need? To figure the expected inventory position after six months, it is easier to convert all figures to a cost basis.

Beginning inventory.....................	$12,000
Purchases..............................	12,000
Total.................................	$24,000
Less cost of goods sold ($26,000 × 0.75).....	19,500
Estimated closing inventory...............	$ 4,500

Since the beginning inventory is admittedly high for the heavy summer months, the closing inventory in a period when the sales months ahead are small is not necessarily low. The banker need not conclude that X has understated his purchase requirements. As this budget shows, considerable room for error exists, and the loan could still be repaid. If sales were as much as 20 per cent less than expected, the loan could be repaid even if purchases were not reduced, as they most certainly would be under such circumstances. A delay of the yard improvement plans would also strengthen liquidity. The budget also shows that the loan could be repaid, or partly so, as early as July and not in September as X had been figuring on. Further, the banker is able to construct an estimated balance sheet for the end of the period.

X COMPANY. ESTIMATED BALANCE SHEET, SEPT. 30, 19—

Cash	$ 4,300	Accounts payable	$ 2,000
Accounts receivable	2,000	Proprietor X*	16,800
Inventory	4,500		
Current assets	$10,800		
Fixed assets	8,000		
Total	$18,800	Total	$18,800

* This is without allowance for depreciation on fixed assets.

This statement shows adequate expectation of liquidity. In spite of the owner's special spring withdrawal, there is a modest increase in the proprietor's balance. The business is in good shape. Thus, even though the current position might look very weak in the late spring months soon after the loan is granted, it turns out to be more a seasonal matter than one of long-run concern.

More Complex Budgeting Cases

When the credit applicant is a larger and more complex business, the responsibility of budgeting is no longer the banker's. Such borrowers may be expected to use budgeting techniques in their business, and the banker can reasonably ask them to have their own accounting departments prepare and present the required statements.

Fully developed budget systems usually are broken down into detailed departmental budgets; in these the banker usually has little or no interest. On the other hand, where the sales budget is derived from many departments, the banker may have some interest in the figures. They may shed light on whether the basic assumptions of the applicant as to business prospects agree with those of the banker. The detailed expense budgets, useful for the assessment of individual and departmental performance, are also of limited usefulness to the banker.

In order to reduce the budget detail to a reasonable level for the credit department to analyze, a bank might find it convenient to make up its own budget form and then ask the applicants to translate their budgets to this form.

One principle sometimes gets lost in the involved techniques of budgeting. Every budget assumes something about business prospects; it assumes that both seasonal and cyclical economic factors will follow the pattern of the past and that business will be better, equally good, or not so good. The nature of these assumptions is, perhaps, more important to the banker than the detailed figures. The banker need not insist that the underlying assumptions used in budget planning square with his own, but he must know what they are so as to judge the prospects. Fortunately for the prospects of dynamic business enterprise, some applicants always hold a perpetually rosy view of the future. It is a fine human quality, but perhaps not the right one for judging bank credit risks.

Following the Budget

Budgets, once prepared, should not be forgotten. They are valuable only if used. The banker should require the borrower to prepare and file such figures as will check actual performance with budget anticipations. This means usually the filing of an estimated and interim income statement as well as balance sheet.

In following the realized results, several circumstances (all disappointing) must be guarded against by the banker:

1. Disappointing results due to a general deterioration in business conditions. When they occur, a disturbingly large share of the loan account may reflect the same characteristic. While

the banker may have the greatest sympathy for borrowers so affected, his first concern must be the survival of his bank. He must be sure that he does not have more trouble than he can carry, and he can hardly afford to carry customers that do not have a good chance of survival.

2. Disappointing results due to a decline in the special line in which the borrower is engaged. This kind of circumstance is less important, unless the bank should happen to be loaded with that type of loan. Every so often, although general business conditions remain good, a sudden sales drop in a given line occurs. If customers have been carefully chosen, they should have a good chance of surviving these special disorders. This sort of circumstance weeds out the weak competitors.

3. Disappointing results due to a weakening of competitive position. This circumstance is something that a bank can hardly tolerate for long. The action required is harsh but simple: collect.

4. Disappointing results due to poor management on the part of the borrower. This may or may not be tolerable. Failure to control costs is hard to cure. On the other hand, an overextended inventory position, though criticizable, can often be worked out. It is not beyond remedy.

5. Borrowing plans sometimes upset by changes in costs outside the borrower's control; for example, the cost of constructing plants and buying new equipment. The banker is almost forced to go along with the borrower in working out of such unexpected circumstances. Modification may be the order of the day, but losses by abandonment of partly completed capital plans are usually worse. As long as foresight is imperfect, this sort of circumstance is bound to arise.

The corrective action that the banker must seek depends greatly on which of these circumstances prevails. When the troubles are traceable to unsatisfactory performance on the part of the borrower and the banker is convinced that the borrower is not likely to reform, the loan should be collected while the collecting is good. If the adverse circumstances are outside the borrower's control, the banker has every reason to be sympathetic; but he should not fail to take such protective action as is required. Often the intelligent banker can plan a sort of economic retreat that, in the long run, works to the advantage of the borrower as well as the bank. The handling of situations of this sort is helped by budgeting because the evidences of trouble are detected earlier than if the banker simply waits for defaults to occur.

THE DISTRESSED BANK LOAN

If banks lend aggressively, they can hardly avoid making a certain number of loans that develop disorders. While the first two stages of successful bank lending—making good loans and keeping them good—are important, banks keep their losses tolerable by vigorous collection systems.

The handling of slow collections depends on the general character of the factors that have caused the loans to deteriorate. Sometimes borrowers suffer from no fault of their own; they are the victims of exceptionally bad luck. This is not an adequate reason for the bank to take too lenient an attitude; nevertheless, the difference between a case that is solvable by a "workout" (where the borrower is supported and his business life possibly saved) and a "liquidation" (in which the business life of the borrower may be sacrificed) is material. It must be an early choice.

The Agonizing Choice: A Workout or a Liquidation?

The first explicit indication that a bank receives from a distressed credit is usually a representation from the borrower that he cannot meet his contractual credit obligation or that to do so would embarrass him mightily. The bank may have, through its process of supervision, seen this difficulty approaching, but the problem is faced squarely when it involves a breach in the terms of the loan contract.

Although many banks have refused at this stage to recognize the choice, it is often right here that they make it: to insist on the terms of the contract even if it embarrasses the borrower or to grant an extension or some other device of working the credit out. It should be emphasized that the choice is often made at this early stage before the creditor is fully aware of the fact that he is making such a choice. After a while the bank is without an alternative and must follow the choice it took in the beginning.

The choice is agonizing because a mistake on the side of severity causes ill will; one on the side of laxness causes losses. A short-term bank loan, well made in the beginning, is usually collectible during its first cycle. The collection may embarrass the creditor, but the bank need not take a loss. If the bank follows the hard-boiled policy and insists "on its pound of flesh," two unfortunate circumstances may result: (1) It has almost certainly lost a borrowing customer who might, after a time of recuperation, turn out to be a very good and profitable one. (2) A less tangible product is that the bank may, by tough collection policies, so increase its reputation for severity that borrowers will tend to shy away from it and seek banks where they hope for more sympathetic treatment.

Thus the choice is always a hard one. In the past a very large proportion of banks probably have erred on the side of sympathetic collection policies. Public reputation not to the contrary, most banks have been easy on their borrowing customers.

Handling a Workout

If the banker elects to "stay with" a customer and to work out some basis for extension of the credit, a number of decisions must be made.

In the first place the choice may be for extending a part of the credit with the remainder to be repaid. Another choice is that of extension of the full amount. There are even times when a banker is forced to consider the possibility of adding further funds to those already outstanding.

The range of choice is great because of the variety of circumstances that may be represented in the affairs of the borrower. If the borrower can repay a large part but not all of his loan, then the first choice is logical. If this involves taking so much of the borrower's cash that he is hamstrung for further operations, it is a poor choice for both borrower and lender. Bankers have sometimes been guilty of such compromises. While they do not collect all their credit, they take enough to tie up the borrower and almost guarantee that he cannot earn enough to repay the remainder. An outright liquidation might have been no harsher in such circumstances, and it might have avoided loss for the bank. The longer liquidation is deferred, if it is going to be done eventually, the less the amount that can be realized from it.

Bankers are often influenced by the action and situation of other creditors. If the bank is just one of a number of creditors, it cannot afford to be generous if it is to do so only to bail out the other creditors and leave itself with the tag ends of the business. On the other hand, if a bank threatens tough collection tactics, it may precipitate a general tightening by all creditors to a degree that forces the debtor business to seek the outlet of bankruptcy or of some one of the various stages of restricted operation that are used in circumstances of financial distress.

If a bank can find a satisfactory basis for a workout which includes the other creditors, then the procedure is not unlike that of a new credit. One of the first things the bank may insist on is the budgeting of all further activity. This kind of budgeting is not unlike that already considered in the treatment of new credits, except that more emphasis is put on the cash budget. The budget in such circumstances usually specifies that all capital outlays cease. Administrative budgets may be severely pared, and the purchase budgets may be adjusted to a basis of rather meager sales expectations.

Almost all workouts require a large degree of supervision from bankers. They are costly even if the funds at stake are all recovered. On the other hand, a banker dealing sympathetically with a competent borrower who is the victim of temporary bad luck will often gain for himself a customer so fixed in his loyalties and affections that the process is worth all the time and trouble it causes.

Handling a Liquidation

When a bank elects liquidation of a slow credit, the step does not need to be precipitate. The choice is rather one of degree. Liquidation has this important difference from a workout: The bank is seeking to get out with the funds it has committed to a given business or as large a part as it can recover. It may be willing to reconsider and grant new credits later on, but at the time liquidation is chosen, this is a remote alternative. In the case of a true workout, the bank is hopeful of keeping one of its good customers viable.

There are various kinds of liquidation programs. If the bank is one of a number of creditors, it may follow a plan which involves only a *creditors' committee*. This is a bit short of full-scale bankruptcy. The major creditors may all agree to this informal and extralegal arrangement, but some minor creditors may hold out. In such circumstances, banks occasionally advance enough funds to the business to pay off the objecting creditors. If the objecting creditors are of any consequence, this course is usually not feasible.

The creditors' committee usually retains the existing management but often installs a representative of the creditors in a strategic post to be sure that its policies are being followed. The banker usually assumes chairmanship of the committee. This is a thankless task but important because the chairman is likely to follow intimately and closely the affairs of the distressed business.

Since a creditors' committee is a relatively mild sort of treatment and does not necessarily contemplate liquidation, it may often be able to put a business back on its feet and return it to the chastened owners. This is the desirable end and the one that is hoped for. In this sense it is like a workout, as discussed above.

The affairs of a borrower are sometimes in a more involved

state and show little hope for recovery. Rather than take the stigma, and expense, of legal bankruptcy, the debtor may offer a *composition settlement* to his creditors. This is an offer of something less than the face value, such as 60, 70, 80, or 90 per cent, of the debts owed in return for a full discharge of indebtedness. Creditors may be inclined to accept such a settlement if offered when the proportion is fairly high because it may be the best deal open to them. If the owner or principal manager were to give up, the creditors might not be able to realize so much in formal liquidation. The going value of the business in the original owner's hands may be higher and his capacity for realization greater than that of the banker or any other creditor.

Of course a banker must exercise the closest of judgment in deciding whether or not to accept a composition settlement. If he is convinced that the borrower is honestly trying to recover as much as possible, that he is not personally profiting from the transaction except in so far as he escapes the stigma of bankruptcy, that his own prospects for liquidation are less favorable, and that the situation of the business is really hopeless, then the acceptance seems to be indicated. Acceptance of a composition settlement may be a lazy act, involve unnecessary loss, and is sometimes offered by unscrupulous concerns that are trying to make a good thing of near bankruptcy.

The view of other creditors is also important. The banker is often looked upon as a leader in the credit community, and his course is followed by others. A composition settlement may save the banker some time, but if it brings with it the unfortunate reputation for "selling out cheap," then it may not be a wise choice. Like all bad choices, it is necessarily a hard one.

An *assignment* is a means by which a collapsing business may be turned over to the creditors. An assignment is very much like a voluntary receivership and, in fact, is a substitute for it on some occasions.

When a proprietor decides that his financial affairs are so involved that he cannot work out of them, he may assign all the business assets (and if it is an unincorporated concern, his personal assets as well) to a trustee, the assets to be liquidated and divided equitably among the claimant creditors. Assignment is often more advantageous than receivership in that the assignee, operating for the benefit of all creditors, has more latitude than in the case of a receivership. If the assignment comes in bad times, the assignee may elect to await better times for liquidation. Also the chances of making a "deal" with another business are often better. The business escapes the stigma of formal bankruptcy, which is a not inconsiderable burden.

In some jurisdictions, the assignment must be recorded in order to make it binding and must be formally received by the creditors.

Equity receivership is still another form of liquidation that falls short of bankruptcy; indeed it is sometimes used as a form of working out a difficult situation. It may be sought for a concern that is solvent in an accounting sense (the value of assets is adequate to meet liabilities), but is illiquid and cannot meet its liabilities as they fall due.

In order to make sure that some nervous creditors do not hasten to collect their claims ahead of the creditors who are trying to take a helpful and constructive attitude toward the business, an equity receivership may be requested. Although the final disposition of the business may be quite uncertain when an equity receivership is asked, there is often a good chance that, once the business has worked out of its worst difficulties, the creditors' claims can be satisfied, and the business turned back to its owner. In other words, the presumption in the case of an equity receivership is that the business will be operated until the choice between liquidation and continuation is clearer.

As is always true, these sweeping generalizations have their exceptions. In some jurisdictions, the equity receivership is used for fairly technical legal purposes.

Complete *bankruptcy*, whether voluntary or involuntary, is the final and complete dissolution of a business. It is a formal legal process, the full significance of which is quite grave. It is sought when other forms of relief are inadequate. Many of the

other forms of settlement already discussed involve a meeting
of minds between the debtor and his creditors and some meeting of minds among the creditors. If this is not possible, resort
to formal bankruptcy may be necessary. This is, of course, the
last resort of a difficult case and is almost always accompanied
by sizable losses. The process itself often puts a stigma, not
only on the bankrupt person but, to a small extent at least, on
some of the assets. The properties of a bankrupt concern almost
never liquidate so well as those of one liquidating voluntarily.
The supervision of bankruptcy costs money; the returns are
often disappointing.

11

The Rate of Interest
Charged on Loans

The average rate of interest earned on loan contracts is the most important factor determining bank profits. Banks operating in major money-market centers charge the "prime loan rate" on a large proportion of their loans. This rate is determined by general economic factors but is set by price leadership within the banking community. In areas outside the primary money market, bankers generally adhere to rates of interest that are considered customary or equitable within those areas.

The major respect in which banks individually determine the rate of return averaged on loans is in choosing which customers are eligible to receive the prime loan rates and which are not. Customers not qualifying for the prime loan rate may be charged a rate that represents a constant differential with respect to the prime loan rate. The determination of differentials, however, necessarily involves human relations risks as well as economic problems. It is galling to the pride of a small but scrupulously honest borrower to be denied the best rate available. Very good cost reasons may, however, make some differential reasonable. On the other hand, a large concern whose credit involves some element of risk may feel that it cannot afford to accept the implied criticism of its financial position by paying more than the prime loan rate. When money markets are easy, banks are frequently persuaded to grant the prime loan rate to customers that are on the margin of earning it. When money markets are tighter, however, banks have more room in which to exercise individual judgment in this respect.

The interest rate charged on bank loans is not a very material matter to most borrowers. A borrower may be incensed at what he thinks is an overcharge, but if he feels fairly treated, interest rates are not a critical cost factor. Although the banker usually has some margin in interest rate policy, he cannot expect good customers to pay rates very far from competitive standards and keep their business. A borrower may or may not be well informed about such market conditions, but if he is a desirable borrower, it is likely that his banking business has been solicited and that he is reasonably well aware of the prevailing level of interest rates.

This brings up early one of the important and pragmatic facts about lending interest rates. The cost of bank money is generally much cheaper than the cost of credit from other sources, such as trade credit when discounts are not taken, commercial finance companies, and the like.

Customers do not often find competing rates in nonbanking institutions; the competition is among the banks themselves. In choosing among banks, all customers ask for is fair treatment. A single bank could not get away with a lending rate for prime customers far out of line with that of other banks. When a general rate change comes, few customers increase or decrease their borrowing plans much. The policy of a bank, therefore, must always stand the test of "fairness"; and this means fairness as judged by customers' standards. If the policy meets this test, a bank can be reasonably assured that it is not losing business for rate reasons. Its general service to customers, its reputation for sticking with good customers during troubled times, will hold business better than rate cutting.

PRIME LOAN RATE

The basic interest rate in the structure of bank loans is the prime loan rate. This rate is a formally and publicly announced rate adopted by about a hundred of the largest money-market banks. It furnishes the anchor point for a great many other interest rates in the structure of bank loans. In general, the prime loan rate tends to be somewhat higher than short-term open-market money rates. The prime loan rate for the past several years is shown in Figure 11-1.

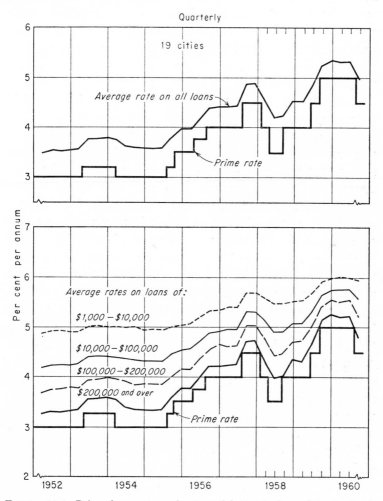

FIGURE 11-1. Prime loan rate and rates of interest charged by banks in nineteen leading cities.

Changes in the prime loan rate are infrequent; there were only 19 changes from 1935 through 1960: 15 increases and 4 decreases. Changes are initiated by announcement of a leading money-market bank and communicated to other leading banks by the "bank" wire.[1] In almost all cases the announcement is made only after it is clear that all other banks are likely to fall in line. The typical experience is that after the initial announcement, the other money-market banks almost immediately make a similar confirming announcement—frequently within minutes or hours. Occasionally, if the change is a reduction some banks show a reluctance to follow; but there has seldom been a false start in the changing of the prime loan rate.

Banks outside money-market centers are less influenced by the prime loan rate and may not even go through the process of making a formal announcement. All banks of intermediate size pay close attention to changes in the prime loan rate, however, and, in fact, make parallel adjustments for their very best customers that might conceivably be recruited by the money-market banks should their treatment of them be felt to be unfair. Furthermore, changes in the prime loan rate are well enough publicized so that the customers of banks are aware of these changes. As a result, adjustments are made by a much larger number of banks than those that are a part of the core process of announcement.

The prime loan rate is related to a number of other bank interest rates by a series of conventional or negotiated differentials. For example, loans to commodity dealers are usually at rates $\frac{1}{2}$ of 1 per cent above the prime loan rate. Loans for construction of commercial properties are usually set by some constant differential to the prime loan rate, such as a 1 per cent margin.

When the prime loan rate is relatively low, a sizable differential may exist between it and the maximum permissible rate under usury laws. When the prime loan rate reaches 5 per cent,

[1] The "bank" wire is a teletype system of communication linking the 200 largest banks in the United States.

however, it is within 1 or 2 per cent of the usury statutes of many states; hence relatively little margin is left for banks differentiating among customers. A variety of other methods of adjustment are used to produce a differential that is more in keeping with economic realities.

THE COST OF BANK LENDING AND LOAN RATES

According to the traditions of economic theory, any long-run price (and interest rates are a special kind of price) should, when competitive conditions prevail, reflect the costs of providing the goods or service. In a very general sense, this does not apply in the banking field; the rates that have prevailed have reflected other factors rather more, mainly the elements of ease or tightness in the central money markets modified by local practices and needs.

Although not generally applicable, one element of cost clearly has entered into bank loan rates. Banks have to get deposits before they can lend. To attract deposits, they must offer satisfactory service to their depositors. This is an implicit cost. An example of explicit costs is the interest paid on savings accounts. When banks have to pay, directly or indirectly, a fairly high price to attract funds from depositors, they are certain to feel compelled to charge borrowers correspondingly high rates. When banks get deposits easily and at low cost (or assess some of the costs of deposits back on deposit accounts as by service charges), then they are disposed to lower loan rates.

Costs enter into bank loan rates in still another sense: some loans involve great possibilities of loss. The only prudent policy for bankers making loans with some risk potential is to charge rates higher than those charged on loans of the same size in order to cover the loss differential. Even though accounting theory has not yet fully accepted the point (it is now accepted by the Bureau of Internal Revenue in permitting banks to charge *estimated* losses to reserve accounts rather than charge realized loan losses as an income deduction), loan losses for institutions such as banks are an expense of doing business—a cost—not a capital gain or loss. More will be said of this matter later.

THE USURY CEILING

The laws of all states contain some sort of usury restriction. The interest rates which may be charged are limited by law. Rates such as 6, 7, or 8 per cent are not uncommon usury rates with certain exceptions such as under small-loan operations. (In some jurisdictions the "legal" interest rate—the rate applied to credit transactions for which a rate is not specified—is also the usury rate.)

In smaller communities the usury rate often serves both as a ceiling and as a floor. On small loans the rate is not high enough to cover costs, but banks are reluctant to turn down good but small loans for this reason. Too many loan rejections create community ill will. The rejected borrowers cannot help but carry away the notion that their credit standing has been impugned by a rejection, no matter how carefully the matter was explained to them. Thus, before the days of separate small-loan operations, many banks carried small and unprofitable loans as a matter of accommodation and public service. For larger loans the legal rate is often ample but, in the absence of strong competitive reasons, there may be little or no incentive for charging less. When the usury rate is also the legal rate, public sanction of this practice is likely to be favorable.

As a result, many banks do not make any too rational distinctions among loans. The large credits of high quality probably do not receive as good treatment as they deserve, while borrowers of smaller amounts and with less implicit security were getting money at about the same rate.

The provisions by which banks are able, for consumer credit lending, to breach the usury limits, together with the more general drift of business loan rates to national levels, have given banks more elbow room in interest rate policy. Modern loan-rate differentials are probably much more reasonable than they used to be.

BANK LOAN RATES
AND OPEN-MARKET MONEY RATES

Anyone who reads the financial press is aware of the volatility of open-market money rates: the rates of "call" loans, the rates prevailing in short-term U.S. Government securities, and the like. Bank loan rates are much more stable, though they tend to lag after open-market loan rates and to move within a smaller range.

Banks located in New York City or Chicago invest funds in the open market. They also have many customer loans that are up to open-market standards. Banks that lend to dealers in government securities or that lend to the large corporations with multiple credit lines cannot but reflect open-market rates in their dealings with these special customers. These customers can shop around; they are fully informed about the market and can bargain face to face with the bankers unflinchingly. Once these special customers force the big money-market banks to adjust their loan rates to open-market conditions, it is natural for other customers of these big banks to feel the influence of money-market changes rather promptly.

Some large cities still do not have well-developed money markets. Banks located there are not subject to nervous short-term influences; they follow the general pattern of interest-rate developments in the money market but not so closely. Banks located in country areas are even more insulated from such influences.

To what extent should the banks which are more remotely located feel compelled to observe money-market levels in setting their loan rates? In most circumstances they have more time and latitude in adjusting their rates. For these banks the reasonable standard for action is probably the competitive one: to make such adjustments (ungrudgingly) as are necessary to keep the good local borrowers reasonably satisfied.

CREDIT RISK AND LOAN RATES

In the opening of this chapter it was pointed out that risk is one of the necessary costs to be covered in the loan rate. Risk, in this sense, has two facets: some loans are quite obviously not as secure as others; almost all loans, no matter how secure they seem, have some element of risk. In setting loan rates, banks must, therefore, make some allowance for risk.

The trouble in making adequate allowance is that the risk inherent in loans does not show up regularly; it tends to bunch. During good times, there may be very few losses; with a shift in times, the losses jump. Depressions may not be wholly the causes of credit losses (they are important but far from the whole cause), but they do tend to be the circumstance that brings losses to the surface and to demonstrate that they exist. Thus there are some years in which the rate of loss is very high; others in which it is low.

Banks cannot adjust their interest rates to correspond to the currently prevailing rate of credit losses, nor would they be well advised to do so if they could. Some sort of steady and regular dependence on a reserve against losses is the best policy.

The importance of the averaging principle has been recognized by the Federal taxing authorities. As will be outlined in detail later, the Bureau of Internal Revenue allows banks to establish and maintain a reserve for loan losses equal to 3 years' losses for the average of the preceding 20 years.

RECLASSIFICATION OF LOANS
TO CHANGE INTEREST RATE

Sometimes banks are able to change the effective interest rate on a loan by reclassifying it. For example, a small business loan that may have been treated as a regular business loan can be transferred into the consumer credit department. If this involves too extreme a change of interest rates, a still different type of system may be feasible. A special department, such as one for handling small business loans, may be established with a standard basic rate materially above the rate available to large commercial borrowers. All small business loans are then transferred to this department. This reorganization of the lending function will improve the technical facilities for handling such credits as well as improve their rate of return.

The higher rate probably will not be resented by customers as long as they believe they are receiving the lowest rate that applies to their class of business. Since small businessmen are not adverse to considering themselves such, the use of the small business loan department where volume of transactions warrants it has a great deal to recommend it as a means of improving income.

INTEREST RATES FOR SPECIAL CLASSES OF LOANS

Banks that are able to assume the risk and to supervise special classes of loans can sometimes earn unusually high rates of return on such lending. As has already been mentioned, loans such as those for construction may be in very large amounts but they involve problems of supervision and control for which the ordinary bank is not equipped.

Another class of special lending for which high rates have been traditional are credits to foreign businesses or occasionally even to foreign governments. This type of business often involves considerable risk, as troubled international developments frequently testify. Nevertheless, those banks with the knowledge and technical equipment for handling these credits may be able to earn a high return. In many cases the profitability of such lending is not limited merely to the high rate of interest charged. Doing such business improves the expertness of a bank in foreign affairs and may equip it to undertake very profitable financing of export business or handling of acceptance credits for exports to or imports from these special areas.

Another kind of lending that sometimes yields unusually high rates of return is supplying credit to the subsidiaries of large corporations. For a variety of reasons, partly legal and partly taxation, some large corporations use separately incorporated subsidiaries for the conduct of special types of business. The parent corporations may wish to undertake borrowing through these subsidiaries rather than to do so directly, and occasionally may wish to undertake this borrowing without giving a guarantee of repayment. Improperly managed, considerable risk exists in credits of this type. With prudent and expert supervision and with knowledge of the character and integrity of the parent concern, these loans may be quite safe though justifying rates of return above the prime rate. Such lending can be a profitable outlet for the large money-market banks with the technical facilities for handling it.

USE OF COMPENSATORY BALANCES
TO ADJUST INTEREST RATES

As mentioned in the previous chapter, the compensatory balance may be treated as an implied form of interest-rate adjustment. Customers who do not supply adequate compensatory balances probably should be charged higher rates. Banks might offer their customers the alternative of being excused from compensatory balances and paying rates somewhat above the prime interest rate or of being given the prime loan rate but being required to meet standard compensatory balance requirements. Faced with this alternative, a customer has less reason to feel that he is being unfairly treated since he presumably has been offered the best arrangement that is available. If judiciously applied, the use of this alternative can solidify customer relationships while helping to improve the rate of return. This is particularly true with respect to the maintenance of compensatory balances by customers when they are out of debt. Compensatory balance is then figured as a percentage of the line of credit rather than of credit outstanding. A relatively modest requirement may be asked but it can be one which will, nevertheless, have the potential of improving bank income materially.

Part IV

POLICIES FOR
SPECIFIC TYPES OF LOANS

The general policies outlined in Part III are applicable to all types of loans. In addition, specifications and details are needed to manage lending of several special types. The diversity of loan types covered in this section reflects the profound changes that have taken place in commercial banking. Before the Great Depression a description of the management of bank funds by standards then prevailing would have been complete after presenting the first two chapters of this section: on working capital and secured loans. A modern banker, however, is not competent unless he is prepared to deal with a great range of lending operations: with loans that have rather long or "term" maturities, with loans that are to and for consumers, with loans that are based on the security of real estate, and with loans to special problem industries such as agriculture. This section devotes a chapter to each of these loan types.

12

Working Capital Loans

Working capital loans are one of the most important forms in which commercial banks extend credit to business. Unfortunately, the statistics of bank loans are not prepared along functional lines. However, almost all the evidence available, such as that in the Federal Reserve surveys of bank lending, suggests the importance of this type of loan. The Federal Reserve conducted three postwar surveys of business lending by member banks: in 1946, 1955, and 1957. Each survey showed that loans with maturities of less than one year accounted for about two-thirds of total business loans. While such maturities are not necessarily related to working capital purposes and while longer term loans may be for such purposes, this evidence supports the presumption that working capital needs dominate bank business lending.

Further evidence can be found in the kinds of industries that borrow from banks. The loan surveys showed that retail and wholesale trade concerns, sales finance companies, processors of consumable goods, and firms in the construction industry were high on the list of bank borrowers. Each of these types of business has large working capital requirements. Further evidence may be found in the fact that the cyclical ups and downs in bank credit are much more closely geared to observed changes in inventories than to changes in capital expenditures. Working capital needs unquestionably play a major role in bank business

213

lending, which fact is also suggested by common-sense observation.

A working capital loan supplies a business with the means of financing the acquisition of either inventories or receivables. Some meticulous analysts have pointed out that a short-term credit for the purpose of providing these current assets does not increase net working capital as it is defined by accountants, since the increase in current assets in the form of cash, inventories, or receivables is fully offset by the increase in short-term liabilities. In spite of this somewhat pedantic objection, credit that enables a business to enlarge its activities by purchasing raw materials for processing, carrying the finished goods for sale, and finally financing their sale serves the purpose of providing working capital as that term is popularly used.

Working capital loans may be and often are unsecured. On some occasions, however, they are secured by the assets acquired, such as inventories or receivables, or even possibly in other ways. To this extent the discussion of working capital loans in this chapter overlaps the discussion of secured bank lending in Chapter 13. The emphasis in this chapter, however, is on the functional nature of working capital loans, whereas the emphasis in the next chapter will be on the problem of provision of security, its cost, and its management.

Working capital loans give an admirable opportunity for exercise of the general tools of credit analysis described in Part III, including the measurement of cash flow. When working capital credit is of a short-term nature, its repayment depends on the flow of cash through these various forms of working capital. In this sense cash-flow analysis for working capital purposes emphasizes the significance of variations in levels of inventory and receivables. It puts somewhat less emphasis on the generation of cash by profits or noncash charges such as depreciation.

Working capital loans may be classified in a variety of ways. The commonest way is to identify them by the cause of the need. The most widely recognized form of working capital loan is the one that grows out of seasonal requirements. As anticipated in an earlier chapter, many businesses experience strong seasonal pressures. Working capital loans also are needed by businesses that have an inherently slow turnover of inventories —usually a case where the technological process of fabrication or maturation takes a considerable period. Examples would include the curing of tobacco leaf or liquor, and the drying of lumber. Still another circumstance involving a need for working capital credit is where an unusual rate of growth is being experienced. Industries that are enjoying an unusual spurt of growth are favorites of investment bankers. However, if great risks are involved these businesses may be unable to secure long-term financing without surrendering a large fraction of profits and possibly stock control. Working capital loans may nevertheless be reasonably safe in such cases. They can be viewed as a transitional device between the early stages of growth and a later stage when long-term financing on more reasonable terms is possible.

Still another kind of working capital loan is the one that grows out of unusual or quite special opportunities. Many examples can be cited, such as unusual contracts involved with national defense production: a fabricator of miniature electronics for missiles, for instance. A business operation may have a unique technological position or talent which suddenly must be utilized to a much larger extent than is normal. It would hardly be worthwhile to bring in long-term capital for an opportunity that might not last. On the other hand, short-term financing may not quite solve this problem. Working capital credit for an intermediate term may be the solution.

Almost all business borrowers seeking working capital loans hope to profit by virtue of "leverage." Leverage is the term applied to capital structures in which borrowed funds are used in the expectation of raising the rate of return on the owner's equity. This is possible when the cost of business borrowing is lower than the rate of earnings on invested capital. A working capital outlay could hardly be justified if its prospective earnings were not at a rate in excess of the rate prevailing on safe and high-grade credit.

While the leverage involved in a working capital loan can increase the earnings of owners, the risks involved in overuse of leverage are never absent. Banks need to observe high credit standards in this as well as in other kinds of credit granting. While working capital loans have less risk than is found in longer term lending, they are not riskless. The amount that a banker can advance for working capital purposes is limited by the amount of the owner's equity; risk protection requires that the owner finance at least some portion of his working capital needs with permanent capital. The amount varies with circumstances such as price risk in inventories and rate of working capital turnover of both receivables and inventories.

THE SEASONAL WORKING CAPITAL LOAN

The seasonal working capital loan is the classic form of self-liquidating bank credit. The unusual demands at the peak of a season for the carrying of inventories frequently is followed by an unusual peak in receivables. These needs may not span the whole year, however, so that permanent capital could not be profitably employed for the entire year. This circumstance offers a first-class use of bank credit. The maturity of the loan can be adjusted to the period credit is needed and promptness of repayment is a test of the propriety of the business operation.

Seasonal working capital loans are also particularly advantageous for banks since they usually involve a minimum risk and require only a relatively simple job of credit analysis. Furthermore, seasonal loans permit a banker to accommodate a wider range of customers. Even when compensatory balance provisions are only mildly enforced, seasonal customers tend to be an important source of funds.

Examples of Seasonal Loans

As already indicated, the foundation of most seasonal loans lies in a basic natural rhythm in activity. The manufacturers of seasonal goods such as woolen blankets, Christmas toys, or agricultural commodities all encounter a peaking of demands in some portion of the year. The cycle of the year may require various kinds of preparation well in advance of the seasonal peak of final sales. In one period the peak may be in inventories of raw materials, in a later period it may be in the inventories of goods in process, and finally the emphasis may be on finished goods. After the merchandising of the finished goods, the receivables that are generated by the seasonal sale of the completed goods may cause still another kind of peak. The dealers in agricultural commodities represent an extraordinarily interesting example of seasonality. The consumption of such commodities is not seasonal or only moderately seasonal, whereas their production necessarily is completed within a relatively short period. Acquiring basic raw materials is necessarily seasonal even if the final sale of the products is not. Such cases may also be complicated by seasonal movements in the price structure both for the basic raw materials and for final products. Working on narrow margins, dealers and processors may be faced with sizable price risks. The extension of bank credit may require provision of adequate security against such price fluctuations by hedging or other form of price protection.

Some seasonal patterns are not related to the natural course of weather or technological factors during the year but to a conventional or customary pattern of behavior. The timing of annual changes in model styles of automobiles, for example, has introduced a seasonal in automobile sales that runs somewhat contrary to the apparently natural season at which people would be expected to make car purchases. (It is thought that scheduling model change-over for the fall has reduced the seasonal pattern of automobile sales.) Accordingly, the financing of automobile dealers frequently involves clearly evident seasonal patterns. Changes by automobile producers in the timing of new models sometimes shift this seasonal.

Form of Seasonal Loans

Because of the uncertain nature of seasonal demands, it is frequently more convenient for both borrower and lender to base these loans on a line of credit. This procedure will be described at the end of this chapter. The top level for a line of credit is usually set at about or a bit above the peak requirement of the business for external financing. The borrowing business then has an option as to the precise time at which it may draw on its line of credit and later retire its borrowings. If, however, seasonal credits involve continuing risks and narrow margins, the lending bank may wish to make each credit transaction a separate action so that it can review business developments and decide whether it wishes to extend its commitment. This policy provides somewhat greater safeguards, but such credit management usually is more awkward and costly.

A seasonal loan may take the form of a simple negotiated promissory note or it may take a somewhat more complex form, such as an acceptance which usually provides some form of security. Secured lending will be dealt with in the following chapter, but it is worth noting here that the use of such special devices not only improves the quality of the credit but also may increase the amount that can be loaned to an individual customer because of the somewhat more liberal laws on loan limits for secured credits.

The Dwindling of Seasonal Lending

While the seasonal credit unquestionably has many advantages for banks and customers, it appears to be a dwindling proportion of total bank credit. The cause may be a variety of business policies that have been aimed at reducing the impact of seasonal variations. Too high a degree of seasonality is an uneconomic way in which to operate a business. Almost every business that grapples with sharp seasonal movements in its principal activity attempts, by various management devices or by diversification, to diminish the degree of seasonality in its aggregate operations. To the extent that seasonality is diminished a business may have more reason for meeting its working capital needs on a permanent or long-term basis and rather less by short-term bank credit.

From the side of banks, seasonal loans are not an altogether unmixed blessing. Very large banks may have sufficient diversification of seasonal lending to smooth out aggregate loan demand and thus produce a steady volume of such business throughout the year. Regional concentration of some types of business, however, may lead to a concentration of seasonal lending in some periods of the year which strains the resources of banks located in these regions but leaves them with idle funds in other periods.

SLOW-TURNOVER WORKING CAPITAL LOANS

Many lines of business experience a slow turnover of inventories and to some extent of receivables purely for technological though occasionally for customary reasons. The tobacco industry, for example, faces a seasonal problem in acquiring raw materials as well as one of slow turnover in the processing of them. Since the basic raw material is an agricultural product harvested in a given season of the year, the period of acquisition of new tobacco leaf tends to be highly concentrated. On the other hand, the period of maturing or aging of the tobacco leaf is quite long. The final sales of the product have virtually no seasonal movement. As a result, tobacco companies require a considerable amount of financing to meet seasonal needs and to cover working capital needs for somewhat longer periods. Another example may be found in the seasonal garment trades where custom sometimes requires long post-dated billings, hence the collection of receivables is very slow. If the product is combined with a highly seasonal product, such as women's swimsuits, the working capital requirement may be a fairly prolonged one.

Both cases are ones in which leverage may be used to advantage. The cost of bank credit usually averages somewhat less than the residual return on business operations. This margin allows equity owners to improve their rate of return. The use of leverage in the tobacco business is safe because of the stability of this type of business. Such stability makes it possible for an intermediate-term kind of working capital credit to be safely extended by banks and profitably used by the tobacco companies. The situation of distilling companies is similar except that the process of production is not seasonal though there is somewhat greater seasonality of sales. In such circumstances, however, a rather better case can be made for providing working capital by more permanent means than bank credit.

Lumber companies experience some seasonality in acquiring basic raw materials, in processing them, and in selling them. Furthermore, the period needed for aging or curing lumber is frequently quite long. Superimposed on these patterns of seasonality is the added risk that the final sale of lumber is subject to rather sharp cyclical influences. Involuntary accumulation in inventory may occur in some periods through no fault of the processor. The lumber industry is also one in which price instability complicates the marketing of the finished product. Extension of bank credit in such cases obviously involves a number of thorny problems.

GROWTH AS A FOUNDATION
FOR WORKING CAPITAL LOANS

An industry may count itself fortunate to face the problems of unusual growth, but the good fortune does not obliterate the problems. In recent years we have seen growth in industries such as electronics, plywood production, aluminum fabrication, pharmaceuticals, and certain specialized types of light chemicals. Some of the most spectacular cases have been companies that started quite small and in which the owner's equity became seriously strained by the very rapidity of growth. Long-term financing often threatens these owners with loss of control since long-term investors are understandably reluctant to participate without being given a sizable voice in control and share of profits. On the other hand, the continuation of growth may be uncertain, so that longer term investors could hardly be expected to participate unless given adequate incentives.

A doubly difficult situation arises when rapidly growing but highly specialized concerns face the risk of losing business to still newer technological developments made by competitors. Rapid growth creates rapid obsolescence.

The Business Problems of Rapid Growth

Businesses that enjoy unusual opportunities for growth have a happy prospect but also face some difficult problems. Growth usually means that provision of added fixed capital must be made simultaneously with increased requirements for working capital. Even though a company in a growth industry may be earning handsome profits, it may be in serious need of financial aid of both kinds. Those in charge of concerns having opportunities of unusual growth frequently are more skilled in technology than in finance. Accordingly, the basic financial position of a concern moving into a period of rapid growth may already be none too shrewdly or conservatively arranged. Under such circumstances the proprietor of an enterprise of unusual growth opportunities may face problems of financial embarrassment in spite of the fine record of growth.

Banking Problems

The banker having a business customer with unusual growth prospects has an opportunity as well as a risk. The risk is that of overextension. The opportunity is that of extending some profitable credit in the immediate future and of securing a very valuable customer for the long run. A banking relationship solidly established during an early phase of growth may give a bank an entrenched position in the affairs of such an enterprise. For this reason unusual efforts to solve the credit problems of growth have extraordinarily great advantages.

All the techniques of financial analysis, including those of cash-flow measurement, can be applied to this problem. In such circumstances the banker will find himself in the position of supplying a great deal of financial advice to such an enterprise. The long-run interests of both the banker and the customer are the same, though they may appear to conflict in the short run. The circumstances of growth require unusual technical competence on the part of the banker. The hiring of engineers as bank credit officers by the larger banks illustrates the specialized nature of the problems.

THE UNUSUAL OPPORTUNITY

Occasionally working capital credit is needed to meet an unusual opportunity which is not expected to be permanent and therefore does not represent true growth. For example, a regular customer may be faced with an opportunity that ordinarily would be considered well beyond his financial capacity. A very simple example would be a dealer in used machine tools who suddenly is given the chance of acquiring a large block of machine tools at bargain prices. Another example would be an appliance dealer who finds that he can buy the complete stock of a bankrupt dealer cheaply. The opportunity to buy a complete business and effect a merger might be thought a similar case, but since it involves more than simply working capital requirements, it is, in fact, a somewhat larger type of special opportunity than is envisaged here. Unusual opportunities also grow out of special orders for national defense products, materials, prototypes, or similar specialized end products.

The Defense Subcontractor

The procurement activities of the Armed Forces have often had to shift rapidly to keep in step with the changing technology of war. The abrupt concentration on space exploration illustrates this kind of shift. Frequently these changes have also been dictated by changes in budgetary policy or perhaps simply by the urgency of international affairs. As a result, large contracts have sometimes been quickly negotiated by these agencies. In peacetime the primary contractors have usually had enough permanent financing so that their credit capacity has not been wholly strained. In periods of national emergencies, however, even the largest prime contractors have often been hard-pressed. The guaranteeing of credits by the armed services in the form of Regulation V loans represented a recognition of the unusual credit needs that might be involved because of these procurement plans.

A less publicized but quite serious problem frequently arises in the subcontracting of portions of these major contracts. Since very few prime contractors can undertake the full scale of fabrication required, the parceling out of operations among subcontracts is a useful device for handling portions of Defense Department contracts. These subcontracts frequently go to smaller operators who have a special competence or unique advantage in handling their portion of a primary contract. This can be an unusual opportunity for both the prime contractors and the subcontractors. Such opportunities, however, may also involve rather serious financial problems. The primary problem faced by the banker is that, although he may be wholly sympathetic with the requirements and possibly having confidence in the integrity and technological skill of the prime or subcontractors, this business does not promise the long-term advantages to be found in a growth company. Accordingly, bankers seldom can afford to undertake working capital loans under these circumstances without rather complete guarantees. Such guarantees may be assignments of the prime or subcontracts or service department guarantees such as have already been mentioned.

Other Unusual Opportunities

The pattern of business developments, while reasonably smooth for the country as a whole, frequently involves rather sharp changes in circumstances for individual medium-sized or small concerns. The dealer in used machine tools and the appliance dealer have already been mentioned. Unusual opportunities may be available to contractors such as those who are manufacturers of automotive parts or manufacturers of style goods in the clothing industry. Manufacturers of special toys or of special garments may suddenly be the beneficiary of a fad, the duration of which is far from clear at the beginning. Faced with such an opportunity a business can hardly afford not to take advantage of the sizable profits that may accrue from it. A banker may have every reason for wishing to support his customer in this quite special but far from stable opportunity. Generally, such flash expansions should involve as much of the owner's own funds as is possible and minimize the extent to which the banker is exposed to becoming the creditor of a concern involved in a deflated fad or a bypassed fashion.

THE LINE OF CREDIT

When a bank has a long-standing relationship with a customer, it may use the line-of-credit arrangement rather than consider separately each new credit application. This is particularly true of concerns that are likely to be borrowers for irregular amounts and for unpredictable periods, concerns such as soy bean processors. The line-of-credit arrangement is essentially a blanket grant of a maximum loan limit. The borrower then can use any portion of his line whenever he wants to and can reduce his loan when the need for funds has passed. This arrangement does not constitute a binding contract on the part of the bank, but most banks expect to honor the requests made under these lines, except as the regular annual review may change the line.

Ordinarily, the line of credit is established by a bank's directors annually after careful review of the case by the credit department and recommendation by the bank's officers. This leaves a flexible arrangement open to the borrowing customer while giving him a reasonable basis for business planning. It is usually expected that the borrowing customer will "clean up" his account at least once during the year, for at least two or three months. The expectation of a suitable compensatory balance is rather more common in the case of a line of credit than it is for occasional borrowers.

The Annual Cleanup

The annual cleanup is a way of disciplining the borrower financially. It is expected to be an assurance that he will not come to depend on banks permanently for a part of his working capital. Borrowers who have a strong seasonal swing in their affairs, either in sales or in need for carrying raw materials or finished product, usually can manage this periodic cleanup without trouble. It follows the natural pattern of their annual affairs.

Some businesses depend more or less regularly on banks for working capital. This may or may not be a good thing, but the practice exists. In such cases the lending banks have one of two choices: to cramp the business uncomfortably at one season of the year in order to make the cleanup possible, or to send the borrower to some other bank. This amounts to a switching of bank credits, but it is not a true cleanup as ordinarily understood.

Multiple Credit Lines

Because a bank is limited in the amount of credit it may extend to any one business, many businesses are forced to seek credit accommodations from more than one bank. This practice is well recognized. It is customary for banks to exchange credit information about such borrowers rather freely. Multiple credit lines have a somewhat unexpected and unfortunate result. Because of them, a borrower can arrange to be out of debt—cleaned up—once a year at each of the banks at which he borrows, without being out of debt at all banks any time during the year. Table 5 shows how this may be managed.

This means that the entirely legitimate matter of multiple lines may be used to promote steady dependence on bank credit. The practice is not necessarily bad, but the banks should not delude themselves into thinking that it is good short-term borrowing in the traditional sense. In many cases

TABLE 5

Month	Indebtedness to			
	Bank A	Bank B	Bank C	Total
January..............	$450	....	$800	$1,250
February.............	400	....	700	1,100
March...............	500	$600	300	1,400
April................	600	700	....	1,300
May.................	550	750	....	1,300
June.................	500	800	....	1,300
July.................	450	800	....	1,250
August..............	....	750	500	1,250
September............	....	700	550	1,250
October..............	....	650	700	1,350
November............	500	....	750	1,250
December............	550	....	750	1,300

the affairs of the borrower would be in much better shape if he were required to negotiate a term loan.

Under such circumstances about the only advantage that the lending banks get from the cleanup is that some other bank has confirmed their credit judgment, but the possibility that Bank A lends because B is willing to do so reduces the value of this sort of assurance.

13

Secured Business Loans

Any banker in extending credit wants to be safe. Unpredictable nature, economics, and human behavior expose him to all the chances he cares to take. Some credits are, by virtue of the financial statement of the applicant, quite obviously well covered, but that is not always true. When the ordinary financial-statement basis for bank credit is inadequate, the banker is disposed to seek collateral or security in some form or other. The secured loans considered in this chapter are confined to those for business purposes. Real estate loans, as the name indicates, are secured loans; they will be considered here only in so far as the security is incidental to some other business purpose. (Thus we shall exclude even the business of holding and owning rental real estate.) Consumer loans, also often secured, will be considered as consumer loans, not as secured loans.

The purview of this section, therefore, is the place of security and secured loans in business finance. To the extent that term loans for business purposes are secured, there is some overlapping with the following chapter. There is even a little overlapping in the discussion of loan policy, but this will be held to a few fragmentary comments.

The extent to which a business can put up security is limited by its assets. Thus the creditor who gets a pledge of specific security is really doing so at the expense of other creditors, or so it would seem. If a business has just so many assets, the granting of security may change the legal priority of creditors but it does not increase the total debt-settling ability.

This is not quite the whole story. As we shall see, there are other reasons for security, not the least of which is that it is sometimes a way of disciplining the borrower. The lender asks for security, not with the expectation of liquidating it (he hopes to return it untouched to the borrower) but rather of using it to enforce the financial policies he thinks desirable.

The traditional form of security was the cosigning of a guarantor. In former days there was the very frequent condition to a loan that the borrower get a "satisfactory" name to go on his paper. It was found, however, that in times of difficulty this was not a very good system. Businessmen exchanged the favor of endorsement, and when one was short of cash, others were likely to be in the same fix. So endorsement was found to have its limitations.

REASONS FOR LARGER USE OF SECURED LOANS

The first systematic statistical survey of the use of security in bank lending was made by the Federal Reserve System in 1946. For data prior to that time students of banking must depend on general comments and a few scattered figures. The general impression is, however, that the use of security in bank lending was at a low point in 1946 because of the unusual liquidity of the postwar economy and the relatively light loan demand. The surveys of bank lending made by the Federal Reserve in 1955 and in 1957 showed a material increase in the use of security. This evidence suggests that when loan demand increases, the insistence of bankers on security becomes considerably more common.

The greater need for security shows itself up more in some business lines than in others. Since current position is one of the leading tests of credit worthiness, a borrower who shows a weak current position is not a good risk for unsecured lending. This so-called "weakness" of current position is not necessarily an organic defect; it may be due to the nature of the business. For example, dealers in U.S. Government securities are among the highest grade, most ethical, and most conservative of businesses. It would be hard to find concerns to which one would be more anxious to lend; but an appraisal of their current position according to conventional standards of credit analysis would make them appear weak. This situation is not really weakness, but a reflection of the nature of their business. They need big inventories of U.S. Government securities if they are to maintain a true dealer's position, and the amount of capital appropriate to such business is not large. Thus, the nature of the business requires borrowing. There is also an added reason for secured borrowing by dealers: giving security raises or eliminates the legal loan limit of the banks at which they borrow. Since full use of several lines of credit is common, the use of security makes it possible for them to deal with fewer banks. It is not that the lending banks do not trust the dealers; far from it. The dealers are among the most trustworthy groups one could find any place; a business where most of the participants are men of high personal as well as business honor.

The use of security to increase loan limits is illustrated by a somewhat paradoxical practice of the Federal funds market. When Federal funds are sold by a very large bank, its capital and surplus accounts are usually large enough that it can sell such funds in the units conventionally employed in this market without breaching its unsecured loan limit. However, if a small bank sells Federal funds to a large money-market bank, it may have to require the posting of security in order to make the sale legal. This results in a kind of role reversal in which large and powerful money-market banks of unquestioned financial strength give security on their purchases of Federal funds to relatively small banks, while in the reverse transactions security is not given.

Security may also be appropriate in a situation where an extreme seasonal peak requires a bunching of inventory at certain seasons of the year. A fish packer cannot even out his

business but must process the fish as fast as he can while the
run is on. Right after a run when his warehouses are jammed
with canned fish, his financial statements are likely to look a
bit bloated. To borrow, security is needed. (This illustrates
why many business lines elect to adopt a fiscal year that ends
at a seasonal low: the current position thus appears advantageous. For example, many department stores have chosen a
fiscal year ending on January 31.)

BLURRED LINE BETWEEN SECURED
AND UNSECURED LOANS

In a strictly legal sense the distinction between a secured
and unsecured loan depends on whether or not a lien on some
valuable property or right has been assigned to the lender as
security for the credit advanced. In economic practice, however, the distinction may be considerably blurred if the lender
executes a loan contract or agreement with the borrower which
restricts the actions of the debtor. Loan agreements may require that other property not be pledged or require the maintenance of some minimum amount of working capital. Such an
agreement may have virtually the same ultimate economic effects as the posting of security even if not the same legal characteristics. It follows, therefore, that the statistics on secured
loans are not by themselves conclusive evidence of the state of
security in bank lending.

SECURITY BY SIZE OF BANK

Each of the Federal Reserve surveys of secured lending in
1946, 1955, and 1957 indicated clearly that security was required more often in the lending operations of small banks than
of large banks. However, security was required by all sizes of
banks, though the character of this security varied materially.
For example, the use of real estate security or cosigners was
quite common at smaller banks. Larger banks were more likely
to use assignments of accounts receivable or of oil runs or of

defense contracts to support financing. The size-of-bank distinction, however, is not at all clear-cut and it appears that differences in individual banks' policies and also in their strategic location may have been more important than their size. The essential point seems to be that large banks demand security from small borrowers just as often as small banks. Large borrowers, however, are required to put up security less often. Since such borrowers are a larger fraction of the customers of large banks, large banks show smaller averages for security required.

SIZE OF BORROWER

While there are certain differences in the use of security between large banks and small banks, there are even sharper contrasts in this requirement by size of borrower. Very large borrowers such as those with assets of $100 million or more seldom are required to give formal security. On the other hand, very small borrowers typically are required to post security. The reasons are understandable. Very large businesses are usually operated with considerable financial restraint. The giving of security is quite unnecessary and would only create needless costs and problems. On the other hand, small businesses, by their nature, present risks. This circumstance is particularly true of small corporations. These corporations may not have assets of their own sufficient to justify credit. Under such circumstances it is prudent common practice to require some form of guarantee. A cosignature by the principal stockholders of such businesses, particularly if closely held, is quite customary. A parent corporation may also be required to endorse or cosign the obligations of its subsidiaries.

MAJOR TYPES OF SECURED LOANS

There are as many kinds of secured loans as valuable property that can be assigned. The classification by type of security is significant for some but not all purposes. Security dealers borrow on stocks and bonds; so might a schoolteacher to buy a small summer business. Therefore, the type of security is not necessarily the most illuminating means of organizing our discussion of secured lending; but since the facts are available in that form and only in that form, that is what has to be done.

Marketable Securities

The borrowings of U.S. Government security dealers have already been mentioned for illustrative purposes. Many others in the financial community also borrow on this basis. This is typical of investment banking firms and of commission brokers. Those who borrow to purchase or hold registered securities are usually subject to one section or another of the Federal Reserve regulations of security loans (Regulations T and U). This is dealt with on page 235.

The investment banking community often makes rather large use of bank credit and always on a secured basis (often for the same reason as government dealers: to increase their line of credit at any one bank). Two different circumstances underlie this use of bank credit: (1) In the underwriting and flotation process, investment bankers are often left with undigested remnants of not-so-successful offerings. To carry these remnants without forcing them onto the market requires bank credit. (2) Most investment banking concerns maintain trading departments and take a dealer's position in some securities. The handling of their inventory of securities for this purpose often requires bank credit.

Marketable securities are used as a borrowing basis by many other business concerns for purposes beyond the limits of our time or space to classify. Many proprietors of small businesses keep some funds which they consider personal investment but which they often use as collateral if in this way they can get better credit terms for their business borrowings. Marketable securities are often used by nonfinancial businesses for the same purpose as in the case of "street" loans: to raise the loan limit.

The one great problem with marketable securities is that any widespread liquidation of collateral may have an adverse effect on the market. For example, the many loans based on stock market collateral in late 1929 created a wave of liquidation when the market started down, and thus the whole process became a vast self-generating cycle. The fact that many investment banking firms may be fairly deep in the commercial banks—and usually on the basis of flotations that have not floated away—often means that the security market is dull or heavy until these outstanding loans are cleaned up. Because the securities markets are sensitive markets, the dumping of collateral can have a sharp impact on prices.

Margins required on loans secured (aside from margins governed by Federal Reserve Regulations T and U) vary with the nature of the security, also with the character of the borrower. U.S. Government security dealers usually are able to borrow the full market value of short-term obligations. The margin required for intermediate-maturity U.S. Government securities is usually only 2 or 3 per cent of market value. For longer term obligations they may be able to borrow an amount equal to 95 per cent of market value.

In the high-grade corporate security market, firms with good names can often borrow on a 10 per cent margin. Other borrowers need slightly more, say, around 20 per cent. The margin is subject to quite a bit of special dickering, and so no generalization is completely safe. Almost anyone ought to be able to borrow on no more than a 20 per cent margin for high-grade corporates; a well-known name in the street could very likely approach a 5 per cent basis.

On more speculative types of securities, the margin widens. For full marketable securities it seldom goes much higher than 40 to 50 per cent for any borrower; some can do better. When the banking community allowed much narrower margins during the late 1920s, they found it caused trouble so, even aside from regulation, they have tended to become more conservative. With more stable markets, there may be a tendency for required margins to narrow.

Many bankers assume that the listing of a stock automatically makes it a marketable security. This is not so. Some listed issues are traded so rarely that the market for them, except for a small number of shares, is very uncertain. While listing usually guarantees that a bid-and-ask quotation is available, the size of the market is not assured. To be truly marketable it has been estimated that a listed issue should be distributed among about a thousand holders and that the market supply of shares should be close to 200,000 shares. This market supply excludes shares in the hands of dominant owners and shares held in trust accounts.

Unlisted shares may be fully marketable if traded in the over-the-counter market. No very satisfactory rules about the size of this market can be stated, but the opinion of a responsible broker can be accepted.

Nonmarketable Securities

The securities of many very fine business concerns, because of close or limited ownership, are seldom traded. Such securities are high-grade but nonmarketable. Banks are often reluctant to lend on the security of such nonmarketable obligations. If a banker is in a position to appraise the real value of such obligations and if, for example, he is intimately familiar with the affairs of the concern, credit can be granted on these securities, but it may be hazardous.

Sometimes holding companies own all or a major part of the securities of an affiliate; thus these securities, no matter how good, have no market. When such holding companies borrow from banks, about the only security they can offer in many cases are these. The transaction can be justified if the banker knows the affairs of both the holding company and the underlying company well enough to be confident of his judgment. But, as many bankers learned during the anxious days of the depression, this is risky business.

Secured Loans Resulting from Exercise of Stock Options

The exercise of stock options by highly placed corporate executives gives rise to one quite special form of security loan. The widespread use of stock options as an incentive device is well known.[1] Many corporate executives, having advanced to their jobs without much personal wealth, require a sizable amount of bank credit in order to exercise these options. Since the corporations they manage may carry very large deposit balances, the banks holding these balances feel they cannot refuse such loans, particularly if they are well-secured and safe loans. No direct compensatory balances are produced by these loans, but indirectly such executives are in a position to influence the location of the balances of the corporations they manage. Without adequate safeguards the loans can become stagnant. The best arrangement is to negotiate a plan of repayment at the time the loan is made and not wait until the first request for renewal to broach the matter. Repayment may become impractical if not arranged in advance.

Bank loans to executives for the exercise of stock options are subject to Federal Reserve Regulation U. When stiff terms are provided under this regulation, permissible loan values may not be very helpful to the applicant executives. Since Regulation U bases loan values on the market value of the stock at the time of the loan, a stock option at a price considerably below the market may, however, present no problem. If the option price is near market value, banks sometimes seek a kind of "overline" assistance on such stock loans from unregulated lenders such as insurance companies. The view is held by some, however, that this is a moral if not a legal evasion of the intent of Regulation U.

Real Estate as Security

According to our opening statement, the only real estate loans to be discussed here are true business loans; residential loans or even those for rental property are not considered.

The use of real estate as security is natural; it is often one of the leading assets of small businesses, one of the few assets that they can "put up" for borrowing. On the side of the lender, real estate may be poor collateral for business

[1] "Financing Stock Purchases by Executives," *Harvard Business Review,* March–April, 1957, pp. 136–144.

loans; it is likely to be of a somewhat specialized sort and not readily marketable. For this reason, the properties of general use—stores and all-purpose factory buildings—are preferred over other types of real estate.

Approximately one out of every nine business loans of member banks is secured by a pledge of real estate. This is a type of collateral available to most firms and acceptable by nearly all banks. Small firms in particular find the pledge of real estate a method for obtaining bank credit when their size or short operating record would warrant only a much smaller loan or perhaps no loan.

Business loans of member banks secured by real estate are largely made to small firms in the retail, service, manufacturing, mining, and "other" groups. The inclusion of real estate companies in the "other" category accounts for the high proportion of real estate loans in that group. Ninety per cent of the number and two-thirds of the amount of real estate loans are to small and very small businesses.

Equipment Loans

For years the railroads have provided themselves with rolling stock by the use of equipment trust certificates. This form of secured financing has had the effect of enabling the railroads to secure new and modern-type equipment even when their finances were otherwise in dubious shape. The use of modern equipment is often so profitable that it can be afforded even when the financial position is otherwise weak.

Equipment is a type of collateral available in almost every business and is more widely used than any other type of security. The purchase of nearly any piece of business equipment, from a calculating machine to an airplane, can be financed by a bank loan on which the title to the equipment is pledged as collateral.

One factor responsible for the increase in this type of financing during recent years may be the substantial increase in the complexity of business equipment and the greater rate at which it becomes obsolete. Before the war, such loans were usually made on a 6 per cent discount basis and, since most of them were repaid in installments, this meant an effective rate much higher than the quoted discount rate: over 10 per cent in many cases.

At the present time, many of the equipment loans to small companies are handled by the personal loan departments, where discount is usually charged against the face amount of installment loans. The effective average interest rate on equipment loans to small borrowers has not gone up, as has been true of other interest rates, so that this form of financing is now often one of the more economical forms of financing available to small businesses.

An overwhelming majority of bank loans on equipment went to the smallest enterprises, primarily in the retail trade, service, manufacturing, and construction groups. The extensive use of this type of financing by the utility and transportation group is largely for the purchase of various kinds of transportation equipment, such as trucks, busses, and airplanes. Equipment loans may have original maturities of from 1 to 5 years. The smaller loans tend to be short-term, while the loans with maturities in excess of 5 years are relatively large in size.

Inventory Credit

One of the most common causes of need for financing is that of holding inventories. It is often difficult to use inventories to secure such financing, but several new ways of doing this safely have been devised during recent years.

Loans secured by inventories are an important source of funds in the manufacturing, mining, wholesale trade, and retail trade groups, where inventories comprise a large proportion of the current assets. Loans for the purpose of carrying inventories are frequently unsecured or secured by collateral other than inventories because the use of inventories as loan collateral presents several problems. The difficulty is that the conveyance of title to the lender may interfere with the borrower's use of the inventories in his processing or distributive operations. Conveyance of title also presents technical difficulties to the lender. For large, identifiable items such as automobiles or household appliances, assignment of title, trust receipts, and chattel mortgages may be used. For bulk goods, some type of warehousing is typically required.

Most bank loans secured by inventories to manufacturing, mining, and wholesale trade companies are on warehouse receipts covering bulk storage, while those outstanding to the retail trade group are largely on the basis of trust receipts, assignment of title, or chattel mortgages on durable goods of high unit value. The latter loans usually are of relatively small size and account for only a small part of the dollar amount of bank loans secured by inventories.

The medium-sized and large manufacturing and mining companies often pledged inventories to secure their loans. That the largest share of the amount of loans on inventory was to medium-sized and large companies is partly the result of the high cost of handling this type of collateral for small loans. Most of the large inventory loans are handled through warehousing arrangements in which the fixed-cost element is large.

Loans secured by inventories are largely short-term since the inventories are pledged only until they can be sold or used in some manufacturing process. Nearly nine-tenths of both the number and the amount of member bank loans secured by inventories were written with maturities of less than six months.

Field warehouse inventory financing has expanded in recent years. It is best applied to lending on kinds of inventory that are too bulky to be conveniently moved to an established warehouse, or where ready and frequent access to the goods warehoused is essential. In field warehousing, arrangements are made to warehouse the goods on the premises of the borrower under appropriate controls. Thus, there is no transportation cost and the borrower can quickly add, withdraw, or substitute inventory as his operations require and the loan terms permit. The expense of installing and operating a field warehouse, which is borne by the borrower, is an additional item of financing cost in this type of loan.

Accounts Receivable Financing

Next to inventories, the current asset most often used to secure financing is accounts receivable. In some lines of business these receivables, even when controlled by the most rigorous collection methods, are still a financial burden. This is particularly true of high turnover lines. Many business concerns and individuals have been, under the impact of high-pressure salesmanship, encouraged to use their open accounts freely and to pay them off none too promptly. Thus the need for financing.

Accounts receivable financing is another type of bank credit to business that has been expanded in recent years. Its use first became important after the depression of the early 1930s when banks were trying to find methods of reducing risk while meeting the credit needs of medium-sized business. Banks went into this business because of competition with lending agencies that had developed financing methods based on this type of collateral.

In some states the law requires that the pledge of accounts receivable is valid and binding only if those whose accounts are being pledged are so notified. Where notification is required, concerns are often reluctant to use this type of financing for fear their customers will regard it as a sign of financial weakness. Another difficulty with accounts receivable financing is that the lender must give considerable attention to the transaction. Because of the risk of fraud, some banks frequently audit the accounts of customers borrowing on this basis. The added expense to the lender involved in handling and supervising this type of collateral, together with the fact that such loans are frequently regarded as carrying above-average risk, accounts for the higher average interest rate on these loans than on most other types of secured loans.

Loans secured by accounts receivable are short-term in nature. Most of them are either demand loans or mature within 90 days. However, some are made with maturities in excess of a year, and a few with maturities of from 5 to 10 years, usually on the basis of revolving credit arrangements. Interest rates on loans secured by accounts receivables are usually a little higher than the rates on loans of comparable size, largely because of the greater costs of handling such credit rather than because of any risk differential.

New Forms of Security

In the postwar period several new and interesting forms of security have been devised. The development of loans to the petroleum industry based on oil runs is an interesting example, as is also the installment loan based on equipment such as machine tools. In an earlier period the development of field warehousing to use conveniently located inventory for security was an ingenious new method of establishing security.

Interest Rates on Secured Loans

Since, as we said in the beginning, the reason for security is usually that the borrower cannot borrow money on an unsecured basis, it is not surprising that the cost of borrowing for the concern which must post collateral is usually higher than average. Exceptions to this rule may be found, such as the security dealers, but aside from these special cases the rule holds.

Part of the higher cost to the borrower is the fact that he must meet the expenses of posting collateral. The handling of securities is almost costless, but when real estate is given, the provision of documentary proof of ownership, the recording of liens, and the related expenses run the cost of the loan beyond the nominal interest. As already indicated, the cost of field warehousing credit and other types of inventory lending is usually high. Accounts receivable financing involves sizable extra costs.

Beyond that, the rates charged by banks on secured loans is greater than for unsecured loans. The business of advancing the funds and of administering, or at least checking and confirming, collateral is so costly that charges must be increased.

Then too, part of the apparently higher cost of secured credit is due to the fact that secured loans are favored more by small banks.

GENERAL POLICY FOR SECURED LOANS

The search for security in credit no doubt induces bankers to ask for collateral in many cases where, strictly speaking, it is neither needed nor very productive of added security. But a great many credits can be extended only with security. Does that mean that a banker should make loans when there is a material chance that he will have to look to liquidation of the pledged collateral for satisfaction of the loan?

That question may not be an entirely fair one; it is never quite clear in the beginning how a credit is going to go. A banker in granting credit may feel collateral necessary without expecting to use it for satisfaction of the debt. Without being too dogmatic, it can be argued that the use of collateral should be viewed by the banker as a means of giving his institution a priority in the event of liquidation, but a loan that probably can be liquidated only by recourse to collateral is a doubtful proposition.

This view cannot be adhered to dogmatically. Suppose, for example, that a banker is approached by an ambitious young man who has inherited some valuable property. Suppose further that he offers it as collateral for a loan he wants in order to set up in business. The banker might have grave doubts about the success of the business; still the collateral offered will satisfy the loan beyond the shadow of a doubt. Should the banker take the loan, or should he advise the young man to liquidate the property and use the funds to start his business? What license has a banker for turning down a good loan?

The question can be asked in somewhat different form. On all unsecured credits the invariable rule of banking is to deal only with honest men. The first C of the credit analysts who speak of the three, four, or six C's, is character. Can or should an amply secured loan be made to an individual or a business concern of dubious reputation, perhaps not an outright crook, but one noted for sharp and close dealings?

There is much to be said for staying clear of this type of deal, no matter how promising it may seem. Perhaps the most important reason is that the customer relationship is one that banks find hard to juggle. When a bank accepts a customer, it often is difficult to get rid of him in times of adversity. Even with government-security collateral, such a customer is not likely to furnish the kind of continuing relationship that is profitable and safe. Gangsters, dishonest businessmen, and racketeering labor leaders have never furnished the kind of business out of which continuing bank profits are made.

The types of loans made and the conditions attached to them should not be influenced by the fact that security is given. A good loan is one that is apt to be paid in the ordinary course of business without special efforts. A conscientious banker will use the techniques of credit analysis to establish the quality of secured as well as unsecured loans. A banker is unquestionably tempted to lean on the existence of security to extend credit when it otherwise does not seem possible. In the long run, however, this is not a desirable practice. Security that does not amply cover the credit involved is particularly dangerous. The giving of security that only barely covers an outstanding credit exposes the lender to risk and may be effective only in disciplining the operations of the borrower.

When the security back of a loan is ample, the risk problem is small. What about the case when the security is somewhat less than adequate? In final liquidation, partial security helps. For example, suppose a bank has U.S. Government securities as collateral for 80 per cent of a loan to a concern which finally collapses into bankruptcy. Suppose the unsecured creditors receive only 50 per cent of their claims. The bank will then realize 90 per cent on its credit (80 plus 50 per cent on the unsecured 20 per cent).

Inadequate security, however, poses a number of problems. Many borrowers feel that if security is given it should be sufficient for full satisfaction of a credit. Suppose a bank has accepted some stock of dubious value as partial security on a loan to a businessman. If affairs go badly, he may tell the bank to go ahead and liquidate the collateral. He is likely to expect this to be full satisfaction for the credit. Even if a deficiency judgment can be secured, the borrower is likely to resist it with great vigor. The position of the bank in such a deal may be misunderstood by the public. In many ways, it is arguable that a bank should either insist on adequate collateral or lend on an unsecured basis. Like most dogmatic rules, this one has numerous exceptions.

Installment or Lump-sum Repayment of Secured Loans

Many secured loans for longer periods are put on an amortization or installment basis just as is done for longer term unsecured loans. The use of amortization is not particularly related to the existence of security but is keyed to the characteristics of the flow of funds which make possible partial repayment and maturity of a longer term debt.

Collateral Added to an Unsecured Credit

Some bank loans start out unsecured but have security added to them subsequently. If a borrower on an unsecured basis gets into difficulties and cannot repay his debts, the banker may insist on the posting of collateral as a condition of not pressing for liquidation. Thus collateral will be given for keeping a loan viable. The net result of this sort of transaction is that of giving the bank a preferred position among the creditors. If, as sometimes happens, the news of this is bruited about, it may precipitate a general tightening of terms by all creditors.

This act often saves a bank from large losses, but it is not always recognized in equity law. If it is decided that such collateral was posted after the business was bankrupt and so had only the effect of giving the bank a preferred position, the court may well put aside the collateral arrangement and order the segregated assets returned to the general assets of the business for settlement of all credit claims. Thus, this sort of deal may not turn out to be so effective as at first it seemed to be.

Maturity Policy for Secured Loans

The several loan surveys show that the maturities of secured loans depend more on the nature of the credit than on the existence of security. For example, loans secured by marketable stocks or bonds usually have very short maturities. On the other hand, equipment loans, and loans for the purchase of plant and equipment, usually have longer maturities. In other words, there is no reason to vary maturity policy because security is available; this policy should be geared to the basic borrowing needs of the customer. But it is true that the existence of security may permit somewhat longer maturities than might otherwise be feasible or desirable. Security may make it feasible to extend a loan for the period needed by the borrower, but it should not be used to do more than that.

14

Term Loans

The biggest single change in the nature of commercial-bank lending since the 1930s has been the growth of term loans. A few years ago these loans were estimated to be about one-third of the business loans of commercial banks. In the big money-market banks, the proportion has often approached and sometimes exceeded one-half.

Not only is the term loan important; it seems likely to remain so. Fundamental changes in the nature of business financial needs may favor the further growth of term lending. Banks, at first cautious in the granting of term credit, have learned how to use and control this new form.

WHAT IS A TERM LOAN?

Term loans have already been defined as business loans with a maturity of more than a year. Though borderline cases exist, this definition brings out the major characteristic of term loans that most people have in mind—the "long" or "intermediate" term nature of the credit. Since they are "business" loans, long-term credit on residential real estate is excluded. Strictly speaking, loans on income-producing residential real estate could be treated as term-loan credit, but it is not customary to do so. The amortization of term loans is so common

245

that it could almost be included in the definition, but not quite. Exceptions occur as we shall see later.

What is the "term" of these loans? When banks first started making term loans, they usually limited the initial maturities to 3, 4, or 5 years. It was assumed that commercial banks probably should not extend credit for periods much longer than this; even 3 years was, after all, a big change from traditional practice. But the terms have lengthened with time. The initial maturity of term loans was found by Jacoby and Saulnier in 1940 to exceed 5 years in almost half the cases (counted by dollar volume of credit).[1] By 1946, a Federal Reserve survey showed that over 54 per cent of the loans had terms of more than 5 years.[2] Since that time further extension of final maturities does not seem to have taken place; in fact, there may have been a retreat from the longer maturities, as evidence later in this chapter will show.

The growth of term lending as a commercial banking practice came mostly after World War II. The National Bureau of Economic Research study estimated that the volume of such loans outstanding did not reach $1 billion until 1937. By the end of 1940, it was estimated by this study that commercial banks had $2.2 billion of these loans. The Federal Reserve survey of November, 1946, indicated a volume of $4.6 billion, or over one-third of all business loans held by member banks. By 1957 the volume of term loans had reached $15.4 billion and by 1960 the estimated volume reached $18 billion.

In many ways this "growth" may be a deceptive measure of the amount of real change. To some extent term lending by banks is replacing loans that formerly were made on a shorter term basis but renewed frequently. It was long suspected that

[1] N. H. Jacoby and R. J. Saulnier, *Term Lending to Business,* National Bureau of Economic Research Inc., 1942, table C-2, pp. 152–153.

[2] The principal empirical evidence on term lending is to be found in three Federal Reserve surveys of business lending by banks made in 1946, 1955, and 1957. These surveys are reported in the following *Federal Reserve Bulletin* articles: "Term Lending to Business by Commercial Banks in 1946," May, 1947; "Business Loans of Member Banks," April, 1956; and "Member Bank Term Lending to Business, 1955–57," April, 1959.

the so-called short-term commercial loans of many commercial banks were neither so short-term nor so commercial as was claimed. This is not to argue that the development of term lending is a bad one; quite the contrary. It rather might be viewed as the abandonment of a fiction which had never been very true or relevant.

In many important respects, the bank term loan can be reviewed as an almost new way of employing money. It is providing a financial service never before adequately undertaken by any financial institution. Much has been said of the credit needs of small business. Many of those who spoke of "small" business units were referring to sizes that are often thought of as more than small and well into medium size.

In the past the investment banking community has not been equipped to serve even middle-sized business. Its financial orientation, its customers, its habits were such that it served mainly the top-flight and top-sized outfits.

The individual investor, the local "capitalist," sometimes filled this gap by investing in small new enterprises. But the concessions that original owners often had to give were so large as to make such an arrangement a last resort. The moderate-sized business often could not get long-term capital on respectable terms.

The term loan for small business has great prospects. It can fill in economically where the machinery of investment banking is too massive. It can be used by owners without the fear of having to surrender all control over their business or all chances of reaping the major rewards for their efforts.

TERM LOANS REPLACED CORPORATE BONDS

Prior to the Great Depression many commercial banks were large buyers of corporate bonds. In many ways the growth of term loans in commercial banks can be viewed as a displacement of their corporate bond investments. Term loans have been made to the same kinds of industries in which bond investments had been made. Term loans have several banking advantages. They bring compensatory balances and can be safeguarded with protective provisions in the loan agreements.

The fact that corporate bonds were marketable was initially considered one of their strong points, but this feature sometimes proved to be more of a disadvantage than an advantage. A marketable obligation has a quoted price. The bonds of well-operated concerns have often been quoted considerably below par, sometimes for money rate reasons but sometimes because of general distrust of business conditions. A term loan without a market quotation may have less liquidity, but it is not exposed to such an invidious kind of comparison.

MATURITIES OF TERM LOANS

Experience over the past several years has shown that the policies of banks with respect to maxima maturities allowed for term loans change with the various phases of the business cycle. When the demand for credit is high and banks are able to accommodate only a portion of the demands on them, they are strongly disposed to limit term loans maturities. In this way it is felt that more customers can be accommodated. On the other hand, when funds are more freely available banks are likely to extend maturities according to the demands of customers. Although banks claim that they do not like to make term loans with a maturity more than 10 years, a portion of term loans frequently exceeds this limit—about 10 per cent of total term loans in recent years.

In the early and experimental period of term lending, maturities tended to be short. Later they were extended as banks became more confident of their ability to extend such credit safely. Recent Federal Reserve studies, such as of business lending in 1955 and 1957, indicate, however, some retreat in this matter. About 50 per cent of the term loans outstanding in 1957 had had an original maturity of less than 5 years in contrast to 40 per cent a decade before that time.

Maturity naturally has to be adapted to the needs of the

individual customer. Borrowers in the petroleum industry, for example, have an obvious and legitimate need for longer maturities, as is also true of term loans to the real estate industry or to many lines of manufacturing. On the other hand, term loans to sales finance concerns, to the construction industry, and to the processors of food products do not need as long final maturities.

The problem for the individual bank is not so much the maximum maturity that it will allow on any one term loan as it is the over-all distribution of maturities within its entire investment portfolio. A substantial volume of incoming payments has advantages of credit prudence as well as of liquidity. If cash flow has been well estimated so that payments are made when due and few extensions are requested, a portfolio of term loans can offer an appreciable degree of liquidity.

WHAT BANKS EXTEND CREDIT
ON A TERM-LOAN BASIS?

So far, large banks have been more active as term lenders than small ones. Small banks have not had the facilities to manage or initiate term loans. They have, however, sometimes participated in them. As will be explained later, some term loans are made jointly by several banks.

The 1946 Federal Reserve survey demonstrated the relatively greater importance of the large banks in term lending, but it also showed that small banks were not entirely idle in this field. Since 1946 an increasing number of banks of intermediate and smaller size have developed programs of term lending. Participation in this market is far more general than it was in initial periods of experimentation. Nevertheless, larger banks continue to dominate the field of term lending. Statistics on this point were not collected in the 1957 Federal Reserve survey of business loans, but in 1955 about 40 per cent of total business loans at the very large banks (deposits of $1 billion or more) were in term form. The corresponding proportion for banks with deposits of $10 million or less was only about one-quarter. Intermediate-sized banks were fairly evenly spaced out between these two extremes.

Part of the reason big banks make more term loans than smaller banks is that big borrowers apparently are more disposed to, or at least more able to, borrow on a term-loan basis than is true of small borrowers. A comparison of all business loans between those on a term-loan basis and those on a short-term basis in 1955, the last time such data were collected, indicates that almost a half of the credit to very large borrowers was on a term-loan basis. Only a third of the credit to very small borrowers was on this basis.

THE PLACE OF TERM LOANS IN BUSINESS FINANCE

The key to term lending is understanding its place in general business finance. If the function of this type of credit in prudent business finance is understood, the problem of the management of term loans by the bank is already partly solved.

The use of term loans has, in a very general way, been about that of other kinds of intermediate or longer term capital. Term loans differ from other forms of credit in at least two respects:

1. They have been sought by and made to businesses that are too small to have access to the central or open capital markets, that is, to be able to sell bond, debenture, or other capital issues.

2. They have been sought by and made to concerns which were seeking term credit as an alternative to going to the capital markets, or were refunding securities outstanding in the market at the more advantageous interest rates offered by banks. The securities refunded were usually bonds or debentures, but some issues of callable preferred stocks were refunded by term credit.

These two groups of borrowers are, by their nature, distinct and separate. The first group seeks term loans from banks because other longer term credit channels are not open to it; the second group, on the contrary, could use the open markets but borrows privately, usually for price reasons. This extremity of groups explains why term loans made by banks show such a wide variety of interest rates. It can be said that in so far as banks extend term credit to business concerns in the second group, they are using term credit as a competitive answer to the private purchases of security issues by insurance companies.

For some purposes a separate segment of this second group of term-loan borrowers may be isolated for special notice. Some borrowers could command open capital market credit but prefer not to disclose such details of their business as would be required in SEC registration statements and prospectuses. The advantage of dealing with a bank which is already familiar with their affairs appeals to them. This adds further evidence, if more is needed, that the foundation of successful bank lending is a position of continuing interest in and knowledge of the business finances of all potential borrowers.

Looked at from the side of the borrower, the use of a term loan is not greatly different from other kinds of intermediate-term capital except for availability and cost. Banks can promote further business in term lending (1) among concerns who could otherwise not get credit or (2) by offering credit on interest rate terms more favorable than those offered by other lenders.

STANDARDS AND PROCEDURES FOR TERM LENDING

Since term loans differ from other classes of business loans mainly in the maturity involved, the credit standards differ from those for short-term credit mainly in this characteristic. In general, the factors of short-term financial strength, so important in short-term credit analysis, are given less weight, and factors of earnings and stability are given more weight.

In making term loans, banks often use the advice and services of engineers and management consultants. They look to the "real" factors more than to the financial factors. Competitive and technological factors are important considerations. Quality of management is more important than a strong current position.

Because the basis of term lending is so very similar to that of security analysis, banks often employ those with experience in investment banking or investment analysis to make term loans. Credit analysis covers:

1. The market for the product of the applicant firm.

2. The personal finances of the principal stockholders in a closely held applicant corporation. This will include an investigation of the provisions to pay inheritance taxes if the principal holders are of an age to make this important.

3. The potential effects of extreme business-cycle fluctuations on the applicant concern.

4. The competitive position of the applicant concern.

5. The inventory position and the possible effect of rapid and sizable price changes on the size of inventory losses and gains.

6. The adequacy of depreciation, depletion, and obsolescence in the face of possibly rapid technological and other changes.

One of the most important strategic advantages that commercial banks have in the competition for long-term loans is their ability to act rapidly. Investment banking procedures tend to be slow and time-consuming. In order to exploit this advantage, however, banks must maintain ample and current credit files with respect to their principal customers in order to process loans rapidly when the need arises.

Use of the revolving credit arrangement is a particularly desirable way of making preparations before money must be advanced since the preliminary credit work has all been arranged and the contract worked out. Large and loosely drawn revolving credit contracts, however, may leave a bank open to some unpleasant surprises if customers call for funds under such contracts unexpectedly.

INDUSTRIES USING TERM CREDIT

In many industries the intermediate character of term loans is well adapted to their basic needs and is also consonant with their basic financial strategy. Many small or moderate-sized concerns need to improve equipment and to expand working capital and have a rate of earnings or of cash generation which make fairly rapid repayment of credit feasible. In such cases a commercial-bank term loan is particularly appropriate. Borrowers can have confidence that a commercial lender will not jeopardize their control of their business as long as their affairs are in good order.

SECURITY FOR TERM LOANS

About 60 per cent of term loans are secured. This proportion prevailed in 1946, 1955, and 1957, suggesting relative constancy in the practices with respect to enforcing security requirements. Security is found somewhat more commonly in small term loans than in large ones. Its use is also concentrated in plant and equipment loans. The assignment of claims is a special form of security used widely in lending to companies in the defense industries. The security is a valid contract with one of the armed services. Subcontracts of such prime contractors are also an effective basis for the extension of secured credit.

Banks are often able to enjoy all the benefits of security without having to go through the formality of establishing a legal lien. As will be mentioned in discussing the loan agreement (which usually accompanies a term-loan credit), other indebtedness or the pledging of property is often prohibited by these agreements. Thus, if other creditors cannot establish a priority or even an equality of position, the term lender, though technically unsecured, has almost as strong a position as if he held formal security.

THE LOAN AGREEMENT

In granting term credit, banks often impose conditions on the borrower by telling him what he must do and what he cannot do. The specific means used for imposing these conditions is the "loan agreement," or the "bank credit agreement." This document is a formal statement of conditions to which the borrower agrees in consideration of the granting of the loan.

The loan agreement is, in many respects, like the indenture that governs most relationships in cases of bond indebtedness. Because the credit is granted by a single creditor rather than by a considerable number, a trustee who acts as agent for the several creditors is not necessary. The financial conditions often tend to be somewhat more restrictive than those appearing in the typical bond indenture. The greater strictness may be due to the fact that the loan agreement is drawn by the creditor, whereas bond indentures are usually drawn by representatives of the investment bankers who may have more stake in debtors' affairs.

The loan agreement usually recites the basic facts about the loan: the conditions under which the credit is extended, the form and period of repayment, provisions making the entire loan due and payable if any portion of the credit is defaulted (the so-called "expediting" or "acceleration" clause), and the warranties. (Warranties are guarantees by the executors of the document that they have authority to act for the borrower if it is a corporation, that the credit does not violate the bylaws of the corporation or any other contract into which the corporation has entered, and that the financial statements furnished and to be furnished—particularly the statements of liabilities— are correctly prepared or fully disclosed.)

The major conditions laid down by the term-loan agreement usually relate to the future financial conduct of the business. The leading conditions usually relate to the maintenance of the current working capital position. Sometimes the borrower agrees to maintain a given current ratio.[3] In some loan agreements the guarantee is not stated in ratio form but rather as a guarantee to maintain a stated dollar amount of net working capital.

The second leading feature usually included in loan agreements has to do with other borrowing. Some term-loan agreements prohibit completely all borrowing from other sources, except possibly through accounts payable. Others are not so rigid and may permit short-term borrowing but prohibit all other long-term borrowing. Unsecured loans are often accompanied with loan agreement conditions which prohibit the pledging, assignment, or encumbrance of property to or for other creditors. This provision sometimes becomes an effective, if indirect, prohibition on other borrowing.

A third major feature usually found in term-loan agreements has to do with the payment of dividends, or, in the case of unincorporated enterprises, the distribution of earnings. As outlined in other sections, the rate of retirement of term loans is more often geared to the cash flow. This means that the amortization of term credit needs to be accompanied by conservative retention of earnings or profits. There are many ways in which the earnings distribution limitation may be stated; for example, as a specific dollar limit on the amount of dividends, or as a specification of the proportion of profits which must be retained or may be paid out.

Other features that are frequently included in term-loan agreements are:

1. Prohibitions on the sale of business assets or of specific assets such as accounts receivable. Sometimes it is provided that if fixed assets are sold, the proceeds (or the proceeds in excess of some minimum amount) shall be applied to the term loan in the inverse order of payment. When this is done, the final payments are retired, thus shortening the maturity of the loan.

2. Requirement for maintenance of all property in good condition.

3. Requirements for maintenance of proper insurance.

[3] See pp. 162–163 for a discussion of current ratio.

4. Restrictions on investment of liquid funds.

5. Prohibitions against consolidation or merger.

6. Prohibitions against the purchase by the concern of its own shares.

7. Restrictions on becoming a guarantor of debt.

8. Requirement that all tax claims be paid promptly.

9. Requirement for the maintenance of adequate accounting records.

10. Requirement for the furnishing of regular financial statements and for access by the lender's auditors to accounting records for the purpose of audit and verification.

11. Requirement for the maintenance of corporate existence and the operation within authorized corporate powers. Activities beyond those engaged in when the credit was granted may be prohibited.

When a corporate borrower has a complex corporate structure or has a number of partly or wholly owned subsidiaries, it may be necessary to make part or all of the loan agreement conditions binding on the subsidiaries as well as on the parent company. When specific current asset or dividend limits are imposed, specific rules as to what consolidated or unconsolidated entity is subject to these current asset or dividend limits may be needed.

When a subsidiary corporation seeks credit, it is customary for this credit to be guaranteed by the parent corporation, and the parent usually is made subject to restrictive covenants such as outlined before.

REPAYMENT PROVISIONS

As pointed out in the opening paragraphs, term loans are usually though not always amortized loans, that is, loans repaid in equal installments over the life of the loan. The period for repayment of the installments is often quarterly, but it can be either monthly, semiannually, or even annually. The frequency of payment depends on the type of business to some extent and the other payment schedules. For example, for a business which has material Federal income tax liabilities retirable by quarterly payments, the term-loan payment may be fixed so as to fall in some other month than the March–June–September–December cycle which governs quarterly tax payments.

A majority of loans are repaid in equal installments which fully retire the obligation at maturity, but at least two variations to this rule do occur. The first is the so-called "balloon" note, or one in which the last payment is a very large one. When the note matures with such a large payment, the borrower may not be in a position to wipe out the debt. The balloon note is also used when the period over which retirement is to take place is longer than the final maturity that the creditor is willing to permit. For example, a business might secure term credit to purchase a building with an expected life of 50 years. It might be prepared to amortize the debt within a period of 20 years, much less than the total life of the property and usually thought of as a conservative retirement schedule; but the creditor does not want to lend money for more than 10 years. The compromise arrangement may turn out to be a 10-year credit but with periodic payments at a rate which would retire the credit in 20 years. This means that the final scheduled payment would be a large one, or a "balloon." In this as in many other term-loan balloons, the implied understanding is that the credit will be repaid by refunding. The lender may be willing to rewrite the credit, or funds may be secured from some other lender.

The second type of repayment plan which does not contemplate equal-payment amortization is the so-called "revolving credit." Sometimes the revolving credit is, in effect, a kind of stand-by credit. It was popular in war finance when concerns would undertake war contracts, the exact financial needs for which were less certain than they would normally have cared to undertake in peacetimes. The sort of circumstance that gives rise to a revolving credit would be one in which a concern is planning expansion but, because of uncertainty, cannot schedule its financial needs closely. In such circumstances a revolving credit will supply funds if and when needed. A revolving credit can be retired if and when the unfunded debt is refunded into some other form. A revolving credit may be arranged to mature into a regularly scheduled equal-payment amortized loan.

PREPAYMENT OF TERM LOANS

Considerable variation prevails in the way in which prepayment of term loans is permitted, encouraged, or penalized. Commercial banks are disposed to encourage prepayment and to permit it without penalty. Insurance companies are less inclined to encourage prepayment and often attach a penalty or premium to it not unlike the excess of a bond "call" price over par. While most lenders applaud the conservatism that permits prepayments out of earnings (and, as already observed, feel that prepayment is required if there is a sale of fixed assets), they do not like to lose a credit by refunding at lower rates. Refundings at the option of the borrower are governed by probabilities adverse to the interests of lenders. If the borrower's affairs turn out well and interest rates go down, the loan is a desirable one; but it is under such circumstances that the loan is most likely to be refunded. If the borrower's affairs do not work out so well and interest rates rise, the loan will not be prepaid. The inclination to attach prepayment penalties grows out of these pairings of odds.

When prepayments are made, it is customary to apply them to the final maturities first. This tends to shorten the over-all maturity of the loan. When a loan is syndicated (explained later) with all participants taking a common share, prepayments raise no problem. When some of the members of a syndicate take the longer maturities (such as a life insurance company) and some take the short maturities (such as a commercial bank), the problem of prorating the payments is awkward. This case should be clearly contemplated in advance and written into the loan agreement so that there can be no later misunderstanding.

ESTIMATING REPAYMENT ABILITY
OF TERM-LOAN APPLICANT

The amortization schedule for a term loan should be geared to the ability of the borrower to repay. If the ability to repay is less than that needed to retire the credit within a reasonable period, this fact should be treated as a warning; the credit is probably a dubious one.

The estimation of ability to repay can be made on either of two bases:

1. A term-loan credit should improve the earning capacity of the borrower. To the extent that it does, these added earnings can be applied to the repayment of the credit without reducing or impairing the income the borrower would otherwise have enjoyed. If the estimate of added earnings is a dependable one and if the amount will retire the credit within a reasonable period, this furnishes a fair basis for credit extension and repayment.

2. The direct result of added income may be isolated only when the term loan is for a specific improvement. When a term loan is not for such a purpose but rather to restore working capital which has been depleted for one reason or another, then the repayment estimate should be based on "cash throwoff," that is, the amount of cash that can be applied to debt repayment without jeopardizing the general condition of the business. The ability to repay debt can be estimated as the amount of net retained profits adjusted for accrued income and non-cash expenses. In figuring "cash throwoff," accrual items which involve segregated assets (such as sinking funds) cannot be counted. This form of estimation has the advantage of requiring repayments which discipline the conduct of the borrower's affairs. A term loan based on a schedule so computed is likely to restore financial health, provided, of course, that the borrower has good basic earning power.

SYNDICATION OF TERM LOANS

Only one factual study has been made of the extent to which term loans are divided among more than one bank. That study was part of the Federal Reserve business loan survey of 1955. At that time about 30 per cent of outstanding term loans consisted of individual loan contracts under which the credit had been extended by more than one bank. The use of multiple participations may arise in either of three kinds of circumstances.

First, a small bank may be faced with a credit demand that is in excess of its legal lending limit, in which case it may seek to dispose of the "overline" credit to its city correspondent. This form of overline lending is a way of accommodating large local customers while at the same time avoiding the competitive risk of losing them to some other city lender. It is generally understood implicitly that a city correspondent will not solicit the business customers of its country correspondents without their permission.

Second, large city banks, hard pressed for reserve funds, often sell portions of their term and other loans to country correspondents. The extent to which this practice is followed varies with the tightness of money markets. In recent years New York has often been hard pressed for funds while country banks have still had unused lending capacity.

Third, some banks prefer participation in lending in order to improve their credit diversification. This circumstance has arisen particularly during those periods in which the demand for special kinds of loans in some areas of the country has been so large that the local banks have become overburdened with this one type of credit. For example, banks in the Southwestern states sometimes have encountered heavy demands for petroleum industry loans. Large-scale syndicates or pools were often formed for the granting of such loans.

One interesting form of syndication occurs when one or more

insurance companies combine with one or more banks in a term-loan deal. The circumstance usually accounting for such a combine is the planning of a term loan with a maturity greater than that desired by a bank. The insurance companies take the long parts of such loans, the banks the short parts. The serial notes held by the banks sometimes bear a lower rate of interest than those held by the insurance companies.

CONTINUING SUPERVISION OF TERM CREDITS

Everything said in earlier sections about the need for continued supervision of a loan after it has been made applies with special force to term credits. Because the period of time involved is so much longer, more can happen; greater deviation from expectations can occur.

The term loan requires more than the one budget prepared at the beginning of the credit. The budget probably should be renewed at least annually with full allowance for changes in conditions. In this type of credit the long view is important. The budget can give early clues to the difficulties and problems that may beset a particular credit. Because the rescue of distressed term loans will almost always take longer, the budget furnishes a more continuous check than would otherwise be available.

The size of the supervisory problem makes term lending fairly costly. As will be argued later, there are good reasons for not trimming term-loan interest rates too thinly; this is one of them. Any effort to short-cut or escape the supervisory problem is false economy.

A term credit that is syndicated is usually of such high standing that the supervisory problem is relatively small. The syndicate head nevertheless assumes a special responsibility that should be covered in its extra compensation. For prestige, if for no other reasons, a bank could hardly afford to be associated with a credit deal that turned out badly for lack of adequate supervision or because of revealed flaws that should have been detected by ordinary supervisory routine.

POLICY FOR TERM-LOAN PORTFOLIO

The policies discussed so far relate mainly to the individual term loan. In addition, a bank should have some policies with respect to the nature and size of the aggregate term-loan portfolio.

1. Diversification, already mentioned in other connections, should be reasonably wide. Since term loans are more subject to the risks of business fluctuations and other unpredictable factors, the need for diversification is particularly great. The usual means to increase diversification is through syndication. Some diversification can be secured by picking and choosing among applicants. However, a bank located in a small or moderate-sized town may not be able to do this; a larger town offers more variety.

2. A bank's capital position affects the degree to which it goes into term lending. A bank with a very thin equity cannot well afford to go very far, perhaps cannot enter the field at all. The applicable rules are discussed in Chapter 23.

3. The shape of a bank's investment account must be adapted to its program of term lending. The more term lending, the less maturity permissible in investment accounts. The credit rating of investments should be kept high if large amounts of term loans are held.

4. Term lending cannot be undertaken unless a bank has adequate personnel. Term lending often requires not only competence in finance but also technological and engineering personnel. The extent to which investment banking and investment counseling concerns have gone over to the side of technological investigation is indicative of the problem.

THE RELUCTANT TERM LENDER

The heavy concentration of term loans, particularly in New York City banks, is traceable in part to the fact that this form of credit is particularly useful to many large corporations. They tend to force term lending on their bankers, even though the banks may be reluctant lenders in this form. The large balances that corporations hold give them a powerful bargaining position. Intermediate credit has a place in business finance not met by the open capital markets. These markets sometimes have rejected issues with early call provisions and have required heavy penalties on later calls. Intermediate-term credit that can be repaid at the convenience of the borrower is particularly useful. This circumstance has made the term loans popular with business concerns that make capital expenditures with large profit potentials but with some uncertainty as to the timing of profits. Nevertheless, such term credit tends to reduce the liquidity and mobility of a bank's portfolio. The one compensating advantage is that if extended in high-interest-rate periods term loans furnish a high-earning asset.

INTEREST RATE POLICIES FOR TERM LENDING

Although commercial banks follow a variety of policies with respect to the interest rates charged on term loans, the commonest policy is that of charging a rate of ½ of 1 per cent in excess of the prevailing prime loan rate. The scanty statistical evidence available suggests that the differential prevailing in practice may be even smaller. Some bankers question whether this is an ample differential. At this rate banks are considerably lower cost lenders than life insurance companies. It should be recognized, of course, that the direct placements made by life insurance companies have considerably longer maturities than the term loans of commercial banks. Nevertheless, the life insurance direct-placement rates are so materially higher that one might conclude that other differences in the credit qualities of the two borrowing groups exist. One offsetting point must be recognized. Banks are able to profit from the deposit balances left with them by term borrowers.

CASH FLOW FROM DEPRECIATION AND DEPLETION

Special tax allowances for depletion given the petroleum extract industries by Congress have tended to stimulate term lending. Because of these allowances a sizable amount of cash is generated before a tax liability emerges. This margin gives lenders a protection they would not enjoy under the same circumstances if normal corporate income taxes were applied.

Equipment loans are often made on a term basis. The constant improvement of business equipment has made it an unusually appropriate basis for term lending. Improved and technically better engineered equipment often has a pay-out period of no more than three or four years, even though such equipment may have a working life many times that long. This payout period almost automatically guarantees cash generation of an amount adequate to pay off a term loan of moderate maturity. Such term loans are frequently made with interest rates computed on the initial amount of credit extended. The practice tends to make the loans very much like the sales finance contracts resulting from the sale of automobiles. Similar arrangements may be found in term loans to railroads, airlines, streetcar, and bus companies. These contracts are very much like equipment trust obligations which involve loans secured by the rolling stock or similar equipment. The loans often use a form of contract (labeled the "Philadelphia plan") in which ownership of the equipment remains vested in a trustee until payment has been completed.

15

Bank Credit to and for Consumers

Until about a generation ago bank credit was traditionally supposed to be extended primarily for business purposes. The origin of this tradition probably was in British banking, where a large part of banking was, indeed, truly "commercial." But reality did not always conform to tradition. Credit was undoubtedly extended to consumers. Evidence of the act, however, was concealed more as a shameful weakness than promoted as a regular part of their business, as is done now. It was widely (and wrongly) assumed that consumers were poor credit risks.

A few scattered banks started regular lending to consumers during the 1920s, but the practice was exceptional and many abandoned this activity in the early 1930s. Weak demand for bank loans and low bank earnings during the later 1930s, however, forced commercial banks to reevaluate their position. During that period they sponsored and paid for the first great research inquiry into consumer installment lending under the direction of the National Bureau of Economic Research.[1] At first commercial banks were decidedly experimental

[1] This inquiry was reported in ten volumes published between 1940 and 1944. The volume most relevant to this study is *Commercial Banks and Consumer Instalment Credit,* by John M. Chapman and associates, published by Princeton University Press, Princeton, N.J., in 1940.

in their participation in the market. As time passed they discovered that this credit produced far fewer losses than had been expected earlier. The business also proved to be extraordinarily profitable. As a result, in the postwar period commercial banks moved enthusiastically into consumer lending. They used several channels for doing so, with individual banks choosing those that were most appropriate for their location, public image, and available personnel.

The activities of commercial banks in extending credit to or for consumers may be classified about as follows: The most direct form is the making of cash loans face to face with consumers in the bank's own quarters. The second form is through the purchase of installment paper generated by the "time payment" sales of automobile dealers or other dealers in durable consumer goods. The third form is the even more indirect process of lending to sales finance concerns or to personal or "small" loan concerns. These concerns then purchase installment paper or make direct cash loans.

Some banks are able to engage in all three types of credit granting, others in only one or two of them, and a few banks do not engage in any form of consumer lending. The total amount of credit originated in these various outlets has come to be an appreciable part of the total volume of bank credit outstanding and an even more important contributor to the earnings of banks.

DIRECT INSTALLMENT LENDING

The bank that makes cash loans directly to consumers engages in the most retail of all forms of banking. The aloof austerity of old-fashioned banking quarters and deportment is no longer appropriate. Banks are dealing with customers who probably are not accustomed to the practices of commercial banking. Such customers may not have had checking accounts, and they may not even have had savings accounts. To make a profit on this business, a reasonable volume of business needs to be generated. Credit-checking practices need to be routinized, and a bank's promotional activity should be geared to the new kind of customer.

When commercial banks promote direct installment lending to consumers, they generally make such loans in somewhat larger amounts than the competing personal loan companies but also generally charge somewhat lower rates. They also attract somewhat higher quality customers than other consumer lenders. This form of lending, where it has been adequately promoted, has frequently become a leading part of a bank's activities. To use these facilities fully, banks try to maintain the volume of activity in these departments at all periods. As a result, the direct lending departments usually have a priority over other departments in the use of bank funds.

Terms for Direct Loans

Direct bank lending is often for the purpose of financing the purchase of an automobile or some other durable good. When this is the case, the terms need to be competitive with those available in directly arranged sales financing. Some banks try to enforce rather higher standards for the loans directly made than applied to purchased paper. Part of the reason for this practice is that when loans are directly made, credit protection, such as that supplied by the reserve account used in sales financing, does not exist. Second, the rates charged by banks are frequently somewhat lower than those available to customers in the case of sales financing. This policy is consistent with the somewhat higher quality of customer sought after and generally secured. A loan made for the purchase of a durable good is generally secured by the good purchased.

The terms and arrangements for direct loans that are not for the purchase of durable goods may be compared with the standards set by personal loan companies. In the first place, such loans are frequently not secured. They may also be somewhat shorter maturities than when the purchase of a durable good is involved. It should not be assumed, however, that this type of credit is closely comparable with personal loan company credit. To some extent the cash-installment lending activities of commercial banks represent a more orderly organization of various kinds of lending activities in which they have already been engaging for many years.

Bank credit practices for cash-installment loans are less uniform than for loans based on the sale of durable goods and depend more on the character of the borrower. Some individual borrowers that had received regular bank loans on a noninstallment basis have been tactfully asked to convert such borrowing to an installment basis. Such a change increases credit security and encourages systematic repayment rather than frequent renewal. It also has the healthy effect of increasing earnings from credit to this type. The only disadvantage is that some customers, particularly those of ample net worth, believe borrowing on an installment basis to be degrading. The social stigma attached to consumer debt has not yet vanished.

Credit Factors in Consumer Loans

The widespread assumption that consumer credit results in sizable credit losses is incorrect. As already mentioned, consumer loans are often slow and delinquent, but many banks have found that the ultimate losses on them are less than those on business credits. Whether this result is a tribute to the basic honesty of the population or to the energetic collection practices of consumer credit grantors, the risk in granting consumer credit has been less than was formerly expected.

The National Bureau of Economic Research made a study of the connection of a variety of factors with the consumer loan risks. The results of this survey are summarized in the following paragraphs.[2]

Personal factors. A study of the relationship of *age of borrower* to the collectibility of loans did not yield particularly conclusive results. It was evident that borrowers over 50 years of age seemed to be materially better credit risks than younger ones. Short of 50, age differences were not very important.

[2] David Durand, *Risk Elements in Consumer Instalment Financing* (a National Bureau of Economic Research study), Princeton University Press, Princeton, N.J., 1941.

The study of *marital status* also yielded inconclusive results. Married borrowers had a slightly better record than single ones, but the difference was small. Since a prejudice among credit grantors against the single borrower has long existed, it is possible that most weak credit risks were weeded out before this sample was drawn. It is believed that the moral risk with single borrowers is greater than with married ones because the single ones are less stable and can move fast and far. It appears that a given amount of income will justify a larger amount of credit for a single person, probably because his needs for current expenses are so much smaller.

A classification of borrowers by *sex* indicated that females are generally better risks than males. Because many borrowers are reluctant to advance funds to females, there is some doubt as to the meaning of these results. The sample of borrowers may have been highly selected. Another special factor was present: consumer credit grantors have always prized schoolteachers as very good credit risks. They are in a respectable profession and have to keep their credit standing good; they can be pressed for collection rather more successfully because a bad credit record is usually taken seriously by school boards in hiring and retaining teachers. Possibly teachers tend to be a bit more honest than the rest of the population. Since a very high proportion of public schoolteachers are females, their good record may weigh favorably the record of all females.

The *number of dependents* did not show a conclusive relationship to credit experience although it appeared that very big families might be poorer than average credit risks.

The years a borrower had lived at one address, *stability of residence,* proved to be a surprisingly good index of a borrower's credit dependability. Those borrowers who had lived in one place at time of borrowing less than two years proved to be poorer than average credit risks; those who had lived at the same address for six years or more had much better than average records. Although the study was not geared to show the point, it is a good guess that stability of residence is connected with stability of employment, temperamental stability, and stable income. No doubt general stability is one of the most favorable characteristics in judging the credit worthiness of consumer credit applicants.

Vocational factors. The occupation of the borrower, as we have already suggested, may be tied into some of the other credit factors considered above, but some very evident and significant differences are implicit in the credit results of loans classified by the occupation of borrower. As already noted, teachers have very good credit records; so do nurses, doctors, technicians, lawyers, accountants, stenographers, and typists. Policemen and firemen have better than average records. At the other extreme, unskilled laborers, salesmen, those classified as "managers and officials," and wage earners in general have poorer than average credit records. As already suggested, stability of income may well be a very important credit factor: in the first group are those with reputedly stable incomes; in the second group, those with less stable incomes.

Similar results are found if the *industrial affiliation* of the borrower is studied. It was found that those borrowers working for banking or brokerage concerns, for public utilities (gas, electric, and telephone companies), in public service (state and Federal government), and in professional services all have better than average records. Those connected with the building trades, driving taxis, or working in filling stations have worse than average records.

Tenure in employment showed the same very positive relationship to credit worthiness as did residence at the same address. Those who had worked at a given job one year or less were poor credit risks; added tenure of employment improved the credit results and those who had worked for the same employer for ten years or more had very good credit records. Since it is to be presumed that the credit grantors had already weeded out a high proportion of applicants with short tenure of employment, this finding is doubly significant. Stability may be nearly the best test of a good borrower.

Financial factors. One of the universally expected results would be that borrowers with high *incomes* would be good credit risks; those with low incomes would be poor ones. Because this factor was no doubt in the mind of the bankers in granting the original credits, this is probably true. But the results of this survey show that while it is not overweighted by these judgments, there is no such clear correlation as would be expected. The survey did show that for very sizable incomes ($4,800 or more, which was quite sizable for consumer borrowers in the prewar era of consumer credit granting) the risks were materially below average. Otherwise the differences were nowhere near so evident. Income is an important but far from conclusive factor in consumer credit granting.

Since gross income by itself might not reflect the burden of borrowing (a small loan may be no more burden on a small income than a big loan on a bigger income), the credits were measured as a *proportion of income.* It was found that any consumer debt more than 20 per cent of annual income had a poorer than average experience. Except for this one fact no clear relationship was discovered. Income did not measure up as an index of credit performance of as great validity as would be expected.

Several other financial tests were applied, most of them derived from the net worth statement of the borrowers. For example, it was found that those borrowers who owned securities, a bank account, or some real estate had materially better than average credit records. Ownership of life insurance, an automobile, and household goods was accompanied by slightly better than average performance. Having a charge account was a favorable sign; having other installment indebtedness was a bad sign.

Characteristics of the loan. The survey also revealed that the character of the loan itself was, to some extent at least, an indicator of its likely credit showing. For example, it was found that loans for $100 or less were likely to be poor risks. Above that size no such clear record was detected. Moderate-sized and big loans showed just about the same experience. Some borrowers may make little effort to repay small loans, figuring that the lender "can afford to lose that much." For this reason as well as the costs of making tiny loans, some lenders have a minimum loan rule.

Single-name loans had a better record than loans with one or two comakers; loans with three or more comakers had relatively bad records. This probably reflects the fact that only the better credit risks were granted loans without comakers; only the poor ones required as many as three or more comakers. It also reflects the fact that credit grantors may have put more faith in the comaker system than it merited. Many modern lenders grant only single-name loans and, by careful selection, do very well indeed.

The survey also showed clearly that short-term loans (under a year and particularly under six months) had much better than average records; long-term loans showed poorer than average results.

In spite of the "remedial" theory of consumer credit loans, it was found that loans for the payment of taxes, for vacations, for household purposes, for the help of a relative, or for the purchase of an automobile had a much better than average record; those for consolidation of debts, for the purchase of clothing, for medical and dental expenses, or for business purposes had a poorer than average record.

Summary of credit factors. To summarize, a good consumer debtor is an applicant who has lived at his present address for several years, who has worked for the same employer (preferably an employer in a stable business line) for five or preferably ten years, who has a bank account, and who owns some securities.

An intangible factor pervades these judgments, of course. A good moral credit risk, one with a will to pay, is likely to be a fine risk no matter what the other factors show; a weak moral risk will fall below the average of those with similar vocational and financial characteristics. The moral basis of consumer credit granting can never be reduced to terms of statistical testing nor its results reflected in studies such as the one presented here; but it is clearly one of the leading factors in good consumer credit granting.

Because of this difference in moral factors, the difference between a bank in a big city and one in a small town should be recognized. A small town bank with its intimate knowledge of local borrowers has a vastly different position from that of a big city bank. The basis for urban credit judgments necessarily has to be somewhat mechanical. Lenders have to depend on the sort of objective tests discussed here. The bank in the smaller town might use these tests, but it has available a background the city bank can well envy: a knowledge of moral factors that the city bank can never quite attain.

Operating Practices

When commercial banks engage in consumer financing, they usually have to organize special facilities for it. If a bank does nothing more than grant credit to sales finance or to personal finance companies, the loans usually can be handled with the existing arrangement of loan officers and credit departments. When a bank discounts consumer paper and grants consumer loans, the personnel and organization must be specialized. Commercial banks frequently try to limit the number of extremely small "small" loans by using lending minima such as $500. Even with such limits, however, the business must be put on a routinized basis in order to make it profitable.

Credit arrangements for the granting of direct consumer loans involve provisions for receiving and interviewing applicants and checking their credit. Since direct loans are often unsecured or secured only by endorsement, the matter of credit checking is taken much more seriously than is the case with sale credits. The bank undertaking to make direct loans usually works out a fairly standard procedure, such as the following:

1. The applicant is received by a full-time interviewer who completes a standard application form during their talk. The interviewer often gives the applicant an informal indication of his view of the credit, possibly going so far as to reject the request without completing the formal application. The credit request is often materially modified during the interview; many unacceptable requests are turned into acceptable ones before

anything is put on paper. The interviewer will then promise an answer at some definite early time. Since most borrowers want their money in a rush, the organization must be geared to prompt action.

2. The application is then turned over either to a special credit checking department or to some branch of the regular credit department. In small banks, of course, the interviewer may also check credits. The credit check will include a search of the bank's own records (when a bank extends consumer credit, it often maintains rather full files on individuals, including notices of legal actions and the like), a check with the local credit bureau, and perhaps a verification of employment. This is often omitted when it happens that known borrowing would prejudice the position of the applicant as an employee. References may be checked by telephone, and sometimes a written follow-up to such references is undertaken. If there is any problem of identification, a post card may be sent to the address given by the applicant with a request for a signature which is compared with that on the application.

3. After the credit checking, the application with the recommendation of both the interviewer and the credit checker will be turned over to a senior officer or sometimes a committee which will give the final approval or rejection.

4. The applicant will be informed of the answer by the interviewer (occasionally the loan will be closed by persons other than the interviewer), and the funds will be advanced.

Among credit applications there is bound to be a certain proportion of rejections. A study of consumer credit granting before World War II indicated that various commercial-bank lenders had rejection rates running all the way from 1 to 25 per cent. Too high a rejection rate is bad; it is likely to create ill will. The rejection rate usually depends on the character of the promotion policy. In advertising consumer credit facilities, it is bad to bring in customers that are likely to be denied loans. The consideration of a rejected application usually takes more time than an accepted one. It costs a bank money to invite poor applications. Some institutions try to reject few loans but to attach conditions or change the terms of the less desirable one so that the borrower is likely to withdraw his application.

Banks have various methods for handling the monthly collections: coupon books, passbooks, and other devices. Some of these are patented systems and are installed by specialized firms who provide the necessary materials. The matter of methodology is important; consumer credit is essentially a small-unit large-volume business. Cutting unit costs is the way to make a profit.

The supervision of consumer credits is not unlike that of other credits. Defaults and delinquencies are perhaps rather more frequent than in the case of commercial credits even though final collections are good. While some loans get "slow," the proportion that go bad is surprisingly small. The chief function of supervision, therefore, is prodding the slow and delinquent debtors into payment. When necessitous factors, unexpected medical costs and the like, drive borrowers to delinquency, the usual practice of credit grantors is, if the moral and income basis for the credit still exists, to take a generous view and rewrite the credit according to the revised needs of the case.

Competition

The foregoing comments bear directly on the subject of competition in the consumer loan field. It is a highly competitive one. When banks enter it, they are leaving the dignified shelter of their more traditional operations. They are inviting a new class of customers into their banking quarters and representing themselves as institutions appealing to a new group of the population. Banks that are willing to adopt such an attitude, to take some chances, to make the shirt-sleeved applicant comfortable, can get along in the business and make money.

Success in consumer lending requires large volume, and the only way to large volume is to go out for business by vivid and forceful promotion, by throwing over some of the traditional banking conservatism, by general and spirited aggressiveness. The bank that is not willing to meet the requirements for success might better stay out of the business.

Small banks have always granted some consumer credit, but it has often been in noninstallment form and only as an accommodation. Such banks can often convert this unprofitable business into a good thing by organizing it and putting it on a standard consumer credit basis.

Legal Regulation of Consumer Lending

The lurid history of cheating, misrepresentation, and oppression by loan sharks has left the field of consumer credit with a considerable harness of legal regulation. Some of these regulations try to protect the consumer from sharp practices; others control the interest rates and terms.

One simple form of regulation is that involved in the so-called "full-disclosure laws." It has been felt appropriate that a credit transaction, whether it originates in a sale or a loan, should be one in which all the facts relevant to it are made quite evident to the creditor. This not only makes the borrower fully aware of the obligation he has assumed, but also supplies legal proof of charges actually made at a later date. The character of full-disclosure laws varies from state to state.

A sharp distinction must be made between the regulation of interest rates on true loans and the regulation of charges on installment sale transactions. Legal doctrine has been that charges involved in the sale of goods were not subject to regulation since they were a part of the price. Except where price control prevails a concern is free to set such prices as it sees fit. The consumer is assumed to be protected by open competitive markets.

In 1957 interest rates on personal loans made by commercial banks were regulated by 35 states. Since new laws are being enacted constantly the number may well be considerably larger by the time these sentences are read. The regulations applying to banks generally allow their transactions to be on a discount basis. The maximum rate of interest is usually stated so as to apply to the total of the original indebtedness. When stated in this way these limits range between 6 and 8 per cent. A few states allow somewhat higher rates, usually, however, for true or "simple" interest.

The first "welfare" regulation of consumer credit grew out of its origins. The charging of interest for the lending of money was banned by the Church in the Middle Ages. Usury was thought to be extortion. Later, although charging of some interest came to be permitted, limitation of interest rates by so-called "usury" laws became common. These usury limits were set at levels which represented a margin, fair perhaps for lending to business concerns, but so low that it made lending to consumers in little dribbles unprofitable. There is nothing older than poverty, human distress, and the unexpected (or imagined) need for money. Money lending to individuals is as old as the hills. The loan shark had to operate outside the law when there were usury laws, but there were often means for evading these rules and making his operations at least semi-legal. All too often the loan shark, operating near the margin of or outside the law, was disposed to exploit his unfortunate "clients." Since ignorance and ineptness in money matters are all too common, this was not hard. The ubiquitous loan shark was often able to keep his clients ("victims") in debt to him for years. The effort to get rid of this social evil led to the adoption of special laws regulating the form and methods by which loans to consumers might be made. The Uniform Small Loan law, widely adopted in many states, was the specific statute by which the small loan companies were authorized to adopt their per-cent-month rules of interest charges.

This regulation has not broadened to cover all types of consumer lenders but, to varying degrees, all lenders must observe various types of welfare laws. It is notable that, while the lenders are generally subject to some type of welfare regulation, those who extend installment sale credit are often exempt.

Economic regulation of consumer credit had existed during three different periods when Federal Reserve Regulation W was in force. Its background was in the economics of war and of shortages. Credit for the purchase of consumer durable goods would have exaggerated the inflationary pressure. The argument for its application at other times is that, when times are good, consumer credit expands overrapidly and helps to bid up prices excessively. When times get bad, the lenders and vendors shorten their credit terms and refuse credit to all marginal borrowers. In other words, the cyclical swing, already very great, is made even greater by consumer credit, and the shrinkage of consumer debt during bad times tends to make the recessions worse and to dig the economy into an even deeper hole.

This is an unsettled debate. It can hardly be doubted that consumer credit tends to exaggerate economic fluctuations. An overly strict control of it, however, might be considered an infringement of personal rights. Many have not just economic, but moral feelings about consumer credit; many who abhor other types of governmental regulation would tolerate this one because they believe the promotion of consumer credit tends to encourage people to buy what they cannot afford.

This rather harsh view can be countered by the fact that much of the development of modern ease and comfort in living has been due to the use of consumer durable goods, that the widespread purchase of these goods would not have been possible without the use of credit, and that productive efficiency and present lower prices would not have been possible without credit. Electric refrigerator prices at present are less than at the deflated lows of 1932.

Should the possibility of being subject to economic regulation restrain a commercial banker from entering the consumer lending field? The technical problems of compliance certainly should not discourage him. His experience in dealing with regulated credits of other kinds provides ample background for working with consumer credits. And since bankers tend to be conservative consumer lenders, economic regulation might have the effect of widening the field of competition open to them. There is little about the contingency of economic regulation to frighten commercial bankers away from consumer lending.

PURCHASE OF INSTALLMENT PAPER

When commercial banks purchase installment paper originated by dealers they compete directly with sales finance concerns that perform a similar service. In this activity the credit granting and managerial operations of commercial banks are closely patterned after those pioneered by sales finance concerns.

Business of this type is secured mainly by solicitation of dealers. In arriving at an arrangement with dealers, the banks must be prepared to undertake a number of servicing functions usually performed for dealers by those who purchase their paper. The major problem is that of reaching a mutually satisfactory agreement with dealers on the terms and quality of paper that will be acceptable for purchase. Dealers are mainly interested in selling automobiles or other goods in maximum volume with minimum price concessions. To achieve this goal they may be forced to make sales to marginal or extramarginal credit risks. Banks, just as sales finance concerns, need to steer a middle course. They must be prepared to accept the kind of credit risks that will make the dealers they service competitive with other dealers, but they should not extend credit of such poor quality that it will produce serious losses. Agreement must be reached also on such matters as the rates charged customers, the terms of the credit itself, and where the risk is to be borne. In earlier periods it was common to require dealers to be contingently liable for paper sold to sales finance concerns or banks. In effect a dealer's own credit was at stake. A more modern device, however, is one in which the installment paper purchased from a dealer is covered by a general reserve for the absorption of credit losses. This reserve is accumulated as paper is repaid. When the reserve reaches certain proportions and experience with credit losses has developed reliable evidence of expected losses, any excess amount in the reserve is rebated to the dealer. In former periods sales finance contracts were sometimes "packed" (excess charges added and then rebated to dealers) so that dealers were attracted by the extra gain implicit in this practice. The pack has now been replaced generally by the rebate of excessive amounts accumulated in the reserve. This rebate furnishes the main profit reaped by some automobile dealers. The advantage of this arrangement is that it gives dealers an effective incentive for maintaining a reasonable quality in the credit obligations they originate and sell to banks.

The maximum maturity allowed and the amount of credit relative to the value of the purchase are fundamental terms on which banker and dealer must agree. This is also largely a matter of competitive standards within the time-sales financing community as a whole. A dealer cannot expect to be fully competitive if his terms are less generous than those of other dealers. Terms tend to be set more by community practice than by individual arrangement.

Agreement must also be reached on a number of managerial or administrative points. When paper is offered by a dealer to its bank for sale, the purchasing bank generally reserves the right to reject unacceptable credits. An agreed limit to the time period in which rejection may be made should be settled. In addition, purchasing banks generally prepare the credit contract forms and make the arrangements for collection of outstanding credits.

Another part of the package of purchasing the paper that a dealer originates is the financing of the dealer himself. The financing problem is usually that of carrying an inventory of unsold automobiles or household appliances. Credit for this purpose may be extended by "floor planning." This is a type of secured loan. The inventory of unsold goods is the security and is held by the dealer on the basis of trust receipts. The bank expects the dealer to retire the credit as soon as an automobile or appliance is sold. Banks normally release the dealer from his obligation under the trust receipt only when specific repayment of the credit is made. Registration of serial number for the goods released under trust receipt and other devices are usually used as a way of verifying such transactions. Close auditing procedures are generally required to avoid nasty surprises. A bank also needs to maintain close supervision of the general financial affairs of a dealer to whom it is extending a great deal of credit since deterioration of his condition can lead to unexpected defections from honesty.

BANK LENDING TO SALES FINANCE
AND PERSONAL LOAN COMPANIES

The third channel through which banks supply money that ultimately finances consumer expenditures is by lending to companies that specialize in buying the installment paper generated by sales or in making of personal loans. In both of these activities banks are, of course, financing companies which directly compete with them. Sales finance companies compete as purchasers of consumer installment paper. Since banks also lend directly to consumers, the personal loan companies could be considered competitors. In practice the credit worthiness of persons who borrow from the small loan companies is typically considerably poorer than is tolerated by banks in their own direct lending activities. Sales finance competition is more direct than small loan competition.

When banks lend to sales finance companies or personal loan companies they are dealing with sophisticated and knowledgeable borrowers. These concerns typically make very large use of both long-term and short-term borrowed funds. Thus, they are, in effect, using leverage to increase the rate of return on their own equity investment. Because these concerns are knowledgeable and sophisticated in the field of financial arrangements, they tend to know the customs of lending and to abide by the rules. As borrowers the quality of their credit is generally very high. At the same time, they bargain sharply and can do so since they have alternative sources of credit. Large sales finance and personal loan concerns typically deal with a wide group of banks so that their relationship with any one bank, except for perhaps one leading bank, tends to be rather more impersonal than is true of other bank relationships. One money-market bank may have something like a true customer relationship with one of these lenders and may act as a kind of leader for the other "line" banks. It is typically true that lines of credit to sales finance companies and small loan companies are used more regularly than is true of the lines of credit to other types of borrowers.

One important distinction may be made between sales finance concerns and personal loan companies in terms of their characteristics as bank borrowers. The business of sales financing or the purchasing of consumer paper has proved to have rather wide cyclical swings. Banks should expect sales finance concerns to be somewhat more volatile borrowers than personal finance concerns, whose volume of bank borrowing tends to be more stable. Personal loan companies, however, have very little reason to maintain appreciable cash balances; therefore bargaining for compensatory balances with them frequently tends to be even tighter than is true in bargaining for the compensatory balances to be held by sales finance borrowers.

Administrative Arrangements

Typical lending to either a sales finance or a personal loan company is under a line-of-credit arrangement. In general, the arrangements for these lines of credit are somewhat more explicit and exact than is true for other lines of credit. In the first place, these lines of credit are almost always accompanied by an explicit arrangement for an annual "clean-up" (complete repayment) of borrowing, usually for a period of one or two months. Furthermore, negotiations for increasing lines of credit (except where the line of credit has already reached the legal loan limit of the lending bank) tend to be bargained more closely. Banks have been known to refuse such increases to sales finance company borrowers of impeccable credit standing because the bank preferred to give local borrowers preference or because it felt the sales finance concern had used its line of credit excessively at moments awkward to the bank. The nature of the compensatory balance expected of such borrowers is likely to be spelled out in more precise terms. In recent years compensatory balances of these borrowers have frequently been expected to be 10 per cent of their line of credit or 20 per cent of outstanding indebtedness, whichever amount is greater. In periods of credit tension some banks have attempted to increase the expected amount of compensatory balance to as much as 20 per cent of the line of credit.

Most sales finance and personal finance concerns, and all the leading ones, command the prime loan rate. A large proportion of the secondary concerns are also given this rating. Direct bargaining on rates is rare and some leading concerns even pride themselves on never having tried to "break" the prime loan rate. Most of the bargaining takes place in the area of compensatory balance terms. Nevertheless, both sales finance concerns and personal loan companies are deeply interested in bank rates. The chief influence of such rates on their policies is sometimes expressed in the extent to which they seek long-term financing from the open market.

Credit Standards

Analysis of the credit of both sales finance concerns and personal loan companies has developed into a fairly complex statistical and analytical process. Since these concerns typically have lines of credit with many banks, the leading "line" bank frequently furnishes copies of their detailed statistical analyses to the other "line" banks. In general, however, most banks are expected to make their own credit analysis and it is considered good banking practice to do so. The analysis form for concerns of this type prepared by the Robert Morris Associates is widely used.

Analysis of the credit of sales finance and personal loan companies is at two levels: (1) the balance sheet and income statement of the concern itself, with special emphasis on the nature of its capital structure, and (2) the quality of the credit granted by the sales finance concern or small loan company. These concerns have tended to use more and more leverage (that is, a higher proportion of debt to equity) as the quality of their credit came to be more widely recognized. Nevertheless, trading on equity excessively is still criticized by most banks. Another feature of interest to credit analysts is the extent to which the indebtedness of the concerns being analyzed is divided between long-term and short-term forms. Banks are also concerned with the extent to which long-term debt may be subordinated to short-term debt. When some portion of long-term indebtedness is subordinated, short-term creditors receive a considerable degree of protection.

The quality of purchased paper and loans may be given a detailed statistical and, indeed, almost actuarial analysis. The credit quality of paper acquired by a sales finance company varies according to the character of customers solicited. Some sales finance concerns have an unusual concentration of customers (dealers) who cater to marginal credit risks. If this is a conscious policy they may have recognized this fact in the character of their capital structure. The quality of small loans varies somewhat less from concern to concern than is true of sales finance paper. The quality of paper outstanding is generally measured by its actual performance in terms of delinquencies or the necessity for repossession. It may also be tested by other features, such as proportion of down payments and the amount of credit in relationship to security. In automotive paper the amount of a contract can be compared with the wholesale value of the automobiles which represents the underlying security.

Credit standards are subject to constant evolution. The person interested in pursuing the subject further usually can find current statistical studies depicting standards prevailing at that time. Leading banks that wholesale credit to sales finance and personal loan companies are the best source for such studies.

Captive Finance Companies

Several large manufacturing concerns have found it useful to establish sales finance subsidiaries which purchase the paper created by the dealers or agents franchised by such manufacturers. These captive finance companies frequently have a somewhat special status as regards credit standards. The bankers for the large and powerful parent companies can hardly afford to apply the same credit standards to such captive finance companies that they normally apply to unaffiliated concerns. Frequently compensatory balances are, in effect, furnished by the parent company so that it is not possible to enforce compensatory balance requirements against these subsidiaries. For the same reason, the capital structure expected of such subsidiaries may contain more leverage than is tolerated for independent concerns. If a captive finance subsidiary does not have adequate credit strength of its own, however, it is not amiss for a banker to ask for a guarantee or endorsement by the parent concern. A legitimately managed parent concern should be willing to guarantee the credit of a subsidiary that it has established, particularly if it has not seen fit to supply it with the amount of capital normal for such concerns.

Related Types of Lending to Finance Companies

Legal loan limits have tended to restrict bank credit extension to sales finance concerns and personal loan companies to the standard form of short-term line-of-credit loans. In general, the sales finance and personal finance companies have not sought intermediate-term loans from commercial banks since such term borrowing would have reduced or exhausted the amounts available for short-term borrowing under lines of credit. It has been thought preferable to borrow on a long-term basis either by direct placements negotiated with insurance companies or by open-market sales of obligations through investment bankers. For similar reasons many banks refuse to buy the open-market commercial paper of sales finance concerns for fear of inadvertently exceeding the loan limits if a line-of-credit arrangement is activated at a time when they might possibly be holding such commercial paper. Another reason banks are reluctant buyers of this paper is that it brings in no compensatory balances.

16

Lending on the Security of Real Estate

For many years it was presumed that commercial banks should not make real estate loans; indeed, many of them did not. National banks, for example, were denied the privilege of making such loans until 1916. This privilege continued to be severely curbed until 1927, when it was moderated slightly. National bank rules on real estate loans have since been further liberalized to some extent but they are still more restricted than those for state banks. It was thought that these loans were not in keeping with the demand nature of commercial-bank liabilities. Accordingly, many state banks, though legally free to do so, elected to make no real estate loans.

The growth of time and savings deposits in commercial banks changed these views. Specialized savings banks had long made real estate loans, and it was thought appropriate to match savings deposit liabilities with the somewhat less liquid but highly regarded real estate loans. So the practice grew until today real estate lending is one of the chief outlets for savings funds in commercial banks.

IMPORTANCE OF REAL ESTATE LOANS TO BANKS

In step with the rapid growth of total bank credit in the postwar period, real estate loans have continued to maintain

286

an important place in the portfolios of commercial banks. They account for nearly one-fourth of the total amount of loans outstanding. As would be expected, these loans are not of much importance in the portfolios of true money-market banks that specialize in the wholesaling of money. More surprisingly, however, they are not of great importance in many very small rural banks. Such banks frequently make more real estate loans on farm lands than on homes. A great share of farm lending on real estate is now done by other lenders, particularly governmental agricultural credit agencies.

The bulk of real estate loans, therefore, is to be found in middle-sized banks. In this group of banks real estate loans are frequently more than a third of total loan portfolios. In some individual banks they have gone to even higher levels. A number of banks located in rapidly growing suburban areas surrounding great metropolitan centers have acquired unusually large portfolios of real estate loans. In addition, trust departments also use real estate loans as investment vehicles.

WHY ARE REAL ESTATE LOANS THOUGHT ILLIQUID?

Why is it that real estate loans are thought illiquid? It is because they are long-term. As long-term credits, the proportion that matures in any given period is bound to be relatively small. About one-sixth or one-seventh of the mortgages outstanding are collected in a given year. During less inflated periods, this collection rate would certainly be smaller. In addition, no well-organized market for outstanding real estate loans exists (though, as we shall see below, this is less true than it used to be). As a result, the chances of disposing of such loans without material sacrifice of real investment value are much less than in the case of marketable even though long-term securities.

The lack of liquidity of real estate loans is in part reflected in the fact that real estate itself—the underlying security—is far from marketable. The market for real estate has been described as "thin, sluggish, and erratic." Since the underlying security has this character, it is hard to make the credit super-structure any more marketable than the value basis for it.

REAL ESTATE CREDIT
NOT AS ILLIQUID AS FORMERLY

Although real estate loans are still not very liquid, they are more so than formerly. The development of mortgage insurance by the Federal Housing Administration (FHA), to be discussed later, established minimum lending standards so that there is a rough homogeneity from loan to loan. In order to encourage building in areas where mortgage money was short, the Federal government bought mortgages through the Federal National Mortgage Association (FNMA). Some of these mortgages have been resold. As a result of these factors, a limited national market for mortgages has developed. While it is not as fluid and fast as that for securities, it offers enough protection to take much of the curse off real estate lending.

ADVANTAGES OF REAL ESTATE LENDING FOR BANKS

Although real estate lending is viewed coldly by many bankers, it has undeniable advantages. The greatest is that the interest rates on real estate loans have usually been moderately good and therefore the income from this source has been relatively high.

Another advantage is that it is one of the constructive uses to which a bank can put some of its funds. Real estate loans are frequently associated with home ownership.

A further advantage of real estate lending should not be overlooked. The fact of limited markets usually would be considered a disadvantage, but it is not always so. Frequent market quotations sometimes make the holder of a marketable security jittery. The holder of an unquoted security—a loan—may have as bad an underlying situation but there are no objective facts to prove it; without the pressure of bad current quotations he may worry less and pursue a more sensible long-term investment policy.

DISADVANTAGES OF REAL ESTATE LENDING

The chief disadvantage of real estate lending—lack of liquidity—has already been mentioned. The next most important disadvantage is the comparatively demanding requirements on a lending bank. The business is so specialized that, according to many experts, it should not be conducted on a part-time or casual basis. It can produce more grief and losses than most other types of lending unless given unusual attention. Whether it is really more difficult than other types may be disputed, but that it has caused frequent banking difficulties cannot be denied.

Still another disadvantage is that real estate credit tends to be quite unstable during the various phases of the business cycle. New building is the main source of demand for credit, and new real estate construction varies greatly from the top to the bottom of the cycle. The range of variation is extraordinarily wide. As a result, the demand for credit is also highly variable. At times a bank engaging in such lending can find lots of real estate use for its money; at other times, somewhat less. Real estate lending was comparatively stable during most years of the 1950s or at least it was not marked by as severe swings as were once experienced. Continuation of this situation, however, is not assured.

Another disadvantage of real estate lending is that such loans usually are not accompanied by deposit balances of significant magnitude. Individuals borrowing to buy a home are obviously not likely to hold large balances. After allowance for activity, the profitability of such balances as they do carry is open to question. Nevertheless, compensatory balances can be secured indirectly in some cases in the process of real estate lending. For example, banks that are active in real estate lending may be more successful in attracting good balances from builders.

They may also be able to attract added business from among the firms that specialize in supplying building materials.

A final disadvantage of real estate lending is the large degree of price and profit instability that is potential in this market. It is hard to overestimate the potential instability in the real estate market and business. The annual increase in structures is small in relation to the total number in use (seldom more than 2 per cent annually in the case of residential structures), and because land itself is a wholly fixed resource, small variations in demand are reflected in larger price changes. When the real estate market is good, prices rise readily; when it is dull, they fall and the volume of sales drops.

In the real estate market, credit is of the greatest importance. Most homes are bought by their owners with credit, and the amount of credit (the reciprocal of the "down payment" put up by the buyer) that is available makes a great deal of difference in the willingness and ability of persons to buy homes. Generous credit terms can stimulate vast real estate speculation. (The Florida boom of 1926 is worth recalling; also the more recent GI housing loan.) Tight credit terms depress the real estate market.

VARIOUS KINDS OF REAL ESTATE LOANS

Real estate loans can be classified in the following ways:
1. On owner-occupied homes
2. On rental-income properties
   a. Residential
   b. Commercial
3. To business for operating properties
4. On specialized properties, such as theaters, churches, or garages
5. For construction

Many real estate lenders prefer to extend credit on owner-occupied homes. Home ownership is a deeply rooted social institution. People are fond of their homes, take pride in them, want to keep them. During severe depressions, market values sometimes dip so that the realizable value of a home is less than the mortgage loan remaining on it. While commercial borrowers sometimes abandon properties when logic indicates that they are "paying for a dead horse," owners often will struggle against great odds to retain their homes. Furthermore, since homes represent the largest use of real estate, there is a broader market for them than for any other type of real estate. The market never quite disappears as it often does with other types of property. A home mortgage is often of a convenient size which permits diversification of risk, something not possible with larger mortgages, except by very large banks.

A mortgage on rental-income properties is not so highly regarded as one on an occupied home. On really good income-producing property, repayment of the credit is well protected. If the lender has to take over the property, the income from it helps in the recovery. The distinction between residential and commercial income-producing property is not of great importance except that the variation in demand for commercial property and its rental income is usually thought to be somewhat wider. Many properties incorporate both types, for example, a flat building with stores on the first floor, or a hotel with space for leasing out to restaurants and shops.

Investors borrow on income-producing property in order to increase the rate of return by trading on a relatively thin equity. As illustration, suppose a private investor has the chance to buy for $120,000 an apartment building with gross rental income of $20,000 (six times the gross rental is a representative ratio). If the costs of operation including taxes and reasonable depreciation are $10,000 a year, the rate of return on the entire venture would be an expected 8.3 per cent ($10,000 divided by $120,000). But suppose that the investor can borrow half of the purchase price at a rate of 5 per cent; he then can net 11.7 per cent on his smaller investment. (Since the interest on the borrowed $60,000 is $3,000, the net return is reduced from $10,000 to $7,000, but the capital required is also cut to $60,000. The net return of $7,000 on the owner's equity of $60,000 is 11.7 per cent.)

The lending to business concerns for the construction of plants or other buildings, or for the acquisition of land, is technically a kind of real estate loan, but it has more the nature of a business loan. Since this type of credit has already been considered under the heading of term loans (page 250), it will not be considered further here.

Many real estate lenders avoid loans on specialized types of property such as theaters, churches, garages, and hotels. These properties have very limited markets. In good times they may sell well enough, but lenders seldom have to realize on such real estate collateral in good times. These are fair-weather properties. Furthermore, in some though not all of these loan classes, the lender takes the risk of an industry that may be subject to technological deterioration.

Construction loans, as their name implies, are made to finance the construction of buildings or other improvements. They are looked upon as a necessary evil by many banks: difficult in themselves but a necessary condition for doing a general real estate lending business and attracting adequate volume of demand in this field. This bad reputation does not apply universally to all types of construction loans. Some banks have been active in making construction loans on large technically complex construction jobs. The risks are considerable, but high rates can be and are charged in such circumstances.

Two types of construction loans are made. The first type is involved in the custom building of a property for an owner. Since the contractor cannot or will not finance the transaction while in the process, it is necessary to give him "progress" payments which are a specified proportion of the estimated work in place (often 80 to 90 per cent). If the owner must borrow to finance the complete project, it is almost certain that he will not be able to finance it during the construction period. In such cases, the lender who expects to secure the final mortgage has to render the service of granting a construction loan. Custom building often costs much more than estimated, particularly if the owner changes his plans while construction is in process. The increased cost means a larger loan than contemplated. If the owner has no resources other than his equity, the lender usually has to advance the added amount. By virtue of this, the borrowed portion of the whole cost may amount to more than had been planned in the beginning or regarded as conservative.

For example, an owner plans a house for $40,000, and a bank agrees to put up 60 per cent, or $24,000. Let us assume that the owner's equity of $16,000 is all he can raise. If in the course of time and plan changes, the property actually costs $50,000 to build, then the $34,000 the bank will probably have to advance will amount to about a 68 per cent loan. Once a building venture is under way, it is hard for a lender to withdraw even if the expected terms do not work out. The same principle applies in construction loans on other types of property.

The second type of construction loan has to do with speculative building. The speculative builder does not have ready buyers but builds with the expectation of selling completed structures. Often the builder does not own the sites he plans to build on but only has options on them. The owner of the land may agree to "release" the land as the buildings are sold. In this type of deal, the element of costs may be under better control but there is not always a ready sale for speculatively built houses. When this is so, the lender may be faced with the necessity of taking possession of security that has so far not proved very salable. Banks make loans for construction of speculative properties, not because they like the business but because, if the venture proves to be a good one, they will have an inside track on the final financing of the properties. In periods during which there is strong competition for mortgage loans, lending for construction may be necessary to get business.

TERMS OF REAL ESTATE CREDIT

Real estate credits are not materially different from other loans in general principles; they are, however, specialized in the sense that some technical conditions of real estate loans differ greatly from other loan types.

A Good and Enforceable Lien

The implicit nature of a real estate credit is that it depends on property for a good part, perhaps the chief part, of its security. A mortgage is a legal way of giving bond for the payment of a loan according to its terms. The problem is basically a legal one and is frequently tied up with the complex laws of real estate title and ownership.

Owner's Equity

As in all other financial arrangements, the proportion of a loan to the value of the security often is a crude measure of safety. If the creditor puts up a small (conservative) proportion of the funds needed in a real estate deal, it means that the owner (who is also the debtor) has put up a sizable (and also conservative) proportion of the required funds.

In the making of real estate loans, the proportion of the credit advanced to the value of the property has always been one of the prime terms or factors in such credit. The proportion is often covered by the laws regulating the lenders. For example, the national banks are governed by Sec. 24 of the Federal Reserve Act, including the following provisions:

Any national banking association may make real estate loans secured by first liens upon improved real estate, including improved farm land and improved business and residential properties. . . . The amount of any such loan hereafter made shall not exceed 50 per centum of the appraised value of the real estate offered as security and no such loan shall be made for a longer term than five years; except that (1) any such loan may be made in an amount not to exceed 66⅔ per centum of the appraised value of the real estate offered as security and for a term not longer than ten years if the loan is secured by an amortized mortgage, deed of trust, or other such instrument under the terms of which the installment payments are sufficient to amortize 40 per centum or more of the principal of the loan within a period of not more than ten years, and (2) any such loan may be made in an amount not to exceed 66⅔ per centum of the appraised value of the real estate offered as security and for a term not longer than twenty years if the loan is secured by an amortized mortgage, deed of trust, or other such instrument under the terms of which the installment payments are sufficient to amortize the entire principal of the loan within a period of not more than twenty years, and (3) any such loan may be made in an amount not to exceed 75 per centum of the appraised value of the real estate offered as security and for a term not longer than 20 years if the loan is secured by an amortized mortgage, deed of trust, or other such instrument under the terms of which the installment payments are sufficient to amortize the entire principal of the loan within the period ending on the date of its maturity. . . .

State banks are often, though not always, limited by similar provisions. The savings banks in New York State, for example, can make amortized loans up to 80 per cent of the value of real estate property.

While considerable attention has been devoted to the percentage that a mortgage loan may be of the value of the underlying property, rather less attention has been given to the way in which this value is to be determined. The law applying to national banks, quoted above, says that the loan must be figured as a percentage of *appraised* value. Since appraised value often (one might almost say "usually" or "almost always") is not the same as the transaction price involved in a market sale, the way in which an appraised value is arrived at is of the greatest consequence.

Appraisal is a value judgment; but the basis for the judgment, how it is rendered, and the standards used vary widely. Sometimes banks retain professional appraisers, sometimes they use their own staff. In small banks, directors are often called on for appraisals. As recounted elsewhere, the directors' legal responsibility in making loans cannot be evaded, and so appraisal, a necessary step in real estate lending, is often looked upon as a directors' function.

The methods used by appraisers vary widely. Their procedure may be as casual as a pleasant drive to the property in question, with a slowing down of the car as the property is passed. Sometimes the car is stopped long enough for the appraisal committee to walk around the property; they may even go inside and look it over.

At the other extreme, some professional appraisers make the business of appraisal a complex and almost mystifying rite. They appear with a great sheaf of papers and a measuring rule. They crawl into attics and under porches; they peer with flashlight at the hidden parts of basements, all the time making innumerable notations on various papers. When finished, they retire to a quiet spot to complete computations and to write up a report of impressive detail and completeness.

The extreme of methods is not so much an extreme of accuracy; the "quickie" look out of the car window by an experienced and wise old fellow may be a better guide to current market than all the impressive detail of the other method. Being hasty, it can also make mistakes. The real difference in the two methods is in the factors emphasized. It is on this point that the results of appraisals tend to vary so widely. This is not to minimize variation in appraisal under the same methods and conditions. Two bank directors in the same car might come up with fairly sizable differences in opinion. Professional appraisers tend to be closer together, but differences are still possible and likely. It cannot be emphasized too strongly that the real estate market is one of individual commodities; each deal is a separate transaction. The matter of value, however conceived, is always open to difference of opinion.

As those who have studied economics know, there always is, even under idealized conditions, room for a number of concepts of value. So it is fruitful to consider, momentarily, the various kinds of value involved in real estate appraisal. The simplest concept is that of current market value. This sort of value naturally fluctuates with changing demand for real estate. It is likely to be the value concept used by the look-out-of-the-car-window bank director appraisers. Another value concept is that of reproduction cost. This is the cost of the property adjusted for depreciation and, perhaps, for changes in building technology and taste. This sort of value is much less variable. When market demand is low, it is likely to be above market price; when market demand is active, it may fall below market price. Since new houses usually can be built (unless there is a war) when the second condition prevails, it is much less likely to exist for as long as under the first condition.

Still other concepts of value may be distinguished. Some appraisers seem to think in terms of market price, but not the current market price. They have in mind a kind of long-term average market price. If pessimistically inclined, appraisers seem to arrive at a figure which represents the price that a property would bring under a relatively weak market. Sometimes they apply this concept in the reverse direction. In very bad times, they may think of a long-term market value which represents potentialities when the market is less distressed. During the early 1930s, the "real" value of a given real estate property was then thought of as being considerably above what could actually have been secured in the then vastly depressed markets. From 1946 to 1948 when buyer demand was very strong, this same concept was used to reflect a value, certainly below the current market, which represented a longer view of market price. These two appraised values are not the same; the one prevailing in bad times will be under the one of good times.

What bearing does the vast difference in appraisal have on real estate lending practices? The chief significance is that some consistent policy needs to be followed. If a bank uses a very conservative appraisal technique, the proportion of appraised value it is willing to lend can be safely higher (within the limits allowed by law, if any). If the appraisal technique yields high or generous valuations, then the proportion of loan to appraised value needs to be lower.

Repayment Provisions for Real Estate Loans

Real estate loans are repaid in two basic ways: (1) by lump-sum repayment at the end of the contract or (2) by the amortized payment schedule. Lump-sum payment has been largely displaced by the amortized loan.

The amortized loan is one that combines interest and principal payments in a single uniform regular payment. These payments may be made monthly, quarterly, or even annually; for loans for the owner-occupiers of homes, monthly payment is most common because most persons receive their income monthly or oftener. Since the payments are all equal, it naturally follows that the early payments are largely interest and the later ones are largely principal.

Many factors favor the use of amortization. Real estate lenders have found that it has greatly improved the quality of the mortgage market. The proportion of original loan to appraised value of property can be higher with safety in an amortized loan than with a "straight" or lump-sum or "old-fashioned" mortgage. Amortization gets the loan paid off very much after the fashion of rent, and often at rates no higher than those for rent. The reason it works satisfactorily even when the owner's equity is small in the beginning is that this equity is increased with fair rapidity. It is usually true that home mortgage loans do not turn sour in their early years while the borrower is still flushed with the pride of home ownership. Defaults, if they occur at all, are more likely after the property has deteriorated and the family composition has changed. As a general proposition mortgages on owner-occupied homes have had far better credit records than other types of real estate credit. Apart from personal pride, the basic need for shelter tends to make this true. This tendency has been demonstrated repeatedly in research studies of mortgage lending.[1]

---

[1] Lintner, *Mutual Savings Banks in the Mortgage Market,* table 41, p. 362;
Wickens, *Residential Real Estate,* D 47, table 1, pp. 290–291; R. J. Saulnier, *Urban Mortgage Lending by Life Insurance Companies* (a National Bureau of Economic Research study), Princeton University Press, Princeton, N.J., 1957, table 22, p. 84.

Interest Rate Policy

The interest rates on mortgage loans have, in general, been competitive. For this reason the bank that undertakes to make mortgage loans usually has little margin of choice; it offers rates in keeping with the market or makes few loans and then very likely only those that others have already turned down.

Within the margin of competitive action, there is usually a moderate range of choice. Commercial banks have generally chosen to take only the best loans, to enforce conservative standards, but to charge low rates. The commercial-bank mortgage is usually a preferred risk. There is much to be said for this policy; if chances are to be taken, other lenders are better situated for such risk bearing.

Interest Rate on Construction Loans

Construction loans are traditionally a high-interest-rate type of credit. If well-supervised they may produce good returns. Large construction loans have frequently been charged 5 to 6 per cent when the prime loan rate has been at the level of 4 to 5 per cent. Smaller construction loans bear even higher rates. At the same time this type of credit requires close supervision so that these rates do not represent gross additions to profits.

Federal Housing Administration (FHA) Insurance of Mortgage Loans

In 1934, the FHA was established by the Federal government for the promotion of home building. One of the promotional devices used was the insurance of mortgage loans that met certain minimum standards. The insurance means that, if the holder of an insured mortgage suffers a default and cannot secure its correction, he can foreclose on the property, convey it to the FHA, and receive all unpaid principal and interest, and even foreclosure costs in some cases. Thus, while mortgage insurance does not guarantee liquidity, it insures against capital loss. (The discussion here relates to Title II coverage.)

The major requirements for an insured mortgage relate to the character of the property. The FHA has worked out detailed appraisal techniques. They try to be assured that the properties on which they insure mortgages are sound and that they fit the needs of the applicant borrowers. Another requirement for an insured loan is that it must be in amortized form.

When the FHA was first operating, mortgage credit had been blighted by widespread delinquencies and default of lump-sum mortgage maturities. The leading innovation of the FHA was to extend the principle of amortization, or monthly payments, to a large proportion of real estate loans. Prior to that time this very useful practice had been largely neglected except by savings and loan associations. As a result, largely of that innovation, almost all new real estate loans are made on an amortization basis.

The insurance of mortgages makes them a much more acceptable asset for commercial banks. At the same time, the more liberal terms available in insured mortgages make the granters of insured credit more competitive with the lenders that have more liberal conventional credit standards. The insurance of mortgages, however, does not constitute a complete safeguard and the lender must observe normally prudent practices. In general, the mortgage-lending practices and appraisal standards established under FHA insurance have tended to improve the quality of mortgages in the market. Their one drawback is that rates on insured mortgages are fixed by law and the FHA, under congressional pressure, frequently squeezes these rates down to the point where they are not in line with other market rates. Discounts in the secondary market have offset some of this disadvantage but have not been a fully satisfactory cure.

The terms under which mortgages may be insured have tended to be dominated by political rather than economic considerations. Liberalization of these terms by Congress has often been in response to pressures of home building and financing trade associations. In general, the terms have been made particularly easy for very small mortgages and generally somewhat easier on newly constructed houses than on existing property. These terms have been changed frequently, usually in an effort to give a new stimulus to housing. Liberalization of down payment and maturity terms has had considerable influence on the terms available on conventional noninsured mortgages.

Two other types of FHA loan insurance programs should be mentioned. First, FHA-insured loans are made for the repair and modernization of homes. Loans up to amounts of $3,500 may be insured, with maturity limited to five years. The true rate of interest on this credit is almost 10 per cent. This type of credit is frequently arranged through building supply materials dealers or specialized home modernization contractors. Second, rental housing loans are also insured by the FHA under certain circumstances. The rate of interest allowed on such credit, however, has frequently made these loans unattractive to commercial banks, particularly since they seldom generate useful customer relationships.

VA Mortgage-guarantee Programs

While the programs of mortgage insurance under the FHA were primarily to stimulate real estate activity, the Veterans Administration program was primarily a special expression of national gratitude to the veterans of its armed services. It was intended to make home buying possible for veterans on unusually favorable terms. The privilege has therefore been limited to those who have served in the Armed Forces. The guarantee of VA loans has also become subject to frequent political intervention. The terms have been liberalized in a series of congressional changes. Loans guaranteed under the VA program tend to be somewhat smaller than the mortgages insured by the FHA. The maximum rate of interest permissible has also been lower. This low fixed rate of interest has tended to make VA loans unattractive in higher money rate periods. Some discounting even of new loans has been a device used to conceal higher true interest rates but official limits to these discounts have often made this evasion ineffective. Banks and other lenders have made funds available for this type of lending more in slack money markets than in tight money markets.

Acquiring Mortgages from Mortgage Bankers

Most commercial banks prefer to extend mortgage credit directly to improve customer relationships. Because of the unit banking system recourse to mortgage bankers as a source of mortgages has not been needed. However, the relatively few banks that do not have local outlets for mortgage funds have found it useful to acquire mortgages from this source. Trust accounts have acquired mortgages in this way when the trustee bank was not in a position to originate the type of mortgages needed. Most of the mortgages originated by mortgage bankers and supplied by them for investment by others have been either insured by the FHA or guaranteed by the VA.

Mortgage-lending Policies

Is the security for a mortgage to be found chiefly in the property on which a lien is held, or is it in the economic status of the borrower? The literature of mortgage lending has emphasized the importance of the mortgaged property as security, but little attention has been given to the borrower. This is unfortunate; lenders have discovered all too often that the foreclosure of mortgage loans was not only expensive and unproductive but also created ill will. A good mortgage lender would prefer to have as few foreclosures as possible. A mortgage loan should be judged by the finances of the borrower as well as by the value of the property as security.

The application of this principle to a business loan secured by real estate is obvious common sense. For the loan on an income-producing investment property, the finances of the investor are important but not predominately so. If a mortgage loan is not satisfied in full in case of foreclosure by liquidation of the property, the lender has the nominal right of securing a deficiency judgment for the remainder. However, experience shows that deficiency judgments are hard to get and harder to enforce. In these cases the property itself is pretty much the security foundation. A good lender should be convinced that a loan on rental property is a good business deal and that it will stand on its own feet.

Loans to home owners fall in a different category. The factors of security here range from questions of the social and moral tenacity in sticking to home ownership, the relationship of income size to debt, the stability of income over various phases of the business cycle, and related factors. An old rule, or various versions of it, relates income to total outlay for a home. The cost of a home should not exceed two and one-half times the annual income of the home buyer. The appropriate ratio for higher income families is sometime thought to be no more than two times. Another version of this rule is that the cost of a home should not exceed two and one-half or three times income *after income taxes*. The exclusion of taxes takes care of much of the difference of income levels.

This rule in its many forms is a good one, but it has exceptions and problems. One of the exceptions is that it depends on the stability of the income. A person holding a secure job, such as a schoolteacher or a middle-income salaried person in a stable food-processing concern, might be justified in pressing the limits of these rules or even exceeding them. On the other hand, a salesman for machine tools probably should not spend too large a proportion of his peak income for a home; perhaps not more than one to one and one-half times his annual income. Salesmen's incomes are notoriously variable and the machine-tool industry varies over phases of the business cycle. For an actress, a horse jockey, a gambler, or anyone else with unstable and uncertain incomes, a good rule would be, no credit! They should pay cash. If mortgage lenders required applicant-borrowers to be prudent in their financial commitments, there would be fewer foreclosed mortgage loans.

How large can the total mortgage loan portfolio of a commercial bank be? A national bank has its portfolio limit settled automatically: it cannot hold real estate mortgages in excess of its capital and unimpaired surplus or 60 per cent of its time deposits, whichever amount is greater. Should some national banks observe limits below this? Should other commercial banks, when not limited by law, adopt some rule of self-limitation? For all commercial banks the amount of mortgages held is about three-fourths what this rule would permit.

Any banks not in a position to promote an adequate volume of mortgage lending might forgo the business completely, but most banks would be better advised to impose limits on the quality of loans rather than on the quantity. A good qualitative limit will usually act as an automatic quantitative limit. If a bank has otherwise made adequate liquidity provisions, the only factor which might argue for restriction of mortgage loans beyond the national bank rule would be a thin capital equity. Even with limited capital but adequate liquidity, high-quality mortgages should be manageable.

Wholesale Credit to Real Estate Mortgage Lenders

The growth of large-scale speculative home building has given rise to the origination of mortgages by specialized mortgage banking companies that are not investors in these obligations. To finance this activity banks extend short-term credit to them. While the great bulk of this credit has been extended to mortgage companies or mortgage bankers, some is also extended to life insurance companies, savings and loan associations, and even occasionally to builders themselves. The purpose of extending "warehouse" credit on mortgages is to bridge the gap between the time when loans are originated and the time when ultimate investors are ready to purchase them. Mortgage bankers usually have extensive and complex commitments or other contractual arrangements with ultimate investors such as life insurance companies or mutual savings banks. However, they cannot always be confident of receiving funds from these investors at exactly the same time when the mortgage credit must be extended. Bank credit bridges this gap.

The amount of this credit has never achieved large magnitude in terms of national credit totals but has varied between $1 billion and $2 billion. Nevertheless, those relatively few banks that specialize in this business have made it a leading outlet for credit.

Commitment arrangements undertaken by banks with respect to the mortgage lenders are somewhat more formal than the line-of-credit arrangements used for other borrowers. Firm commitments are usually given only when there is the payment of a fee. The volume of commitments has averaged roughly one-half the volume of credit outstanding.

17

Lending to Farmers

Nowhere is the art of bank lending more casual than in rural areas. The scientific analysis of balance sheets and income statements, the exchange of credit reports, systematized credit analysis are needed in the city. Country lending is more by rule of thumb. Because of this characteristic, very little of its nature can be communicated by book, article, or precept. It is, as all arts, learned by the doing. This fact, doubtless, explains why bank examiners with a city background sometimes view with mistrust the apparently unsystematic and hazardous way in which country banks make loans, and, it must be admitted, when farm lending is done carelessly the results can be bad. Many country bankers go on in their apparently aimless way, extending credit, carrying some slow loans, it is true, but seldom suffering large losses.

Agricultural credit is important to the banks and to the agricultural community. Some of the more profitable and as yet unexploited opportunities for banking lie in the remaining profitable agricultural areas. The sustained profitability of some Southern and Western agriculture in the last few years, in spite of general agricultural problems, is evidence supporting this general view.

SPECIALIZED NATURE OF AGRICULTURAL PRODUCTION

General statements about the extension of credit to farmers may be of relatively little use because many banks have to deal with highly specialized types of agriculture for which general rules cannot be set. For example, in recent years the production of eggs has come to be a quite specialized business. It approaches factory production methods in many of its aspects. Granting credit to this type of operation has highly specialized requirements. A similar situation prevails in the raising of broilers. Again, rather than select seed from among their own crop, many farmers depend on the product of specialized seed producers. Another agricultural specialty is the feeding or finishing of beef. This business is a relatively old one, but the technology of feeding, the use of antibiotics and other new devices have tended to shorten the feeding period—a development that has been encouraged by changes in consumer taste for somewhat lighter beef.

The influence of these changes on financial requirements has been partly to increase the specialized nature of capital equipment. Such highly specialized capital may be useful only in the hands of a few skilled farm managers. The increase in specialization has also tended to expand the amount of short-term credit that is needed. The farm is no longer as self-sufficient an economic unit.

PROSPECTS FOR DEMAND

The demand for agricultural credit is subject to a number of conflicting influences. Some factors have tended to reduce the demand for credit. The number of farmers has been declining steadily for quite a few years. The greater productivity of the individual farmer and the natural limits of the human stomach have combined to diminish the number of farmers needed. This naturally has tended to reduce the demand for agricultural credit. In addition, during periods of prosperity some farmers have been able to accumulate considerable net worth so that they can conduct large-scale farming operations with little resort to outside financing.

Other factors have tended to increase demand. The business of farming now requires larger farms and more equipment. The number of farmers has been reduced but the remaining farmers have increased the average size of their land holdings. New and complex machinery has been needed to increase productivity. These two factors have tended to increase the demand for long-term agricultural credit. The new methods of farming have also tended to increase the proportion of cash expenses relative to gross recepts. Farmers spend more for fertilizers, fuel, insecticides, and operating costs of such specialized projects as irrigation. This increases the ratio of cash expenses to receipts and tends to increase the demand for short-term agricultural credit.

PRICE INSTABILITY: ITS EFFECTS ON FARM CREDIT

In the alternation of good and bad times, most businesses respond to lowered prices by some curtailment of output. This helps to keep prices from dropping even further. In farming, quite the opposite seems to be true. Farmers seem to produce about as much during bad times as during good times; sometimes it seems as if they produce more. Many reasons account for this phenomenon: The productive cycle is longer than in most other lines. The cycle of agricultural production—crop rotation, the balancing of stock food with livestock production, the long life cycle of livestock—makes it difficult for a farmer to change plans and almost impossible for him to do so quickly. Farmers sometimes seem to increase production in order to overcome the loss of income due to lower prices. As the result, the full impact of lowered consumer demand is taken out on prices. Agricultural prices therefore tend to be highly variable. Egg and broiler production may approach modern factory methods in the techniques used, but the prices of eggs and broilers are far more variable than the prices of most factory products.

Unstable farm prices make agricultural income highly variable. It is also reflected in farm-land prices, which vary through a wide range. There have been times when the prices of agricultural land have gone up far more than agricultural income seemed to justify, but there have been times when the land could not be marketed except at sacrifice prices. The fortunes of farmers are extraordinarily variable.

It is this price instability that makes agricultural credit uncertain. A banker may judge accurately all the other credit factors, but farm price prospects are always uncertain. Because farming prices can move both rapidly and widely, there is often little that the banker can do to protect his institution or help his customer to protect himself. Since this great variability is due to outside forces, bankers are always reluctant to use harsh methods of collection against decent, responsible, well-intentioned, and competent farmers.

Federal governmental programs for the support and guarantee of agricultural income have, of course, modified this situation materially. While the shape of these programs has been changed many times, the continuance of some sort of program seems almost assured. The platforms of the two major parties vie with each other in making promises to the farmers; the only choice is as to which one offers more, more sincerely.

How much assurance do support programs give the banker? They have large elements of political horse trading in them. The programs usually are firm for one year in advance but not longer. Short-term agricultural credit is very much guaranteed by these programs but not long-term credit.

Long-term loans for a type of agriculture that is overextended as a result of highly artificial price supports create serious problems. For example, many more potatoes are grown than are needed. With growth of income and prosperity, it is usually found that consumption shifts from low-cost foods like potatoes to more expensive ones like meat. The outlook for potatoes may grow even bleaker in course of time. For a brief while a support program for potatoes was followed but it ended in dismal and evident failure. The position of potato farmers was even worse than it would have been without the effort.

THE KIND OF CREDIT NEEDED BY FARMERS

Credit for agricultural use includes all three maturity categories: long-term, intermediate-term, short-term. Maturity has fully as much significance for agriculture as for any other credit-using group, perhaps more.

The *long-term* credit needs of farmers are usually associated with the purchase of land. Land is, of course, the chief productive asset of most farming ventures. The problems of land and its relationship to agricultural need vary so widely that generalization cannot be accurate. In some areas agricultural land is cheap; land that sells for $5, $10, or $15 an acre is not unknown. Often cheap land is associated with poor agriculture, a low level of farm income, and general rural poverty. Bank lending under such circumstances is bound to be difficult and risky. Sometimes, however, cheap land is associated with extensive types of agriculture: grazing land for livestock or the dry "dust-bowl" land which nevertheless in some years produces good wheat crops. There are good profits in these lines but lots of risk.

The other extreme is that of highly specialized agricultural land: the citrus orchards and irrigated specialty croplands worth thousands of dollars an acre. Here agricultural income is usually high, the system productive. Such a situation has its special risks. Highly specialized crops are about as subject to the vicissitudes of untamed nature as other farming ventures. An unexpected blight, a new insect pest (or the disappearance of a protective insect due to overuse of insecticides such as DDT), and similar hazards arise without warning. When they do, the losses are very great. Lending on land in such areas can lead to great losses because of such unexpected developments. Both types of land are associated with special agricultural problems with which the banker must be fully familiar before extending credit.

Still another type of risk for highly specialized agriculture must be recognized. Sometimes this specialization is due to the fact that a certain area seems to be uniquely adapted to certain crops. For example, it may be found that head lettuce can grow in a certain valley. The temperature cycle and the rainfall needed for this crop are better combined than in any other area. Later a new irrigated area proves to be adaptable to this crop which makes the rainfall requirement unnecessary and opens up new land for this special use. Land in the older production area loses value. Since long-term credit to agriculture is usually based on land, the hazards of land use are reflected in the banking risk of such credit. For this reason some banks require that the owner's equity be rather larger than in the case of stable urban property.

The hazard of highly specialized farming land can be illustrated by still another example. In days gone by, the farms near cities often commanded a premium for the growing of "truck" crops, that is, the highly perishable vegetables that must be sold promptly. The development of high-speed refrigerated trucking and transportation reduced the special value of this land.

Partly because farm lands have been used by city investors as inflation hedges but also partly because farmers themselves have been trying to increase the size of their holdings, the current yield on much farm land is lower than on urban real estate. This high price of farm lands relative to income produced creates a financing problem. The margin of safety left for the coverage of long-term credit has become smaller. Where thinly protected long-term credit is outstanding, the protection of short-term credit is likewise somewhat reduced.

Because of the general banking reluctance to go in for long-term credit, the lending to agriculture on this basis has often been left to other financial agencies. Life insurance companies at one time were large lenders on the security of farm land. Governmental credit has been important in this field. Banks are less reluctant to lend on this basis than formerly, but the risks are undoubtedly as great now as ever, possibly higher because of high land values.

The *intermediate-term* credit needs of agriculture are associated with the provision of machinery and livestock, sometimes also for farm improvements such as soil-conservation programs. Since this latter case will be illustrated later, it is not covered here.

With the increasing mechanization of agriculture, the provision for required machinery becomes a much greater financial problem. In years gone by, agriculture was on a handicraft basis; it used a technology that was only moderately advanced from that of our grandfather's time. Within the past generation, it has gone through a technological revolution of as yet unappraisable proportions. This was not because the scientific basis for increased productivity suddenly emerged; the scientists and agricultural engineers had been preparing the groundwork for this change for many years.

Economic pressure brought the change with a rush, the compelling factor that hastened the rate of change being the higher price for agricultural labor. Farmers found that they could no longer supply their labor requirements by raising large families and expecting them to stay on the farm; city life drained off this source of labor. Higher city wages made it impossible for the farmer to get the traditional hired man for a few dollars a month plus "findings." The supply of seasonal labor on which farmers had depended to handle peak requirements—the "oakie" and "wet-back" hordes—are no longer available when the labor of the country is fully employed.

Machinery is the answer. Labor, including the farmer's own labor, has to be used more efficiently and economically. The technology of scientific farming, which has been accumulating for years, is called into active use.

The financing of machinery for farmers has sometimes taken a form not unlike that employed in the financing of industrial machinery, or that of consumer financing. The installment form of credit can be adapted to farm loans, but the system of monthly amortization is not always applicable. Some forms of agriculture, such as dairying, produce year-round income and are adaptable to the system of monthly amortization. Most agricultural pursuits, however, are not of this type. Even quarterly amortization is not usually very applicable. To an increasing extent, bankers and other grantors of credit are working out individual or "tailor-made" credit arrangements. They calculate the periods of high income during the year and arrange payment plans that will concentrate the larger payments at those times.

The use of intermediate-term financing to build up livestock herds is not uncommon. Again, this is a highly specialized type of lending. The banker needs to have as full a command of the technical problems as the borrowing farmer, and perhaps even more of the long-term economics of stock breeding. Such credit is often highly constructive for the income and welfare of a community, but it is not without hazard.

Short-term credit has a regular place in agriculture. The annual cycle of nature makes agricultural credit traditionally appropriate to commercial banks; it is short-term (less than a year), self-liquidating in the true sense of the word, and automatically backed up with security—the farm crop or product itself. True short-term credit for agriculture is somewhat longer than common in other forms of traditional commercial credit. That was recognized in the original Federal Reserve Act when the allowable maturity for agricultural paper was 9 months, whereas the allowable maturity for commercial and industrial loans was 90 days.

The use of security for short-term farm loans depends to a considerable extent on the section of the country. In the South, for example, security for short-term borrowing is frequently required. Chattel mortgages on livestock and farm equipment are common. Security for short-term farming loans is rather less frequent in the Middle West, but more common in farm loans than in urban business loans.

CONVERSION OF SHORT-TERM LOANS INTO LONG-TERM CREDIT

All bankers are familiar with the process by which borrowers, normally asking for short-term credit, end up converting this short-term loan into a long-term credit by applying retained earnings to capital expansion. This conversion is a particularly great hazard in farm finance. Farmers are often rather unsophisticated about financial affairs. The only protection a bank can give itself is to enforce strictly its requirements for budgeting and repayment scheduling and to insist on an annual cleanup of all short-term credit. This sort of policy may seem harsh, but it is the one way in which the danger of conversion can be adequately met.

Scheduling of a short-term loan to avoid the risk of conversion of it into long-term credit can be illustrated simply. Suppose that a farmer goes to his bank on July 1 and applies for a loan. During the course of the interview he discloses the following facts: he expects to have a corn crop of about 6,000 bushels, to sell one-half of it for cash in September and October, and to keep the rest for feeding. He expects to market about 100 hogs at 225 pounds, half in December and half in January. Assume corn prices are $1 a bushel and hog prices $20 a hundred. Cash costs of "making the crop" are expected to total about $3,600, half of which normally falls in June, July, and August. Family living expenses average about $200 a month. The farmer has now drawn his checking account down to a working minimum and wants to borrow to meet his requirements but pay back as soon as possible.

A budget could be worked out as shown in the accompanying tabulation.

Month	Income		Outgo		Net of income and outgo	Cumulative, starting with July
	Corn	Hogs	Crops	Family		
July.........	......	......	$ 600	$ 200	$− 800	$− 800
August.......	......	......	600	200	− 800	−1,600
September....	$1,500	......	200	200	+1,100	− 500
October......	1,500	......	200	200	+1,100	+ 600
November....	......	......	200	200	− 400	+ 200
December....	......	$2,250	200	200	+1,850	+2,050
January......	......	2,250	200	200	+1,850	+3,900
February.....	......	......	200	200	− 400	+3,500
March.......	......	......	200	200	− 400	+3,100
April........	......	......	200	200	− 400	+2,700
May.........	......	......	200	200	− 400	+2,300
June.........	......	......	600	200	− 800	+1,500
Total......	$3,000	$4,500	$3,600	$2,400	......	$+1,500

Since it was said that half the crop outlay fell in June, July, and August, it is assumed that the other half should be spread evenly over the remaining months. This is, of course, better than a rough guess. Assuming this happens, a loan of $1,600, half disbursed in July and the rest in August, could be paid off partly in September and retired completely in October. The farmer can, unless conditions change, stay out of debt for the remainder of the year.

When the loan plan contemplates payments for more than a year, the same sort of device could be used for estimating the normal flow of farming funds.

CREDIT ANALYSIS: INFORMAL
OR AGRICULTURAL STYLE

Although, as was said in the beginning, the paraphernalia of formal credit analysis as practiced by city banks does not work any too well in farm lending, some informal catch-as-catch-can devices can be used by a banker in analyzing farm finance. The opportunities for practicing such analysis are improving.

The difficulty has been that farmers, though really small business units, have seldom kept satisfactory financial records. Under the constant prodding of state agricultural colleges and extension units, some farmers have established bookkeeping systems, but these have often been more technological than financial in nature. A farmer, once started on a program of dairy herd improvement, may keep milk production records; the keeping of cost records is less likely. The failure of farmers to maintain adequate accounting records is not unnatural. The good farmer is a technician, not a financier. The mysteries of modern insecticides with their complex chemical backgrounds floor most of us; a modern farmer rattles off these chemical names as if he understood them. But not balance sheets! As a result, the basic financial records needed for credit analysis are seldom available.

Income taxes, of course, increased the pressure for farm accounting records. Few farmers paid income taxes before the recent war. While the number is still smaller than one would

FEDERAL RESERVE BANK OF MINNEAPOLIS—Form No. CR3.   STOCKMAN
                                                                                                        OR
                                                                                                      FARMER

NAME_____   ADDRESS_____
                    (Typewrite full name and address)

To_____
        For the purpose of obtaining loans and discounting paper with you and otherwise procuring credit from time to time, I furnish the following true
and accurate statement of my financial condition.
        I agree to and will notify you immediately in writing of any materially unfavorable change in my financial condition and in the absence of such
notice or of a new and full written statement, this may be considered as a continuing statement and substantially correct, and it is hereby expressly
agreed that upon application for further credit, this statement shall have the same force and effect as if delivered as an original statement of my financial condition at the time such further credit is requested.

        Financial condition as of_____19_____
                            (Fill all blanks, writing "No" or "None" where necessary to complete information)

ASSETS			LIABILITIES		
		(omit cents)			(omit cents)
LIVESTOCK: Number			ENCUMBRANCE ON LIVESTOCK AS FOLLOWS:		
_____Steers and heifers, 1 year old, @ $_____per head $_____			To_____ $_____		
_____Steers and heifers, 2 years old, @ _____per head_____			Dated_____19_____due_____19____		
_____Steers, 3 and 4 years old, @ _____per head_____			Covering_____		
_____Cows_____@ _____per head_____					
_____Calves (19____)____@ _____per head_____			Personal property taxes paid to_____19____		
_____Bulls_____@ _____per head_____			CROP MORTGAGE AND TO WHOM		
_____Horses_____@ _____per head_____					
_____Hogs_____@ _____per head_____			OTHER BORROWED MONEY (itemize)_____		
_____Sheep_____@ _____per head_____					
_____@ _____per head_____					
_____TOTAL NUMBER SUB TOTAL $_____			ACCOUNTS PAYABLE_____		
FEED ON HAND_____					
GRAIN AND PRODUCE FOR SALE_____			AMOUNT DUE RELATIVES (itemize)_____		
CASH IN BANK_____					
GOVERNMENT BONDS AND LISTED SECURITIES_____			INCOME TAX UNPAID_____		
NOTES RECEIVABLE (ALL GOOD)_____			ALL OTHER DEBTS_____		
TOTAL CURRENT ASSETS $_____			TOTAL CURRENT LIABILITIES $_____		
MACHINERY AND EQUIPMENT_____			ENCUMBRANCE ON REAL ESTATE_____		
ALL OTHER PERSONAL PROPERTY AND OF WHAT COMPOSED_____			To_____		
			Dated_____19_____due_____19____		
REAL ESTATE:			Interest paid to_____19____		
City or town_____			Covering_____		
(Including homestead _____$_____) .			Taxes paid to_____19____		
Farm real estate_____					
(Including homestead _____$_____)					
_____acres in_____County @ $_____					
_____acres in_____County @ _____					
			TOTAL LIABILITIES $_____		
			NET WORTH_____		
TOTAL ASSETS $_____			TOTAL LIABILITIES AND NET WORTH $_____		

Describe contingent liabilities: Guarantees, endorsements, litigations, etc._____

SUMMARY OF INCOME AND DEDUCTIONS COMPUTED ON A CASH RECEIPTS AND DISBURSEMENTS BASIS
For period from_____to_____

Sale of livestock raised_____	$_____		Expenses_____	$_____	
Sale of produce raised_____			Depreciation_____		
Other farm income_____			Net operating loss deduction_____		
Profit on sale of livestock and other items purchased_____					
GROSS PROFITS $_____			TOTAL DEDUCTIONS $_____		
			NET FARM PROFIT $_____		

(OVER)

FIGURE 17-1. Interview statement prepared by the Federal Reserve Bank of Minneapolis and recommended by them for farm lending in that area.

REAL ESTATE

DESCRIPTION	IMPROVEMENTS	MARKET VALUE	MORTGAGES
		$	$
TOTALS		$	$

GENERAL INFORMATION

Name of person in whom real estate title is vested

Nature of ownership (fee simple, leasehold or under contract for deed)

Details of lease for any rented land

Yearly rental $ Paid to

Amount of any unsatisfied judgments Details

Fire insurance in force $ Windstorm insurance $

Life insurance $ Beneficiary Loans on life insurance $

Details

Names of partners

Details of partnership agreement

Place of residence Since Former residence

Age Married Children boys, ages to girls, ages to

Names of other persons who are acquainted with your personal and financial condition

Remarks and other information

I, the undersigned, hereby certify and declare that the foregoing statement and representations constitute a true and accurate account of my financial condition as of the date first above given.

Date signed 19 Signed

Statements submitted to Federal Reserve Bank must either be signed originals or certified copies. If copies are furnished, the following certificate should be signed on behalf of the submitting bank by an authorized officer.

WE HEREBY CERTIFY THAT THE FOREGOING IS A TRUE AND EXACT COPY OF A SIGNED FINANCIAL STATEMENT OF THE ABOVE NAMED APPLICANT FOR CREDIT NOW ON FILE IN THIS BANK.

(NAME OF MEMBER BANK)

(OFFICIAL SIGNATURE)

(Title)

(Over)

expect from an observation of farm prosperity, it has grown. Once a farmer has to file an income tax return, he needs at least a simple system of record or bookkeeping. If he is to be assured of having his expense deductions allowed, he needs to have confirming records.

It is possible for a good banker to prepare sketchy *pro forma* statements in the process of interviewing farm customers. The farmer will tell what he owns and what he owes, and these figures can be converted into a simple proprietary balance sheet. The farmer is usually able to tell how much his gross revenues are. When this is combined with some account of costs, a rough nonaccrual statement of earnings can be computed. The form for such an interview statement is shown in Figure 17-1. This form, prepared by the Federal Reserve Bank of Minneapolis, has rather complete detail on many points that are not generally applicable. While the form appears to be complex, it can be prepared quickly. When an area has special farming problems, a form appropriate to the area and reflecting these special problems should be devised.

If a banker collects *pro forma* balance sheets for a number of years on a consistent valuation basis, he can, after making allowance for family consumption of the farmer, check the accuracy of his direct estimates of net income with changes of proprietary worth in the balance sheets.

Not only are records of this sort useful to the bank in its credit analysis; they are often lifesavers for the farmers themselves. They give a better notion of progress (or lack of it) than could be evident without such estimates.

GOVERNMENT COMPETITION

More than in any other field of credit, the Federal government has entered into lending to farmers. The agricultural credit agencies date back to 1916, but their biggest growth was in the early 1930s. The number of different Federal agencies that lend to farmers is large and impressive. The proliferation of agricultural lending agencies has been due to the political potency of the farmer. For years, farmers blamed their troubles on a "shortage of money" and were correspondingly distrustful of banks. They felt themselves being discriminated against in the credit sphere.

The competition of the governmental lending agencies has usually been more about rates than any other factor. Many of the agencies offer rates below those that banks can, or feel they can, afford. In terms of services, the banks are almost always better equipped to beat the agencies; they are not hampered by formalities and rigid rules.

AGRICULTURAL LOAN POLICIES

The problems of loan policy for agricultural credit are not unlike those of other fields, but they assume special guises and forms with which the banker must deal.

For example, the banker who is located in an agricultural area and who grants farm loans must often face the problem of a crop failure. This is not unlike the problem that an urban banker must face when dealing with borrowers who are reliable and effective but who suffer from hard times. The banker's choice is often this: If he presses for the collection of his loan immediately, he is likely to be able to recover the amount lent without loss. If he does so, he is likely to embarrass borrowers and invite the customer's enmity; he may even earn the unwelcome reputation of being a "hard man." For all the supposed hardheartedness of bankers, this is almost always quite the opposite of their intentions. In practice, they have usually been generous about extensions in such circumstances and have often gone to the extreme of endangering their own institution rather than undertake harsh collection policies. In the case of a crop failure, a banker often can feel that because of this act of nature, he should not proceed within his contractual rights but renew and extend or even increase loans as needed in each case. The trouble is that a crop failure is likely to hit most farmers of a given area in about the same way at the same time. It is not isolated cases of trouble with which the bank must deal. A severe agricultural failure in an area can produce an "adverse balance of payments." More is paid to outsiders than is collected from them. The pressure on a bank of possible adverse balance of payments cannot be dismissed, no matter how sympathetic the banker may be. Crop insurance can be purchased for some products. Insurance against hazards such as hail damage to cereal grains or hurricane damage to citrus fruit is available. Where this is true, the foresighted banker may require his farm borrowers to buy insurance.

Another problem of farm loan policy is that of farmers' holding their crops after harvest for a more favorable price. Such speculation is practiced widely. In some lines, the practice is so widespread that existing commercial storage facilities could not accommodate the whole crop if it were marketed soon after harvest.

There is a widespread belief among farmers that crop prices are lower right after harvest than at any other time. Statistical studies indicate that agricultural prices for stable and nonperishable farm products sometimes have a moderate seasonal pattern, but this pattern is often negligible, at times being less than the cost of storage. Thus, all that a farmer may make by holding his crop beyond the early marketing season may be no more than the storage fee. On-farm storage, while widely practiced, cannot be expected to save this fee. Farm storage facilities are often makeshift and poor. Shrinkage losses or loss of quality more than offset the normal storage fees. But farmers persist in holding crops after harvest just as some men persist in trying to fill inside straights. Because the profits are occasionally very attractive, even if the odds are against the practice, they keep on doing it, again and again.

What view should banks take of this practice? Naturally, the farmer who holds after harvest is not able to liquidate his loan as promptly as the one who does not. In general, the banker might take the view that in dealing with a secure farm loan, it is not his place to run the farmer's business. He can advise but should not impose his views. Where the short-term credit extended by a bank is a material proportion of the value of the crops that the farmer proposes to hold beyond harvest, the banker has good reason for insisting on prompt liquidation and credit retirement. The rich can afford to speculate; the poor cannot.

What view should banks take of the essentially constructive loan to a young and beginning farmer? Such a person often has very little capital. This sounds like bad credit, something to be avoided; but if bankers had always refused to make such loans, many now prosperous and productive farmers could not have got started so rapidly or at all.

The problem comes up in farm lending more often than elsewhere because it has been the tradition to start farming with less capital than most other businesses. The basic cost for the smallest plant in many small manufacturing lines is less than the cost of a minimum-sized farm. Yet those who would hesitate to start a manufacturing enterprise without a reasonable amount of capital sometimes try to start a farming enterprise.

SOIL CONSERVATION LOANS: AN EXAMPLE

Many types of agricultural loans are more important than those for soil conservation. This type of credit, however, illustrates excellently several facets of bank lending problems.

One of the great agricultural problems in this country is the erosion of soil. We live, literally, off the few inches of our topsoil. Topsoil is produced by decaying organic matter accumulated over long years. Without this thin layer of topsoil plants would hardly grow at all; the world would starve. When land is unused, this topsoil is protected by grass, weeds, or other surface plants; naked topsoil can be carried away by either wind or water, the great eroders.

When sloping land is first plowed, perhaps to be used for row crops with the rows running down the slopes, the stage is set for erosion. Running water washes off the topsoil. Those who have seen the ravages of the dust bowl or the eroded slopes of some of our older farming communities know what this means: bare gullied soil no longer able to support plant life. To keep on living well, we must conserve our soil.

Agronomists have developed techniques for stopping the waste process. By seeded waterways, terraces, and contour planting, they can stop erosion and reverse the direction of fertility change. This process, however, is costly. It often requires the use of specialized conservation contractors and may involve forgoing cash crops during the developmental stage. Time after time it has been shown that soil conservation programs pay off well; but they take money.

A bank that has space in its loan portfolio for some intermediate-term credit can provide the money. To do so safely, however, it must be prepared to handle all aspects of this kind of credit. First, it needs to have an officer who understands fully the techniques, costs, and rewards of soil conservation. Second, it needs to be able to develop and supervise a budget and repayment schedule for such an operation. Finally, it needs customers who have the technical ability, integrity, and perseverance to stick with a program for which the rewards may be rather slow in appearing.

FINANCING IRRIGATION

Irrigation is another important technological development in improving the productivity of farming. This is particularly true in those areas in which natural rainfall is light. Although practiced for centuries, recent development of lightweight aluminum and plastic pipe combined with better trenching machinery has greatly widened the potential range of applications for irrigation. The resort to irrigation, however, increases demands for both long-term and short-term credit. Long-term credit involved in irrigation is substantial when large-scale trenching, the installation of deep wells, and costly pumping and distributing equipment are required. Short-term credit may be needed to meet the considerably heavier seed and fertilizer costs, particularly for nitrogenous fertilizers when the balance of plant food requirements is changed by greater availability of water. Operating costs also may include fuel as well as repairs, maintenance expenses, and added labor in the operation of irrigation equipment.

The financing of the short-term portion of such credit requirements generally offers substantial opportunities for commercial banks. When irrigation is practiced by experienced and competent farm managers it can be quite profitable. It may, however, create considerable risk because the technology of irrigation is often complex.

PROMOTION OF AGRICULTURAL CREDIT

Most banks located in farming areas lend to farmers to some extent. The lending policies vary as widely as the bankers who frame them. Of recent years a rather more systematic pattern for making farming loans has emerged. A number of banks have developed outstanding programs for granting agricultural credit.

More and more, banks are employing one or more trained *farm representatives*. These representatives, as might be expected, work outside the bank the greater part of their time. However, they usually spend a part of their time in the bank on market days. The extent to which they are active and responsible loan officers in their own right varies, but in most cases they have much of the real responsibility, even if on an informal basis, for lending to farmers. The farm representative is also particularly useful to a bank which has farm loans that are in trouble. As a matter of fact, some farm representatives were first hired to work out such distressed loan problems and later retained to avoid their recurrence. They can help to supervise farm operations and, if need be, manage farm properties taken over by the bank to satisfy claims.

Banks are also finding that the promotion of agricultural credit is helped by their county agricultural agent. He can be used extensively by the bank. His opinion is usually available on technical problems, and his advice on economic problems is worth respectful attention.

Some banks have used spectacular promotional devices for selling the loan services of their institution to farmers. One banker, for example, promoted dairy herd improvement (and incidentally made many a good loan) by buying a purebred bull, the services of which were made available to customers' dairy herds by artificial insemination. Another banker mounted a power paint-spray outfit on a small trailer and lent it to farmers for painting their buildings. In addition to creating good will, the improved value of the property which secured the bank loans was probably enough to compensate for the use of the equipment. Still another bank provided an enclosed auction trailer, where payments and other auction details could be settled. This bank also served coffee and doughnuts at the auctions its officers clerked. This is promotion in the style of Main Street, not Madison Avenue.

Part V

INVESTMENT MANAGEMENT

Some elements of investment management have already been considered in Part II, Chapters 4 to 7, where liquidity was the first consideration, income was secondary. Liquidity uses of investments, however, do not exhaust the subject. Where and when loan demand does not pinch available funds, funds may be invested primarily for the purpose of providing income. Such residual investment operations, while not central to commercial banking, are important to some banks. Investment policy inevitably provides one of the most interesting and critical paradoxes of banking. The background circumstances of a situation where loan demands do not exhaust available funds imply a need for income. Pressure of "need" for income, however, often tends to cramp an investment officer in pursuing a successful program. To serve income needs in the long-term sense he often should be free from pressure to produce income in the short run. Part V describes the various policies that are used to resolve this conflict of considerations.

Part V

18

General Investment
Practices and Policies

Priorities in the management of bank funds were discussed in
Chapter 1. It was suggested there that the second priority in
the application of bank funds is provision of an adequate degree
of liquidity for the operation of a bank. This is usually achieved
by investing in short-maturity money-market instruments. The
fourth priority for the use of funds is to salvage income from
investments when loan demand does not exhaust available
funds. Since the third priority—that of having funds available
for lending directly to banking customers—lies between these
other priorities, it can be said that the investment operations
of commercial banks straddle their lending operations. On one
side they provide the liquidity that makes it possible for commercial banks to operate and to have funds available for lending when such are needed. On the other side the investment
process employs such residual funds as cannot be employed in
loan operations.

To some extent the investment operations of banks tend to
be divided along the lines suggested by these priorities. In
large banks management of the money position is usually
delegated to a special function. Those operating this function
have at their disposal the part of the investment account which
is used primarily for liquidity purposes and secondarily for

income. The residual or income maximizing investments are handled by a different group. In medium-sized and smaller banks, however, such division of function is not common. Even if not administratively recognized, the dual functional role of investment operations is just as important in small banks as it is in the money-market giants.

One operational requirement is sometimes put on the investment account: that of providing an adequate volume of securities for collateral. Government deposits and purchases of funds from small banks in the Federal funds market require the availability of security collateral. This requirement sometimes determines the practical minimum size of the investment account.

HISTORY OF COMMERCIAL-BANK INVESTMENT OPERATIONS

Prior to World War I it was generally believed that commercial banks should not purchase or hold investment securities. Some exceptions existed, such as the securities used as collateral for the issuance of national bank notes. Commercial banks did, however, hold other securities, but this was generally felt to be a violation of commercial banking principles in theory if not in practice. Self-liquidating commercial loans were believed to be the proper outlet for monetary reasons and the safest asset for practical reasons. World War I caused a sizable expansion of public debt, and commercial banks were encouraged to buy some of these securities. Furthermore, a new theory of banking gained some following. Emphasis was shifted from the desirability of self-liquidating commercial paper for banks to the concept of liquidity achieved by "shiftability." A shiftable asset was, in effect, a readily salable asset. Since securities were obviously more salable than loans, this concept suggested that securities were superior bank assets.

In practice, commercial banks stretched excessively the standard for what was shiftable. Widespread abuse of the con-

cept took many forms: Commercial banks engaged in investment banking operations and bought many lower quality
corporate long-term securities as well as real estate and foreign
bonds. As a result, when banks were suffering liquidity difficulties during the early 1930s the investment excesses of the
1920s were criticized. Nevertheless, low loan demand during
the 1930s put pressure on commercial banks to augment income in some fashion. The principal response to this pressure
was the purchase of securities, mainly those of the United
States government. During World War II commercial banks
bought U.S. Government securities, partly because other outlets did not use available funds. Since that time commercial
banks have reduced their holdings of securities as loan demand
revived.

The composition of bank investment portfolios has changed
greatly from that prevailing in the 1920s and the 1930s.
Corporate securities have almost vanished from banking portfolios. Term loans have largely replaced corporate bonds.
Foreign securities are no longer held in appreciable volume.
The two principal types of securities now purchased by banks
are both governmental: either those of the Federal government or those of state and local governmental units. Separate
chapters will be devoted to each of these two types of obligations.

GENERAL INVESTMENT POLICY

The framing of investment policy for an individual bank
depends on its circumstances. General comments about investment policy may be dangerous and even misleading. Investment
policy should be tailored to the strength, seasonality, and character of loan demand faced by each bank. Banks that experience sharp seasonal movements in their deposits or in loan
demand need more liquidity than banks that have stable
deposits and relatively unfluctuating loan demands. Once the
character of a bank's loan expectations has been determined

its general investment policy can be framed.[1] The general aspects of bank investment policy will be dealt with in the following sections, particularly with respect to the quality of securities that banks should buy (which at the present time is applicable mainly to their tax-exempt portfolios) and also the nature of diversification and the general maturity policy. It is with this latter feature, maturity policy, that the most critical features of bank investment policy are concerned. Accordingly, a separate chapter has been devoted to this subject.

The Investment Program

Almost every investment operation needs a goal. The program for achieving it can be worked out only after the goal has been selected. In personal plans, a young man might set up an investment goal of maximum capital appreciation with little or no emphasis on current income. The goal almost defines the program that is consistent with that end. A trust officer of a bank in planning a program of investment for a widow might make safety and income the primary goal. The program for achieving that would differ greatly from our young man's program. The goals and programs of life insurance companies, of fire and casualty insurance companies, of university endowment funds have their own characteristics. Within these general groups, programs must be even more precisely adapted to the goals of the individual institutions. *Each* insurance company, *each* endowment fund, and *each* commercial bank has its own unique problems.

The very first step in a bank's investment operations must therefore be definition of goal: income, liquidity, and flexibility, for example. Which factor to emphasize must be decided by each bank. While we have strongly urged that income needs cannot be decisive in bank investment decisions, their importance cannot be dismissed. A bank that can make a satisfactory income without investment income has the potential

[1] See Chapter 6 for a discussion of the determination of seasonality of deposits and loan demand.

of a much more flexible position, of being able to take advantage of income opportunities as they arise.

Once the goal is set, some sort of program for its achievement is needed. This is partly a matter of staff work. Detailed investment plans cannot be easily framed by a group as large as a board of directors. The written investment program developed by the staff and considered, modified, and finally adopted by the directors is perhaps the best way of crystallizing the investment program.

The Written Investment Program

Long experience has shown that when an exact understanding among men is needed, the written form of agreement is superior to any oral form. Contracts, treaties, and—so students say—even professors' lectures are more intelligible in written than in oral form.

The written investment program is only an extension of this idea. It has a unique place in bank management and is one of the few situations in which detailed advance planning is feasible. Bank loans, as has been said before, come to banks from borrowers who are local to a given bank. A bank can, within limits, control the distributional character of its loan portfolio. But these limits are not wide. A bank's loan portfolio cannot always be tailored to its wishes. Its investment policy, however, can be planned, and, as other parts of this section try to make clear, planned around the kinds of loans that are available.

The written investment program is just what the phrase says: a written document setting up standards of the investment practices which are elsewhere discussed in this general section. Some investment programs are very concrete; others are rather more general. Room should be left for maneuver by the investment officer, but all matters of general policy are determined by the board of directors.

The written investment program is to be considered the grant of authority from the board of directors to the investment officer. It is not, however, to be used by him as an alibi. For example, the permission to own securities down through a certain rating grade does not mean that this permission is to be fully used at all times. If, however, the investment officer feels that the program sets too long maturity standards or too low-quality standards, this should be adjusted by revising the investment policy with the board of directors, not by persistent failure to use the permissible margins.

OPERATION OF A BANK INVESTMENT PROGRAM

In order to make an investment policy effective, the internal organization of a bank needs to be geared to the problem. The first or invariable requirement of organization for investment purposes is that there should be some active and preferably full-time officer to whom investment responsibility is delegated. In a small bank this may be only a part-time function for one officer; even in very large banks, the number of persons needed is relatively small. At smaller banks a full-time officer would be neither feasible nor profitable. In banks with total assets of $50 million or more, however, a full-time investment officer is not only needed, he should be able to earn more than his salary by superior investment management. No question about responsibility should prevail, and a clear delegation of authority should be made to the investment officer.

It goes without saying that investment operations are specialized and that training and experience in this field are as important as in any other field. Even with a written program of a fairly specific sort considerable room for discretion should remain. The investment officer exercises this discretion; it is both his license and his responsibility.

In small banks, the investment officer is likely to be the leading full-time executive officer. In larger banks, this is not so likely to be the case; he may be of subordinate rank. While he need not be independent of the authority of the leading full-time executive in the bank, he should have direct access to the board of directors of the bank. This is particularly true in cases when the leading full-time executive officer has limited competence in investments. Ultimate investment policy must be shaped by the board of directors. At the same time education of the directors is needed, and the investment officer should be given the opportunity to make his influence felt.

The degree of detail by which the directors set investment policy and the margin of latitude within which the investment officer may operate vary from bank to bank for good reasons. If there is a likemindedness of the investment officer and the board, there need be no problem; if not, the change needed is more fundamental than that of reorganization.

Relationship with the Trust Department

In most large banks, the investment operations of the trust department are completely separate from those of the banking department. In small banks this may not always be the case. Where the investment officer of the bank also gives a part of his time to the trust department, special safeguards should be erected. Because of the rigid rules prohibiting self-dealing (the banking department cannot sell assets to trust accounts—a practice that might lead to abuse), the two phases of the individual's work need to be clearly separated.

The best rule is no connection at all.

Use of Outside Investment Advice

Most banking institutions make some use of outside investment advice. The various agencies that compile statistical data about securities are almost all engaged, in varying degrees, in selling investment advice. It is also the practice of most dealers in securities to offer free investment advice. The city correspondents of country banks offer the same service; some have elaborate programs for analyzing country-bank portfolios.

More than in times gone by, banks can depend on this advice to be both competent and disinterested. On the other hand, bankers should recognize the limits within which these agencies operate. Their advice is bound to be conservative; perhaps more so than is required. If they are bold and make recommendations which cause capital losses, they are blamed. If they are overcautious, they are not blamed for the income forgone. In the long run, every bank, like every person and every institution, is better off to have made its own choice and program and to have managed the adherence to this program. No one else can assume final responsibility.

The regulation of bank investments by the Comptroller of the Currency (with similar or almost identical regulations being applied by the other bank supervisory agencies) depends on the rating classification (Aaa, A1 +, etc.) assigned to securities by the rating agencies. The influence of the rating agencies (Moody, Standard-Poor) has thus come to be considerable. Most of these agencies have investment advisory departments as well as the rating departments, and many banking institutions subscribe to and use their services. These investment advisory agencies have competent staffs and have adopted ethical standards of conduct which make them dependable sources of information and advice.

It has already been mentioned that dealers and underwriters in securities offer investment advice to the institutions that are their customers. Because of the abuse of this relationship in the late boom days of the 1920s, this advice is occasionally still treated as suspect. In general, most of the leading houses have tried, within the limits of human frailty, to resist the excess of salesman enthusiasm, but this is not altogether possible. The problem is not one of honesty but of basic conviction. An underwriting house probably would not handle an issue if it did not feel that it was a reasonable buy for the customers at the price offered and under the conditions of the market at the time of offering. With the best of intentions, the temperament needed for successful promotion, which is the essence of underwriting, is not the cool and often critical temperament which is the heart of investment judgment. For this reason nonunderwriting dealers (who have less special interest in specific issues) are more likely to be sources of impartial investment advice than those houses that combine dealing with underwriting.

investment obligation in question will be serviced with its interest payments as they become due and that the debt will be paid at maturity. Insurance companies can afford to concentrate on this point because they expect to hold their investments to maturity. Even though commercial banks may be able to hold a fair proportion of their obligations on through to maturity, they cannot be *certain* of doing that. During the Depression of the early 1930s, many banks had to realize on their investments by market sales. Not only must investment obligations owned by banks be of high quality, but the high quality must be so universally recognized that the market will not discount their soundness even in bad times. The high-quality but small issue that has escaped general market attention—the great favorite of the insurance company investment analyst—does not have quite the same appeal to the commercial banker.

4. Marketability means rather more to banks than to other investors; standards of marketability must be higher. Quality and marketability are not quite the same thing as averred above but very nearly so. Banks need the sort of marketability that is certain and rapid. They need to be able to dispose of a sizable block of a given issue quickly without depressing market quotations materially. Many fairly high-quality issues can be sold without too much concession if enough time is taken. Alternatively, some issues can be sold quickly if a moderate price concession is made. For both features to be present in a given security, it must be of the very highest quality.

5. The special requirements of banks arise, in part at least, from the fact that they face their severest demands for liquidity under the most trying circumstances. A bank that has made normally adequate provision for liquidity usually does not have to resort to its long-term investment account except when there are large and unusual drains, such as runs and currency hoarding waves. But then the investment market takes the dimmest view of credit risks and asks the highest premiums for carrying them.

DIVERSIFICATION

One of the most venerable rules of investment policy is diversification. If risk cannot be avoided altogether, it can at least be reduced to manageable proportions. If unanticipatable losses occur according to pure chance, then the holding of investment issues spread over a wide enough area will tend to reduce the losses to about their average probable value. But losses reduce to a random-chance basis only when the elements of risk are "independent" and can be spread out. A simple analogy will illustrate this point. If a fire, tornado, and other casualty insurance company should concentrate its operations in a single town, for which there might be some very real operating advantages, it would be taking an unconscionable risk. Tornadoes do their damage in one area, and occasionally large fires spread widely before being brought under control. Concentration of risk can ruin an insurer and does so occasionally. (Great local disasters have several times bankrupted local casualty insurance companies.) On the other hand, if a company insured 1 per cent of the houses in each of 100 similarly sized towns, it would be spreading its risk. Over the long run, losses should average out without any serious bunching at one time or place.

The analogy to investments of such a concentration of risk is not quite accurate because investment risk is not of the entirely accidental sort. Economic instability is the great precipitating factor for investment losses, and diversification cannot offset that. Risks of declining industries, or industries suddenly adversely affected by new developments, can be offset by diversification, and competitive changes where one company advances while another declines can also be offset in part. So diversification has a place in bank investment policy. The need for diversification in portfolios of state and local government securities is just as great as the need for spreading risk in portfolios of corporate obligations. Geographic diversification, however, is the principal form such risk spreading takes.

Maturity distribution is logically a kind of diversification. To the extent that gains and losses on investment securities are due to changes in interest rates, a bank needs to put new funds into the market at fairly regular intervals in order to average out the experience of the market. This matter will be handled in the next chapter, which considers maturity and yield.

Diversification does not mean "taking a little bit of everything that comes along." It does not mean that a bank needs to add the issues of a state or city that borrows rarely to round out its portfolio. Another false meaning of diversification is that of having a large number of securities. The major elements of diversification can be secured in a portfolio that can be listed on one sheet of paper. The advantages of being able to follow each security carefully far outweigh the advantages of more detailed diversification. Some large banks, of course, may want longer lists simply for the purpose of keeping their commitment in a single issue or company within an amount that can be marketed without difficulty. When a bank is that large, however, it will have an investment staff adequate to supervise a large number of issues.

One more false meaning is sometimes attached to diversification. Since diversification minimizes the risks that borrowers will not perform according to contract, the practice is more useful in dealing with middle-grade than high-grade securities. Of course, the highest grade can deteriorate, and so diversification is useful there, too. But the most important feature of diversification is in dealing with investments which are not fully sheltered from risk. Thus, the banker who said, "I have too many U.S. Government securities, I need to diversify my account," had missed the meaning of diversification.

Probably the leading principle of diversification that a bank needs to follow is that of not duplicating its loan account. It has been said before that banks are generally not able to diversify loan accounts as much as they might wish. Under a unit banking system, only the very largest banks make loans throughout the country. Other banks do most of their business near home. (This tends to be true in part of the very largest banks.) Thus, the loan accounts of most banks are concentrated geographically. However, the problem is not only geographic. Some banks, by virtue of an excellent connection through a director or an officer, may lend an unusual amount in a given industrial field. The results are fine, and by concentrating in that field, a great deal of good business can be done. Some banks get to be known as "oil" banks, others as "utility" banks, still others as "textile" banks.

Such concentration in lending not only is unavoidable, but is natural and to be expected. In planning investment operations, banks need to offset this loan concentration. One of the tests of diversification of investments is to find out the extent to which the investment portfolio, *combined with* the loan account, gives a reasonable over-all balance. This usually means that a bank should not purchase the open-market securities of nearby industries. This might be considered unfortunate since the banker may be well prepared to judge the intrinsic value and performance of such issues. But such investment would add to its geographic concentration. Likewise it seems perhaps stubborn and unreasonable for a bank not to buy the investment securities of an area it knows thoroughly from lending activities; yet there is much to recommend this restraint.

INVESTMENT POLICY FOR SPECIAL BANKS

The generalizations about investment policy made above have wide but not universal applicability. Some banks face exceptional problems. The bank that looks carefully at its special problems may find that the general principles stated above apply to it only if allowance is made for some exceptions. No two banks are alike any more than any two persons.

The observations that follow, therefore, are more illustrative than definitive. They present special cases, but they do not exhaust the list, or the problems of these special cases. They may help banks that do not fall in these categories to solve the problems they face.

Banks with a Large Volume of Savings

Our first case is hardly "special" because it is fairly frequent: the commercial bank with a relatively large savings department. This case is important. In many sections of this country no other savings or thrift institutions are within a reasonable distance. The mutual savings banks are located mainly in the Northern Atlantic seaboard states. The savings and loan associations are more often urban than not. The little all-purpose commercial bank has shrunk in number but not in importance. When it has quite a few savings accounts, it becomes a community institution.

Savings banking is materially different from commercial banking. The savings departments in commercial banks are also quite different from pure savings banks. The investment of funds received as savings accounts requires special policies. As recounted in an earlier chapter, the random movement of savings deposits is much more sluggish than that of demand deposits; but the cyclical variation can be almost as great. Savings deposits generally must be paid interest, and that puts income pressure on the bank in arranging its investment policy.

The rate of interest paid on savings accounts necessarily influences investment policy. When a bank pays a high rate, it is likely to feel compelled to try to recover that rate plus its operating costs in investment operations, even if other banking operations are profitable. The entire rate of interest does not have to be covered in the excess of investment returns from savings funds over investment returns on commercial funds. Savings deposits are not so costly to manage or operate as demand deposits. While there are no adequate statistics to show the difference, a rough guess would be that savings accounts are at least $\frac{1}{2}$ of 1 per cent less costly to operate than demand deposits.

Still another feature makes the comparison not quite precise. The prime business of commercial banks is commercial; because of overhead costs, the addition of some savings business to a commercial bank does not require that the savings business contribute pro rata to profit. Even a partial recovery of fixed costs means some gain. In fact, some banks take the view that savings as a desirable social institution should be encouraged. Profit is less the prime goal than in commercial operations.

It is generally assumed that all or almost all real estate mortgages should be considered as an investment of savings department funds. The National Bank Act which limits real estate mortgages to 60 per cent of time deposits (the capital account limit is usually smaller and less effective) sanctions this idea. Investment policy must then be framed about the totality of mortgages and securities, with the general presumption that, up to the point of liquidity needs, the application of funds to mortgages will be given a priority. In a few areas, banks enjoy such good mortgage demands that no investment problem exists beyond the relatively simple one of providing liquidity. A few banks take all the available mortgages and still have a residue. Such a bank must look to other outlets for the employment of its money. Local mortgages involve a direct customer relationship and banks must allow for this factor in the granting or refusal of requests for such mortgage loans. Mortgage loans acquired in the secondary market or through mortgage bankers from other areas, however, can be viewed as an investment outlet and as impersonally judged as other investment forms would be judged.

During part of the 1930s when interest rates were low, many bankers could find no satisfactory outlet for funds. Since they held excess reserves, they could see no point in accepting savings deposits—certainly not in promoting the business. Some kept their facilities available and thought of them as an unprofitable public service, but they did not promote them.

There are undeniable advantages to this sort of off-again-on-again policy. If savings are promoted only when interest rates are high, a bank will naturally invest the money when received. Over good and bad times, it averages to get a higher return on funds received through savings accounts. If such a bank cuts savings interest rates during low-rate periods, these higher returns accrue to the bank owners in better profits. Alternatively, such a bank can keep on paying a better rate to the savings depositors that came to it in good times, this being true so long as it does not dilute its accounts with very much new money seeking investment. The policy is probably a profitable one; the whole question is whether it is justified on other grounds. Some bankers feel not. But it illustrates one of the paradoxes of banking: The bank that promotes savings steadily may not be able to pay so good a rate to its savings customers as the bank that promotes them mostly when interest rates are high.

Banks in Boom Areas

For one reason or another, various areas sometimes enjoy (or suffer) unusual booms. The location of a missile base, the discovery of uranium or another rare mineral, the opening of an irrigation project, almost anything that brings in a rush of money and increased income may cause it. Banks located in such an area are almost sure to enjoy (but precariously) a rapid increase of deposits, far beyond the rate of advance for other banks. Sometimes a boom will be accompanied by a proportionate expansion in loan demand, but often the nature of the loan demand is such that the banker feels able to accommodate only a part of it even if he has ample funds.

What should the investment policy be for such a bank? The end of some booms, such as war plants, may be foreseeable; for others it is indeterminate, such as the uranium boom proved to be. The cautious banker would do well during the early stages of enjoying a rapid deposit growth to wait a bit before committing his institution to a larger and larger investment account. There will be time later on. Sometimes the investment market moves against such a bank, but just about as often for it. If the prosperity of the area keeps up, the loan demand, whether or not it developed in the beginning, will help solve the income problem. After a bit, the banker can appraise the loan risks better. He is in a more strategic spot if he has kept his investments short.

Very Small Banks

By now the reader must have discovered that the formation and administration of a good investment policy for a bank are fairly complex matters. The active manager of a small bank (often the cashier if the president is inactive or honorary) may agree in principle to the need for a full-dress investment policy and program, but question whether the kind of detailed investment planning suggested in these chapters is practical for a small bank. The number of senior officers in a small bank is limited; they must attend to various kinds of duties and cannot specialize in just one. The environment in which the officers of most small banks are trained is not one to develop sophistication in the intricacies of money and capital markets. The yield improvement that even the most skilled investment managers can produce safely is not large; it must be reaped from a rather large portfolio in order to make such specialization profitable.

These are relevant considerations. A good compromise for the small bank is to maintain higher standards of both quality and maturity than are observed by larger banks. A very simple investment program is needed, one that can be operated by a part-time investment officer with a minimum of time and study. Even more so than in large banks, small banks should not look to investment portfolios as the source of a great deal of income; the most important source of income is in the loan account. The higher interest rates on loans available to many small banks makes this differential view even more compelling. The small bank with weak loan demand represents a special problem; too often, however, this has really meant a small bank with weak loan promotion or excessive conservatism in its lending operations.

Small local tax-exempt issues can be considered an exception to the foregoing argument. Although capital markets do a fairly good job in handling small issues in public offerings, the very small issue usually can be sold only at higher interest cost, even if of fine quality. A local bank is in the position of being able to judge the credit quality more skillfully than outsiders because intangible factors are so important in appraising such issues. A small bank usually can afford to put a moderate amount of money into such high-quality but also high-yielding local tax-exempt issues. Although it may not engage in regular underwriting of tax-exempt issues, a bank may participate in syndicates, particularly if local investors in such obligations are a logical market for them. Investment in these obligations, however, is quite illiquid even if the quality of the issues is high. Such investments partake somewhat of the nature of term loans. A bank that is active in investing and marketing local tax-exempt obligations often has a persuasive argument when seeking to secure the deposits of public bodies.

Even the smallest bank cannot avoid one investment operation: management of its money position. While small banks can use correspondent balances to meet week-to-week needs rather more than larger banks, they cannot depend on this source for true seasonal or cyclical swings. Some small banks manage money positions by carrying ample amounts of excess reserves. This is understandable, but it is a wasteful practice and not defensible if needed earnings are sacrificed. Choosing a truly liquid market investment for money-position management purposes is not difficult; Treasury bills furnish an excellent vehicle adaptable to the needs of the smallest bank. But figuring the timing of such needs cannot be evaded.

Banks with Thin Capital Accounts

Wartime deposit expansion only hastened an apparent trend of more than a generation: the steady thinning of bank capital ratios. Bank capital has increased in absolute amounts, but the balance sheet footings have raced even faster. In the sense of ultimate solvency, banks have less margin than in times gone by.

The thin capital margin is exaggerated in certain banks. Unusually rapid growth, the pinnacle of banking success by most standards, is likely to be the cause of an extra-thin capital ratio. There are two sides to this position: (1) Because of the greater leverage in such a bank, the average net earning rate on assets may be smaller than average and still yield a higher than average return when calculated on capital; (2) the presumptively higher earning power of the bank with thin capital means that it can restore its capital position. A bank may excusably have a thin capital position, but it should not stay far out of line with other banks indefinitely.

Even though the supervisory agencies do not require banks to use the market value of securities held in judging solvency, banks are disposed to do so in making their own computations. The corporate customers of large banks have also favored the market value basis. Since swings in security prices have been rather wider in recent years than in the early postwar years, thin capital accounts have become a problem of real concern for some banks. The presence of the problem has been felt most sharply in periods of high interest rates and low security prices because it is in such periods that loan demands have been highest and the value of corporate deposits at their greatest.

There is another side to the matter. If a bank constricts its investment operations because of thin capital, it provides more liquidity than is needed. Except for confidence creation, there is nothing about a thin capital equity that requires a stronger liquidity position. The things that create confidence are hard to gauge. Meticulous corporate treasurers, in analyzing the banks in which they keep big accounts, look for and prefer to find a good capital account; few others understand the significance of bank capital. Both probably heed liquidity more than any other factor.

The real danger of an overcautious investment policy because of thin capital is that it tends to perpetuate the very situation that causes this policy. The great bulk of added bank capital comes from retained earnings. Some banks have grown so rapidly that they have outrun their original capital. Earnings have not yet restored this position.

The usual way for such a bank to expand its capital is by retaining its earnings (not paying dividends), which means it would have a hard time selling new shares. If it keeps earnings small for the sake of safety, it may keep capital growth small and thus never escape this dilemma. There is no simple guide to how far such a bank can go; it might liberalize investment policy, at least moderately. If deposits are reasonably stable, it can do so safely.

Banks with Small Loan Demand

It has been averred in earlier chapters that the loan demand met by a bank is usually the product of its own promotional effort. The bank that hunts for loans usually finds them; the bank that stays home gets only the loans that "fly through the transom."

This is true but there are exceptions. Some banks are located in declining areas where loan demand is small. In towns with departing industries, without new building or new businesses locating there, where the population is increasing in average age (the youngsters being attracted to newer, livelier areas), the loan demand is likely to be small no matter how promotional the banker.

It is not uncommon to find banks in older suburban areas in this situation. Without industry there is little business loan demand and, if the area is an older one without much new real estate development, there may be little mortgage loan demand and no real outlet for consumer credit.

In such an area, the investment account is not just a safety device and an adornment of the balance sheet; it is bread and butter and meat and potatoes. Without it, the banks so located could not earn expenses or survive.

Can such banks relax some of the restrictive rules that have been proposed for investment operations? Enough has been said about qualitative factors to make it reasonably clear that a great deal of relaxation is not always possible, nor does it promise to help much incomewise since losses may offset the gains. There are, however, some margins to which such a bank can work. It can, for example, hunt for the small local securities that have great strength but limited appeal (though the number of these good but obscure securities is declining). The amount that can be gained by this means is not very large.

Nor does maturity elongation offer much help. Such a bank must be as safe as any other bank, and it has no license for chance taking. Perhaps the remedy it seeks lies in still another direction, higher service charges and less free service for customers. These are more appropriate ways of making up the difference. Investment liberalization, no!

Legal Regulation of Bank Investment Operations

The chief legal regulation of bank investment practices is the Comptroller of the Currency's regulation of bank investments. Its present form has been in force since 1938, together with some amendments made in 1949. This regulation, although applying primarily to national and state member banks, has by informal agreement become the standard of regulation which is applied by the Federal Deposit Insurance Corporation in its control of bank investments, and many of the state banking authorities have done likewise.

The essential features of this regulation are:
1. The credit quality of bank securities must be high.
2. The marketability of securities is given some emphasis.
3. Significantly, it contains no maturity limitation.

How far does the Comptroller's regulation go in providing the sort of rules that might be used to guide bank investment policy? In general, not very far. The provisions that cover the matters of credit quality and marketability are, in general, even lower standards than most prudent bankers would employ. The other factors of diversification and maturity that would so concern bankers are not mentioned in any degree, with one exception. As with loans, a bank cannot put more than 10 per cent of its capital and unimpaired surplus in the securities of any one corporate obligor.

While the Comptroller has not used the security rating services directly in the definition of quality, the ratings are mentioned in the regulation and many have assumed that listing in the top four grades (down through Baa, or B1 +), confirmed by two services, makes a security eligible for a bank.

19

Investment Policy: Maturity and Yield

The significance of maturity in bank investment operations is relatively simple and direct: Banks cannot be assured of holding the securities they purchase until their ultimate maturity; they may have to sell them in advance of maturity. In this they differ from the great majority of other investing institutions which generally can and do hold the securities they purchase until final maturity. Banks may need to sell because of loan demands or to take advantage of tax-swapping opportunities.[1] Ultimately, of course, the need for liquidity may arise because of deposit losses, but this is a more remote need. Regardless of which factor gives rise to the need to sell in advance of maturity, the distribution of maturities within the group of securities available for sale becomes a critical factor to a bank when sale is contemplated.

INVERSE MOVEMENT OF YIELD AND PRICE

One of the simplest facts of the mathematics of investment is that yields and prices of fixed-return obligations always move in opposite directions. The foundation for this relatively simple mathematical fact is readily found in any description of the

[1] See Chapter 20 for an explanation of tax swapping.

present value. When the fixed return from an
...rity must be discounted at a higher rate of
...sulting present value is naturally lower. One hun-
...due one year from now is worth one dollar less
...ounted at a 6 per cent rate than if discounted at a
...ate ($95).

...slightly more complex mathematical fact is that
...ven movement in interest rates, movements in price
of securities having relatively short maturities are smaller than
of securities having longer maturities. In other words, if a bank
holds short-maturity securities, it is usually able to sell them
without material loss should the need arise. The other side of
this fact, of course, is that the opportunities for capital gains
in short-term securities are correspondingly limited. Price movements of long maturities may be substantial. The risks are
greater; but so are the opportunities for capital gains and almost always for current income.

RANGE OF INTEREST RATE FLUCTUATIONS

The history of interest rates shows that short-term interest
rates move through a much wider range than long-term interest
rates. The simple mathematical facts about bond yields outlined in the preceding section are the basis for the economic
rationale of this fact. Since short-term securities present fewer
risks of capital losses, investors use them as a refuge when they
are uncertain about alternative investment outlets. The converse
is that when other investment opportunities become more certain and attractive, short-term investments tend to be sold in
large volume or allowed to mature. Thus short-term rates tend
to be volatile. The effect of this is that banks, depending on
income from short-term open-market securities, experience considerable volatility in their rates of earning.

This tendency is amplified by another observed economic
fact: short-term open-market interest rates move considerably
more than the negotiated short-term customer rates for bank
loans. In other words, if banks should limit their investment

operations wholly to very short-term obligations they subject themselves to the risk of great variability of income even though they avoid the risks of capital losses on their investment portfolio.

The facts outlined above are readily evident in Figure 19-1a, which compares long-term and short-term interest rates during the present century. Figure 19-1b shows a relatively briefer period, but with interest rates charted on a weekly rather than an annual basis. This part of the figure indicates even more dramatically the sharp fluctuations in short-term interest rates. Within the period of less than a decade three drastic moves in short-term interest rates took place, all of which had material bearing on the rate of bank earnings.

The volatility of short-term interest rates promises to be a continuing feature of money and financial markets. The extensive use of monetary policy as an instrument of economic stabilization tends to put a considerable pressure on markets and to increase the scale of these movements. Fiscal policy, another instrument of government in economic stabilization, also has sharp and varying effects on the rates of interest prevailing in the investment markets.

THE PATTERN OF RATES AND THE YIELD CURVE

Our analysis of interest rate relationships can now be converted into more systematic terms. These historical facts—that short-term and long-term interest rates move up and down roughly at the same time but with a wider range of movement in the short rates—can be reduced to a simple schematic diagram as in Figure 19-2. This diagram shows not only the extremely short and long rates; for the sake of completeness, the movements of intermediate rates are also illustrated. The diagram is of a time series; that is, movement from left to right represents the passage of time. If we were to take a single point of time, we should be able to show a more precise relationship between interest rates. This is done in Figure 19-3. We have selected a single date in the time series used above (left-hand

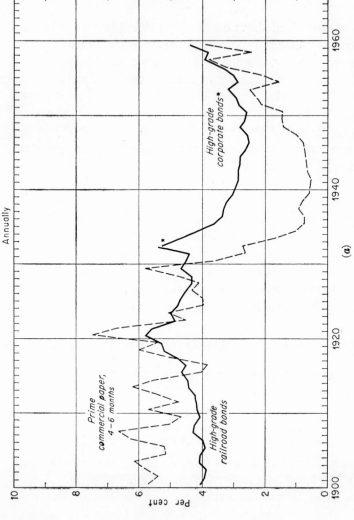

FIGURE 19-1. (a) Long- and short-term interest rates. *Standard and Poor's composite Al. (b) Money rates. (Source: Board of Governors of the Federal Reserve System, *Historical Chart Book*, 1960.)

354

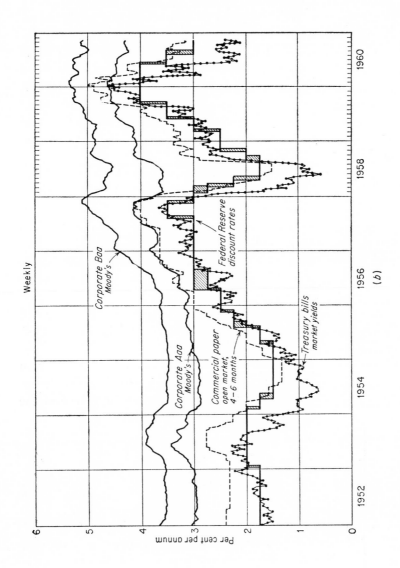

Weekly

Corporate Baa
Moody's

Corporate Aaa
Moody's

Commercial paper
open market,
4–6 months

Federal Reserve
discount rates

Treasury bills
market yields

Per cent per annum

6   5   4   3   2   1   0

1952   1954   1956   1958   1960

(b)

side of chart) and derived a chart of interest-rate relationship for that date. This is a chart *as of one date;* it is not a time series. In the right-hand side, horizontal distances represent the period to maturity for various classes of credit instruments. This abstract chart of relationships is a "pattern of rates" or a "yield curve." The more common, but also complex, form is the one based on real market quotations. Figure 19-4, a real yield curve, is taken from pioneering research study in this field; the crosses and dots represent actual market yields for various securities.

The abstract illustration (Figure 19-3) and the parallel factual illustration from the Durand study (Figure 19-4) are of a high-yield period, when the short-term rates are above the long-term rates. The converse is shown in Figure 19-5 and the related Durand chart for 1937 (Figure 19-6).

This second case is the one which has been much more common in recent years. Indeed, for almost two decades now the upsweeping pattern of rates has prevailed.

A still more complex kind of yield curve has been prepared from the prices of U.S. Treasury securities in Figure 19-7, taken from the *Treasury Bulletin.*

Some believe the upsweeping yield curve to be more common —more "normal"—than downsweeping curves. This presumption has some logic, but it certainly has not been true of the

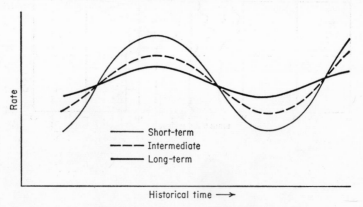

FIGURE 19-2. Hypothetical illustration of interest rate fluctuation.

past. As nearly as the facts of interest rates can be interpreted, there have been about as many years of downsweeping yield curves as there have been of upsweeping curves. Many years have been neutral. Figure 19-8, also taken from Durand, shows

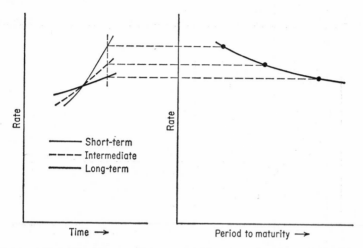

FIGURE 19-3. Deriving a high-rate yield curve, based on hypothetical interest rate fluctuation.

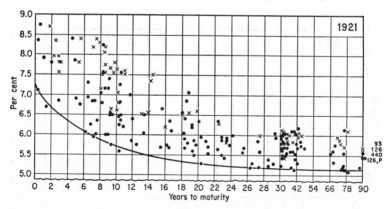

FIGURE 19-4. A "real" yield curve. (Reprinted by permisson of the Natonal Bureau of Economic Research: *Basic Yields of Corporate Bonds, 1900–1942*, by David Durand, Technical Paper no. 3, p. 29, 1942. See also *Basic Yields of Bonds, 1926–1947: Their Measurement and Pattern*, by David Durand and Willis J. Winn, Technical Paper no. 6, 1947.)

the superimposed yield curves of the forty-three years from the beginning of the twentieth century.

The existence of "patterns of rates" has important implications for the investment analyst; the curve can be used to guide investment maturity policy.

The Durand curve for 1937, shown in Figure 19-6, is one in

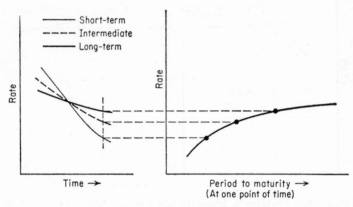

FIGURE 19-5. Deriving a low-rate yield curve ("pattern of rates"), based on hypothetical interest rate fluctuations.

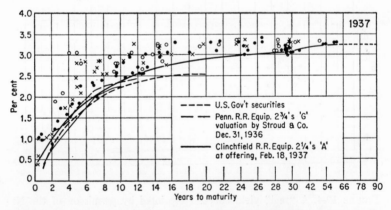

FIGURE 19-6. A "real" upsweeping yield curve. (Reprinted by permission of the National Bureau of Economic Research: *Basic Yields of Corporate Bonds, 1900–1942*, by David Durand, Technical Paper no. 3, p. 33, 1942.)

which the ascent is gradual. The curve for 1960, which appears in Figure 19-7, shows a much sharper rise. Such a sharp slope in the early years of a yield curve is rather rare. One of the earliest and most striking examples of such a circumstance occurred in 1935. The Durand yield curve for that year is shown in Figure 19-9.

This faster rise in the yield curve might be termed "shoulder"; it is a reflection of the relationship of intermediate interest rates to the two extremes. If intermediate yields are evenly spaced between the short and the long ends of the curve, there is very little shoulder (as in Figure 19-6); when intermediate-term interest rates are closer to long-term rates, then there is quite a bit of shoulder.

How is shoulder to be interpreted? It has the clear and important market significance of being a measure of the rewards and risks faced by the banker who is considering changing the maturity distribution of his portfolio. Let us focus our attention on the two years chosen for illustration. The year 1935 has quite an upright shoulder. The long-term interest rate was about $3\frac{1}{2}$ per cent. This was less than it had been since the early part

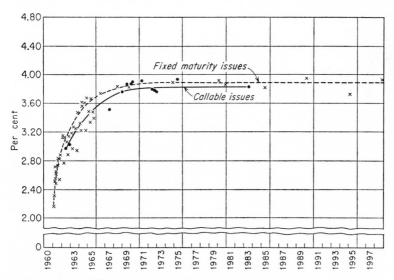

FIGURE 19-7. Yields of taxable Treasury securities, October 31, 1960.

of the century, a span of thirty years. Many then mature business and financial men were yet too young to have any recollection of rates as low as that. We were coming out of a severe depression, but many of its aftermaths were still in evidence. There was still much unemployment; between 8 and 11 million men did not have jobs during that year. On the other hand, there were some signs of recovery.

The New Deal was on the rise. The atmosphere was a mixed one, but many viewed it as a traditional recovery from depression. Short-term interest rates were low, but that was a fairly normal thing. This lowness was not uniquely the result of New Deal policies. It was thought natural, as indeed it was, for short-

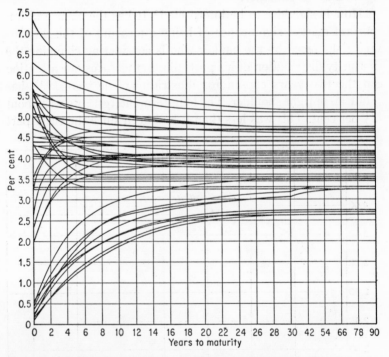

FIGURE 19-8. Superimposed basic yield curves, 1900–1942. (Reprinted by permission of the National Bureau of Economic Research: *Basic Yields of Corporate Bonds, 1900–1942*, by David Durand, Technical Paper no. 3, p. 17, 1942.)

term rates to be low. While short-term interest rates were at and below 1 per cent, the 5-year rate was $2\frac{1}{2}$ per cent and the 10-year rate about 3 per cent.

The implication of the yield curve was that investors expected the level of interest rates to rise within five years. Thus, there is considerable shoulder to an interest rate curve when investors expect the change to come fairly soon.

The point can be made all the more evident if we look for contrast to the yield curve for 1937 shown in Figure 19-6. There is very little shoulder on this upsweeping curve; it is fairly flat. Why this change? It is hard to recapture the intangibles of the period, but there was almost certainly a change in what might be called "political sentiment." The later part of the year witnessed a sharp recession piled on an already depressed economy. There had been a break in Federal government security prices during the early part of the year, but most of it had been recovered. Investors and others were by no means so sure of the fairly early return of higher interest rates. The demand for intermediate-term securities drove their yield down relatively

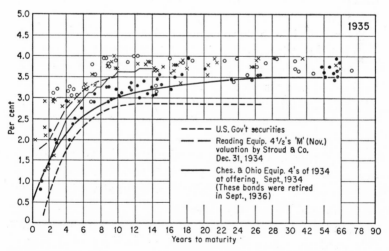

FIGURE 19-9. A yield curve with "shoulder." (Reprinted by permission of the National Bureau of Economic Research: *Basic Yields of Corporate Bonds, 1900–1942*, by David Durand, Technical Paper no. 3, p. 33, 1942.)

more than that of the long-term rate, although this rate was down. Investors and banks were not quite willing to take the prevailing rates of very short-term obligations; they still did not want to go far out into the very long-term obligations. Thus a "flat" yield curve reflects an expectation that the yields are going up but not necessarily in the near-term future. It is a curve of uncertainty.

The period 1952–1953 furnishes a similar illustration. In the fall of 1952 uncertainty prevailed in the market for U.S. Government securities. The Treasury–Federal Reserve "Accord," announced more than a year and a half earlier, had given the money market some experience with price freedom. In November, 1952, the Federal Reserve took a further step toward increasing market freedom: it ceased to support new Treasury financing operations. In this prevailing state of uncertainty, the yield curve showed a very shallow slope from yields of about 2.0 per cent at the short end and 2.3 per cent at the 5-year maturity to about 2.7 per cent at the long-term end. The amount of income improvement available to commercial banks by extending maturities was small; the loss of income from shortening maturities was also very little.

Six months later a sharp change had occurred. Yields of short maturities had increased only to 2.2 per cent but 5-year maturities yielded over 3.0 per cent and the yield curve went out to about 3.2 per cent at the long end. Few banks had funds with which to extend maturities but those few that could and did improved income materially. Even more important, they put themselves into a position to reap capital gains later if they had been so inclined. Another six months later, short-term rate had declined to 1.3 per cent, the 5-year rate to under 2.0 per cent, and the longest end of the yield curve was at about 2.8 per cent. Note that the long-term yield in the fall of 1953 was *above* the yield in the fall of 1952, but short-term rates were much lower. The yield curve then had quite a bit of shoulder.

The period of 1957 and 1958 presents a quite different case. In the summer of 1957 high yields prevailed but the range of rates along the yield curve was small. The shape was "hump-backed." Short-term rates were about 3.5 per cent; this was also the rate prevailing at the long-term end of the curve. The intermediate 5-year maturities, however, yielded about 3.8 per cent. While a bank might have been tempted to move into the intermediate maturities to increase income, the improvement would have been small.

Eight months later short-term rates and intermediate-term rates were both down materially, short-term rates at about 1.2 per cent and the intermediate rates at 2.6 per cent. Long-term rates, however, were still only moderately under the high level of the preceding summer; they were about 3.2 per cent. A bank might have felt starved for income by the short end of the market; it might have felt tempted to extend maturities to improve income. But what would have been the result?

By the end of October, 1958, all interest rates had increased, but the most drastic move of all was in intermediate-term rates. A flat yield curve prevailed from the 5-year to the longest end at roughly a 3.8 per cent level. Short rates had moved up to 2.5 per cent.

Can a moral be drawn from this experience? The future never repeats the past but in virtually all periods during the last quarter of a century, an extension of maturity when income was "needed" would usually have proved dangerous. On the other hand, banks were presented with good opportunities to increase income further several times *when income was already high.* If any moral can be safely drawn from recent history it is that income need is the most dangerous of all reasons for justifying an increase in portfolio maturity at banks.

Humpbacked Yield Curves

Although yield curves in most periods display either smoothly rising patterns or smoothly falling patterns (such as appear in Figures 19-4 and 19-6), exceptions occasionally occur. In some periods the yield curves have developed a peak which lies between the very short end and the long end. This is the so-called "humpbacked" yield curve, one in which intermediate maturities have the highest yields of all. The curve is illustrated in Figure 19-10, drawn from the official *Treasury Bulletin*.

Humpbacked yield curves seem to appear only in secondary markets and primarily in the market for U.S. Government securities. (For this reason, the phenomenon is also dealt with in Chapter 20 devoted to securities of that type.) Humpbacked yield curves have not appeared in the markets for either corporate securities or tax-exempts. The hump in intermediate yields is of special concern to commercial banks. Tax-loss selling, which is concentrated in intermediate maturities, is presumed to be the primary cause of this phenomenon.

The existence of the humpbacked yield curve emphasizes the practical fact that intermediate maturities are frequently almost as risky to hold as very long-term obligations. The potential of capital losses is rather greater than the potential of capital gains as long as banks bunch their investment in intermediate-maturity securities during periods of monetary ease. The possibility of capital gains is open for those few banks

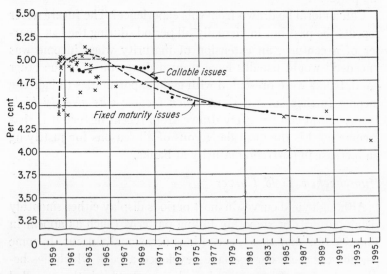

FIGURE 19-10. "Humpbacked" yield curve. Yields of taxable Treasury securities, December 31, 1959.

having funds to invest in the intermediate-maturity range during the brief periods when high yields prevail.

Interpretation of Up- or Downsweeping Yield Curves

The significance of the slope of interest-yield curves is of the greatest importance to investors. Commercial banks are specially concerned because the maturity distributions of their portfolios usually are concentrated along the sloping portions of these curves. Why do investors accept a lower interest rate for short funds (when the interest rate pattern is upsweeping) rather than get the best or the long rate? It is because they fear the loss of capital involved in an increase in interest rates. Conversely, why invest long-term when the short rate will yield more with a higher degree of liquidity? If an investor expects interest rates to fall, he may accept the relatively lower long rate to protect against its fall. If he expects the long-term rate to go up within the next year or two, he can much better afford to take a low current yield (or none at all and just hold cash) and buy the long-term security when its yield is higher and its price lower.

This point can be illustrated very simply. Suppose the current 20-year yield to be 4 per cent; suppose, also, an investor expects this rate to rise to 5 per cent within the next two years. The minimum price fall this would represent would be from 100 (the price for a 4 per cent yield basis) to 88.22 (the price for a 4 per cent coupon security within 18 years to run and selling on a yield basis of 5 per cent). Since the 8 points of interest (4 per cent for two years) are less than the 11.78 per cent capital loss involved in this shift, the investor could afford to hold cash and earn nothing rather than buy. Any short-term interest is just that much surplus.

Of course, no investor is ever sure that the interest rate will change in any given direction; he just thinks it is likely to go one way or another. A bank investment officer, no matter how well informed, cannot be sure; he certainly cannot stake his reputation and base his policy on such a firm conviction. He has to treat the matter as one of probability. Thus, we may make a more refined statement than the one already given. An upsweeping interest rate curve reflects a consolidated judgment of investors that an increase in the long-term interest rate is more likely than a decrease. A curve with a shoulder shows expectation of an early change in rates; one that is flat shows more uncertainty as to how soon the change is likely.

To some extent the slope of a yield curve may be viewed as betting odds implied by the actions of the investment market. For example, if a security maturing in two years yields roughly $\frac{1}{2}$ of 1 per cent more than a security maturing in one year, this can be viewed as a reflection of a market judgment that one-year yields are likely to rise $\frac{1}{2}$ of 1 per cent during the next year. The holding of a 1-year maturity puts the investor in a position to make a higher-yielding purchase at the end of the year. Although this interpretation of yield curves may be made, it is not a realistic one. Slope in the yield curve usually represents operation of the general insurance principle that the greater uncertainty of a more remote maturity is worth a slightly higher yield. On the other hand, changes in the slopes of yield curves probably do have some probability significance, though not of such a refined nature as to be subject to a precise and mathematical interpretation.

A downsweeping curve is interpreted just the reverse: it reflects the expectation of a drop in yields. One might ask: Why should any investor accept the hazards of long-term investment when he can get an even better rate for a short-term? The investor thinks that high rates cannot last and, if he takes the current high rate for the short term, his investment may mature later when interest rates will very likely be lower. Then he will be forced to reinvest at a poorer rate. Better take a $5\frac{1}{4}$ per cent yield on a high-grade 30-year obligation than about 6 per cent on a 5- to 10-year one. The full $5\frac{1}{4}$ per cent for 30 years is better than 6 per cent for $7\frac{1}{2}$ years and then 4+ per cent for the remaining $22\frac{1}{2}$ years.[2]

Still another characteristic of yield relationships should be

[2] The interest rates chosen in this illustration represent the actual levels and relationships that prevailed in 1921.

mentioned here. All investment and financial institutions have not been equal competitors for the securities of all maturities. The market always has been and continues to be, though less than formerly, a specialized one. Insurance companies buy "long." Commercial banks buy "short." Individual investors and trust funds have variable policies, depending on market conditions and on special and individual circumstances. Because of these institutional differences, the long-term market may be strong (yields low) when the insurance companies and pension funds have lots of money looking for a job; the short-term market may be strong when the commercial banks have ample reserve funds, but weak (yields high) when reserve funds are being pinched. The shape of the yield curve may reflect who has, and who does not have, funds looking for investment.

We might ask still a further question: Is a slope either up or down "normal" for interest-rate yield curves? A review of the Durand series[3] shows that 10 of the 43 years covered are of "no-slope" curves and that there are at least a half-dozen other years in which the slope is nominal. For about half the years since the turn of the century there has been a clear distinction between long and short rates on corporate obligations; in about half, or slightly less than half, of the years there has been no difference or a nominal one.

This is an imponderable. It is like asking: How many "normal" years can we expect? How many of extreme inflation *and* deflation? This is not just a rhetorical question. Business conditions supply a lot of the answers about the shape of yield curves. If we have a stable full-employment economy without extremes of inflation and deflation, we might settle down to an interest rate pattern that showed little choice between long and short.

A factor which might result in a bias toward the side of generally upsweeping interest rate curves has emerged. For many years prior to World War I, commercial banks were a small factor in the bond market. In the next decade or so, they were

[3] David Durand, *Basic Yields of Corporate Bonds, 1900–1942,* Technical Paper No. 3, National Bureau of Economic Research, Inc., 1942.

not leading factors but their relative importance was growing. In spite of large loan demand the commercial banks have continued to be important factors in the bond market; in the short-term section of it they are dominant. If one presumes that commercial banks will continue in this role, then an upsweeping interest rate pattern seems more likely than not. Since corporate flotations tend to adjust to the demands of the market, this may not be a persisting influence. It is already observable that corporate issues are shorter-term than they used to be; they may shorten up even further, or more may be offered at the very short end.

What Terminal Maturities Are Appropriate for Banks?

Our study of yield curves to this point must have made it clear that maturity differences in yield beyond the 20-year limit are small, negligible beyond 30 years. This makes one point reasonably clear: There is seldom any advantage to a commercial bank in investing funds in a maturity more remote than 20 years. Most banks do not go that far.

On the other hand, the margin of gain from the 5-year to the 10-year has often been material in recent years; likewise the gain from 10 to 15 years.

A study of the curves will also show that there have been times when the very short-term rate, such as that on less than 1-year maturities, has been so low that just a little extension of maturities would have increased income materially. In 1939, for example, the 1-year rate was only about $\frac{1}{2}$ of 1 per cent; the $2\frac{1}{2}$-year rate was about $1\frac{1}{4}$ per cent. If, in secondary reserve management, a bank had elected to put a *part* of secondary reserve funds at $2\frac{1}{2}$-year maturity, it would have been both safe and profitable. In making this sort of choice, there is a subtle distinction between the part of secondary reserves that a bank is likely to use within the year, and the part it may use but for which the need is none too likely. It is the "none-too-likely" portion that can be spread out a bit under extremely low rate circumstances.

On the other hand, in a period such as mid-1949, the odds

in favor of stretching maturities were by no means so promising. The 1-year rate was slightly over 1 per cent. This could be increased to about 1.2 per cent by going out to $2\frac{1}{2}$ years. This is a pretty thin margin for possibly forgoing the chance at distinctly better yields. The roughly $\frac{1}{6}$ of 1 per cent premium for $1\frac{1}{2}$ years of maturity could mean forgoing the chance at a material income improvement. If there were, for example, a chance of one in ten that yields were to go up sharply in the next two years, then the shorter maturity is the better bet. In this world of uncertainty, dismissal of any alternative as less likely than once in ten times seems unreasonable.

The foregoing paragraph, written in 1949, proved to be prophetic; sizable interest rate increases were not expected at that time, but they came. The slope in the 1960 yield curve shown in Figure 19-7 can be used to make the same point. The small improvement in current yield could hardly offset the risks of loss should interest rates turn up again.

The maximum maturity that a bank can afford in its investment operations is not some one single figure—3, 5, 10, or 15 years—the allowable maximum changes with circumstances. Banks that have competent investment control can afford to take considerable liberties with the strict rules of maturity spacing and maximum maturity and follow discretionary policies. Risk spreading is desirable, but good investment policy requires knowing whether the reward for risk taking is material or trivial. When the cost of a short maturity policy is trivial, it may be the wise thing; when the cost is material, it may be a poor choice.

The value of a short position often cannot be evaluated in precise terms. For example, if a person had only $100 to his name, would it be worth while to take a one-in-five chance of getting $1,000? An unimaginative person would tell us that a one-in-five chance at $1,000 is worth $200. Although it would be a profitable gamble for a person of considerable means, the person with just $100 to his name cannot take (or certainly should not take) chances like that. If he loses his $100, he may be sunk. A bank with a thin capital position or with other factors making chance taking undesirable should not go for the income of long maturities even if the market favors such a bet. A bank with ample capital may be justified in going out a way.

Spaced Maturities for Protective Investment Policy

Bankers have sometimes felt themselves faced with a serious conflict in investment policy. If they followed a policy of great conservatism—invested "short"—short-term interest rates yielded them a meager income. The risks of long-term investment were possibly excessive. The device used by many bankers to resolve this dilemma was "spaced maturities," a kind of diversification of maturity. When a bank followed this device, it always had some short-term, some intermediate-term, and some long-term securities. Because of the concentration of very short maturities at one end for liquidity reasons, it often meant that there were not equal amounts in all the brackets; if the excess of short maturities—probably to be considered secondary reserves—were kept on one side, the remainder might be divided equally among the future years up to the maximum maturity point.

When an investment account starting from cash is converted to a spaced (sometimes called "rotating") maturity basis, it is necessary to buy short-term securities as well as long-term ones. If the account to be converted consists solely of long-term securities, then some have to be sold, and "spaced" short- and intermediate-term replacements are purchased. If the account is unequally distributed, sales are made from the over-quota maturities and purchases made to round out the under-quota maturities.

Once an account has been put on a spaced basis and as long as there are neither additions nor withdrawals from this investment account, the proceeds from the securities which mature each year can be reinvested in securities of the longest maturity admitted to the account. Since time itself tends to shorten the maturity of the account, this reinvestment tends to keep the average maturity of the account constant.

The principle can be illustrated very simply. If a bank had

an investment-for-income account of $10 million and had decided as a matter of policy that this account should not exceed a 10-year maturity (which would give it an average maturity of 5 years), then when the account is established, $1 million may be invested in maturities of each of the following 10 years. The account would look something like Figure 19-11.

If the bank maintained a $3 million secondary reserve investment account in a maximum maturity of 3 years separate from the investment-for-income account, then the total of the two accounts would look something like Figure 19-12. There are even suggestions for classified kinds of secondary reserves, not unlike the suggestions made in earlier chapters.

The great merit of the spaced maturity plan is that it permits a bank to earn income at the average of rates which prevail at the long end of the yield pattern where reinvestment is made but produces a portfolio of considerable liquidity and with an average maturity of half the maximum.

The liquidity of the portfolio with spaced maturities is due in part to the fact that a sizable proportion of the portfolio matures every year but also to the fact that there is a constant replenishment of the supply of short-term but not yet matured issues. As we argued in an early chapter, the more remote liquidity demands do not come suddenly and without warning. In the great bank liquidation of the early 1930s, a $3\frac{1}{2}$-year period lay between the collapse of the stock market in the fall of 1929 and the banking holiday in 1933. Some banks were subject to earlier pressure, but there was a period of deterioration and warning for all institutions.

The point can be sharpened by use of a very simple illustration. Suppose that a bank maintained a 10-year spaced maturity plan. If in a 3-year period it had to liquidate 60 per cent of this portfolio for liquidity reasons, this could be done by selling securities having an average maturity of $1\frac{1}{2}$ years. The remaining portfolio at the end of the 3 years still had an average maturity of 5 years. Sales of high-grade securities with average maturities of no more than $1\frac{1}{2}$ years can never hurt a bank very much.

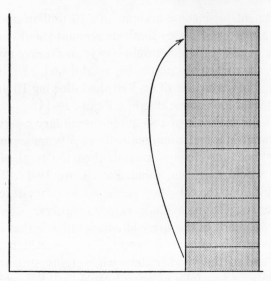

FIGURE 19-11. Maturity spacing, simple case. With a maximum maturity of 10 years, one-tenth of the portfolio matures each year. This portion is reinvested in 10-year securities. Average maturity is constant at 5 years.

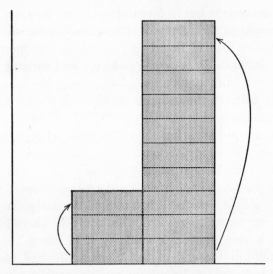

FIGURE 19-12. Maturity spacing, complex case. Part of the portfolio is 10-year; part is 3-year. Maturing portions of each group are reinvested at the appropriate maximum.

While the spaced maturity idea is simple in theory, it has a number of practical complications. A bank investment account is never the unchanged fund which was assumed in our illustration. Sometimes more funds are becoming available; at other times the account must be shrunk for liquidity or loan demand reasons. Also the market supply of securities is such that an exact spacing of maturities is seldom truly practicable; some degree of approximation is needed.

One of the first problems is the one we have already used for an illustration. If a bank is losing funds at a more rapid rate than is met by maturities from the investment portfolio, should it sell the very longest term or the very shortest term securities? (In our illustration we assumed that they sold the shortest maturities.) If a bank sells from the short end, this tends to increase the average maturity of the remaining segment of the portfolio; if it sells from the long end, the portfolio shortens. If a bank wanted to maintain an unchanged average, it should dispose of proportionate amounts from all maturity segments of the portfolio.

No invariable rule can be defended; all choices have elements of speculation. If a bank sells from the longer maturities, it improves its liquidity position but weakens its earnings position. Perhaps as good a choice as any is to try to maintain the average maturity in the portfolio. If the maximum maturity has been chosen well in the beginning, it should not be abandoned without good reason.

Fitting Spaced Maturity Plan to Yield Curve

In discussion of the "spaced" or "staggered" maturity plan, we indicated that this scheme, while having merit for some banks, nevertheless was not the sort of device that could be accepted without qualification.

For a bank to hold rigidly to a staggered maturity plan, without regard for the shape and conformation of the yield curve, would be to close its eyes to the opportunity for improving its protection at little cost, and very likely for improving its long-run income with added safety! If a plan of spacing up to, say, 15 years is adopted for the residual or nonliquid portion of a bank's investment account, that margin may be quite safe. But should a bank make replacements at the long-term end of the maturity schedule if, for example, the income margin between the 12- and the 15-year maturity has shrunk to a small amount?

In most recent years putting one-half of an investment portfolio into 1-year obligations and one-half into 4-year obligations would have yielded more than an evenly spaced 4-year portfolio. The larger proportion of short-term obligations would have given a bank more funds with which to take advantage of the yield changes that occurred.

This is correct, but it has one flaw. If a rate change should come in the near-term future and then be reversed well before the 4 years were up, the device would leave the bank at the end of the period with a slightly lower average earning rate. If the rate change should come in, say, about 3 years, however, the proposed two-way split of the portfolio would be an advantage, assuming that the bank kept the long half of the portfolio and let it approach maturity, rather than maintain it at the constant maturity of 4 years.

Still another difficulty mars these special "scalping" plans. Bank directors are often not very well equipped to appreciate their subtle points. Spaced maturity is a plan they can understand and adhere to. While complicated investment plans, such as the formula plans that have enjoyed such a vogue in investment management, have much merit, they are not always easy for nonprofessional directors to administer.

FEDERAL RESERVE CREDIT POLICY

Maturity policies pursued by commercial banks should be enlightened by a sophisticated interpretation of Federal Reserve credit policies. During the early postwar years when the Federal Reserve supported the prices (and therefore kept down the yields) of long-term U.S. Government securities, commercial banks could extend maturity *as long as they had confidence that this support policy would be continued.* In fact, however, the policy was terminated in 1951. This experience illustrates the general injunction that banks probably should look more at fundamental economic pressures than at official statements when forecasting the direction of public policy.

The Federal Reserve is committed to a policy of anticyclical credit action. This means that credit is tightened whenever general business conditions threaten to get out of hand. Conversely, money markets are eased when business activity recedes. These actions have complex and disputed effects upon interest rates; nevertheless, the short- and intermediate-term interest rates which are the ones most important to banks are clearly affected by such policies. Indeed, movements in interest rates are thought by some to be one of the principal instruments of monetary policy, since modest increases in rates are assumed to "lock" banks into holdings at the time of the increase because of their reluctance to realize losses. In practice, this "lock-in" effect probably has been weaker than its early expositors expected it to be. Tax-swapping may have weakened its influence so that it has less bearing on banks than on other investment institutions. Nevertheless, Federal Reserve policy intentionally produces considerable variation in both short- and intermediate-term interest rates and probably increases their range of fluctuation. Accordingly, banks should expect a cyclical movement in interest rates in planning their investment operations.

20

U.S. Government Securities

The role of U.S. Government securities in bank portfolios is primarily that of providing liquidity. Such investment also provides some income, the amount of which is not secondary but is subsidiary to liquidity protection. To the extent that a bank has free funds to invest solely for the sake of income, better yielding outlets are generally available. Investment in tax-exempt securities, for example, usually yields substantially more after taxes than is available from U.S. Government securities. Such an investment, however, sacrifices liquidity.

The type of liquidity supplied by holdings of U.S. Government securities is intermediate and longer term liquidity as well as the short-run or day-to-day kind of liquidity. As mentioned several times earlier, loan demand is subject to a considerable degree of cyclical variation. The rhythm of these cycles since World War II has been in irregular intervals of roughly two to four years. The provision of liquidity to meet loan demands at the peak, therefore, has required a form of investment from which banks can escape with the minimum of loss when such is needed.

One other small role is played by the portfolio of U.S. Government securities—that of providing collateral. Certain banking transactions, such as holding government deposits, purchasing funds from smaller banks in the Federal funds market, and borrowing from Federal Reserve banks, require the posting of acceptable collateral. While other types of collateral can be used in some circumstances, U.S. Government securities provide the form most commonly and conveniently used. In recent years, some banks have started to use tax-exempt securities for collateral, a practice which is workable by banks willing to take the trouble.

THE SUPPLY OF U.S. GOVERNMENT SECURITIES

The supply of U.S. Government securities is large. The legacy of war and depressions is an enormous public debt, a large fraction of which is in marketable form. While most of these securities are lodged with firm investors, a sizable supply is generally available in the secondary market. In other words, this is a market in which commercial banks can meet their investment needs without waiting for new issues. Even the very largest banks can generally find all the securities of the type they need without too extended or costly a search. What is more, many issues of Federal government securities have maturities consonant with bank investment policies.

The types of marketable U.S. Treasury securities issued include Treasury bills, certificates of indebtedness, Treasury notes, and Treasury bonds. The *Treasury bill* is the most liquid of all these instruments. These bills are discount obligations with initial maturities of from 3 months to 1 year. Bills with maturities of 3 and 6 months are auctioned by the Treasury Department each week. Amounts up to $200,000 can be obtained by noncompetitive bidding each week. Cumulated to $5,200,000 over a twenty-six week cycle this amount should meet the needs of a large majority of banks. In practice, it is generally possible to find Treasury bills of all outstanding maturities in the secondary market. The principal exception is when a special tax date may cause a shortage of a particular maturity. Treasury bills can be traded in large blocks, such as from $5 million to $25 million. These amounts frequently can be sold immediately on the telephone at or close to the prevailing bid side of the market.

Certificates of indebtedness are limited to a 1-year maturity. The certificate of indebtedness enjoys a fairly broad market but cannot be traded in as large quantities or with as little turnover cost as is true of Treasury bills.

Treasury notes have initial maturities of from 1 to 5 years. These obligations enjoy a reasonably broad market but they cannot be sold (or purchased) in as large quantities as either certificates of indebtedness or Treasury bills. Treasury notes can give rise to appreciable capital gains and losses, whereas Treasury bills produce only current income and certificates only trivial gains or losses. A later section on tax swapping will bring out the significance of this factor.

Treasury bonds have initial maturities of 5 years or longer. In recent years almost all new Treasury bonds have been given single maturities and without advance call provisions, but some bonds, issued in earlier periods in which there were call options that could be exercised by the Treasury, are still outstanding.

The Treasury securities described above are direct obligations of the Federal government. In addition, a number of governmental agencies issue securities: the Federal National Mortgage Association, the Federal Land Banks, the Federal Home Loan Banks, the Federal Housing Administration, the Federal Intermediate Credit Banks, and the Banks for Cooperatives. While the securities are not directly guaranteed by the Federal government, it is widely assumed that these agencies would not be allowed to get into financial difficulties. Their credit quality is generally assumed to be nearly as good as that of Federal government obligations. Although a few of these agency issues are sold with long initial maturities, most of them are relatively short-term. They generally offer yields that are moderately higher for any given maturity than those available on ordinary U.S. Government securities. The gain in income involves relatively little loss of liquidity. While large blocks of agency issues cannot be sold as readily as direct obligations, the quantities dealt in by most banks are not large enough to strain the resources of this market.

The supply of U.S. Government securities, apart from the

secondary market, depends primarily on the nature of Treasury finance. The largest part of this supply arises out of the debt refunding and exchange operations of the Treasury. New cash issues are also sold by the Treasury, but their supply is not as regular as the supply of exchange issues.

The Treasury is constantly having to refund a large volume of maturing debt. A steady supply of new securities can be purchased indirectly by the exchange process. A commercial bank wishing to get a new security offered by exchange has merely to buy the maturing security to secure the exchange privilege. In earlier years when interest rates were low and the demand for investment outlets was high, these "rights" were often a rather costly way of acquiring new securities. At the same time, some banks made some handsome quick profits speculating in these "rights." In recent years, however, "rights" values have usually been small or even negligible, so that investment access through this channel is reasonably priced.

In addition, the Federal government from time to time has deficits which require financing by new cash issues. Because of awkward seasonal characteristics of Treasury cash receipts, the Treasury has frequently had to borrow in the fall of the year even in fiscal years in which the budget was balanced overall. Years in which budget deficits are planned or appear as unwelcome events also require cash financing.

COUNTERCYCLICAL NATURE OF SUPPLY

The supply of Treasury securities displays one special characteristic that is both an opportunity and a risk to commercialbank investment in such obligations. Cash financing by the Treasury tends to be concentrated in periods when general business activity is low. This is partly a result of the conscious fiscal policy of the Federal government: the management of expenditures and receipts. In addition, deficits tend to coincide with a lower level of business activity because tax revenues automatically decrease in a recession, whereas expenditures such as those for unemployment insurance tend to increase automatically.

Offhand this seems like convenient timing for banks since it means a larger supply of Treasury securities at a time when loan demand tends to slacken.

This circumstance contains some inherent risks. Periods of deficit in Treasury finance which coincide with easier business conditions are also likely to coincide with periods in which the Federal Reserve System is encouraging ease in the money markets. In other words, such financing is likely to take place in relatively lower interest rate periods. Furthermore, during recent years Treasury financing in periods of money market ease has tended to be of a longer term nature. The Treasury is naturally tempted to extend the maturity of its debt during a period in which sales opportunities are favorable and interest-rate costs are low. The commercial bank that passively accepts the securities offered in new Treasury financing is thereby likely to be induced to extend the average of its portfolio maturities in low interest rate periods.

The converse, of course, is that when business conditions revive loan demands, commercial banks then may need to sell such low-yielding securities on a market in which prices have gone down and yields have gone up. The appropriate Federal Reserve policy of credit restraint in a period of boom and high loan demand seems to have had unusually sharp impact on the prices and yields of intermediate-term securities—the type most common in commercial bank investment portfolios. This "hump-backed" type of yield curve was shown in Figure 19-10.

A passive maturity policy based largely on the character of new Treasury offerings in recent years would have almost automatically led to investment losses. This issue will be dealt with later, but it suggests that in its investment policy with respect to U.S. Government securities a bank should not follow the passive policy of merely taking what is offered by the Treasury in its new cash offerings. More than is true of most other types of investment operations, banks have many reasons for conducting much of their U.S. Government investment operations in the secondary market for such securities. Fortunately this market is a "good" one: a market of narrow spreads between bid and asked prices and prompt execution of large transactions. It is a volatile market but technically well organized.

CHARACTER OF THE MARKET
FOR U.S. GOVERNMENT SECURITIES

In dollar volume the market for U.S. Government securities is larger than that for any other type of financial obligation by a very wide margin. Nevertheless, this market is relatively little publicized outside professional circles. Less than twenty full-fledged dealers operate in this market, and not all of them "make markets" in the whole list of U.S. Government securities. Special departments of five leading money-market banks offer formal dealer service, and a few other banks act as limited or informal *de facto* dealers. A dozen nonbank specialized dealers are now in business, less than half of which covers the whole range of Treasury obligations.

A commercial bank of any size usually maintains access to more than one dealer. Almost all the leading dealers recognize their responsibility to act as principals. They quote both bid and asked prices with relatively narrow spreads between these prices, and in normal circumstances support these bids and asked prices (make them "good") by genuine offers for more than token amounts particularly for the customers they value. This means that they will, in fact, buy reasonable amounts at their bid prices and sell reasonable amounts at the offered price. What is considered a "reasonable" amount, of course, depends on the maturity of the issue. As already indicated, a reasonable amount for a bill transaction may be quite large, whereas a reasonable amount for a note or bond would be considerably smaller. Dealers do not expect to have all the business of any one of their customers. It is considered proper for customers to shop about to some extent and compare prices. On the other hand, customers who try too diligently to shave prices by restlessly shifting their business among many dealers build up the reputation of being "shoppers" and therefore not truly favored customers. In normal periods very little can be saved by such

extensive comparison shopping. In troubled times a high standing with two or three dealers can be an asset of considerable
value. A bank may find it to its advantage to concentrate quite
a bit of its business in the two or three dealers who seem to give
it the best service. A small bank may do best to pick one dealer
and stick with him. In periods in which markets are quite volatile, dealers are often unwilling to buy securities offered for
their own position or to sell the securities that are sought.
Strangely enough, the second can, in some circumstances, be
more of a problem than the first. Since dealers cannot carry inventories of all securities, the particular security being sought
may not be owned by a dealer. If the market supply of this
issue is thin (as is true of some of the smaller Treasury issues),
he may hesitate to sell short for fear of being unable to replace
the security and of having to "fail" on delivery.[1] Under such
circumstances dealers may accept orders only on an agency
basis. Most dealers try hard, expertly, and honestly to execute
agency orders to the advantage of customers. It is only natural,
however, that they should make their very best efforts at execution for those customers that they consider "good" customers:
those who have given them a substantial amount of business in
the past.

TAX AND LOAN ACCOUNT UNDERWRITING

The Treasury Department carries most of its cash balances
in the form of deposit accounts in leading commercial banks.
These balances are known as "tax and loan" accounts. Almost
any insured commercial bank willing to qualify may become a
depositary. The receipts from tax collections and borrowings
are paid into these accounts under fairly detailed rules and regulations. The amount of taxes deposited is not contingent upon

---

[1] This event is not quite so drastic as the phrase indicates. It means that the
"failing" seller pays the coupon return on the security that had been sold to
the buyer without requiring the customer to pay cash for the security until
it is, in fact, delivered.

participating in new Treasury offerings, but the amount deposited from security sales does depend directly and to a major extent on the purchases made by a depositary bank. The funds in these accounts tend to be drawn out fairly promptly by transfer to the Treasury account in the Federal Reserve so that the life of these deposits is relatively brief. The relative speed of turnover is indicated roughly by the following facts: In recent years Treasury Department deposits in commercial banks have ranged between $2 billion and $10 billion. Most of the time, however, the balances have been between $4 billion to $6 billion, and $5 billion may be accepted as a rough average of such holdings. If this figure is compared with annual Treasury expenditures of about $80 billion, the normal period over which Treasury balances are carried in tax and loan accounts works out to be one-sixteenth of a year, or roughly 23 days. Although a relatively short period, it is enough to make many commercial banks think it worthwhile to try to maximize the amount in tax and loan accounts. The principal way of doing this is by participating in the underwriting of the sale of Treasury securities, particularly the shorter term obligations. Tax anticipation bills and certificates, two of the most popular forms of such obligations, are auctioned by the Treasury. The average bid yield on these securities has usually been lower than the yield at which they sell on the open market after issue; in other words, the price paid is higher than the open-market resale price. This means, in effect, that in order to secure deposits by this means, banks have had to accept some offsetting losses. This has made the profit margin on such underwriting particularly narrow; the amount depends on accurate estimation of the period that such deposits were likely to be available in tax and loan accounts. Dealers and others in the money market have complicated methods for estimating the "life expectancy" of amounts so secured for deposit. In practice, however, these estimates have been subject to considerable error. Treasury financial needs are not wholly forecastable. The underwriting gains from longer term securities are also potentially risky. Although quite volatile, banks clearly view tax and loan accounts as profitable. Most banks solicit the deposit of withheld tax payments aggressively.

These observations are only a warning, however; they should not discourage participation in cash financing. Such participation has some real advantages. When a bank has a known investment need, participation in the new-offering market is usually the cheapest way of meeting this need. Participation in the auctions of Treasury securities also has important indirect advantages. Some important customers of banks, such as nonfinancial corporations, are themselves sizable investors in short-term Treasury securities, particularly bills. These customers occasionally bid directly to meet their needs but more often than not they look to their banks to be agent buyers for them. When this is the case, participation in the auction equips a bank to service its customers' needs in a more sophisticated fashion and, with luck, to make more profit in doing so.

TAX SWAPPING

Prevailing tax legislation includes a special provision applying to commercial banks that has given rise to the practice known as "tax swapping." In brief, through this special tax situation commercial banks are permitted to charge losses on securities sold against current income. They can, however, charge only *net* capital losses in a given tax-computation period ("fiscal year"), that is, the excess of capital losses realized over capital gains realized during the same period. On the other hand, long-term net capital gains (the excess of long-term capital gains over capital losses) are taxed at only 25 per cent, less than half the standard corporate income tax rate. A sale which establishes a capital loss reduces income taxes. An immediate repurchase sets the stage for recovery of the loss in the form of a long-term capital gain which is taxed at a lower rate. The only problem is the timing of sales to establish losses and gains. Because of the required netting, a bank needs to concentrate establishment of losses by sale during one tax-computation period in order to achieve the maximum benefits of tax swapping, and to avoid realizing capital gains during that period. Conversely, realization of capital gains by sale should be concentrated in another tax period and realization of losses should be avoided in that period.

Simultaneous or nearly simultaneous purchases and sales may be made if they are not purchases and sales of the same or closely similar security. Swapping the same security requires a 30-day gap. Thus a tax swap can be used as an occasion in which to make a change in investment policy. Since the supply of U.S. Government securities contains many quite similar securities, a bank can establish either losses or capital gains and make nearly identical replacements if so desired; but it can also use the occasion for seeking replacements in a different maturity range. Reinvestment in low-coupon securities is usually particularly advantageous inasmuch as a larger part of the gain in them tends to be realized as capital gains and less as coupon or current income. (Banks are required to amortize premium securities but they are not required to accumulate discounts.)

The determination of whether a given fiscal year should be one in which capital gains are realized or capital losses taken depends on economic forecasting. To some extent the pressure to forecast may arise during the early part of the tax-computation period. Sometimes it is preferable to defer both purchases and sales early in a tax-computation interval until the situation is clarified, but delay is not always practical. For example, what appears to be an extreme high or low price may come early in such a period. A bank would clearly gain by taking advantage of such a price if it seems clear that the remainder of the tax year will have the same characteristics. For example, if a very high yield and low price appears early in January or February (for a bank which computes its taxes on a calendar-year basis) this low price may be an excellent occasion for taking a capital loss.

Once having taken the capital loss, however, the bank is largely committed to treating the remainder of that year as a loss year so that sales involving capital gains should not be

made in that year. This might seem no problem since prices
would tend to be low in such a year. It is possible, however,
that a bank might have some assets on its books at less than
market value and their sale (or maturity) might involve realization of a capital gain. In practice it is not likely that this will
be a serious handicap. Rising security prices are likely to be
accompanied by reduced loan demands and so a bank is not
likely to be under pressure for funds in such a circumstance.

The converse is equally true; if very high prices and low
yields turn up in January or February, it is unquestionably
desirable to make sales for the purposes of establishing long-
term capital gains. If banks should hesitate and delay, prices
might turn down and such gains could not be realized. Once
having made the plunge and having sold to realize a capital
gain, the bank is to some extent committed to treat the remainder of the period as one in which long-term capital gains
are taken and capital losses are avoided. Since a revival of loan
demand can occur fairly soon after a high-price low-interest-
rate period, this second circumstance can pose an awkward
dilemma for the investment manager of a bank.

Once a bank is committed to either a gain or a loss year, repeated use of this device can be made. For example, if early in
a tax-computation period the investment manager of a bank
decided that securities had reached a low in price and a peak in
yields, he might sell to establish capital losses and reinvest
according to his prevailing needs. If, however, this judgment
proved to be false and prices should slide still further, the
banker would be well advised to make further sales in order to
establish still further capital losses. Since no tax distinction is
made between long-term and short-term capital losses, this action can be taken promptly whenever new lows are reached. The
only cost of this policy is the small dealers' margins taken by
the market.

In a gain year the decision is not quite as simple. The establishment of a long-term capital gain early in the period would
usually be accompanied by replacement with other securities.

If prices go up still further any gain taken within a six-month period would be a short-term capital gain for which there would be no tax saving. Accordingly, the timing of sales to establish capital gains is generally rather more critical than the matter of establishing losses at the bottom side of the market.

FEDERAL AGENCY BONDS IN BANK PORTFOLIOS

The United States government has sponsored a number of governmental-purpose corporations that finance their activities by borrowing on the open capital markets. These corporations include the Farm Loan Banks (FLB), the Federal Intermediate Credit Banks (FICB), the Federal Home Loan Bank Board (FHLB), the Banks for Cooperatives (COOP), and the Federal National Mortgage Association (FNMA; also known colloquially as "Fannie Mae"). Their obligations are not directly guaranteed, but the market regards them as having a measure of governmental support. Some banks are investors in these obligations as well as salesmen of them in the groups that market these bonds. Although statistics on bank ownership of these obligations are compiled only rarely, the amount owned is estimated to be equal to about 5 per cent of direct U.S. Treasury obligations. This proportion probably varies cyclically since banks may not use these obligations for liquidity purposes quite so actively as they do direct obligations. The statistics of U.S. Government security trading suggest that the market in these issues is slightly less than 5 per cent of the total U.S. Government security market.

The credit quality of these securities is unquestionably high. Even in the absence of a direct guarantee the moral responsibility of the United States government is believed to exist. The more practical question is the degree of marketability that the securities enjoy and their appropriate place in liquidity holdings of banks. The market for the securities appears to be a good one. For a variety of reasons governmental agencies have tended to issue relatively short-term obligations so the relative proportion of short-term agency obligations is even higher than in the total marketable U.S. Government debt. One of the reasons these issues have proved to be quite marketable is that the dealers receive a small but welcome underwriting commission for participating in selling groups organized by the issuing governmental corporations. As a result, the dealers generally feel some obligation to make markets in these securities. While large blocks might not move readily, the spread of bid and asked quotations is only faintly wider than those prevailing on regular U.S. Government obligations. The amount which may be handled in single transactions is satisfactory for all but the very largest banks.

As a result of the popularity of agency issues, a large part of their yield advantage has been bargained away. Yields were formerly 10 to 40 basis points higher on agency issues. In recent years, however, the yields prevailing on agency issues have approached those prevailing on direct obligations and therefore their advantages have all but disappeared except on the very longest maturities. Banks that participate in the selling groups probably should own some, but the advantages of these issues for others are no longer so evident as they were years ago for banks without money market sophistication.

PORTFOLIO ROLE OF U.S. GOVERNMENT SECURITIES

Portfolio policy of a commercial bank with respect to U.S. Government securities consists of two major problems: The first problem has to do with the proportion of total funds committed to U.S. Government securities, and the second problem is the average maturity to be given the portfolio.

While no general rules can be stated for determining exactly how much should be committed to U.S. Government securities, the following observation may be helpful. U.S. Government securities have the unique advantage of being quickly salable in large quantities when funds are needed. They furnish an excellent resource on which to lean for a bank that is seeking to cover its unexpected needs for liquidity, which in modern banking is primarily the need to meet loan demand. A bank may use its general policy as to the maximum size of its loan account as a guide to its holdings of U.S. Government securities. This possibility arises because the amount of capital in a bank tends to be a more direct limit to the size of its loan account than to its holdings of high-grade securities (see Chapter 8). Whenever a bank has fewer loans than the amount that it considers the maximum possible size of its loan account, the difference between this maximum and loans actually held might well be covered by investment in U.S. Government securities. Additional amounts, however, would be only for liquidity needs associated with deposit movements. As already seen, such amounts tend to be small. Funds in excess of these amounts may be more profitably employed in tax-exempt securities or mortgages or possibly even in term-loan participation. None of these forms, however, have the liquidity needed to arm a bank to meet its maximum loan demands.

Maturity policy within the security account has already been generally discussed in Chapter 19. The choice is between a policy of varying maturity according to the state of the money markets and an automatic or nondiscretionary policy such as that of spaced maturities. Since forecasting is imperfect, a bank may be ill advised to try to outguess the business cycle. On the other hand, the policy of spaced maturities may be a mistake since it does not equip banks to meet the rhythm of changes in loan demands. A reasonable compromise policy is one in which a bank buys the longest maturity that it is willing to sell within the next two to four years in a low-price high-yield market. On the other hand, a bank need not hesitate to lengthen its average maturity when yields are quite high, nor need it refuse to contract maturities when yields seem relatively low by historical standards. This policy may not yield the highest income in the very short-run, but over the long-run it will both avoid losses and produce the type of portfolio that is consistent with the larger profit goals of a bank.

As said before, profit maximization is not attempted in this sector of a bank's accounts but rather in its over-all lending activity.

TRADING POLICIES

Most of what has been said before has been by way of caution against too aggressive trading policies. Knowledge of the future is denied all natural men. A winning proportion of right guesses is possible for only a limited few. Nevertheless, *some* portfolio managers in *some* institutions have made profits trading in U.S. Government securities in *most* years. Where trading profits are not a major goal, a flexible attitude toward portfolio management can, nevertheless, minimize or avoid losses. Strangely enough, trading opportunities sometimes are better for a medium-sized bank. It can get its trading done without disturbance to the market, whereas a large bank often cannot move its portfolio in volume without affecting relative prices by the impact of its large offerings and bids.

A number of trading operations can be conducted with relatively little risk. For example, a careful student of this market frequently observes shifts in relative yields among individual securities so that swaps could improve earnings without increasing average maturity. If a tax swap can be combined with such a shift, the transaction is all the more advantageous. This is not exactly market arbitraging as practiced by professional dealers, but it is related to it in terms of the circumstances that make such opportunities possible. In other words, an alert portfolio manager may be able to make these shifts in such a way as to improve return without increasing risk.

Superiority of yield for a given issue within its maturity range is not always the complete story. For example, short-maturity certificates do not have as active or large a market as do bills with the same maturity. It thus follows that the higher yield on certificates under some circumstances should not be considered a true improvement of income. Greater concessions may be required if these obligations must be sold prior to maturity for liquidity reasons. Since such yield differentials are sometimes available in the market only for a few days and occasionally only for a few hours, the manager of the investment portfolio needs to have a broad grant of authority from his board of directors to engage in such swapping activities. At most it probably would not be feasible to get approval of a body larger than a skeleton executive committee within the bank.

Sometimes trading may be advantageously done in a way that shortens average maturity without loss of income; occasionally it is even possible to increase income. The "humpbacked" yield curve, commented on before in this chapter and illustrated in Figure 19-10, is the circumstance that makes this possible. Under such circumstances securities having maturities longer than the peak point on the hump might be reasonably swapped for securities having short average maturity. This action would improve income. This action, however, is not without danger; the existence of a hump usually indicates an abnormal state of the market. If the market is one of unusually high yields and low prices, it may mean that it is about to take off on an upward price movement. If this be the case, the securities with somewhat longer maturities beyond the hump point in the yield curve may enjoy more price appreciation in the following period. A bank agile enough to change its position might still take advantageous action. So far a substantial upmove in the market has not taken place until the hump in the yield curve disappeared. But a bank engaging in such a sensitive operation must be prepared to relengthen maturities quickly if such be indicated.

Occasionally increasing average maturity is quite appropriate. This will be particularly true just as a boom period turns into a recession. Security prices may start to jump actively, and rather appreciable capital gains may be in prospect. The portfolio manager who is sensitive to general economic developments can turn this circumstance into an opportunity. But such action also has its risks. If temporary strength in the U.S. Government security markets proves to be only a false move before the conditions of the economy turn strong again and move into an even higher boom, lower security prices probably will return. Another risk is that even if the judgment involved in this action is right in the short-run, the downturn in business may prove to be only short-lived. If a recession is relatively brief, as in 1958, a bank must reverse this average lengthening of maturity within a few months to solidify its profits in realized form. Some of the banks that waited to take their capital gains on a long-term basis saw the gains disappear as the market went down after the middle of that year.

If portfolio trading is an approved strategy, a number of tactical problems should be kept in mind. Frequently an apparent spread in prices may have relatively little real substance. An offering in any sizable volume would drive quotations before the seller; aggressive bids would drive up prices quite rapidly. The portfolio manager, therefore, cannot take prevailing bid-and-ask quotations as being a completely satisfactory measure of the market situation. Under such circumstances the normal practice is to test the market with experimental sales or purchases. If a bank has a good relationship with a dealer—one to which he is willing to disclose his general plans—this dealer may be able to make his switches for him, which leaves the matter of market tactics to the dealer. The portfolio manager, however, should be sensitive to the problems encountered by the dealer and understanding of them so that he can fairly judge whether he is being given a good or an unsatisfactory marketing performance by the dealer.

A few incidental devices are available for making some modest extra income from a U.S. Government security portfolio. While "rights" values (discussed above) no longer amount to very much, on occasions they can produce a little extra income. A bank that has clear-cut liquidity plans can sometimes purchase bonds and notes (which are more likely to be offered a long-term exchange) as they approach maturity but some time before they start to show active rights value in the market. Such a period is usually six to nine months in advance of maturity. Such issues may be available at fully as good yields as are otherwise available. It must be recognized, however, that until rights trading becomes active, these issues do not have quite the same degree of marketability as Treasury bills. The amount of rights value is speculative, but if basic income is satisfactory a chance of a bonus return exists.

Still another way in which the U.S. Government security portfolio may be used for incidental gain is in the lending of securities to dealers, primarily to cover their short sales. The customary lending rate is $\frac{1}{2}$ of 1 per cent per annum. This return may be added to the yield already accruing to the owner of the loaned securities. The portfolio manager who lends securities for short sales, however, should recognize that he has foregone liquidity for the contractual period for which the securities are loaned. Sometimes securities are loaned on a day-to-day basis, but they may also be loaned for specific contractual periods. Whatever the contractual period may be, the portfolio manager has lost some measure of flexibility during this period.

21

Tax-exempt Securities

For more than a quarter of a century the most important investment outlet of commercial banks has been the securities of the Federal government. For an equally long period the second most important outlet has been the tax-exempt securities of state and local governments, commonly known (but not quite accurately) as "municipal" bonds. Over 21 per cent of commercial bank investment portfolios are now in this form, an amount equal to almost 9 per cent of total earning assets. In some recession years, such as 1954 and 1958, these securities have been bought by commercial banks in very large volume.

Tax exemption is the principal feature that makes these securities attractive to commercial banks. Prior to World War II commercial banks seldom paid appreciable amounts of Federal corporate income taxes. Tax exemption was then available on Federal Government obligations and the level of bank income had been reduced by the Great Depression. That situation, however, has since changed greatly. Banks now pay Federal income taxes on a large part of their income. Tax rates are also higher than they were before World War II. Tax-exempt securities are the principal tax-reducing outlet available to commercial banks. In recent years tax-exempt securities have generally yielded an after-tax income materially above that available on fully taxed securities of a given quality and maturity. An added advantage to a commercial bank of investment in tax-exempt securities is that, being an active investor in such securities, it is better able to participate in the underwriting of such obligations. Investment has also sometimes been the opening wedge by which banks have been able to attract increased deposit of public funds. Although cynics generally assume that the deposit of public funds is governed primarily by gross political considerations, this is not always the case. Many governmental units concerned with borrowing problems have felt beholden to those banks that were active purchasers of their securities. Those that also participated in underwriting the sale of such securities may have gained even more public funds. The advantages of investment in tax-exempt securities, therefore, cannot be fully measured simply by the arithmetic of comparative after-tax yields.

One of the shining merits of state and local government obligations for bank investment purposes is that, being issued in serial form, they offer a much wider, more flexible choice of maturities than that offered by almost any other market obligation. In this respect they exceed the flexibility of corporate bonds (excepting rail equipment obligations which are generally issued in serial form). Another factor making state and local government obligations an unusually desirable bank investment vehicle is that the steady stream of them coming into the market provides frequent opportunities for investment. The investor in corporate obligations must sometimes wait weeks before an obligation of the type he is seeking may be available in the new-issue market. This is seldom the case in the market for state and local government obligations.

The chief offset to these very real advantages of state and local government obligations for bank investment lies in their relatively low liquidity. Under some circumstances these obligations can be sold fairly readily, but the spread between bid and asked prices is frequently so great as to reduce net realized income appreciably. This high cost of turnover inhibits the use of these obligations in a highly flexible and mobile investment operation.

Small banks having net taxable income of $25,000 or less on which the marginal tax rate is only 30 per cent rather than 52 per cent under prevailing law do not have quite so great an incentive to buy tax-exempt obligations as larger banks. Even for these banks, however, tax exemption may be quite valuable, particularly if it permits net taxable income to be kept under $25,000.[1]

TYPES OF STATE AND LOCAL GOVERNMENT OBLIGATIONS AVAILABLE FOR BANK INVESTMENT

More than 100,000 local government units exist in the United States, of which at least 25,000 appear to have been borrowing in 1957. The number is doubtless greater now. Because of so many issues and issuers, the number of types of obligation is bound to be very large. Only general groupings of these obligations need to be distinguished for purposes of investment planning.

State vs. Local Governmental Units

The obligations of the fifty states constitute a very special class of obligation. Although defaults of state bonds have not been unknown, the credit of most states is high. As sovereign bodies, they have almost unlimited power to cover debt service. On the other hand, governmental units below the state level are of several quality grades. Cities and school districts are the most frequent borrowers; other units such as counties and townships less frequently. The credit quality of most of these bodies is also generally high, but exceptions exist. The record shows that very few "municipal" bonds have ever become hopelessly worthless, but defaults have occurred and could occur again. The general taxing power of these intermediate units gives them a solid ultimate value in most cases. In the short-run, however, it is not always possible to marshal this power

[1] The first $25,000 of income of all banks is subject to taxation at the 30 per cent rate, but all income above $25,000 is taxed at the 52 per cent rate. This marginal rate of taxation, not the arithmetic average rate, should govern all decisions relating to investment management.

effectively. Limited-purpose government authorities or districts such as for installing and operating sewers, sanitary systems, toll roads, toll bridges, or parking lots also have the privilege of borrowing on a tax-exempt basis. The obligations of most of these units, however, are not based on a general authority to tax; they are "revenue" obligations.

General Obligations vs. Revenue Obligations

A majority of the obligations of governmental units are a direct responsibility of the issuing unit and are based on their general credit. These "full-faith and credit" obligations command as high a credit rating as can be earned by the issuer.

While most general credit obligations are based on unlimited authority to tax within the jurisdiction of the issuing body, some are based on a limited tax authority or only on the authority to levy special assessments. Obligations based on unlimited power to tax obviously are stronger than those where the authority is limited. If the basic and assessed value of the aggregate property or income subject to taxation is limited, however, then an unlimited taxing authority may provide less protection than a limited tax authority applying to valuable property on which outstanding debt is low or to a large flow of income or transactions. The character of the underlying tax authority is a necessary starting point for credit analysis.

Revenue obligations are those that are not based on a general tax foundation but are serviced only by the special receipts from projects such as toll roads, toll bridges, parking lots, or other utilities which were financed by these obligations.[2] Revenue obligations, depending on the power of a given property to produce earnings, should be analyzed in about the same way corporate securities or business properties are analyzed. The analogy to public utility operations is quite close. Toll bridges, toll roads, parking lots have a monopolistic power to

[2] Some obligations issued for the purpose of financing projects such as these may nevertheless be general credit obligations. For example, New York State has unconditionally guaranteed some bonds of its toll road authority.

set prices subject usually to review by a higher authority, but they must also be limited in their pricing policies by the elasticity of user demand. The price elasticity of demand for public parking lots is obviously much greater than that for strategically located bridges.

PREVAILING CHARACTER
OF BANK TAX-EXEMPT INVESTMENT

Bank participation in the market for tax-exempt securities has tended to be on the side of high credit standards and general conservatism. As a result, the rates of earnings realized by banks from this source have been rather low. Several factors other than conservatism, however, appear to account for much of this result.

Timing of Purchases

Commercial-bank purchases of tax-exempt securities have generally been concentrated in years of relatively low loan demand. Interest rates tend to be low in such years and so commercial banks have, by virtue of this fact, concentrated their purchases in years of relatively low yield. Since yields on tax-exempt securities are particularly volatile, the returns from securities acquired dominately in such periods are particularly low. Table 6 shows the net acquisitions of tax-exempt securities during the postwar years and the ratios of these changes to changes in total earning assets. Individual banks presumably have made even sharper shifts in their portfolios than can be detected in the aggregates reported by all commercial banks.

The Quality of Tax-exempts Held by Commercial Banks

The formal published statistics give very few clues to the quality of state and local government securities purchased by commercial banks. The best evidence, which is admittedly indirect and not wholly satisfactory, is contained in the expressions of opinion of the underwriting firms that have had con-

TABLE 6

COMMERCIAL-BANK INVESTMENT IN TAX-EXEMPT SECURITIES
(Dollar amounts in millions)

Year	Holdings at year-end	Net increase during year	Changes in amounts held as a ratio of changes in earning assets (per cent)
1946	$ 4,395	$ 425	*
1947	5,276	881	39.3
1948	5,661	385	*
1949	6,548	887	15.0
1950	8,118	1,570	24.2
1951	9,198	1,080	18.2
1952	10,189	991	11.0
1953	10,821	632	15.6
1954	12,586	1,765	17.3
1955	12,698	112	2.3
1956	12,901	203	4.8
1957	13,915	1,014	20.5
1958	16,505	2,590	17.3
1959	16,958	453	8.9
1960	17,570	781	6.1

* Total assets declined.

SOURCE: Roland I. Robinson, *Postwar Market for State and Local Government Securities* (a National Bureau of Economic Research study), Princeton University Press, Princeton, N.J., 1960, table 11, p. 82 (with figures since 1957 added).

siderable experience selling these securities to banks and also in the opinions of the supervisory agencies. The general testimony of these groups is that the quality of tax-exempt securities purchased by most large and well-managed banks is high, generally higher than the average of these securities issued. On the other hand, some smaller banks apparently have bought lower quality state and local government obligations. This is particularly true of banks in remotely located areas that have concentrated their purchases on essentially local securities, sometimes of rather poor quality. The frequency of such concentrations is not disclosed though the public statements of the supervisory authorities warn that such practices do exist. The securities of small governmental bodies are not inferior *per se;* indeed some are excellent. Banks should not be dissuaded from buying such securities when the quality is adequate. But special objectivity is required of a banker in the judgment of quality in local obligations.

Some quantitative evidence on the investment quality is shown indirectly by the yields of tax-exempt securities held by banks. Table 7 shows the estimated yields for the portfolios

TABLE 7

COMPARATIVE AFTER-TAX YIELDS FROM GOVERNMENTAL SECURITIES
HELD BY COMMERCIAL BANKS

Year	Tax-exempt securities	U.S. Government securities*	Year	Tax-exempt securities	U.S. Government securities*
1946	1.51	0.93	1954	1.85	0.94
1947	1.59	0.93	1955	2.04	1.01
1948	1.82	0.97	1956	2.24	1.10
1949	1.75	0.98	1957	2.22	1.26
1950	1.57	0.86	1958	2.35	1.23
1951	1.60	0.80	1959	2.57	1.34
1952	1.74	0.86	1960	2.87	1.49
1953	1.92	0.95			

* U.S. Government securities earnings are averages for member banks (see various *Federal Reserve Bulletins*) multiplied by arithmetic reciprocal of prevailing corporate tax rate.

SOURCE: Roland I. Robinson, *Postwar Market for State and Local Government Securities* (a National Bureau of Economic Research study), Princeton University Press, Princeton, N.J., 1960, table 12, p. 85 (with 1957—1960 data supplied).

of tax-exempt securities held by insured commercial banks for the past decade and a half. The yields in each case can be compared with the after-tax yields of U.S. Government securities held by commercial banks. Tax-exempt yields, while favorable compared with after-tax earnings on U.S. Government securities, suggest high-quality investment on the average.

Maturity of Securities Purchased

The maturities of tax-exempt securities held by banks were surveyed twice in official call reports during the past 15 years. The call report for all insured commercial banks in 1956 surveyed the distribution of maturities, as was also done for the year 1947. These data are shown in Table 8.

TABLE 8

MATURITY OF STATE AND LOCAL GOVERNMENT OBLIGATIONS HELD BY INSURED COMMERCIAL BANKS, JUNE 30, 1947, AND JUNE 30, 1956

Maturity	Amount in millions		Per cent of total	
	1947	1956	1947	1956
Maturing in 1 year or less.......	813	1,931	16.9	15.2
Maturing in 1 to 5 years........	1,420	4,437	29.5	34.9
Maturing in 5 to 10 years.......	1,269	3,825	26.3	30.0
Maturing in 10 to 20 years......	945 ⎱	2,539	19.6 ⎱	19.9
Maturing after 20 years.........	381 ⎰		7.9 ⎰	
Total......................	4,828	12,732	100.0	100.0

SOURCE: Insured bank call reports for 1947 and 1956.

As Table 8 shows, commercial-bank holdings have been concentrated in the maturities of 10 years or less. Less than a fifth of such holdings are in maturities of more than 10 years. The 1956 data show no division beyond this maturity, but in 1947 a very small proportion of the securities then held matured in more than 20 years. For reasons outlined below, it is unlikely that portfolios turn over very much by sale prior to maturity. Commercial banks presumably tend to concentrate their initial purchases in the 10-year maturities. A few buy even longer term securities. The slightly larger concentration in early maturities represents a combination of the shortening of maturities by the passage of time and some initial purchase of earlier maturities.

*Link between Underwriting and Investment
in Tax-exempt Securities*

Commercial banks that are members of the Federal Reserve System may not underwrite the sale of securities except those of domestic governmental units. This prohibition was adopted in the early 1930s because of several disastrous experiences of banks in underwriting corporate and foreign securities in the late 1920s. Since the securities of the Federal government are not formally underwritten, member banks can formally underwrite only the general obligation of state and local governmental units and those of Federal government agencies.

Some banks participate in the underwriting business in a large way. About two dozen banks have fully staffed underwriting departments which both head and join major syndicates for the purchase and resale of large tax-exempt issues. These banks compete vigorously with the investment banking houses that have tax-exempt underwriting departments. In addition, about fifty other banks regularly participate in underwriting groups, frequently concentrating their attention on the securities of public bodies located near where they operate. This is not as much of a limitation as might seem at first; the Bank of America specializes in and confines itself to underwriting California obligations. Within this limitation it manages to stay near the top of the national list of underwriters year after year. Some banks without formal departments or trading arrangements participate from time to time in underwriting the sale of local issues about which they have direct knowledge and perhaps interest. The amount of this activity is unknown.

Underwriting activities are usually carefully separated from the investment operations of a bank. The investment departments of some underwriting commercial banks direct very little business to that department; most of them deal with their bank's underwriting department only at arm's length. Trust departments frequently direct all of their business to outside dealers to avoid suspicion of a conflict of interests. It is fairly evident, too, that the portfolios of the banks operating extensive underwriting activities do not necessarily tend to be larger than those of banks less active in this field. There are exceptions; some of the more vigorous underwriters also have exceptionally large portfolios of tax-exempt securities. The opposite is also true: some active underwriters hold rather small tax-exempt investment portfolios.

POLICIES FOR INVESTMENT
IN TAX-EXEMPT SECURITIES

The ways in which banks use tax-exempt securities as investment outlets vary widely. Since the needs of individual banks also vary widely, divergence of policies is to be expected. A discussion of investment policy must, therefore, be conducted in somewhat general terms.

Use of Tax-exempt Securities for Liquidity Purposes

Tax-exempt securities do not enjoy a particularly good secondary market. In addition, their price often shows a considerable degree of short-term volatility. The tax-exempt market can dry up one week and then move briskly the next week. These securities, therefore, cannot be used extensively as liquidity reserves. To a considerable extent tax-exempt securities tend to be purchased at time of issue and to be held until final maturity. Nevertheless, a secondary market of sorts exists and well-known and recognized issues can be sold in reasonable-sized blocks. The marketing costs of such transactions are usually an appreciable deterrent to trading but not beyond consideration, so that shifting is sometimes feasible. At the same time it must be recognized that limited marketability is the rule rather than the exception; hence primary dependence on these securities for liquidity purposes would be hazardous.

The principal exceptions are a few widely known issues of tax-exempt securities for which good secondary markets with reasonably close price spreads exist. For example, the notes of the Public Housing authorities enjoy a reasonably good market; large blocks of these securities can be sold prior to maturity without excessive cost. A certain limited number of other tax-exempt securities, principally those of well-known and highly regarded issuers, also enjoy reasonably good two-way markets.

As a general matter, therefore, commercial banks are ill-advised to use tax-exempt securities for first-line defense liquidity. Under some circumstances shifts can be made, but the cost is generally so great as to limit such shifts to quite necessitous or profitable purposes.

Quality Standards for Tax-exempt Securities

In general, a high degree of conservatism prevails in commercial-bank investment in tax-exempt securities. To a considerable extent this is logical and the following paragraphs should not be read as encouraging banks to depart from true conservatism. It is possible, however, that traditional standards of conservatism may have led banks to depend too much on external evidence and not enough on their own initiative in investment analysis. Some banks seem to depend on the ratings assigned by the leading investment services as guidance in making security selections. The investment rating services have generally been fairly conservative in their rating of tax-exempt securities. Some feel that they have been more cautious in rating tax-exempt securities than in rating corporate obligations. Those securities given high investment ratings can be counted on as being quite high in quality. The middle ratings, however, such as "A" or "Baa," are really rather broad bands of quality, with a security at the top of a band far better than one at the bottom. In addition, ratings are assigned only to the larger issues; the numerical majority of issues are not rated. Thus a bank cannot really evade its responsibility to evaluate the credit quality of the tax-exempt securities it acquires.

A discerning bank willing to exercise independent judgment and to study carefully the real economic factors lying back of unrated issues frequently can acquire such securities having excellent investment characteristics and at yields considerably better than those obtainable from rated securities. It must be recognized, of course, that such securities do not enjoy as high a degree of marketability as fully rated securities. No bank would be justified in putting more than a modest part of the funds it commits to tax-exempt investment in unrated securities. Nevertheless, an investment of some funds in well-selected unrated securities offers some income improvement.

What characteristics should a banker look for in unrated securities? By and large, the principal characteristics are a good tax-collection record, moderate debt burden, and promise of stability or growth. Since rating services depend almost entirely on past performance, they frequently do not allow enough weight for the strength of growing communities. Rapidly growing communities frequently are faced with difficult financial problems and accumulate debt rather fast in the early stages of growth. In the long run, however, sound growth is far better security than stagnation. The securities of small but growing communities frequently offer the greatest challenge as well as the greatest rewards for the acute analyst of investment quality. One paradox of this kind of situation is that the banks best able to judge the soundness of growth are those located in or near these areas. Such banks, however, are likely to encounter relatively strong loan demand and so have fewer funds available for investment. Conversely, banks located in receding areas are more likely to have funds available for investment.

Analysis of State and Local Government Credit

Within the space that can be devoted to this subject here it is impossible to describe adequately the principles of credit analysis that apply to state and local government obligations, or "civil obligations" as they are frequently labeled in this context. The literature on the subject, however, is extensive and a bank officer involved in supervision of a portfolio of these securities can find ample study sources from which to develop his skills in this type of analysis.[3]

The basic factors governing the credit analysis of state and local government obligations do not differ materially from those applying to other kinds of credits. First, the credit of a governmental unit is superior if it is a responsibly organized and managed entity. States and municipalities that are well-managed and largely free of corrupt politics obviously are superior credit risks. Second, the relationship of debt to basic value and taxing power needs to be moderate. Third, the cash flow of a governmental borrower needs to be adequate to cover debt service with considerable margin to spare. Finally, a well-managed local governmental unit should be able to finance some portion of its capital expenditures from current tax revenues. This may be awkward for a small school district but possible in most other cases. The statistical standards for testing these facts are outlined in the texts referred to in the preceding footnote. They are relatively simple applications of principles that any bank investment officer who has gained facility in analyzing other credits can apply.

Credit Files

National or state member banks investing in tax-exempt securities are required to maintain credit files for such securities.[4]

[3] R. E. Badger, H. G. Guthmann, and H. W. Torgerson, *Investment Principles and Practices,* 5th ed., Prentice-Hall, Inc., Englewood Cliffs, N.J., 1961, chap. 17. Also G. W. Dowrie, D. R. Fuller, and F. J. Calkins, *Investments,* 3d ed., John Wiley & Sons, New York, 1960, chap. 22.

[4] See Digest of Opinions of the Office of the Comptroller of the Currency Relating to Operations and Powers of National Banks: Investment Securities Par. 355, August 1957, Section 3(g) investment securities regulation:

All investment securities shall be supported by adequate information in the files of the bank as to their investment quality.

Each national bank is required to keep in its files supporting information and data which will enable the management to exercise informed judgment in determining whether each issue of securities should be purchased or retained in the investment portfolio and to permit examiners to determine that the investment securities purchased meet the requirements specified in the Investment Securities Regulation.

This principle is just as important with respect to general obligations of

The dictates of prudence as much as law should also require that such files be maintained. This may seem to be duplication of effort when only rated securities are purchased; nevertheless, since the quality of state and local government securities can deteriorate after purchase, acquiring and recording the basic analytical information is a good precaution. Investment supervision should not be passive, it should be active. Fact-finding is a central element in such supervision.

Geographic Diversification

Most sizable portfolios of state and local government securities attempt to reduce the risks of area blight by geographic diversification. Most banks necessarily have loan accounts that are concentrated locally. If this is particularly true of a bank, it probably should purchase a fairly large proportion of its tax-exempt securities from issuers located in other areas. Offset against this advantage, however, is the probability that the credit analysis of securities issued by remote localities cannot

---

municipalities even though exempt from the restrictive provisions of R. S. 5136. The minimum information to be retained and analyzed in support of a proper credit judgment of municipal obligations is as follows:

A. Statement of debt, including overlapping, floating and full faith and credit obligations.

B. Assessed valuation, including basis of assessment.

C. Property tax rates.

D. Tax collection record.

E. Receipts and disbursements.

F. Sinking fund operation and requirement.

G. Future debt service requirement.

H. Population (whether well balanced or otherwise).

I. Economic background.

J. Default record.

K. Per capita debt.

With respect to each issue of investment securities the minimum information to be maintained in the banks' files should include reasonably current financial and operating statements. Although the rating services and investment counsellors play an important part in the intelligent and informed acquisition of securities by banks, management may not under any circumstances delegate its responsibility for maintaining a sound investment account to a rating service or any other individual or entity. Therefore, it is incumbent upon management to use all necessary and available sources of information to keep informed and the data obtained should be retained for ready reference.

be as discerning as that of securities issued by nearby governmental bodies. The value of extensive geographic diversification
may be questioned; prudence only requires that the portfolio
manager avoid too much local concentration. Avoiding concentration in securities of very small governmental units is also
wise, even if moderate use of them may be profitable. The
types of difficulties likely to assail full faith and credit obligations are not so randomly distributed that a large number of
issues is required to effect a satisfactory degree of diversification. A selection of securities in a few well-selected areas should
suffice to meet a prudent standard for geographic diversification.

Maturity Policy for Tax-exempt Investment

Commercial banks are faced with a perplexing dilemma in
framing a maturity policy for investment in tax-exempt securities. In periods of high loan demand very small amounts
of funds are available for investment in any form of securities,
including tax-exempt securities. Table 6 demonstrates this point
strikingly. Past experience has demonstrated, however, that
periods of high loan demand are likely to coincide with those
periods in which the yields on tax-exempt securities are most
favorable. On the other hand, when loan demand is sluggish,
the yields on tax-exempt securities are frequently driven quite
low by the sudden convergence of commercial-bank demand on
this essentially volatile market.

Under such circumstances should a commercial bank attempt
to cling to a policy of spaced maturities? Purchases that fit its
general schedule of spaced maturities tend to create a potential
of considerable capital losses in later periods. On the other
hand, a concentration of purchases in short-term obligations
under such circumstances would reduce future earnings. If an
investment officer can retain the confidence of his directors
over several years of lean profitability, it is quite likely that
forgoing income in the short run can add to profits in a worthwhile way in the long run. Investment of free funds in periods
of slack loan demand in very short-term securities, whether

tax-exempt or not, would leave an investment officer with funds which might then be converted to longer term tax-exempt investments in periods of high loan demand and correspondingly high yields.

It must be recognized, of course, that this policy is not without dangers. If periods of slack loan demand should prove to be longer than they were in any of the postwar recessions so far experienced, considerable income might be lost by this policy. On the other hand, a great deal can be said in support of the policy on general grounds. As suggested many times in the preceding pages, the primary business of banks is making loans. A bank that has followed a reasonably aggressive loan policy will have built up a fundamentally strong earnings position. Against this background it should then be able to forgo some current earnings. The increase in liquidity and mobility created by this policy would make a bank strong, no matter which direction economic events might take.

Some supervisory authorities urge banks to limit their purchases of tax-exempt securities to terminal maturities of 5 to 7 years. This would result in a maturity distribution not unlike that governing holdings of U.S. Government securities. The argument for this policy is the conventional one that it reduces the potential losses in the event of forced sale.

This argument is perfectly valid. In so far as banks have remote liquidity needs which are not covered by other liquid assets, there is a possibility of the need to sell tax-exempt securities. If this should occur, it would be preferable to have maturities within this range. However, as already said at various points, the potential liquidity of these securities is limited at best. Depending on these securities for liquidity might tend to reduce total earnings considerably. It is quite likely that total earnings would be increased if banks depended wholly on U.S. Government securities for liquidity needs, forgoing earnings to the extent necessary to keep those portions of portfolios liquid, and candidly treating the tax-exempt segments as frozen but profitable assets. Shortening the portfolio of U.S. Government securities would not limit income nearly as much as would shortening of tax-exempt portfolios. The yield curves prevailing for state and local government securities have often had rather shallow slopes, so that maturities of 5 to 7 years yielded considerably less than the income obtainable from slightly larger maturities. The yield curves for U.S. Governments have generally had much more sharply ascending slopes for early maturities in the postwar period. In any event, the purchase of evenly spaced maturities within the 5- to 7-year range does not increase liquidity by virtue of ultimate maturity in any very important degree. With either policy the amount maturing within a 6-month period is small in relation to total assets. A 6-month period is a relatively long one for measurement of liquidity needs. A preferable policy probably is to have an extra concentration of relatively short-term securities combined with allowance of maturities of 10 years or 12 years for the remainder of the portfolio. Such a policy should result in considerable improvement in yield and still have, in fact, higher liquidity potentials than an evenly spaced maturity policy.

Promotion of Deposit Balances
via Investment in Tax-exempt Securities

Cynics not to the contrary, the banker most likely to develop a satisfactory and profitable business in handling public funds is the one who is informed about, and sympathetically disposed toward, public financial problems. Such a banker can combine investment in tax-exempt securities with a general interest in policies of public finance of local governmental bodies in a way which will make him a natural depositary of public funds. The knowledge of cash flows of state and local government units is a good test of the ability of these governmental units to service their debt obligations. More important, this knowledge gives a banker the necessary planning information for management of the liquidity needed to cover the movement of public funds.

Promotion of public balances as a professional activity has

not been widely practiced by bankers in the United States, but it has proved profitable in a number of outstanding cases.

Tax Swapping[5] of Tax-exempt Securities

Tax-exempt securities do not furnish as natural a vehicle for tax swapping as is true of fully taxable securities. They qualify, strictly speaking, only on the loss side of the swap since capital gains realized from their sale are taxable even though coupon income is not. However, capital losses realized by selling tax-exempt securities can be charged against regular income under prevailing tax laws; thus one-half of the tax-swapping cycle may be practiced advantageously.

There is, of course, no point in taking losses only because the government absorbs half of them. Some other purpose should be served by the taking of these losses, if they are to be taken. Alternative uses of funds for lending would qualify as such a purpose. Tax swapping cannot be profitable except for obligations that can be sold without serious concessions from their true market value as reflected by yields prevailing on similar securities at the time of sale.

Banks that practice tax swapping aggressively probably should carry an adequate volume of more marketable tax-exempt securities, such as those of the Public Housing authorities. When funds are needed these securities can be sold with minimum turnover costs and the losses charged off in the tax accounting. In order to have an inventory of securities which is accessible for tax-loss selling, it must have been acquired in an earlier period.

Tax-loss selling of tax-exempt securities has one quite special facet. Low-coupon tax-exempt securities often show particularly heavy losses when yields are relatively high because part of the true yield in such securities must be taken in the form of capital gains. When banks are buying longer maturity tax-exempt securities, it sometimes pays them to select low-coupon

[5] See Chapter 20 for an explanation of tax swapping.

obligations which sell at large discounts, provided the basic quality and yield are adequate.

Shrewd investment management of such details often improves income appreciably. In recent years, the low-coupon tax-exempt securities have tended to sell on a better yield basis because so many investors want current income from their tax-exempt holdings. This is particularly true of individual investors. For this reason, banks can well afford to depart from the preferences of the market and buy low-coupon obligations when offered on an advantageous basis. Such securities are usually available only in the secondary market, but shrewd buyers sometimes can find moderate-sized blocks of them. This possibility is rather less practical for very large banks whose investment requirements cannot be readily met in the secondary markets.

Part VI

PROFIT MANAGEMENT

A primary goal of commercial-bank management is profits. Most bankers have some choice in the way in which profit is sought and also the way in which profit is used. But the choice may be a hard one: Should short-run profits or long-run profits be maximized? One is tempted to say that the choice should always be resolved in favor of long-range profits. A successful bank officer, however, must retain the support of his directors and stockholders. They may prefer short-run profits.

The way in which profits are used also presents a conflict of considerations: a choice between long-run and short-run gains. The final chapter suggests a set of priorities for guiding the top management of a bank through these paradoxical choices.

22

The Determinants of Bank Profits

The unstated goal of almost every policy and plan discussed in the foregoing chapters has been to improve bank profits. In most cases, however, the discussion has been centered on the effects of the single subject at hand on profits. More often than not the practical problem is that of choosing from among a number of mutually exclusive and complex alternatives. The purpose of these two concluding chapters is to discuss in summary form how the various policies pursued in the management of bank funds should be balanced so as to maximize aggregate bank profits.

The importance of an over-all view of profit management is hard to exaggerate. Bank profits are achieved mainly by balance, precision, and consistency in management rather than by isolated bold strokes of business planning. In many lines of industrial activity some single unique idea—a striking marketing device, an unusual product, a unique location—may be sufficient foundation for large profits. The opposite side of the coin, of course, is that a fairly large proportion of industrial and commercial concerns show losses even in the very best of times. The business of banking, however, is one of more modest but more assured profits.

Comparatively few banks sustain losses. Evidence with respect to the distribution of bank profits is relatively indirect. A special study made more than a decade and a half ago for the year 1944 showed that less than 1 per cent of commercial banks suffered net losses. Since this was a wartime year, the evidence is not conclusive with respect to peacetime conditions. However, more recent if less direct evidence suggests about the same conclusion. The Statistics of Income prepared by the Bureau of Internal Revenue based on income tax returns give some clues, though not as clean evidence as would result from a special inquiry. Their evidence, however, suggests little dispersion in banking profits. Tax returns filed in the fiscal year 1958 (most of which were for the calendar year ending December 31, 1957) indicated that more than 95 per cent of all commercial banks had taxable net income. Some of the remaining 5 per cent doubtless had net income less than total tax-exempt interest. The number of banks suffering losses was thus undoubtedly small—probably not more than 1 or 2 per cent of all commercial banks. The amount of loss reported by banks having net losses was less than $\frac{1}{2}$ of 1 per cent of compiled net income of all banks. The evidence, therefore, suggests that money-losing banks are uncommon and are mainly relatively small banks.

The other side of this picture is, of course, that exceptionally large profits are equally rare in banking. Examination of the profit records of the large banks indicates a far closer bunching of the rate of earnings on invested capital than is true, for example, of manufacturing enterprises of a similar size. In many ways banking profits are like public utility profits: They are reasonably assured but they are also generally limited.

The fact that relatively few banks suffer large losses, however, should not give bank managements much comfort. Quite the contrary, to achieve satisfactory levels of profits bank managements must be thoroughly on top of all aspects of their business. It is the function of this chapter to suggest the way in which the various aspects of the management of bank funds are joined together at the level of top management in the pursuit of an over-all profit goal.

A casual observer of banking profits, particularly in the years since World War II, would be struck by an apparent stability of such profits. Profits were also unusually high in several depression years, such as 1954 and 1958. He would be tempted to conclude from this evidence that banking profits are relatively immune to the business cycle.

This would be a wrong conclusion based on misleading evidence. The accounting for bank profits induced by prevailing tax legislation conceals a very considerable degree of cyclical variability. For one thing, the tax swapping of securities, described in earlier chapters, tends to concentrate banking profits in years in which money rates are declining and security prices increasing. A second factor is that transfers to reserves on loans tend to be concentrated in years of high loan demand. Both factors tend to obliterate evidences of cyclical variability in bank profits. For these reasons, reported banking profits have not only been sustained but have, in fact, bulged slightly in such years as 1954 and 1958.

A critical review of the statistics of bank earnings after allowance for these factors shows that bank earnings still contain a pronounced cyclical pattern, a pattern that conceivably might become larger rather than smaller in the future. In other words, banks may have been lulled into complacency, feeling that they were in a cycle-proof industry. This is not true; banks continue to be quite fully exposed to the influences of fluctuations in the level of economic activity.

The discussion in this chapter will be broken into three major sections. The first will consider the gross income of banking, the second the expense side, and the third the matter of capital gains and losses in banking. These three sectors contain the principal factors that determine the levels of banking profits.

GROSS BANKING INCOME

The principal determinants of the gross income received by banks are: (1) the rates of interest on both loans and investments, and (2) the composition of bank assets. A simple but incomplete measure of the second factor is the ratio of loans to investments. Service charges also have some bearing on bank earnings and will be discussed briefly in this section. Such factors as trust earnings, foreign department earnings, and earnings from other banking functions such as safe deposit rentals will not be discussed.

Rates of Interest Received

As many preceding comments should have made clear, rates of interest received are a principal determinant of banking profits. These rates of interest are subject to powerful external forces which are resolved in the money and capital markets, forces that are largely beyond the influence of the individual institution. Interest rates on loans are largely fixed by the external competitive factors of the market. Banks not located in central money markets have more latitude in the fixing of loan interest rates, but no bank is free from the influence of competitive alternatives. Banks can classify customers and charge higher rates to those customers not qualified for the very best credit rating, but the power must be cautiously exercised. Interest rates on investments are almost wholly determined by the money market. Furthermore, investments bring no compensatory balances with them.

The point to be noted above all others is that the rates of interest prevailing on loans, even without adjustment for the influence of compensatory balances and with full allowance for the greater cost in making loans, are nevertheless considerably higher than the rates of return from investments. The principal way in which managerial judgment can be exercised is in the composition of the asset account. The range within which bankers can set the interest rates charged customers is rather narrower. Nevertheless, the exercise of managerial judgment within this range influences the profitability of lending considerably.

Ratio of Loans to Investments

For a long period there has been debate but no agreement as to when a bank is "loaned-up." As commercial banks entered the 1960s, however, an increasing proportion of them seemed to find themselves near the highest point of comfort and financial convenience. The ratio of loans to investments has risen in the postwar period, but it has not reached or exceeded the levels that prevailed in earlier periods, such as before World War I or even in the 1920s. A bank cannot, of course, control precisely the ratio of its loans to its investments. Some banks are located where loan demand is strong, and they have access to customers with growing needs; they are able to go about as far as they wish in the development of loan business. Other banks, however, are not so fortunately located and must either promote lending vigorously or content themselves with investment income. The bank that must promote aggressively admittedly has to offer inducements whether they be in the form of price or of service to secure added loan volume. Nevertheless, the strength of postwar loan demand suggests that most individual banks, except the very remotely located ones, probably should not blame external events but rather their inactivity if they do not have just as large a volume of loans as they desire.

One of the intangible but important determinants of the appropriate ratio of loans to total assets is the quality of loans in a bank. A portfolio of very high-quality loans can unquestionably be a larger proportion of assets than one that contains loans marred by some credit doubts. For example, a portfolio primarily of consumer loans or loans to small business concerns certainly could not stand up against a portfolio of open-market paper and loans to prime corporate risks. No statistical devices exist for establishing the quality of a loan portfolio, but the extent to which the portfolio tends to produce real losses may be a guide.

Various kinds of ratio tests are used to measure the pressure of loans on total bank resources: ratios of loans to total assets, to earning assets, and to capital accounts. Each of these ratios measures a somewhat different analytical point. Ratios of loans either to total assets or to earning assets have somewhat different analytical significance than ratios of loans to capital accounts. The ratio of loans to either total or earning assets is primarily a test of liquidity. If the loan account itself has a relatively low liquidity quotient (as usually should be assumed), working liquidity must be found in the nonloan assets, either in cash or in investments. In other words, the appropriate ceiling of a loan account when measured as a ratio to assets should be determined by the character of total liquidity needs, whether they are for deposit fluctuations or to meet outstanding but unexercised commitments to make loans. The ratio of the loan account to the capital account is really a measure of the extent to which ultimate realized losses may be safely accepted without jeopardizing the continuing viability of a banking institution. In general, this ratio should be interpreted in light of the quality of the loan account. Since the two principal kinds of ratios have differing significance, the fruitful way to use them is to compute both forms and to determine that the loan account meets both tests. It is possible that, in practice, rather too low ceilings are set when only one ratio test is applied; somewhat higher ceilings can be employed if the loan account is made to qualify under both types of tests.

Investment Management to Maximize Income

The discussion of investment policies in the preceding chapters contained a number of devices for improving investment income. These devices are all legitimate and have been successfully used by many banks. Nevertheless, it is important to put them in their proper perspective: They are not of the highest order of importance in the long-run determination of banking profits.

One of the commonest investment devices for improving bank gross income is that of stretching out the average or maximum maturity. When yield curves have a considerable degree of upward slope to the right, this device unquestionably improves earnings—for the time being. If one takes a longer look at total bank earnings, however, one may ask whether, in fact, maturity stretching has paid off in the long run for the majority of banks that have practiced it. As was pointed out in Chapter 19, dealing with maturity and yield, the principal pressures to extend maturity have arisen in periods of relatively low interest rates which, of course, meant relatively high security prices. Banks may have exposed themselves excessively to the risks of realized capital losses in this process. Alternatively, and possibly even more seriously, they may have exposed themselves to the risk of being unable to make profitable and desirable loans.

Occasionally, maturity stretching can be practiced safely and profitably. The best opportunity comes at the peak of the business cycle, at which point the highest tension in the money markets usually prevails. Doing this successfully is a superb act of investment daring and the rewards are substantial. Banks equipped with the necessary money market sophistication, with sufficient courage, and with an adequately tolerant board of directors to engage in such daring tactics are relatively rare. Many banks question whether the policy is as dazzling as it first seems to be.

Tax swapping has unquestionably improved bank income. It should be practiced by every bank that has enough in its portfolio to make the swaps practically feasible. Nevertheless, tax swapping does not, except in rare circumstances, improve investment income to the point where it equals the income available from good lending. Tax swapping should be used by a bank to the extent that it properly must have a secondary reserve portfolio for somewhat more remote contingencies. It is dubious, however, whether a portfolio should ever be larger than it would otherwise be simply to take advantage of tax swapping.

Investment in tax-exempt securities is also a dubious competitor with lending for limited bank funds. The after-tax yields of tax-exempt securities have unquestionably been attractive in many periods. It must be admitted, however, that a tax-exempt portfolio tends to be a relatively illiquid one. Tax-exempt investing is an excellent second choice but it is seldom a good first choice.

Service Charges

Commercial banks learned about making service charges in the 1930s when earnings were unusually low. During the more prosperous postwar years they have extended the practice. Service charges planned according to rational schedules are unquestionably fair and equitable. They avoid the servicing of unprofitable accounts and encourage maintenance of larger balances. On the other hand, some banks, avid to increase their margin of earnings, have pushed service charges to the point where they have become a voiced or unvoiced annoyance to many customers. In figuring the value of an undisturbed balance banks have frequently used much lower rates of interest than those prevailing in the money markets. Judicious customers have been prompted to calculate ways of minimizing both activity and balances. The exact influence of service charges cannot be determined, but the question must be raised whether or not some banks have carried service charges beyond the point of diminishing returns.

EXPENSES OF COMMERCIAL BANKS

A discussion of the management of bank funds is not an appropriate place in which to make any extended comments about the operating practices of banks, the factors that account for bank expenses. However, a few observations about bank expenses may help top management to establish more rational goals of income determination.

Bank Expenses Are Largely Fixed

Banking is essentially a service business. Like many service businesses its operating expenses are to a very considerable extent fixed, at least over the period of time in which most managerial decisions are made. That means that expenses do not vary closely with the volume of business done or with gross profits. Fortunately, the relative stability of gross profits in recent years has so far avoided making this fixed nature of bank expenses a critical factor. Nevertheless, with the continuance of cyclical swings, the fixed nature of bank expenses could cause them to become more important in the future than they have been in the recent past.

Because of fixed expenses banks may experience fairly sharp variations in net current earnings. The correct goal, however, is to maximize the long-term profits of a bank rather than merely to stabilize them year by year. Bank stockholders and directors may have been deceived by the relative stability of reported earnings in recent years. As a result, top managements might panic if faced with a drop in profits. Under such pressure they might curtail developmental and educational expenses that are needed to develop long-term profits. The only cure for this situation is education in the financial facts of life, an education which will start in the first year in which a serious reversal of banking profits occurs. This education has to start with the board of directors and the top management itself.

Personnel Costs

Many banks survived the years of lean earnings before World War II largely by virtue of loyal staffs who continued to serve them faithfully though paid less than their true value in competitive open markets for skilled labor. This was not altogether an act of beneficence; those who have spent long years in banking often tend to be timid and conservative by nature and thus hesitate to take the risks of shifting to other jobs. Recently this disparity has been corrected somewhat. The problem remains acute, however, since salary and wage levels generally go up as economic productivity goes up. Just maintaining relative place means a fairly steady rate of wage and salary improvement.

In the long run commercial banking will not maintain its competitive place unless it keeps up the quality of its personnel. Some savings in quantity are possible but not many. Automation and other devices will reduce routine physical work such as transit operations and bookkeeping. It is hard to imagine, however, any degree of automation that can successfully replace the skill and competence of middle-management bank officers and senior nonofficial employees who have long-standing contacts with and personal knowledge of customers. If bank profits are to be sustained it is through maximizing income or through savings elsewhere, and certainly not by resorting to any new wave of salary economy, should bank profits slip.

Interest Paid on Time and Savings Accounts

Since the mid-1950s bank policy with respect to interest paid on time and savings accounts has often been solved by Regulation Q. Some banks have been below the regulatory ceilings but, under pressure of competition, these ceilings have been approached by a fairly large number of banks.

Rate policy below the regulatory ceilings is basically a competitive matter. The value of money to a bank is determined by the characteristics of the loan demands it faces and the amount of capital it has to justify further increases in loans. An aggressive policy with respect to time and savings deposits, including an attractive rate on them, may be quite profitable for a bank that can use more funds. On the other hand, such added funds are by no means clearly profitable for other banks. A good rule: Pay what money is worth, neither more nor less. Don't follow external competition; follow internal cost accounting.

CAPITAL GAINS AND LOSSES

Capital gains and losses do not represent for most banks an important feature in the final determination of profits. Nevertheless, differences among individual banks in this factor may be relatively more important than is indicated by aggregate profit figures. To some extent the reported figures of capital gains and losses have been obscured by the several tax features already mentioned: tax swapping and transfer to loan reserves. Although technically and correctly reported as capital gains, the second cycle of a tax swap produces interest income in economic terms. The artificial nature of estimated losses in tax-induced transfers to loan reserves should also be recognized. True capital gains and losses have been of small proportion in postwar commercial banking.

The Striving for Capital Gains

Aside from the types of reported capital gains growing out of special tax situations, should banks strive to improve their earnings by investing with the goal of capital gains? If capital gains are sought by investment in securities of lower quality, the wisdom of this policy is extraordinarily dubious. It is hard to believe that the policy ever has any merit. The one circumstance in which banks can seek capital gains is to run counter to the movement of money-market interest rates by lengthening of maturities. This policy has already been discussed. As the earlier discussion should have made clear, the successful achievement of capital gains under such circumstances is accessible only to the most unusual skillful and sophisticated of market traders. In other words, capital gains promise relatively little hope for improvement of bank earnings. Loans, of course, provide no true capital gains.

Capital Losses

The first impulse is to say that banks should seek to minimize capital losses under all circumstances. This is partly but not wholly true. Some institutional investors such as insurance companies have discovered that by liberalizing their credit standards and increasing the rates charged customers, they have been able to improve their rate of earnings considerably. It is hard to enunciate precisely a standard that expresses the extent to which more aggressive lending policies are appropriate for banks. It is entirely possible, however, that if banks were willing to work harder at the lending process and to safeguard their loans by more carefully devised protective features, they could make more loans at premium and profitable rates of interest. If lending of this sort should produce greater compensatory balances, the policy is particularly desirable. In other words, capital losses should not be *minimized;* rather they should be *optimized* in relation to the maximization of interest returns on loans.

A bank should not feel compelled to make capital gains cover capital losses; the two factors are quite unrelated under existing conditions. Each should be judged by the standards appropriate to it.

The Influence of Growth and Size on Bank Profits

Businessmen have always been aware of the importance of growth. In recent years, however, growth has become even more than a business goal; it has become a national preoccupation. We worry about relative national growth rates and debate at length the economic policies needed to stimulate growth.

Banking has not usually been thought of as a "growth" industry. Some banks have grown faster than others, however, and it would be expected that more rapid than average growth should have increased profits accordingly. Surprisingly enough, this has not always proved to be the case. The Federal Reserve Bank of Kansas City made a study of the relationship of growth and earnings at individual commercial banks.[1] The study found that the more rapidly growing banks did not have higher earnings than banks that had grown less or not at all. The more rapidly growing banks had higher gross rates of earnings, but they also had higher expenses. Although this hypothesis can be neither proved nor disproved by the statistics, it may explain these facts: The more rapidly growing banks were spending much more to gain deposits and can improve their earnings whenever they taper off these expenditures. The survey was based on the postwar years from 1947 to 1959, years marked by quite special influences on both industry and agriculture. It is conceivable that after growth has been stabilized the banks that had achieved more growth will be able to get expenses under control and to transmute the benefits of growth into profits.

This evidence suggests that growth by itself is not a guarantee of profits. On the other hand, it does not make a case against

[1] *Monthly Review* of the Federal Reserve Bank of Kansas City, July, 1960.

growth. It suggests that there is an optimum rate of bank growth which is probably positive but not necessarily the maximum rate of growth.

Influence of Size on Banking Costs

A related research inquiry of the Federal Reserve Bank of Kansas City developed some evidence suggesting that the costs of doing business at big banks were appreciably lower than those at smaller banks.[2] The finding is hardly unexpected but the specific causes of this result might not have been surmised without statistical evidence. The study showed that the primary reason for lower costs at large banks was a lower ratio of salaries and wages to total assets. Interest costs and other expenses of large banks were not appreciably lower than those of small banks. The greater economy in salaries and wages at large banks is all the more notable since large banks pay higher salaries, even for routine clerical posts, and offer more diversified services, such as in foreign departments or trust operations, than do small banks.

The inquiry also showed that the sharp differences by size of bank were mainly in the very small banks. Operating expenses of banks with less than $5 million of total assets were relatively greater than those of banks with $25 million. As size increased above $25 million costs decreased slightly but the amount of decrease was moderate.

The individual bank does not have the option of choosing its size; it can only observe the economic facts of costs and profits. Nevertheless, the value of growth to a bank may be judged to some extent by application of these facts. A quite small bank can put a higher price on growth than a bank that is already large enough to achieve many of the economies of scale.

[2] *Monthly Review* of the Federal Reserve Bank of Kansas City, February, 1961.

23

The Uses of Bank Profits

The profits generated by a bank are distributed according to a sequence of priorities. The order of sections in this chapter might be considered a suggested statement of such priorities. The first use of profits is to establish special earmarked reserves, particularly reserves for losses on loans. In addition, a bank may establish other functional reserves such as those covering litigation costs on trust department operations or special losses on foreign operations.

The second priority in the use of bank profits is to increase bank capital. This priority is a practical rather than a theoretical necessity. Theoretically, added capital could be raised from the new-issues market. Practically, this has been done rather infrequently by banks. Retained earnings have been the major source of bank capital during the past generation.

Third, dividends may be distributed to stockholders. The treatment of dividends as a residual item may seem a bit ironic in view of the purposes of a business corporation: that of producing profits for the owners. The paradox is more apparent than real. If the first two priorities were not met, the residual earnings accruing to owners would not grow and might shrink, a result that would be against the long-run interests of owners.

Although the sequence of sections is intended to indicate a general pattern of priorities, some variations in them can be made legitimately. For example, the establishment of functional
428

earmarked reserves may not necessarily command a priority over adding to the general capital account, particularly for a bank that feels it needs to show an enlarged or strengthened general capital account for legal or publicity reasons.

EARMARKED RESERVES

The strategic value of earmarked reserves is that they permit a bank to realize and charge losses without disclosure or any sense of embarrassment. Earmarked reserves are intended for specific purposes, and they can be used for such purposes without reproach. For example, if a bank wishes to promote consumer lending aggressively, it must necessarily expect a certain amount of losses in that type of operation. The establishment of earmarked reserves furnishes a ready outlet for the charge-off of these losses without any particular discredit being attached to the action. Although this distinction is not entirely logical, charging of losses directly to bank capital accounts is viewed apprehensively by stockholders.

Earmarked Reserves for Loans

Almost all lending involves some credit risk. The amount varies widely among types of customers. Losses of this type are likely to be brought to light by bad times, even though credits have been degenerating unnoticed for a long time. For this reason a bank is likely to be faced with the need of recognizing sizable losses in bad years and fewer at other times.

It would be folly to argue that the losses belonged just to the income of those bad years. For that reason, the use of some device to provide for likely, though as yet unascertained, losses is recommended. This principle has been recognized for banks by the Bureau of Internal Revenue (BIR), which now allows the regular charging off of estimated losses on loans for tax purposes.

Although the BIR rule for providing for loan losses might be improved, it is nevertheless the leading one in use and is probably superior to any other device that has ever had widespread usage. This rule, therefore, furnishes a good point of departure for the consideration of loan loss provision out of current income. The BIR plan may be summarized as follows:

1. A bank may determine its loss rate by a moving average of the losses of the past 20 years. For statistically minded technicians, there are two ways of establishing the loss rate: (1) the 20-year moving average of losses divided by the 20-year moving average of "admitted" loans, or (2) the 20-year moving average of the loss rate. Since large losses are usually determined and booked in bad years when loan volume is low, it is likely that most banks would gain by using the second of the two alternatives!

2. The loss rate is applied to the current loan volume; the resulting dollar figure is then credited to a special loan valuation reserve.

3. All losses as they are realized are charged to this valuation reserve.

4. The valuation reserve account may be increased until it is three times the current level of losses as estimated in step 2 above. If the valuation reserve becomes excessive because of a shrinkage of loan volume, for example, it does not have to be reduced; but no further additions can be made until it is below this level.

Just how much current income should a bank devote to the amassing of a reserve for losses on loans? Is the BIR rule adequate? While a bank is building up its allowable reserve according to BIR rules, the amounts credited to the reserve are likely to be fairly ample. What about the bank that has reached or is approaching its maximum reserve allowance according to BIR rules? Three years' average loss is apparently a fairly adequate rule, but the record of the past shows a number of depression years in which a single year's charges would have exhausted the reserve accumulated by this technique.

To what extent is this record a good guide for future events? A great many of the bases for expectations have been vastly changed. Bank credit practices have improved, but they have accepted loan business which they used to reject. Public policy with respect to economic depressions has changed. Some factors indicate lower loss expectations; some indicate greater loss expectations.

Several factors indicate that bank loan losses in the future may be less than in the past. For example:

1. The art of credit granting has been vastly improved.

2. The liquidity of business concerns has increased. Credit risks for business as a whole are probably smaller than in any past times.

3. Depressions probably will be opposed by more vigorous public efforts at alleviation than has been true in the past.

4. Banks face fewer liquidity problems than they faced in past depressions. Many loan losses were not due to inherent weakness in the loans, but rather to the fact that banks, suffering great pressure for cash, have to press for liquidation of credits in a fashion quite contrary to their tastes and better judgment. A different way of making the same point is that any strong tendency toward liquidation is cumulative; once it starts, its effects are transmitted to otherwise good credits. Such momentum or cumulative effects were clearly in effect during the early 1930s.

Only one factor indicates that bank loan losses may be greater in the future than in the past: Banks hold larger amounts of capital loans than in the past.

Generalizations derived from the experience of all banks do not necessarily apply to the individual bank. The BIR rule is for an individual bank, but it takes account of the past only. As a matter of policy, a bank may change the character of its lending operations. When, for example, a bank undertakes to compete for real estate loans, it is taking on a new and different kind of risk. History of the past is not applicable. Such a bank might feel compelled to make larger loss provisions than past records indicate.

No rules, no statistics, will yield a completely satisfactory answer. Judgment is the final guide. A bank should take a clear-minded view as to the relative kind and character of the lending risks it is assuming and then charge enough in its inter-

est rates to cover this kind of risk adequately. The excess
amount so charged should be set aside in a loss reserve for
operating purposes. This should be done even if the amount
exceeds that allowed as a tax deduction. Only after considerable
experience, including probably one full swing of business conditions, should a demonstration of excessive provision for loss
be taken as conclusive.

Earmarked Reserves for the Investments Portfolio

While a fairly sizable earmarked reserve for losses on loans
is justified, it is hard to envisage any sizable need for earmarked reserves to cover losses on investments. Bank investments are used primarily for liquidity purposes and only secondarily for income. Under such circumstances the ordinary
use for reserves as a pool on which to draw when losses occur
should not exist in any large degree. A small reserve, of course,
may be useful. A bank engaging extensively in tax swapping
may not wish to display this fact in its published statements.
Some question may be raised, however, whether two sets of
records should be maintained. Tax swapping, however, is an
established practice and should be undertaken when it increases
income. If the directors understand the process thoroughly,
there is no reason why the disclosure of the "losses" it generates should create any embarrassment.

BANK CAPITAL

If all the needs for reserves have been met and a bank has
satisfactory earnings left, the question then faced is: How much
should be used to increase bank capital? The relationship of
banking earnings to capital is direct. In any business, the proprietary funds are the result of either the original owners' investment or the retained earnings. In commercial banking, the
amount coming from the first source has dwindled so much that
bank capital is increased mainly by retained earnings. As a

result, a review of dividend policy means first a review of bank capital policy.

Function of Bank Capital

The function of capital in commercial banks, and in financial institutions generally, is quite different from that in most other business enterprises. In a manufacturing or a public utility concern, the function of capital is to finance (provide funds for) the acquisition of the brick and mortar and other real ingredients needed for the business. In banking, the function of capital is primarily that of a guarantee fund. The capital funds of commercial banks insured by the Federal Deposit Insurance Corporation on December 31, 1959, were $18.8 billion; on the same date the investment in bank buildings, furniture, fixtures, and the like amounted to $2.5 billion. In other words the "real" uses of capital amounted to only 13 per cent of the total capital accounts. Since the "hidden" capital reserves of some banks take the form of undervaluation of fixed assets, this percentage may truly be higher, but hidden capital reserves are also concealed by other means. To the extent that other means are used, the true ratio would be lower.

Capital performs the guarantee function for other enterprises but not so dominantly. The capital of a manufacturing concern is something of a cushion for long- and short-term creditors to fall back on, but this is only one of its purposes. Bank capital has almost no other purpose.

Because of this guarantee function, supervisory agencies— the Comptroller of the Currency, the FDIC, and the state banking departments—have strongly urged increases in bank capital on the grounds that the public deserves the protection. For years there was a general belief that a bank's capital should not be less than one-tenth of its deposit liabilities; stated the other way around, deposits should not be more than ten times the capital. How old this rule of thumb is no one knows; it was used in a California law as early as 1909 and was proposed in a report of the Comptroller of the Currency in 1914.

Bankers' Attitude toward Capital

Whatever the nature of supervisory policy, banks have to choose their own capital (and therefore dividend) policies. What should the guiding standards be? Banks should and do take a responsible view toward their obligations. The responsibility of banks to discharge liabilities according to contract is overriding. Banks cannot exist if they are not safe. Concrete public guarantees like deposit insurance and the more general guarantees implicit in central banking and fiscal policy do not relieve banks of their obligations. If banks lean on these public guarantees to any great extent, they will soon be public wards. The only debate then is not how complete the protection should be, but how protection is measured and what protection is.

Whatever the long-run advantages of increasing bank capital by sale of new shares, the short-run effect is almost always to decrease per-share profits. When a manufacturing, public utility, or related business concern decides to raise new capital, it is usually with the expectation (hope, at least) that the added capital will increase earning power enough to pay its cost. The raising of new capital may mean an expansion of plant facilities or the use of more economical means and methods, but in some way it is tied up with profitability. Adding capital to a bank does not increase its earning power materially; as a matter of fact it affects stockholders adversely. In a bank with a 5 per cent ratio of capital to assets, which is not uncommon in view of the fact that the average for commercial banks is about 6.6 per cent, the sale of enough capital to bring this bank to the average of all commercial banks would be equal to 32 per cent of capital accounts. The transaction would dilute earnings almost one-fourth but would add only 1.6 per cent to available funds. This point is illustrated in Table 9.

The only important way in which additional capital can contribute materially to increased earnings would be by influencing the lending or investing policy. If a bank with added capital could pursue a more liberal lending policy or broaden, perhaps lengthen, security portfolios, some increase in earnings would

TABLE 9

HYPOTHETICAL EXAMPLE SHOWING EFFECT OF ADDED CAPITAL
ON EARNING CAPACITY

Assets	Before capital adjustment	After capital adjustment	Percentage change
Bank assets.............	100	101.6	+ 1.6
Deposits..............	95	95.0	0.0
Capital accounts........	5	6.6	+32.0
Earnings leverage........	$\frac{100}{5}$ or 20	$\frac{101.6}{6.6}$ or 15.4	−23.0

result. This, however, would be a gross, not a net, increase; the risk costs of such programs are indeterminate but often material. If more capital should attract more deposits, then it would increase profits. There is little evidence, however, that deposits follow bank capital.

Ratio Tests of Bank Capital Not Meaningful

If each dollar of bank assets had the same risk potential, ratio tests of bank capital would be meaningful; but to state this assumption is to expose its fallacy. In some banks the character of assets is extraordinarily safe, only a very low risk potential exists; in others the potential risk is much higher. This is not necessarily a matter of bad or good performance on the part of the banker–managers; the differences may result from the character of the area in which the banks operate. Banks in one-crop agricultural areas must reconcile themselves to the fact that their credits are riskier than those of urban banks with diversified loan accounts. The Comptroller of the Currency now recognizes this in his new capital policy.

In the Short Run, Liquidity, Not Capital, "Protects a Bank"

The contingency that generally must be protected against is a great concentration of depositors' demands. When depositors demand cash, only cash satisfies their claim. An insolvent bank, in the sense that the dollar value of its assets is less than the dollar amount of its liabilities, may remain open if it is adequately liquid, while a solvent bank without adequate liquidity may have to close. This is not just theory. During the Great Depression many solvent banks undoubtedly were forced to close because they were not liquid. Some temporarily insolvent but liquid banks stayed open and weathered the hard times.

This is not a defense of insolvency, but it does suggest a standard that should guide banks: The tests of adequate liquidity, which were considered in earlier chapters, should be based on adequacy during the worst possible times; the test of solvency does not need to be so pessimistically based if there is adequate liquidity. Banks need to be solvent according to asset valuation standards of reasonable times, not of severe depressions.

Risk Can Be Adjusted to Capital

A bank can follow either of two policies: (1) It can adjust or raise capital to cover the risk implicit in its assets, or (2) it can manage its assets so as to reduce the risk implicit in them to a level consistent with the capital they have.

The second policy has much to recommend it. Added bank capital dilutes earnings. If supervisory agencies put pressure on a bank for added capital, it might well respond by seeking an asset-management policy in keeping with the capital the bank has.

There are, of course, some limits to this sort of policy. A bank, particularly a medium-sized or smaller one, makes local loans primarily. The chances for controlling the character of loan risk are limited, as already admitted, but each bank can adjust its investment policy to its capital position. A bank with a slender capital position but good loan outlets may adjust to this responsibility and opportunity by following a very conservative investment policy.

Retained Earnings vs. Raising New Capital

While bank capital has been built up chiefly by the retention of earnings, the improved market for bank shares in recent years has made it possible to raise capital on respectable terms by offerings in the new-issues market. Usually these offerings are made on a pre-emptive basis to existing shareholders. The choice between earnings retention and sale of additional shares raises a kind of paradox. If a bank wishes to raise capital from the market on favorable terms, it may be wise to establish a generous dividend on its shares. This action runs contrary to the purposes of earnings retention. At one time this choice was more critical than it has been in recent periods; stockholders have become increasingly sophisticated with respect to the advantages of retained earnings. Frequently a bank, particularly one with a sophisticated body of shareholders, can offer new capital stock successfully even if its current dividend is only a modest portion of earnings and the dividend yield is not particularly attractive on the basis of the prevailing market price for the shares of the bank.

DIVIDEND POLICY

The dividend policies of most business corporations depend on the rate of their growth and the health of their finances. In the 1920s, banks paid out a fairly large proportion of earnings in dividends, generally over two-thirds, but the losses of the banking holiday were a great shock to the entire system. It has retained more than half its earnings since the banking holiday, and in the war and postwar years only about one-third of earnings have been paid out in dividends. Recently the proportion has increased moderately and is now somewhat above one-half of net profits.

As already indicated, the possible sale of additional capital shares may create a dilemma for dividend policy. The basic reason is that some shareholders do not want higher dividends, while others clearly do. There are great differences among banks in the utility of their dividends to the owners. Some are very closely owned. The tradition of banking families is strong; there are many institutions, including some very big ones, still dominated by a single family, or by the third or fourth generation descendants of an original owner, if such can be called a family. A sizable proportion of the capital stock of such a bank will be represented at the directors' table. It is not uncommon to find that the directors may own or control from 50 to 90 per cent of the outstanding stock. When this is the case, the directors are justified in looking directly at their own situation: How will the distribution or retention of earnings affect their taxes? When should a reserve for inheritance taxes be accumulated? How urgent is the need for current income? What alternative investment use of the funds can the owners make of distributed income that is not needed for consumption? Banks do not have a great deal of room for tax-reducing maneuvers.

An increasing number of banks are publicly owned and the number of shareholders in publicly owned banks is increasing. Some big banks have thousands of shareholders. In them, the directors may not own or control a fraction of much more than 10 to 25 per cent of the outstanding shares. In such circumstances the directors must take more of a trustee attitude: What is the interest of and desire of shareholders as well as the needs of the bank? Here the dividend distribution practices of large nonfinancial corporations apply.

Constancy of Dividends Is Desirable

Any corporate stock is made a more desirable investment medium for holders if it manages to make its distributions fairly constant. Banks have been good performers on this score. The use of a "regular" rate, with "extras" when special earnings justify, has the effect of making dividends fairly constant in real value terms. Extra earnings are much more likely in good times when prices are higher, but since this means a lower value of money, the "real" income distributed may not be much increased by this policy.

Since, ordinarily, the great determinant of bank profits is the level of business conditions, a policy of dividend stability is primarily one aimed at averaging out the return of good times and bad times. In so far as fluctuation of loan volume is one of the chief determinants of bank profits, the level of business conditions is the most important element. In former times interest rates fluctuated with business conditions; they were up in good times and down in others. This tended to cause some swing in bank profits. Of recent years, this has not been so true.

Growth Justifies a Conservative Dividend Policy

A bank that is growing more rapidly than the banking system as a whole has more than ordinary reasons for building up its capital account. It needs to consider prospective as well as present liabilities. Thus, growth is a good reason for larger than ordinary retained earnings. For a new or recently established bank, such a policy of conservatism is, of course, necessary. There occasionally arises a circumstance in which this rule is not exactly applicable. A bank that wants to raise capital from the market because of an extraordinary rate of growth may need to establish a dividend policy that will attract new capital. For a limited appeal to sophisticated investors, the nonpayment of dividends is no bar; for broader appeal, this would not work so well.

Dividends from Profits on Securities Sold

One of the commonest rules has been that, while ordinary earnings might be the basis of dividend distribution, profits on securities sold should be retained against the potentially countervailing losses. This point has already been considered briefly in the preceding chapter, but a few added comments can be made here. When capital gains are the result of unusual or special circumstances, a dividend distribution of the results is of doubtful wisdom. When there is an upsweeping yield curve, however, tax-swapping operations tend to book capital gains. These are the result of "riding the yield curve" and can be considered a regular part of interest income. The income is realized in the year of sale rather than in earlier years. They are a special form of interest return and are the proper basis for dividend distribution.

Dividend Policy Adjusted to Type of Stockholders

Widespread public ownership in the shares of a bank is likely to be accompanied by more generous distribution of earnings as dividends. Where shares are closely held, a larger fraction of earnings is usually retained. Wealthy owners of bank stocks frequently prefer that earnings not be distributed. Retained earnings, if recognized in the appreciation of market value, produce better after-tax income than the distribution of earnings through dividends. The relatively closer relationship of the market value of bank shares with respect to book value than with respect to dividend yield suggests that a reasonable fraction of retained earnings tends to be recognized in market values. Although this logic is appropriate for shareholders of considerable means, it does not apply to small shareholders. If a bank has many small shareholders, it cannot submerge their interests in meeting the preferences of the few large shareholders.

If a bank wishes to screen the character of its shareholders, a special technical device may be employed. To encourage widespread public shareholding, it should divide its shares by stock splits to the point where the market price makes such shares accessible to popular ownership. The dividing point for this policy would be somewhere from $100 to $200 a share. A bank, however, which wishes to discourage widespread ownership should consciously avoid stock splits and dividends so that the capital account is divided into a relatively small number of shares. The market value of individual shares will then be quite high. A high market value for individual shares is an effective way of discouraging widespread stock ownership and is likely to attract only ownership by stockholders who can well afford to avoid dividend distribution. The principal difficulty with this prescription is that the stock of a bank selling for a high unit value may not, in fact, sell for quite as high a ratio with respect to book value as is true of a bank whose stock has a market value more nearly approaching commonly accepted unit prices.

Index

441